D1533238

This Book Comes With a Website

Nolo's award-winning website has a page dedicated just to this book, where you can:

KEEP UP TO DATE – When there are important changes to the information in this book, we'll post updates

READ BLOGS – Get the latest info from Nolo authors' blogs

LISTEN TO PODCASTS – Listen to authors discuss timely issues on topics that interest you

WATCH VIDEOS – Get a quick introduction to a legal topic with our short videos

You'll find the link in the introduction.

And that's not all.
Nolo.com contains thousands of articles on everyday legal and business issues, plus a plain-English law dictionary, all written by Nolo experts and available for free. You'll also find more useful **books, software, online services, and downloadable forms.**

Get updates and more at
www.nolo.com

11th edition

Stand Up to the IRS

Tax Attorney Frederick W. Daily

ELEVENTH EDITION FEBRUARY 2012

Editors	DIANA FITZPATRICK
Cover Design	SUSAN PUTNEY
Book Design	TERRI HEARSH
Proofreading	SUSAN CARLSON GREENE
Index	BAYSIDE INDEXING
Printing	BANG PRINTING

Daily, Frederick W., 1942–
Stand up to the IRS / by Frederick W. Daily. — 11th ed.
    p. cm.
Includes index.
 Summary: "Contains strategies and insider tips to help readers deal with the IRS, whether
for an outstanding tax bill or audit."—Provided by publisher.
 ISBN 978-1-4133-1328-4 (pbk.) — ISBN 978-1-4133-1706-0 (epub ebook)
 1. Tax protests and appeals—United States—Popular works. 2. Tax auditing—United
States—Popular works. 3. Tax courts—United States—Popular works. 4. United States.
Internal Revenue Service—Popular works. I. Title.
 KF6324.D345 2012
 343.7304'2—dc23

                        2011032245

> **Please note**
>
> We believe accurate, plain-English legal information should help you solve many of
> your own legal problems. But this text is not a substitute for personalized advice
> from a knowledgeable lawyer. If you want the help of a trained professional—and
> we'll always point out situations in which we think that's a good idea—consult an
> attorney licensed to practice in your state.

Acknowledgments

Everyone who gave me thoughtful suggestions on writing, and then improving, my first book, *Winning the IRS Game*—your comments were considered and incorporated into *Stand Up to the IRS*.

My partner in life, Brenda, and my son and cartoonist, Derick.

Alan Rosenthal and John Raymond of San Francisco for their assistance with the (very tricky) bankruptcy issues in this book. John maintains a law office in San Francisco where Alan works as a paralegal.

Bobby Covic, E.A., of Incline Village, Nevada, who greatly assisted in the tax collection area of this book and is one of the top experts in this field.

My editor Diana Fitzpatrick, head Noloid Jake Warner, and all the other nice people at Nolo.

About the Author

Fred Daily graduated from the University of Florida College of Law in 1968. He later received a tax law degree and is now a practicing tax attorney in Nevada, Florida, Idaho, and California. He is a frequent speaker at continuing education programs for tax professionals and is a former professor at Golden Gate University's Graduate School of Taxation and arbitrator for the American Arbitration Association. He has appeared on numerous radio and national television programs, including Good Morning America. He strongly believes that an educated taxpayer can beat the IRS at its own game. In his free time, Fred does some world traveling, enjoys numismatics and Shakespeare, and rides his motorcycle.

The author appreciates feedback from readers. You can check his website at TaxAttorneyDaily.com or contact him in writing c/o Nolo, 950 Parker Street, Berkeley, California 94710, or by email: suirs@aol.com.

Table of Contents

Your Companion for Dealing With the IRS

Chances are that you will have trouble with the taxman at least once in your life. Nearly everyone will face an audit, receive a bill for back taxes, or have some other serious dispute with the Internal Revenue Service. If your number comes up, you will need to understand how your adversary—the IRS—is organized and the rules it plays by.

Contrary to what you might think, you don't have to be a tax expert to successfully deal with the IRS. It usually isn't necessary to know anything about the tax law. However, you do have to know how the IRS works—its rules and procedures. This book gives you the tools you need to successfully deal with IRS. Really.

We address all of the issues people have most frequently faced with the IRS, including:

- what to do if you are behind in filing tax returns
- how to handle an IRS audit, from start to finish
- appealing when you don't agree with an audit report or other IRS decision
- taking your tax problems to court
- negotiating with an IRS tax collector when you can't pay
- settling a tax debt through the Offer in Compromise program
- removing tax liens and levies
- self-employed and small business tax issues
- avoiding tax scams and phony tax experts, and
- invoking the Taxpayer Bill of Rights.

We'll also discuss ways to lower your audit profile, legally protect your assets from IRS seizures, and reduce tax penalties and how to deal with the IRS in the event of divorce or the death of a loved one. In addition, we'll go into the most serious of all tax issues—tax fraud, and the likelihood of your ever being charged with a tax crime.

Every action recommended here has been tested and is 100% legal. So, this book isn't for you if you're looking to learn how to cheat on your taxes, claim the income tax law is unconstitutional, or hide from the IRS.

Can you really stand up to the IRS yourself without hiring a tax expert? For over 90% of the tax problems the average person is likely to face, the answer is a money-saving, big Yes. We know that some types of IRS and tax problems might be over your head. In these cases, we will tell you so and how to find the right kind of professional tax help.

Many self-help people who have failed in their IRS encounters did not bother to learn and follow the IRS procedures. These people are the ones who try to handle IRS issues with casual phone calls or rambling letters. This is a recipe for failure. What these unfortunates should have done was filed the correct IRS forms, contacted the right IRS department, or furnished some vital information to the tax agency. And, of course, they didn't read the book in your hands. Don't let this be you. We have the prizewinning recipes. We explain the process and show you what steps to take, what IRS forms you need to file, and the right way to fill in those forms.

We know that just receiving an envelope with "IRS" stamped across it makes your heart skip a beat. The IRS knows this too and tries to use this intimidation factor to gain the psychological advantage. Don't let this happen to you. This book will level the playing field by providing practical and supportive advice every step of the way. Yes, you can *Stand Up to the IRS*.

Get Updates to This Book and More on Nolo.com

When there are important changes to the information in this book, we'll post updates online, on a page dedicated to this book: **www.nolo.com/back-of-book/SIRS11.html.** You'll find other useful information there, too, including author blogs, podcasts, and videos.

Inside the IRS: What You Need to Know About IRS Operations

L et's take a look at the Internal Revenue Service, or IRS. The IRS's stated mission is to "Provide America's taxpayers top quality service by helping them understand and meet their tax responsibilities and enforce the law with integrity and fairness to all."

A chart of the main IRS divisions appears below. Here is a description of the divisions and offices you are most likely to encounter.

National. The IRS is a branch of the U.S. Treasury Department, with headquarters in Washington, DC, and is ruled by a commissioner appointed by the president. About 1,900 folks work at the national office. The IRS brain is contained in the National Computer Center. The national IRS office sets tone and policy, while procedures—especially audits and collections— are left to the regional and local offices.

The IRS is divided into four operating divisions, but only two concern most of us: the Wage and Investment Division and the Small Business/Self-Employed Division.

IRS campuses. IRS campuses (formerly called service centers) annually process over 200 million tax filings, including over 145 million individual income tax returns. IRS campuses collect over $1 trillion in tax payments each year. Regional campuses are located in Andover, Atlanta, Austin, Cincinnati, Fresno, Brookhaven, Kansas City, Memphis, Ogden, and Philadelphia. They mail out tax notices, collection notices, or bills; tax return problem notices; and tax forms. Contacts with the IRS campuses are usually by mail or fax, or occasionally by telephone.

Automated Collection System, or ACS. This program communicates with taxpayers who owe the IRS. It is a highly computerized collection system staffed by personnel working by phone and mail. You may talk to an ACS person, but you will never meet one.

Local offices. Local IRS offices sit in major cities with suboffices in smaller cities. You can bet one is near you.

Each local office is divided into several departments, four of which you may encounter: examination, collection, criminal investigation, and Taxpayer Advocate Service.

Let's look at these departments in more detail:

- **Examination** personnel perform audits, or examinations in IRS-speak. The people who audit tax returns are either tax auditors working inside the local IRS office or revenue agents if they come to your home or business, which is called the "field." The term auditors in this book refers to both.

- **Collection** personnel collect tax dollars from people who haven't voluntarily and timely paid. Local IRS collectors are called revenue officers. If your case goes to collection, you or your representative will meet with a collector face to face. The IRS campuses and Automated Collection System are also part of the collection apparatus, but they do not employ revenue officers.
- **Criminal Investigation** is the police force of the IRS, and its employees are called special agents. If you ever meet an IRS criminal investigator, it means that you or someone you know is under investigation for a tax crime.
- **Taxpayer Advocate Service** has the IRS troubleshooters to call on when you can't get tax problems solved through normal IRS channels. These officers are found at IRS campuses and local IRS offices. Taxpayer advocates hold powers to cut through red tape and get things done quickly.

The total number of IRS permanent and seasonal employees at all levels is approximately 95,000, making it our largest federal bureaucracy. Auditors make up 25%, collectors 15%, and criminal investigators 3%. The other 57% make policy, run the computers, answer taxpayer inquiries, and God only knows what else. The IRS has been downsized by one-third since 1988. The explanation is the increased reliance on IRS electronic data processing.

If you're confused about the structure of the IRS, don't worry—you're not alone. The following example, shows how the various divisions work.

EXAMPLE:

1. On April 15, Arnold and Aimee Tyson file their income tax return by mail with their IRS campus.
2. The information on their return is transmitted to the National Computer Center for analysis and given a potential audit score. If the score is high enough (it is), the return is screened at the IRS campus. If the return is then deemed to have a high enough audit potential (it does), it is sent to their local office.

3. At the local office, the Tysons' return is scrutinized again and selected for examination (audit). An IRS agent calls the Tysons or sends them an examination notice.

4. The Tysons make an appointment with a tax auditor at the local IRS office. (Or alternatively, a revenue agent comes to the Tysons' business to conduct the audit.)

5. The auditor looks at the Tysons' records and suspects fraud. He refers their file to Criminal Investigation for handling by an IRS special agent. The audit is temporarily suspended. A criminal investigation is very rare.

6. The special agent concludes that the Tysons made many errors, but they were not serious enough to be criminal acts. He sends the file back to the auditor.

7. The auditor concludes the audit and sends the Tysons an examination report. The report states that they owe the IRS additional taxes, interest, and penalties. The Tysons disagree with the report.

8. The Tysons file an appeal, or protest, of their audit.

9. The appeal is heard at the nearest IRS Appeals Office. The appeals officer upholds the auditor, and the Tysons file a petition in tax court. Tax court is independent of the IRS. The Tysons win a partial victory in tax court.

10. After their tax court hearing, the Tysons still owe the IRS. Taxes, interest, and penalties are formally entered, or assessed, in the Tysons' IRS computer records.

11. The Tysons receive their first series of computerized collection notices from their IRS campus. They don't pay or make only a partial payment.

12. The IRS campus eventually gives up. Next, collection notices and telephone calls come from an IRS call center.

13. The Tysons still don't pay. The IRS call center sends the file to a revenue officer at the local office.

14. They try to work out a payment plan, but the collector is unreasonable and threatens to take their wages and property. The Tysons seek help from the Taxpayer Advocate Service.

15. With the help of a taxpayer advocate, they arrange a monthly install-ment plan. Assuming the Tysons make the payments on time, the case will be closed.

Tax Return Processing

From January to May, regional campuses operate around the clock, processing income tax returns, extension requests, and tax payments. Many temporary workers are hired, trained on the job, and paid little more than the minimum wage. IRS officials admit that many processing mistakes are caused by these seasonal employees.

First, machines open tax return envelopes and remove tax returns and checks. Human transcribers scan the returns for completeness and enter the key tax return data into a computer; the computer then checks for arithmetic accuracy. A second transcriber double-checks the first transcriber's workup by inputting the same information into the computer again.

Tax return data is sent to the National Computer Center, where each return is computer scored for its "audit potential." About 10% of all individual (nonbusiness) income tax returns are selected by the National Computer Center for further review. These files are sent back to the regional campuses. There, IRS classifiers (human beings) weed out most of the 10% scored for audit, based on their opinions of the most problematic tax returns. So, roughly ½% to 1% of all individual tax returns filed are selected for further taxpayer contact. (For more information on how returns are selected for audit, see Chapter 3.)

IRS Inefficiency

If you have never dealt with a bureaucracy, the IRS will give you a lesson in how one operates. The IRS machinery moves slowly and often breaks down. Internally, the IRS is very specialized, which can create problems right at the outset. Often, your first challenge is to locate the right department and person to talk to. Because most IRS employees don't know or care how the IRS operates outside of their own small area, IRS personnel often don't know where to direct you.

Here are the major challenges you will encounter in dealing with the IRS.

Bureaucracy. Civil servants in the IRS bureaucracy are not usually self-starters. For many, the IRS provides an escape from the long hours and competitive pressures of the private business world. Others are gaining work experience or biding their time until a better job comes along. All this results in a paint-by-the-numbers approach which can drive any taxpayer nuts. In contrast, you are highly motivated in your IRS dealings—it's your pocketbook at stake. What's important is that you hang in there. Success with the IRS is possible, especially if you are armed with the information and strategies suggested in this book.

Computers. The IRS loves its computers and would replace all its people with machines if possible. Sometimes your file gets lost in the computer— usually through human error. Often this is good—for example, if you want to delay dealing with the IRS. In many cases, however, it is better to get your file out of the computer and into human hands. Every individual taxpayer's IRS file is electronically stored by tax year or period and is computer accessed by Social Security number (SSN), not by name. Returns filed by a business with employees are accessed by the business's employer identification number (EIN).

The ultimate computerization goal of the IRS is totally paperless tax returns. The IRS reasons that if all your income, deductions, exemptions, and credits were electronically reported, a paper tax return would be unnecessary. Information returns, such as W-2 and 1099 forms filed by employers, banks, and the like, on paper and electronically, already make it possible for the IRS to prepare tax returns for nonfilers. And electronic tax filing allows tax refunds to be processed quickly without a paper filing.

Complexity. Americans have the dubious honor of having the most complex income tax laws in the world. The IRS was created to see that we follow the rules. But nobody, including the IRS, understands all of them. It's no wonder—given that the tax code is full of contradictions and hopelessly unclear provisions. Blame Congress. It is far easier to pass a tax law than to administer it or to teach a taxpayer or tax professional how to apply it. Each major tax revision produces unworkable tax provisions that are revised or repealed in the next term of Congress.

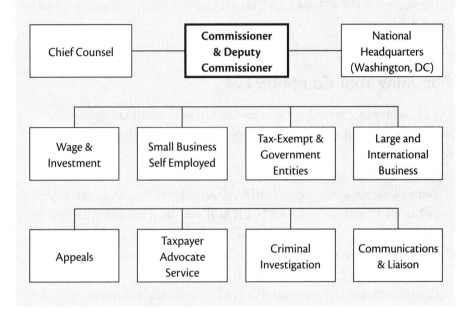

IRS Organizational Chart (Short Version)

The IRS structure is far more complicated than the chart below indicates. Only the top-level divisions you are most likely to encounter are included. The IRS publishes its own chart showing the entire organizational scheme, but you'll probably be more confused than educated if you try to read it.

Communicating With the IRS

If you need to communicate with the IRS, try the telephone first. A specific IRS number should be on the notice that's causing you concern. If not, call 800-829-1040, the IRS's toll-free number.

If calling doesn't work, get out your pad and paper. However, be warned: Letters, which the IRS refers to as white mail, are not the best way to communicate with the IRS. The IRS gets millions every year from earnest, well-meaning taxpayers with legitimate IRS concerns (in addition to letters from cranks). IRS employees are trained to respond to IRS forms, not letters.

TIP

Before contacting the IRS, find out if there is an IRS form for your problem. The IRS has a form for just about everything. For example, you can request a payment plan on Form 9465, *Installment Agreement Request*. The clerk who opens the mail will route the form to the proper department right away, but may leave a letter with the same request to languish in a pile. To find out if the IRS has a form for your concern, call 800-829-1040, ask a tax advisor, or check the IRS website at www. irs.gov.

Obtaining Your Computer File

The IRS computer includes statements of accounts of all taxpayers—individuals and businesses. These accounts show the dates the IRS claims you filed your tax returns, any assessments of penalties and interest, and payments credited to your account.

You can obtain a copy of your IRS accounts by calling and asking for your Master File Transcript, or MFTRA. If you are a business, also request a Business Master File, or BMF, transcript. Call the IRS Taxpayer Service (800-829-1040), visit your local IRS office, or write to your regional IRS campus where you file your tax returns.

Give your Social Security number (and your spouse's if you're married) or your federal employer identification number (if you have a business), as well as the tax years requested. Include your telephone number and mailing address and a photocopy of some form of identification, such as your driver's license.

Within days or, more likely, weeks, you'll receive a copy of your MFTRA or BMF. Don't be discouraged if you can't easily decipher it. It's replete with IRS codes. Read it carefully and note all items you don't understand. Then call the 800 number (800-829-1040) and ask for explanations or report any mistakes you found, such as payments not credited to your account. If that doesn't work, contact a taxpayer advocate (see Chapter 8) or a private tax professional.

Access to Tax Data Under the FOIA

All federal governmental agencies are subject to the Freedom of Information Act, or FOIA. This law guarantees access to all data the IRS has in its files about you and about internal IRS operations. You are not entitled to information about other taxpayers, which is protected from disclosure by the Privacy Act. And sensitive information, such as how the IRS conducts criminal investigations and whether you are under investigation, is exempted from the FOIA.

The FOIA gives you access to the contents of your IRS files, such as notes of IRS agents, workpapers, computations, and opinions. This information is particularly useful if you are contesting an IRS decision, including an audit or a bill.

Getting information under the FOIA involves making a simple written request. (A sample letter is in Chapter 4.) If you are lucky, the IRS will respond to your request within 30 days. Unfortunately, however, the IRS gives a very low priority to complying with FOIA requests; after all, this is not a function that brings in money. Typically, the first response you receive is a letter stating that the IRS needs more time to get the materials.

Delayed responses are not the only problem; the IRS edits out materials it doesn't think you are legally entitled to—which may be exactly what you are looking for. Frequently, a person who doesn't understand the FOIA, such as an auditor or a collector, is given the file to decide what you will get. Often, you have no way of knowing what was left out. The form letter accompanying what is sent to you routinely states that materials were withheld under certain statutes. Occasionally, you'll get all the materials with blackouts on the pages. I have seen some documents 90% blacked out! This is usually the case if you have been the subject of an IRS criminal investigation.

You can appeal, but the FOIA Appeals Office is several years behind in deciding appeals. Thus, many taxpayers are forced to proceed without having the IRS provide all documents as required under the FOIA.

A sure way to counter the IRS's disregard of the FOIA is to file a lawsuit against the IRS in federal court. Going to court is prohibitively expensive for most people. But nine times out of ten, the IRS complies with your original FOIA request within days or weeks of your filing the lawsuit, without your having to get near a courtroom.

How Your Tax Information Can Become Public

The federal Privacy Act prohibits the IRS from disclosure of an individual's tax records. However, there are four notable ways your tax information can become public:

Tax lien. The IRS may file a tax lien in the public records if you owe back taxes. You see this occasionally in the news, especially when it happens to celebrities like Willie Nelson and Nicolas Cage.

Tax crimes. If you are charged with a tax crime, the government will break the news. Personal tax information will come to light at a public trial. Actor Wesley Snipes's tax history became an open book in his trial—and conviction.

Taxpayers and others. There's nothing to stop you or me from telling others about our private tax life. And, other third parties can bring your tax secrets to light. Take Congressman Charles Rangel. A public interest group reviewing certain required financial disclosures by members of Congress found and made public some questionable tax items in Rangel's tax filing. The publicity around the disclosure ended up in Rangel's giving up his chairmanship of certain committees and he was reprimanded.

State tax and law enforcement agencies. The IRS shares taxpayer data with 49 states (Nevada is the exception). Also, under certain circumstances, your tax information is available to law enforcement agencies.

Obtaining Income Information

Your MFTRA won't show income reports the IRS has in its computer on you—that is, any 1099 and W-2 forms reporting how much you were paid by employers, banks, and the like. Income data is available, however, if you know how to ask for it. Call 800-829-1040 and ask for an Information Returns Program (IRP) transcript for each year of concern.

IRP data is helpful if you have lost W-2 or 1099 forms and need to prepare a tax return. The information also lets you match your records against what others have reported to the IRS to let you check for discrepancies. Also, if you are ever audited, the auditor will have this IRP data in hand.

Getting Your Tax Data From the IRS

Can't find an old tax return or don't know the balance on an unpaid tax bill? Here are two ways to get tax account information from the IRS:

- **Tax returns.** Call the IRS Taxpayer Service (800-829-1040) or visit an IRS office and ask for the Tax Return Transcript for whatever tax year you need. This computer printout is not a copy of your return, but it shows key parts including income reports from sources such as banks and employers. The transcript also shows that you filed (or didn't file) a tax return for a specific year. If you want a complete copy of an old tax return, it will cost you $57. Use Form 4506 to make the request by mail or online (available at www.irs.gov). Expect to wait six to eight weeks for the return copy.
- **Tax bill records.** Call the IRS Taxpayer Service (800-829-1040) and ask for a Statement of Account for your tax ID number (usually your Social Security number). This computer printout should arrive by mail in a week or two. Sometimes a local IRS office will make this printout for you on the spot.

Rules of the Game—Tax Laws

Congress writes the tax laws, which become part of the Internal Revenue Code, IRC, or tax code for short. The tax code is amended every year. The present tax code is over 8,500 pages long. It's hard to keep up, even for a tax advisor. Thankfully, most of the tax code isn't applicable to the average citizen taxpayer.

Part of the problem is that many tax laws are passed for purposes other than raising money. For example, tax laws can have a *social* goal, such as attempting to alleviate the housing problem by giving tax breaks to those who invest in low-income housing. Or there might be an *economic* goal to stimulate manufacturing by allowing rapid tax write-offs to buyers of new business equipment. And there are purely *political* reasons for tax laws. Many special interest groups, such as oil companies, horse breeders, broadcasters, insurance companies, and even major league baseball clubs, have gotten tax laws passed designed to give them special treatment. These special provisions of the tax code outnumber the laws of general application.

The Income Tax: Past and Future

Our income tax has its roots in the Civil War when Honest Abe asked Congress for money to finance the war effort. Enacted in 1862, the first tax law lasted until 1872. The Supreme Court struck the second income tax law down, which led to the passage of the 16th Amendment to the Constitution, which led to the basic law we have today.

In 1913, the tax rate was just 1% on all corporations and individuals. But few people paid income taxes, because the standard exemption was $3,000 for single people ($4,000 for married couples), and almost no one earned this much. In fact, only one out of every 271 Americans paid any income tax the first year. By 1919, another war had broken out, and the maximum rate soared to 77%.

Today, the highest federal income tax rate is 35%, but through the subtle workings of the tax code, it is actually several percentage points higher for top earners. With Social Security, Medicare, and various state income taxes added on, the total tax can be as high as 50% for individuals.

The one-size-fits-all flat tax is a constant political issue. The flat tax is simple, pure, and has a lot of appeal. Is it likely to become law? My guess is that Congress knows that even small changes to the tax code have widespread repercussions—to the banking, real estate, housing, manufacturing, and charitable industries—affecting just about everyone. Once the big money special interest groups gear up to protect their niches in the tax code, things won't change all that much. I don't see the IRS going out of business or the tax code ever becoming comprehensible.

Interpreting the Tax Code

Congress has given the IRS the power to interpret the tax code. This is done primarily through a series of IRS regulations and other pronouncements. The regulations are expanded versions of some tax code provisions, with illustrations of how the law is applied in different situations. The regulations are about four times the length of the tax code itself. The IRS also publishes revenue rulings, revenue procedures and letter rulings, which provide guidance to taxpayers.

There are thousands of situations where it is not clear exactly how the tax law should be applied. In these gray areas, disputes often arise between the IRS and the taxpayer. This is where the tax professionals earn their keep—by fitting the tax code most advantageously to a client's case. Or put another way, if the tax case is analogized to the fence around Farmer Brown's cabbage patch, the perimeter has gotten so long and twisted that a self-respecting rabbit may have a decent chance of finding enough room to wiggle through or under it.

The IRS is not the final word on interpreting the tax code. The federal court system, composed of the U.S. Tax Court, federal district courts, the U.S. Court of Federal Claims, and U.S. Bankruptcy Courts, all have the power to decide, on a case-by-case basis, how Congress intended the tax laws to be applied. Any taxpayer or the IRS, unhappy with a court's tax decision interpreting the tax code, can appeal to a circuit court of appeal, and in rare cases to the U.S. Supreme Court.

Self-Assessment of Income Taxes

The U.S. income tax system is based on a self-assessment theory. You are responsible for reporting your income and telling the government how much tax you owe. You assess your own income tax every time you file a tax return. This doesn't mean that the system is voluntary or that you have a legal choice whether or not to assess taxes against yourself. Despite what some tax protestor organizations contend, you must file a tax return if you earn above a specified annual minimum income amount.

The IRS's job is to determine whether or not you obeyed the self-assessment principle and the tax code by:
- reporting all your income
- stating the correct amount of taxes due, and
- paying the taxes due.

If the IRS suspects that you have violated your self-assessment obligation, you may be audited and billed for an additional assessment. If you do not file a tax return, the IRS is empowered to calculate and assess the tax for you.

Winning the IRS Game

If you file and pay your taxes on time and never get an IRS notice, then you are already winning the IRS game and probably don't need this book—at least not yet.

The rest of us who encounter the IRS up close and personal still have a chance to win, or at least to not lose disastrously. This means keeping your income and assets away from the IRS and staying out of jail. And this is one game where, despite your coach having told you "It's not whether you win or lose, it's how you play the game," you darn well want to win.

Great, but you won't win the IRS game unless you know the rules. This book tells you the most important rules—written and unwritten—and helps you develop a game plan.

Let's call the IRS team the Goliaths and your team the Goodguys. On paper, the Goliaths look unbeatable, but on the playing field it comes down to the strengths and weaknesses of the individual players. Here's an analysis of the teams and players.

Goliaths have experience. You are a rookie, so even the weakest IRS team member is ahead of you. But he or she probably can't make it a runaway—the IRS is characterized by low morale and a high rate of employee turnover. Score seven for the Goliaths in the first quarter, 7-0.

Goodguys have motivation and the advantage here every time. Coaches say that motivation is the key to winning. The Goliath player gets the same pay, win or lose, while the Goodguys are playing to keep their money. Score seven for the Goodguys in the second quarter. It's tied at the half, 7-7.

The game will be decided in the second half. You have to be prepared to go the distance. Know what you are doing and show strength and perseverance to the IRS. Keep your cool and don't beat yourself. Remember the words of Pogo, the comic strip philosopher: "We have met the enemy and he is us."

A Costly Victory—the Wrong Way to Play. One way to lose is to play the IRS without bothering to learn the rules of the game, preparing, or devising a game plan. You'll lose if you ignore IRS contacts or respond incorrectly, miss deadlines, or lie to IRS employees. Charlie is a prime example.

EXAMPLE: Charlie had been having IRS problems for five years when he called a tax professional, Sheila. He had lost an IRS audit, an appeal, and then in tax court. When the tax bills came, he threw them away. Charlie believed he was right, and he was sticking to his principles.

An IRS collector repeatedly warned Charlie that his business assets were going to be sold at auction to pay the tax bill. Sheila asked when the sale was to take place. "Tomorrow," Charlie replied. She agreed to try to help Charlie but made no promises—the game was just about over and he was behind by several touchdowns.

Sheila called the IRS and got a postponement of the auction for 30 days to give Charlie a chance to get a home equity loan to pay the taxes. He tried, but the bank didn't approve the loan. The IRS refused another postponement and sold the business assets for $92,000.

The sad part is that if Charlie had sought tax advice at the beginning of the game, he would have been able to settle with the IRS for $7,000. By stubbornly refusing to meet the problem, he lost his business. And he cost himself $92,000 in taxes, penalties, interest, and tax professional fees. Charlie needed to know the rules and needed a plan before playing the IRS game.

RESOURCE

The Internal Revenue Service *Annual Report* provides a wealth of information about IRS organization and performance. View or download it at the IRS website at www.irs.gov.

Chapter Highlights

- The IRS is an inefficient mega-bureaucracy and not the all-knowing Big Brother it would like us to believe it is.
- Successfully dealing with the IRS comes from knowing basic IRS procedures and following those procedures.
- It is possible to beat the IRS at its own game by perseverance and going up the IRS ladder to solve problems.

Filing Tax Returns

O ver 50% of all people file annual federal income tax returns before April 1 of each year. Most of the rest file in the first two weeks of April, but 5% get an extension to October 15.

According to the IRS, about 10% don't file at all. My guess is that the number is even higher. In any case, millions of folks are either illegally not filing tax returns or are filing beyond all extension dates. This number is so large that some nonfilers may never get caught—but don't bet on it. In this electronic age, it is increasingly difficult to stay below the IRS radar forever.

How Long Must You Worry About Not Filing a Tax Return?

The tax code sets out time limits, or statutes of limitations, for the IRS to pursue nonfilers.

Criminal. The government can only bring criminal charges against a nonfiler within six years of the date the tax return was due. For example, after April 15, 2012, you can't be prosecuted for failing to file a 2005 tax return that was due on April 15, 2006.

Civil. There is no deadline, however, for the IRS in going after nonfilers and imposing civil penalties—in addition to any taxes owed. This means that while you can't be put in jail for not filing a 1988 tax return, you will forever owe the IRS a return—as long as you earned enough to have had an obligation to file. And fines—penalties and interest—on unfiled tax returns run forever.

IRS policy. Don't worry too much about that missed tax return after six years. The IRS usually doesn't pursue nonfilers after six years from the filing due date. The IRS materials on Taxpayer Delinquency Investigations (*Internal Revenue Manual* 0021; IRS Policy Statement P-5-133) read as follows:

> *Taxpayers failing to file returns due will be requested to prepare and file (them). All delinquent returns … will be accepted. However, if indications of willfulness or fraud exist, the special procedures for handling such returns must be followed …. Factors taken into account include, but are not limited to: prior history of noncompliance, existence of income from illegal sources, effect upon voluntary compliance and anticipated revenue in relation to*

the time and effort required to determine tax due. Consideration will also be given to any special circumstances existing in the case of a particular taxpayer, class of taxpayer or industry.

Normally, application of the above criteria will result in enforcement of delinquency procedures for not more than six years. Enforcement beyond such period will not be undertaken without prior managerial approval.

The IRS can still request a tax return for a period more than six years ago. But if you tell the IRS that you don't have enough information to prepare a return, the agency usually will drop the request. If the IRS computer shows income information on you, such as a W-2 or 1099 form, however, the IRS may calculate and assess the tax anyway.

Don't Forget Your State

Unless you live in Alaska, Florida, Nevada, New Hampshire, South Dakota, Tennessee, Texas, Washington, or Wyoming, the IRS is not the only tax agency to worry about. All 41 other states have their own income tax reporting requirements, and a few cities do as well. In many cases, if you haven't filed a tax return, you may be contacted first by your state tax collector, not the IRS. If this happens, you can bet the IRS is not far behind. If you had income from jobs in more than one state, you may need to file multiple state tax returns. All states except Nevada have agreements with the IRS to trade tax information about their residents. In this electronic age, the exchange occurs automatically; if one taxing authority finds you aren't filing, the computers will turn you in to the other. If you file a late IRS return, be sure to file a state return as well.

Consequences of Not Filing

It is a crime not to file a tax return if taxes are owed. By contrast, there is no criminal penalty if you file but can't pay your taxes. You'll owe interest and penalties, but you won't be sent to jail. So even if you don't have two dimes to rub together and owe a bundle of taxes, file your return.

If you ignore this advice and fail to file, you can be fined up to $25,000 per year and/or sentenced to one year in prison for each unfiled year. Our justice system, however, doesn't have enough jails to put away even 1% of the nonfilers, so going to jail is highly unlikely—even if you owe hundreds of thousands of dollars.

IRS Hunting for Nonfilers

The IRS looks for nonfilers through its computerized Information Returns Program (IRP). This tremendously effective operation matches information documents—W-2 wage statements and 1099 income reports from payers (such as your client or the bank where you earn interest on your deposit account)—against tax returns you have filed. If the computer search fails to find a return, the IRS initiates a Taxpayer Delinquency Investigation, or TDI. A TDI is an IRS search to find out why a taxpayer didn't file a tax return.

TDIs usually begin with computer-generated notices. If you don't respond to the notices, your case is eventually turned over to a taxpayer service representative for telephone contact or more letters. If the IRS is really serious, your file is assigned to a revenue officer at your local IRS office who goes out looking for you. (See Chapter 6 for more information on collection contacts with a taxpayer.)

If you're an independent contractor, earn investment or interest income, or sell real estate or stocks, the IRS receives payment information on you annually. The IRP will probably catch that you didn't file. The IRS is about 12 to 24 months behind in notifying the nonfilers it discovers. So don't think that because you haven't heard from the IRS within a year or two after the filing due date you are home free. The IRS will catch you—it's just a matter of time.

IRS Notifying Nonfilers

How the IRS contacts you is the key to how seriously the IRS views your case. There are four ways you can be notified—and they are not mutually exclusive. If the IRS tries one of the following methods and you don't respond, it will no doubt try another:

- **Written requests from the IRS over a 16-week period.** Most nonfilers are initially contacted in this relatively nonthreatening manner. Threats come later if you ignore these notices. These notices usually mean that you aren't targeted for criminal nonfiling.
- **Telephone call or letter with a deadline** to get your returns filed, usually within 30 days.
- **Visit or call from an IRS agent.** The officer will give you a deadline to file the missing returns directly with him or her, or will offer to help you prepare your return. If you still don't file, *the IRS can legally prepare a return for you, based on any information it has and guesses it makes.*
- **Visit by a Criminal Investigation Division agent.** This is the very worst way you can be contacted. This means that your nonfiling is the subject of a criminal investigation. This usually happens only if the IRS suspects you of not reporting hundreds of thousands of dollars in income over multiple years.

IRS Questioning About Unfiled Tax Returns

Someone from the IRS may ask you by phone or in person if you filed income tax returns for all years.

This creates a dilemma. If you haven't filed but you answer "Yes, the IRS must have lost them," you will have lied to the IRS, a crime punishable by up to five years in prison. But if you answer "No," you may have confessed to the crime of failure to file a tax return. *The best response* is to say you'll get back to the IRS after you check your records or speak with your tax adviser. You can't get into trouble with these magic words.

The IRS might keep pressing but just politely repeat "I'll get back to you."

Regardless of your answer, the IRS will set a deadline for you to respond or file your tax returns. Ask for 60 to 90 days to do it and talk with your tax adviser, if necessary. Then, you should start working on getting the returns prepared right away.

> ⓘ **CAUTION**
> **The IRS has no tax amnesty program, so no penalties or interest on taxes are forgiven for those who file late.** The IRS typically adds the maximum penalties and interest to the taxes found due.

When the IRS Prepares Your Tax Return for You

The IRS has the power to, in effect, prepare and file tax returns whenever you don't file. (Internal Revenue Code § 6060.) In IRS-speak, this is called a Substitute For Return, or SFR. Usually, it is not to your advantage to have the IRS do this. IRS preparers may give you the bare minimum—one exemption, no dependents, and the standard deduction. The IRS can guesstimate your tax liability, usually from W-2 forms and 1099 informational reports. If these are not available, the IRS can impute income to you based on tables from the Bureau of Labor Statistics showing income needed to sustain a minimal lifestyle by area of the country. This can result in a much higher tax bill than you would have had if you had prepared your own tax return.

If the IRS prepares an SFR, it will mail a copy to your last known address asking you to sign it and return it. It may not be in your best interest to sign, even if the figures are accurate. Instead, prepare a return yourself and send it to the IRS with a copy of the SFR letter it sent you. Request that your return be accepted in lieu of the SFR. If your return looks okay, the IRS will accept it. The IRS can audit it first, but this doesn't often happen.

Another reason to prepare the return yourself is because the normal statute of limitation rules for auditing a filed tax return don't apply with SFRs. If the IRS prepares an SFR, it will be able to audit it forever, unless you sign the SFR and agree to the tax liability. But, if you prepare a tax return, the IRS normally has only three years from the time you file it to audit you. An IRS-filed tax return does not start the normal ten-year statute of limitations on collecting any taxes due. (See Chapter 6.)

A final reason for filing your own return has to do with qualifying to discharge (eliminate) your tax debt in bankruptcy.

If you don't offer your own return, the IRS finalizes the SFR, whether or not you sign it. Any taxes due, plus penalties and interest, will then be formally assessed against you.

Nonfiling May Be a Crime

Very few people are put in jail for not filing a tax return, but it can happen. A willful failure to file a tax return is a misdemeanor if you owe taxes. You can be sentenced for up to a year in jail and a $25,000 fine—for each year of nonfiling. (Internal Revenue Code § 7201.) If your failure to file is deemed to be part of a scheme to evade taxes you can be charged with a felony, a more serious tax crime, which carries a maximum punishment of five years in prison and a monetary penalty of $100,000—but rarely is anyone criminally prosecuted for this felony. (Internal Revenue Code § 7201(1).) The felony crime requires a deceitful act beyond the nonfiling, such as intentionally using a false Social Security number. The misdemeanor doesn't require any additional deceitful act.

If you are contacted by an IRS agent about your nonfiling, but you are not asked to file a return, start worrying. This may mean that you're on the way to the IRS Criminal Investigation Division, or CID. This does not guarantee you will be prosecuted, only that you might be. A small percentage of nonfiling cases result in criminal prosecutions. But, you still have to get your past-due returns prepared and filed. (Criminal investigations and other criminal matters are covered in Chapter 10.)

In deciding whether or not to recommend prosecuting a nonfiler, the CID considers many factors, including:
- the number of years you haven't filed returns
- the amounts of taxes due
- your occupation and education
- your previous history of tax delinquencies
- whether you are in a business largely done by cash, and
- how truthful you were during the investigation.

Certain types of nonfilers, such as reputed crime figures and politicians, may be prosecuted regardless of any other factors. And lawmakers are held to a higher standard to maintain taxpayer confidence in the tax administration system.

CAUTION

If your nonfiling case is referred to the CID, there is little you can do to influence the IRS agent's decision regarding prosecution. If you try to talk your way out of it, you will only make matters worse. In short, if you suspect that the IRS is investigating you, see an attorney. If an agent calls you, don't consent to an interview—in fact, don't say anything except that you want to speak to an attorney. Then, find a tax or criminal attorney immediately and have no further direct contact with anyone at the IRS. Don't talk to your friends or associates about it either.

It's Better to File Before the IRS Contacts You

If you haven't filed a tax return for a year or more, it's never too late. The IRS has a policy of not criminally prosecuting those who file before they are contacted by the IRS. (IR-92-114.) Also, the IRS is often more gentle in collecting from voluntary filers than from the ones they catch. When you file your return on your own accord, the somewhat remote IRS campus initially handles your file. But if the IRS has sought you out, your local IRS office probably has the file and can put more pressure on you than a campus.

> EXAMPLE: Uncle Jack worked in construction for 50 years. He bragged that he never filed a tax return or got an IRS notice. He changed addresses with the seasons and used many different Social Security numbers, none of which were his own. Because the IRS relies primarily on Social Security numbers to keep track of taxpayers, it never found Jack. He didn't get Social Security benefits either. If Jack were around today, his chances of outrunning the IRS computer would be slim— better than beating the house in Las Vegas, but not by much.

Suggestions for Completing Late-Filed Tax Returns

Most people have a hard enough time getting their tax returns prepared and filed every year. It is even more difficult if you are trying to do it for years long past. The most difficult tasks are getting the correct forms and finding the information that you need to fill them out.

Obtaining Lost W-2, 1099, and Other Tax Forms

Longtime nonfilers tend to lose their old W-2 and 1099 forms. Those forms show how much money was paid to you by businesses and are vital to filing an accurate tax return. If you have this problem, start by asking the business that issued the 1099 or W-2. Many businesses don't keep these old records around or won't go out of their way to furnish them to you. They met their legal obligation by sending the forms to you when due; you're out of luck.

Surprisingly, you can't get copies of W-2 and 1099 forms from the IRS. You can, however, get an IRS computer printout with the information on it. Call the IRS at 800-829-1040 and request income data for the missing tax years. It may take several weeks to receive a written response. All your income may not be reflected on the transcript, but it will show the minimum amount you must report on your tax return.

Another way to handle missing W-2 data when filing a tax return is by reconstructing your salary records on Form 4852, *Substitute W-2,* available from the IRS. Attach it to the front of your tax return and file it. For missing 1099 income data, make your best guess. There is no separate form for 1099 payment reconstructions.

CAUTION

Use the correct year's tax form. You must use updated tax forms each year. For example, you can't use 2011 tax forms and change the year to 2012; the IRS makes major and subtle changes to its tax forms each year.

You have several options for obtaining past years' forms:
- Download the forms off the IRS's website (www.irs.gov).
- Check a tax software publisher like *TurboTax* (http://turbotax.intuit.com).
- Call the IRS form department at 800-829-FORM (3676). The forms will be mailed in a week or two. The form center shouldn't pass your name along to other departments—such as the collection or criminal division.
- If you don't want to risk your name being passed along, have a friend or relative—who did file on time—call for you.
- Visit your local IRS office. You won't be asked why you want the forms. You won't even be asked your name.
- Ask a tax professional for forms, although the person may not provide them unless you agree to hire him or her.

If your state has an income tax, remember to get those old forms, too.

Preparing Late-Filed Tax Returns

Your local IRS office will help you prepare late tax returns. The question is whether this is wise. The IRS is not interested in making sure you get every deduction, exemption, or credit to which you are entitled. If you can't afford to hire a tax preparer, see if any local tax professional or nonprofit groups donate their time to low-income or otherwise needy people or ask at your local IRS office.

Getting Your Returns to the IRS

Get your late return to the IRS by the following means:

Hand filing. It's safer to hand file tax returns at a local IRS office than to mail them in, especially late returns. If you file in person, ask the IRS clerk to file-stamp a copy of the first page of the tax return. This shows irrefutably that the return was filed and the date of the filing. And it is better than a post office return receipt or card which shows only that something was sent to the IRS on that date—but not what was sent. Take along your own extra copy for the IRS to stamp; the IRS won't make a copy for you.

Mailing. Late-filed returns are more likely to get delayed in processing or lost by the IRS than current ones. If you plan to mail in your late returns, send them by certified mail, return receipt requested, to the IRS. Again, hand filing is the better way to go.

Electronic filing. You can electronically file a late return. Get an electronic receipt back from the IRS and keep it for your records. Check the IRS website for instructions on how to do this.

Another free or inexpensive option is to use computer tax preparation software, such as *TurboTax*. (Check Turbotax.com to see if you are eligible for the free version.) This program has helpful hints of what to do—and not do—and can take data directly from personal finance recordkeeping programs, such as *Quicken* (Intuit). Some even have built-in tax guides that offer advice on finding deductions and flag questionable items. The IRS has a bias in favor of computer-prepared tax returns. Computers don't make math errors and the IRS itself relies heavily on computers—although much of its reliance is undoubtedly misplaced. You will probably have trouble locating older years' computer tax programs, although tax professionals keep programs back as far as ten years.

Your best (but most costly) choice is to hire a tax preparer. Over 50% of tax filers do. A professional decreases the chances of mistakes and, consequently, that the return will be audited. Late returns are hand-screened by specially trained IRS personnel. In contrast, a return filed on time is seen only briefly by a human being who enters data into the computer and then sends the return to storage. IRS personnel are presumably more likely to let a return go through without question if it bears the signature of a CPA, an enrolled agent, or a tax attorney. (See Chapter 13 for more information on tax professionals.) Also, a good tax professional can offer advice on what you can do in the future to cut your taxes or reduce your audit risk.

Voluntary Filing to Minimize the Chance of a Criminal Investigation

The government policy is not to prosecute most citizens who haven't filed. The IRS claims that the typical nonfiler hasn't filed for three or more consecutive years and owes about $70,000.

Who does the IRS criminally prosecute? The most likely candidates are public figures, such as sports stars or entertainers or known criminals. But some are more ordinary folks with years of nonfiling and hundreds of thousands in taxes owed. My advice to most nonfilers is to simply start filing their tax returns—without first contacting the IRS.

Tax attorneys typically handle the cases of high-profile nonfilers in one of three ways:

- The attorney writes the local IRS office and makes the voluntary disclosure for the client. The lawyer then files the tax returns.
- The attorney calls the local chief of the Criminal Investigation Division and requests a meeting. There they discuss the case without naming the client and the attorney asks if the client would be prosecuted if a voluntary disclosure was made. If the chief says no, the attorney makes the disclosure. Legally, the chief cannot bind the government here, but I know of no one criminally prosecuted after making this kind of deal.

- The tax attorney does a "quiet disclosure." He or she prepares the returns for the last six years and files them, without contacting the IRS first. The tax attorney gets a power of attorney from the client—a form authorizing the attorney to act on behalf of the client—and uses the attorney's address, not the client's, on the tax returns. This ensures that any further contact about the late returns from the IRS comes to the tax attorney directly.

The advantage the tax attorney has is the attorney-client privilege. Under this ancient legal doctrine, neither the IRS nor any other government agency can force your attorney to disclose anything you say. There is also a tax practitioner-client privilege, but it does not apply to crimes—meaning the IRS can force a nonattorney tax professional to divulge client confidences.

What Will Happen When You File Late

The IRS can punish you for filing tax returns late by imposing civil penalties, criminal penalties, or both and by denying refunds due you.

> **TIP**
>
> **Ask for an extension if you are going to file late.** Send in the simple IRS Form 4868, *Application for Extension of Time to File Individual U.S. Income Tax Return*, if you aren't filing by April 15. You'll avoid the late filing penalty and get six more months to file. However, if you owe a balance you'll still have to pay interest and late payment penalties.

Civil Penalties and Interest Added to Your Tax Bill

If your seriously late tax return shows taxes due, you will probably be fined 5% per late month, up to a maximum of 25% for five months past April 15.

> EXAMPLE: Your return was due April 15 and you file on October 1 of that year. You may be charged 25% extra on the amount of any taxes you owe. If you file on August 16, you will be charged 20%—four months times 5% per month. There is no daily proration of the penalty,

so one day late costs the same 5% penalty as does 29 days. After five months, the late filing penalty stops increasing.

That's not all. In addition to the *late filing* penalty, the IRS can impose a *late payment* penalty of ½% to 1% per month. And here's a little more bad news: Interest is running all the while. Interest changes quarterly, and is compounded daily. And interest is charged on the penalties, too. (In recent years, the interest rate has hovered around 4%–6% per year.)

Tax bill interest is not deductible on your tax return, unless it's for a business-related tax debt. Penalties are never tax deductible.

The lesson here is to pay the IRS as soon as you can, even if you have to borrow to do it. Getting out of paying these penalties is not easy, but can be done under certain circumstances. (See Chapter 12.)

RESOURCE

For thorough information on paying all kinds of debts, see *Solve Your Money Troubles*, by Margaret Reiter and Robin Leonard (Nolo).

The one bit of good news is that penalties and interest are added *only* if you owe taxes, because they are based on a percentage of the tax due. So, for example, a business with net losses for the year can generally file as late as it wants without incurring penalties and interest. This is not to say that it is good to intentionally file late—you may lose refunds or other tax benefits granted only to timely filers. Nevertheless, over one-third of all late filers don't owe anything—and may even get refunds. Many people who dread preparing and filing returns because they think they owe the IRS get a pleasant surprise.

Filing Foreign Financial Accounts (FBAR)

You must file Treasury Department Form 90-22.1 by June 30 every year if you own or have an interest in any foreign financial accounts outside the United States. This form is not attached to your income tax return but is filed separately. In tax lingo, this is called an FBAR form.

An exception applies if the total value of your foreign accounts is less than $10,000. The law applies to owners and anyone with authority to conduct transactions on behalf of the account owner. Of course, any income from these foreign accounts, such as dividends or interest, must be reported on your income tax return as well.

The FBAR form is not overly difficult to complete. Nevertheless, it's a good idea to go to a tax pro for help, at least the first time you file. You must provide the account information and name a location of the financial institution.

The IRS strongly enforces the FBAR law. If you haven't filed FBARs in the past—and you should have—see a tax attorney. In the past few years the IRS has become very serious about pursing nonfilers. There are severe civil and criminal penalties for willfully failing to file an FBAR.

Criminal Charges May Be Brought

As mentioned earlier, nonfiling can be a crime. You can be sentenced to one year in prison and be fined $25,000 for each year you didn't file, up to six years. You cannot be criminally prosecuted for nonfiling a return once six years pass from its due date. However, you can be civilly fined beyond six years. (See Chapter 10.)

Refunds May Be Denied

Statistically, late filers are more likely to be deserving of refunds than to owe tax balances. The tax law (Internal Revenue Code § 6411(a)) prohibits the IRS from issuing a refund if your individual income tax return is filed more than two years past the original due date (usually April 15).

EXAMPLE: Andy filed ten years of back tax returns at one time. For the first five years he was due refunds, but in the later five years he owed taxes. Andy requested that the IRS offset the taxes owed with the refunds due. The IRS denied the request because all the refund years were beyond the two- and three-year cut-off periods.

There are two exceptions to the "no refund" law:

- If you pay any of the tax after the due date of the return, the refund time period is extended to two years from the payment date. For example, your tax return was due April 15, 2012. Instead of filing the return, you file an extension request. On August 15, 2012, you file another extension request and make a payment for the amount of taxes you think you will owe. You don't file your return on October 15, 2012, and in fact don't get around to filing it until June 2014. That's more than two years after the April 15, 2012 date, but less than two years from the August 15, 2012 date when you made a payment. You discover that your August 15, 2012 payment was too much. When you file your return in June 2014, you'll be entitled to a refund.

- If you can show that you suffered from a physical or mental impairment at the time the return was originally due, the IRS can grant the refund—at its discretion—if you file the return within three years of its original due date. You will have to document your impairment with a supporting letter from a medical provider.

For more information on refunds due for returns that were filed late, see Internal Revenue Code § 6513.

Bells Won't Go Off When Nonfilers Start Filing

If you haven't filed for many years and decide to hop back in with this year's return, don't worry about the IRS automatically checking for all the other years you've missed. IRS computers aren't set up to do this, primarily because the IRS doesn't want to discourage nonfilers from starting to file again. So nothing will happen if you file anew even after a ten-year hiatus. If you later get a notice asking about tax returns for other years, chalk it up to coincidence—most likely due to income information already on file (W-2 and 1099 forms) in the IRS computer.

Requesting an Extension to File

The only good reason for filing your tax return by April 15 is if you need a refund quickly. If you are getting large refunds, however, that is a sign that your wages are being overwithheld or you are sending in too much in estimated tax payments. If you look at tax refunds as a kind of forced savings plan, realize that you are making an interest-free loan to Uncle Sam. It may make more sense to adjust your withholding or quarterly estimated payments so that you break even or even owe a little to the IRS instead. In the meantime, you can invest the money and collect the interest, which, of course, is taxable.

The alternative to filing by April 15 is to apply for an extension to October 15. Each year about 5% of all taxpayers request extensions to file their tax returns. It's no big deal and won't get the IRS excited or increase your chances of being audited.

To get an extension to file, complete Form 4868, *Application for Automatic Extension of Time to File U.S. Individual Income Tax Return*, and send it to the IRS by April 15. This form changes each year. You can get a current copy from the IRS website, your local IRS office, or by calling 800-829-3676. Your extension is granted automatically until October 15, and you won't incur any late-filing penalties.

If you live outside the United States, you get an automatic two-month extension to file to June 15. In the past, anyone physically outside the United States on April 15 could get the automatic extension. The law was changed to disqualify day trippers who made short April trips to Mexico and Canada just to get the extension. Even if you live outside the United States, however, you do not get extra time to pay the taxes you owe.

Some tax professionals contend that filing tax returns on extension decreases your chance of being audited. They reason that the IRS local offices fill their annual audit inventories before the returns on extension are processed. The IRS denies it works this way, but at the same time, the agency won't say that returns filed on extension have a higher audit frequency. At worst, extensions are a neutral factor; they can't hurt and just might help. I always file my own return on extension—and I've never been audited. Maybe just a coincidence.

(!) CAUTION

An extension to file does not extend your time to pay. Pay all expected tax due with your extension filing forms. Otherwise, you'll get hit with late payment penalties and interest for the underpaid amount. It is very difficult to get an extension of time to pay without incurring an underpayment penalty. Try by filing IRS Form 1127, *Application for Extension of Time for Payment of Tax* (available on the IRS website), by April 15. Follow the instructions on the form, but don't get your hopes up.

Filing a Return When You Can't Pay What You Owe

If you owe taxes, but don't have the money to pay the full amount, file a return and send what you can. Remember—you can incur up to a 25% fine for the first five months you're late. Any partial payment will cut down on the penalty and interest owed.

(💡) TIP

When sending a partial payment, don't send a personal check. The IRS always records your bank account number with your payment. If you ever owe the IRS and can't pay on time, the agency can easily seize this account to get the balance of the taxes owed—and cause your outstanding checks to bounce. (See Chapter 7.) Instead, use a money order, cashier's check, or an attorney's trust fund check to make payments if you anticipate any future IRS collection problem.

Keep photocopies of the check or money order you send to the IRS. Write your last name, Social Security or employer ID number, type of tax—income or payroll—and year of tax in the lower left-hand corner of the payment instrument. If you want your payment credited quickly, use the payment slip and bar-coded envelope provided by the IRS for payment.

Filing a Tax Return When You Live Out of the United States

The long arm of the tax code does not stop at the U.S. border. If you live abroad and have income, you will still have to file a tax return (by June 15). You must also have taxes withheld or pay quarterly estimated taxes if you are working abroad. But the tax bite may be substantially reduced if you qualify for a foreign earned income exclusion, the foreign housing exclusion, and the foreign housing deduction. (See IRS Publication 54, *Tax Guide for U.S. Citizens and Resident Aliens Abroad*.)

You may also owe taxes to the government of the country where you reside. Some countries give you credit for taxes you pay to Uncle Sam; others won't. Also, estate and inheritance tax laws vary widely across the globe.

Renouncing your U.S. citizenship to beat the IRS won't work, either. You remain subject to U.S. tax laws for ten years after renunciation! Norman Dacey, author of *How to Avoid Probate*, found this out when he became an Irish citizen. He challenged this law in the U.S. federal courts—and lost.

There is one bit of good news. While you are subject to U.S. tax laws, it is very difficult for the IRS to grab your wages or assets located outside of the United States. Some countries, mostly in Europe, have treaties with the United States in which their tax agencies can cooperate with the IRS to collect from Americans, but most governments place a very low priority on working these kinds of cases. You claim the foreign earned income tax exclusion on IRS Form 2555.

Reducing the Chance of an Audit When Filing

There is no surefire way to audit-proof your tax return, though you can cut the odds. Nevertheless, a messy return—cross-outs, sloppy handwriting, smudges—almost screams "audit me." This tells the IRS that you are careless and disorganized. So does the use of round numbers for deductions—$1,000 or $12,000 instead of $978 or $12,127. It's an indication that you are estimating things rather than keeping good records.

Here are some suggestions which may—or may not—work to reduce your audit risk:

- If you claim large deductions for unusual items, such as an earthquake, flood, or fire loss, attach documentary proof to the back of your tax return. Copies of repair receipts, canceled checks, insurance reports, and pictures are advisable. This won't stop the IRS computer from flagging your return. These attachments, however, should catch the attention of the IRS classifier who next screens computer-picked returns for audit potential. If the person thinks your documentation looks reasonable, you won't get audited.

- Avoid filing an income tax return with Schedule C, *Profit or Loss from Business*, that reports a net loss from a small business venture. IRS auditors go after these returns like bees toward honey.

- Report side-job income as other income on Line 22 of your tax return. This should be done only if this income is relatively small, and you are not claiming any business deductions against it. Technically, side-job income is usually reported on a Schedule C, *Profit or Loss from Business*. But filing a Schedule C undoubtedly increases your audit chances.

- Prepare your tax return by computer. A neat, computer-prepared return looks more official to IRS classifiers and avoids math errors, which catch the IRS's attention. Most professional tax preparers now use computers. There are also tax preparation programs, such as Intuit's *TurboTax*, that you can use to prepare your own return.

- Don't use electronic filing or the IRS preprinted address label on your tax return. These enable the IRS to get your return into the processing cycle, including the audit cycle, more quickly than otherwise would happen. Anything that slows down the IRS machine can't be bad. On the flip side, using electronic filing or the label usually means that any refund will come faster. If you expect a refund but fear an audit, you'll have to weigh the pros and cons.

- Live in a low-audit area. Your audit chances are radically different depending on where in the United States you live. For example, Nevada taxpayers are audited four times more than people in Wisconsin. While this is extreme, it might make sense if you travel most of the time or have addresses in several areas. If you have flexibility in choosing your tax reporting address, choose the one with the lower audit rate. If you're really interested in this, ask a tax professional or check the IRS website for audit statistics.

- If you can, report less than $100,000 in total positive income from salaries, self-employment, and investments. These people have the lowest audit rate.
- Don't report less income than is shown on your W-2s, Form 1099s, and other third-party forms you receive. If one of them is incorrect, get the issuer to correct the form and reissue it.

Amending Tax Returns

You can change your tax return, or amend, in IRS-speak, after you've filed it. You can voluntarily correct a mistake, such as an overlooked deduction, to get a refund. If you fail to report income, the tax code requires you to amend. The sooner you do so, the less penalties and interest you'll be charged.

To amend your return, file IRS Form 1040X, *Amended U.S. Individual Income Tax Return*.

To get a *refund*, you must file a 1040X within three years from the date the first return was filed or within two years from the date you paid the taxes due on that return—whichever is later. For example, if you filed your 2010 tax return on April 15, 2011, you can file a 1040X any time up until April 14, 2014 and still get a refund. If you filed an extension, you can add the extended period on as well. One exception: If you file an amended return to claim a refund based on a worthless security or bad debt loss, you have up to seven years after you first filed.

How to Amend a Tax Return

File Form 1040X, *Amended U.S. Individual Income Tax Return*, with documentation to support your changes. (If you don't feel comfortable with or understand this form, hire a tax preparer or use a software program like *Turbotax*.)

It's best to hand deliver the 1040X to the nearest IRS office and get a stamped copy as your filing receipt. If you use the mail, send it certified, with postal return receipt requested, to the IRS where you now file your tax returns.

Don't forget to amend your state tax return at the same time. Get the proper forms from its tax department. If you don't feel comfortable or understand Form 1040X (it's a little tricky), hire a tax preparer to do it.

Audit Alert for Amended Tax Returns

Filing amended returns claiming refunds slightly raises your audit likelihood —and not just for the amended items, but for the whole tax return. This is partly because 1040X forms are scrutinized by IRS employees rather than just computer processed.

On the other hand, the IRS ordinarily has only three years to audit a return from the date it was filed. An amended return filing does *not* extend the time the IRS has to audit the first return. Filing an amended return near the three-year audit deadline gives the IRS very little time to audit your tax return and it may simply pass it through.

This ploy can backfire on you, however, as the IRS is not legally obligated to accept an amended tax return. If you file an amended return near the three-year audit deadline, the IRS may be willing to accept it only on the condition that you agree to extend the time for audit beyond the three-year deadline. If you're considering this strategy, you may want to talk to a tax professional first. (See Chapter 13.)

A Word About "Aggressive" Tax Filing

A question I am often asked is, "What deductions and tax benefits can I safely take, and which ones are risky?" The best answer is that it depends on your personality. Are you very conservative? Or are you a risk-taker by nature? Most people have at least a little of each trait in their personality. In the end, go with your comfort level.

Aggressive tax filing means interpreting the gray areas of the law in your favor—and taking the chance that you will either not be audited or survive if you are. It doesn't mean making up numbers. You may want to peruse Chapter 3 first to find out what happens at an audit if you cross the line.

Tax professional litmus test. I have never met two tax professionals who agreed on the meaning of aggressive. Find out how aggressive your tax adviser is by asking the person's opinion on deducting something. For instance, if you are self-employed, ask about deducting business lunch expenses, a combined business and pleasure trip, or health club dues. Or, if you have investment income, ask about financial publication expenses and trips to check out investments.

How tax advisers respond clues you into how aggressive or timid they are. If a person repeatedly says "you can't do that," instead of offering advice on how to make that expense deductible, then he or she may be too government oriented. At the other extreme, if the response is always not to worry, deduct anything you want because chances are you won't be audited, this approach could get you into trouble.

Comfort level. When I first interview a tax return preparation client, I check out the person's IRS comfort level. I ask outright how concerned he or she is about facing an audit, and if it happens, whether he or she will be able to document all the benefits claimed on the tax return.

I do not counsel tax cheating. But there is a fine line between being aggressive and being dishonest. No reputable tax return preparer will sign a tax return that the person believes is a work of fiction. And, if the preparer is not reputable, you don't want that name and identification number on your return. The IRS tracks crooked tax preparers and may reward you with an audit for choosing one.

Finding and using a tax professional is covered in Chapter 13. Some things to look for and types of preparers to avoid are covered there. Don't take picking a tax preparer lightly.

The people most often concerned about audits are small business owners wanting to know how far they can go in taking deductions. Generally, the tax code lets you take a deduction for just about any expense that helps you produce income. On the other hand, the expense must be ordinary and necessary. For aggressive tax filers, this means that as long as there is a reasonable basis for claiming a deduction, they will take it. (For more information on business deductions, see *Tax Savvy for Small Business*, by Frederick W. Daily (Nolo).)

EXAMPLE: Dennis, a lawyer, buys and deducts an antique $10,000 grandfather clock for his home office. He could have bought a reproduction for $500 or a simple wall clock for $25—the $25 clock with the quartz movement probably will keep the best time. The tax question is, does the $10,000 clock help Dennis produce more income? If he is ever audited, Dennis could argue that the clock is ordinary and necessary because it conveys the impression to his clients that he is successful. Will Dennis get this by an auditor? In similar cases, the courts have upheld the right of professionals to take this kind of deduction—but it's a close call.

Tax Shelter Investments and the IRS

Higher-income people, meaning six-figure earners, are often targets for tax shelter investments. These deals promise great tax benefits by using tax losses and deductions to offset other taxable income. Don't get me wrong, this can be perfectly legitimate. For example, the depreciation write-off for a rental property you own can be a great tax shelter. If the property you rent out produces a paper or tax loss, you can use that loss to offset other income.

IRS problems are more likely to arise with investments in exotic-sounding products, like foreign currency options, that promise tax benefits that exceed the amount of your investment.

The IRS now scrutinizes these investments to make sure their underlying purpose is not to avoid paying taxes. To pass muster, the investment program "must possess a reasonable possibility of profits beyond the tax benefits." Or, as other courts have put it, "the transaction must be entered into for a business purpose other than tax avoidance."

If the deal doesn't pass scrutiny, it is termed an "abusive tax shelter" and any tax benefits will be disallowed, with penalties and interest tacked on. As with most things in life, if it sounds too good to be true ....

(!) CAUTION

Creativity has its limits. In the example above, Dennis would have gone too far if he had:

- bought the antique clock and put it in his bedroom, or
- bought the clock for $1,000, added a zero to the receipt and claimed a $10,000 deduction.

In these examples, the deduction would no longer be gray, but black—it would be fraud. Where creativity ends and fraud begins is covered in Chapter 10.

(💡) TIP

Beware of joint filing. Never sign a joint tax return if you know your spouse is cheating the IRS. Your separate income and assets may be fair game if the IRS discovers the fraud. (See Chapter 9, "Filing Tax Returns—Joint or Separate?")

Chapter Highlights

- Not filing a tax return can be a crime if you owe taxes; most nonfilers, however, are not prosecuted if and when they are caught.
- If the IRS asks you if you filed returns and you haven't, don't lie, but don't answer. State that you want to consult a tax professional or check your records first.
- Filing before the IRS catches you is the safest policy.
- The time limit for criminally prosecuting a nonfiler is six years. The time limit for collecting from a nonfiler is ten years, but the clock doesn't start until you actually file a tax return.
- Penalties and interest for late filing are substantial and rarely forgiven. (There is no penalty if you didn't owe any taxes, however.)
- Don't file a tax return while you are being audited. It gives the auditor another year to look at it.

Winning Your Audit

We call them audits; the IRS prefers examinations. Whatever term you use, it describes one of life's most dreaded experiences—having the IRS probing into your financial affairs.

This chapter deals with the types of IRS audits—both correspondence and face-to-face—that individuals and small business owners are most likely to face. The IRS also has a Large and International Business Division for auditing business with assets over $5 million, as well as a Tax-Exempt and Government Entities Division.

The vast majority of individual and small business tax returns are accepted by the IRS without question. Your chance of being contacted by the IRS about a discrepancy on your return in any one year is only one in a hundred. But if you are self-employed, the odds of at least one IRS examination in your taxpaying lifetime are closer to 50%.

As your income increases, so does your audit likelihood. If you regularly earn over $100,000 per year, your probability of an audit has increased every year over the past decade. And when your time does come, expect it to cost you—over eight out of ten people who are audited owe additional taxes. A few people get tax refunds after an audit, but don't count on it. The amount of money the IRS assesses in audits is 32 times greater than the amount given back.

Federal courts have long held that if the IRS determines at an audit that you owe taxes, there is a rebuttable presumption that the determination is correct. This means that you have the burden of proof when up against the IRS. Critics have said that it really means you are guilty until proven innocent. While this is the standard in audits, it is not the standard in court proceedings where the IRS has the burden of proof. If you take the IRS to court, the government must show that you were wrong on a disputed factual issue, not vice versa. (See Chapter 5.)

Audit Rates Are Rising

In 2010, the IRS audited 1.58 million income tax returns, an 11% increase over 2009. This also marked the highest level of audits in the first decade of the 21st century. Moreover, the amount of this so-called "enforcement revenue" topped $57 billion, up 18% from the previous year.

How Long Do I Have to Worry About an Audit?

Generally, your tax return cannot be audited after three years from its original *filing* date. If you filed before the due date, April 15, the three years starts running from April 15 of the year it was due.

There are a few exceptions, however:

- If you understate your income by 25% or more on your tax return, the audit deadline is extended to *six* years.
- If you file a fraudulent return, there is no time limit on an audit. Tax fraud is conduct meant to deceive the IRS, such as using a false Social Security number. A really big mistake, if done negligently, not intentionally, isn't fraud. The burden of proving fraud is always on the IRS. And the IRS seldom audits returns after three years even if fraud is suspected.
- The audit time limit period, called a statute of limitations, starts to run *only* if and when you file a tax return. Nonfiled tax years are always open to audit. If, however, you haven't filed and haven't heard from the IRS within six years of the due date of a tax return, you have probably escaped the audit net.

TIP

Audit notices are usually mailed between 12 and 18 months after you file your return. Generally, if you haven't heard from the IRS within 18 months, you won't be audited. IRS audit notices are sent by first class mail and never by email or telephone contact.

The *Internal Revenue Manual* directs auditors to complete audits within 28 months after you file your tax return. Legally, the IRS has 36 months. The 28-month internal deadline is imposed, however, to allow eight additional months for the IRS to process any appeal you might request. (Appeals are covered in Chapters 4 and 5.)

These internal IRS time limits usually work to your benefit. Audit cases are often delayed within the IRS for various reasons—backlogs, agent transfers, postponements, complex issues, and lost files. The older your file gets, the more anxious the IRS is to close it. Auditors can be fired for missing the 36-month deadline, known as blowing the statute, but it still happens.

The Audit Burden Is on You, Not the IRS

An audit is the process by which the IRS determines whether you properly reported all income—from earnings and investments—and took the correct deductions, exemptions, and credits. If the IRS finds that you didn't, you will be assessed additional taxes, interest, and—usually—penalties. An assessment is the formal entry of a tax liability in your records.

To do its job, Congress has given the IRS wide powers to inspect your financial records and to ask you and others about your financial affairs, to determine whether you are cheating Uncle Sam. (Internal Revenue Code §§ 7601 and 7602.) The IRS will investigate the items listed on an audit notice checklist given to you and scrutinize any other areas deemed questionable. And the law specifically places the audit burden on you to demonstrate that the information shown on your tax return is correct—think of the IRS as the Show Me state of Missouri. If your dispute gets to court, however, the burden shifts to the IRS under certain conditions (see Chapter 5).

Proving the correctness of your tax return may not be that easy. The IRS wins over 80% of all audits, mostly because taxpayers can't properly verify the information on their tax returns. IRS auditors say that the biggest reason for adjustments is poor record keeping, not taxpayer dishonesty.

Stopping an audit once it begins. Once the IRS sends an examination notice to your last known address, the audit has begun. It is difficult to stop an audit. Even if you die, your spouse or the executor of your estate is obligated to carry on the audit.

You may be able to slow down—or even stop—an audit, however, if you ask for a transfer of your file to another IRS district. Audit transfers are discretionary with the IRS, and you need a good reason to get one—such as a location more convenient to that of your tax documents.

EXAMPLE: Janiel, who lived in Pennsylvania but had a jewelry business in New York, received an audit notice for Pennsylvania. She requested a transfer to where her business was located. Janiel told the IRS that her records were at the business location in New York, which was true. The transfer was granted, but the New York office's audit plate was already full and the office never got around to Janiel's audit. The three-year statute of limitations expired and Janiel's worries came to an end.

What to Expect at an Audit

Will the auditor discover the money I made from playing the organ at weddings?

I lost my records in a move last year—what am I going to do?

Was I entitled to claim my mother as an exemption?

Will the IRS question my home office deductions?

Is the IRS going to put me in jail if they find out I've been cheating?

These are common taxpayer concerns. So, let's look at what really goes on when the IRS decides to audit you. We'll look at the two primary issues in every audit:

- Did you report all income?
- Were you entitled to the deductions, exemptions, and credits claimed?

IRS Publication 17, *Your Federal Income Tax*, explains the audit process—from the IRS point of view.

Do I Have to Learn Tax Law to Win My Audit?

The Internal Revenue Code, or tax code, contains 8,500-plus pages of very fine print. Add to that IRS regulations, revenue rulings, letter rulings, manuals, and official publications, all of which add another 100,000 or so pages of tax law. Finally, there are thousands of court decisions telling us how the tax laws should be applied in individual cases. The total number of tax law pages exceeds one million!

How will I ever understand the tax laws?

You won't. But that may not be as much of a disadvantage as you might think. Tax law is so voluminous and complex, most IRS auditors don't know it well either. Moreover, the training and experience level of IRS personnel is declining while the law is getting more difficult to master. This means that auditors normally stick to predictable audit issues. A taxpayer with very high income or an intricate tax issue, however, may be assigned an auditor with more training and experience. But normally, if you are well prepared, you will come out okay—experiencing the minimum damage—most of the time.

In a few hours, you can learn the basic tax law for your particular audit issues. The information is in this book and other sources mentioned in Chapter 13. And you can—and probably should—consult with a tax professional before taking on the auditor.

The truth is that most people succeed in an audit without knowing any tax law at all. This is because many audit issues are factual, not legal. The distinction will become clear as you read this chapter. And it's as important to know IRS procedures—the rules of the game and your rights in dealing with the IRS—as tax law. This book explains the rules to follow and a psychology for dealing with the IRS as well.

Audit Selection—Why Me, O Lord?

You just got an examination notice from the IRS. Are you merely unlucky, or are there more sinister forces at work?

Computers and Classifiers

The IRS computer is to blame for most audits. Each year, your tax return data is sent to the IRS National Computer Center where it is analyzed by a computer program called the Discriminant Function. Your tax return is given a numerical DIF score—the higher the score, the more audit potential the return has.

The DIF program is super secret—few people even in the IRS know how it works or why a return is given a particular score. Outsiders guess that hundreds of variables on a return are weighed by the IRS computer. One known variable is called "total positive income," which means everything you took in from your services and investments, before any deductions or exemptions. If this number is over $100,000, your chances of an audit double (roughly). If you earn more than $1 million, your audit rate is nearly 10%. The key variable is believed to be the percentage of deductions and number of exemptions claimed.

Are You Claiming More Deductions Than the Norm?

One of the chief components of the IRS DIF scoring system is how close your tax return is to the norm of others with similar deductions. According to author Amir Aczel (*How to Beat the IRS at Its Own Game*, $14.95, Four Walls Eight Windows Press), the IRS is most likely to audit you if your return shows a high ratio of deductions to income on three schedules:

- Schedule A, *Itemized Deductions*
- Schedule C, *Profit and Loss from Business,* or
- Schedule F, *Profit and Loss from Farming.*

Aczel claims that, as a rule, as your deductions approach 50% of your income, your audit likelihood rises. He lists precise ratios based on a study of 1,200 audit cases. For example, he claims that taxpayers filing a Schedule C are rarely audited if they claim expenses of less than 52% of gross business income, but are often audited when claiming expenses of more than 63%. If you include a Schedule A with your tax return, Aczel claims you are safe from an audit if your deductions are less than 44% of your gross income. While his book is interesting, don't use it as a manual to avoid a tax audit. I say if you are entitled to a deduction, take it, no matter what the chances of audit are.

The IRS has a second computer scoring program to catch people not reporting all of their income. This is a slightly different approach from the DIF program, which relies heavily on deductions and exemptions claimed. This program is called the Unreported Income Discriminate Information Function (UIDIF). It scores individuals based on a high-expense/low-income ratio. In plain English, the tax man is looking for folks who look like they are living beyond their means. For instance, you and your spouse report income from your jobs of $40,000 and you claim mortgage interest and real estate taxes of $35,000. Even assuming that you didn't owe any taxes that year, it would be tough to live on $5,000—so the IRS believes. Of course some people have down income years and simply borrow or dip into savings to get by. These explanations can always be made to an auditor, if necessary.

One in ten tax returns—those with the highest computer scores—are initially selected for further review. IRS classifiers (human beings) then look at this batch and recommend approximately 10% for audit.

The final say-so on who gets audited face-to-face is made at local IRS offices by examination group managers. These people supervise and assign the auditors, often according to their experience and expertise. Managers decide whether you will be audited at the IRS office or will get the more rigorous field audit.

IRS field offices have their own audit-screening selection process which takes into account income and expense levels in their communities—for instance, people are more likely to claim car expenses for business in Los Angeles than Manhattan. Group managers select less than 10% of the returns received from the IRS classifiers—the 10% of all tax returns—to be audited. Historically, the net result is that only about three-quarters of 1% of all returns are actually audited.

The computer is not the only way the IRS picks its audit victims. See, "Other Reasons for Audits," below for other ways your number might come up.

According to the IRS Manual, only *significant items* should be examined. What is considered significant depends on the IRS's overall view of the return as well as particular items that seem questionable. Factors that are likely to figure into the audit selection process include:

- **Comparative size of an item to the rest of the return.** A $5,000 expense on a tax return reporting $25,000 in income would be significant; the same expense on a $100,000 income return wouldn't be.

- **An item on the return that is out of character for the taxpayer.** A plumber claiming expenses relating to a business airplane would cause suspicion.

- **An item that is reported at an inappropriate place on the return.** For example, $2,000 of credit card interest is reported as a business expense. The IRS might suspect that you improperly deducted personal interest as a business expense.

- **Evidence of intent to mislead on the return.** Filing a tax return with missing schedules or not providing all information asked for on the forms raises an IRS classifier's eyebrows.

- **Your gross income.** The IRS scrutinizes higher earners. If you make over $100,000 per year, your audit likelihood is one in 20 versus one in 100 for the general population.

- **Self-employment income.** The IRS is most suspicious of people in business for themselves. Sole proprietors are four times more likely to be audited than wage earners.
- **Losses from businesses and investments claimed on the tax return.** If your business and investments show losses on your tax return, the IRS may want to know how you paid your bills. Most likely to be audited are taxpayers reporting a small business loss.
- **Sloppiness and round numbers.** A messy return, especially if hand-written, attracts the attention of a classifier who may think you don't take your tax-reporting responsibilities very seriously. Use of round numbers—for example, $5,000 for business advertising, $2,000 for transportation and $1,500 for insurance—is a dead giveaway that you are estimating, not reporting from records.

TIP

Why me? Although you may never know for certain why the IRS zeroed in on you, try to figure it out before the audit date. If you know what the IRS suspects, you can better prepare—or get professional help early on. An experienced tax professional can spot probable audit issues in a tax return or from discussing your situation with you.

Living Beyond Your Means

The IRS targets some people for financial status audits. These are special techniques to detect unreported income, including the UIDIF computer scoring program described above in "Computers and Classifiers." The IRS looks to whether the income on the tax return supports the financial condition of the taxpayer. The IRS is looking for "economic reality" by approximating expenses for personal assets and living expenses. You might have to explain how you eat at the Ritz on a fast-food salary.

The IRS can't randomly conduct financial status audits. Financial status audits aren't to take place unless the IRS sees a "reasonable indication" of a likelihood of unreported income—a fairly vague limitation. (Internal Revenue Code § 7602.)

How the IRS Investigates Your Lifestyle

You can understand the IRS's focus on lifestyle audits by looking at the IRS training materials for auditors. They look at the following lifestyle-related issues.

The standard of living of a taxpayer:

- What does the taxpayer and dependent family consume?
- How much does it cost to maintain this consumption?
- Is reported net income sufficient to support this?

The accumulated wealth of a taxpayer:

- How much capital/assets has the taxpayer accumulated?
- When and how has this wealth accumulated?
- Has reported income been sufficient to pay for these items?
- If not, how did taxpayer obtain and repay credit?

The economic history of a taxpayer:

- What is the long-term pattern of profits and return on investment in the reported activity?
- Is the business expanding or contracting?
- Does the reported business history match with changes in the taxpayer's standard of living and wealth accumulation?

The business environment:

- What is typical profitability and return on investment for the taxpayer's industry and locality?
- What are the typical patterns of noncompliance in the taxpayer's industry?
- What are the competitive pressures and economic health of the industry within which the taxpayer operates?

Other nontaxable sources of funds:

- Do claims of nontaxable sources of support make economic sense?
- How creditworthy is the taxpayer—how many claimed loans?
- How did the sources of claimed fund transfers obtain those funds? For example, it is unlikely that subsidies will be obtained from countries where dollars are hard to obtain.

Goal: Do the taxpayer's books and records reflect the economic reality of his or her personal and business activities, or has the taxpayer omitted income in order to minimize tax liability?

Lifestyle Questions and Suggested Answers

The following sample questions are taken from IRS training materials. The suggested answers are strictly legal—and from me. Note that I never use the word no, but I don't give the IRS what it's fishing for, either. Unless otherwise noted, the auditor's questions should relate to the year or years you are being audited for, not the year the audit takes place.

1Q. (*If applicable*) Can you show me a copy of your tax return extension for the past year?

1A. "I don't see how that is related to the year under audit." (It's not.)

2Q. What is the educational background of you and your spouse?

2A. "I don't see how that is related to the year under audit."

3Q. What is the name of your previous employer and dates of employment?

3A. "I don't see how that is related to the year under audit."

4Q. Can I see the purchase documents on your home?

4A. Show only if you are claiming a casualty loss for your home, you sold it, or you are claiming a home office deduction.

5Q. What other real estate do you own?

5A. Show only if you are earning income from renting it or taking a depreciation deduction or another tax benefit from the ownership.

6Q. How many autos do you own, and what are the payments?

6A. If your cars are registered in the state of the audit, you might as well give in on this one as the auditor can easily check state records. Ditto with boats and planes.

7Q. Do you own any other large (over $10,000) assets?

7A. "I don't see how ...."

8Q. Did you sell any assets, and if so, for how much and to whom?

8A. Answer this only if you sold an asset, such as shares of stock on which you claimed a gain or loss, if there is a question about whether you reported enough income on your tax return to live on, or if the auditor asks the source of money deposited in your bank account. Otherwise, "I don't see how ...."

9Q. Did you lend anyone money?

9A. (Unless you had interest income from the loan for that year) "I don't see how …."

10Q. How much cash do you have on hand at your home or business, in a safety deposit box, or buried in the back yard?

10A. "I don't see …." (As a rule, never answer this question.)

11Q. Did you transfer funds between different accounts?

11A. Answer only if the auditor is questioning the source of deposits into your accounts. Otherwise, "I don't see …."

12Q. Were you involved in cash transactions exceeding $10,000?

12A. This is a tricky one. If you say yes, then you may have had an obligation to file a Currency Transaction Report with the IRS. If you didn't make this filing, you just confessed to a crime. If you say no, it had better be the truth, or you just broke an even more serious law. Stay mum or ask a tax lawyer how to answer if you are in doubt.

As the above hypothetical questions and answers indicate, try to answer economic reality questions with questions of your own, or don't answer them at all. Politely remind the auditor that the questions don't relate to the tax return, that you were merely selected for an audit, and that you shouldn't be treated like a criminal. Suggest that if the auditor wants to make an adjustment based on economic reality, you'll appeal. More likely than not, the auditor won't call your bluff.

Market Segment Specialization Program

The Market Segment Specialization Program, or MSSP, is a cornerstone of the IRS process. The MSSP focuses on specific industries or groups of taxpayers believed to be in significant noncompliance with the tax law. Accordingly, the IRS provides specialized training to its agents and issues *Audit Technique Guides* for its auditors.

The IRS has made these guides public; if you fall into one of the targeted categories, you will know what the IRS is after. So far, over 100 guides have been issued on topics from architects to veterinarians. You can locate these guides:

- at a law library
- from a tax professional
- by calling the IRS (at 800-829-1040), or
- on the IRS website, at www.irs.gov (search "Audit Technique Guide").

Can You Get Audited If You Don't File a Return?

Don't think that because you didn't file a return that you will escape the IRS audit telescope. If you are in the IRS's computer, the IRS will eventually request that you file—if the IRS can find you. If you ignore them, the IRS has the legal authority to file and, in effect, audit a tax return in your name. The *Internal Revenue Manual* directs the auditor to come up with a reasonable and substantially correct tax return—which gives the auditor a license for invention.

In addition to whatever information may be in the IRS records—typically income reports on W-2 and 1099 forms—the auditor may rely on tables from the Bureau of Labor Statistics (BLS) to estimate your income and expenses. This is often done when either the income sources on record show an impossibly small income, such as $4,000, when you live in a penthouse apartment in the Beacon Hill section of Boston, or when there is no income record at all. BLS data shows the government's estimate of the minimum amount of income necessary to live on, taking into account your geographic area, family size, and probable standard of living.

To approximate income from a business, the auditor may rely on industry standards. For example, the auditor may use averages for sales and profit margin on all U.S. auto parts retailers to estimate how much Simon's Auto Parts World made.

After the auditor's report of a nonfiled return is completed, the IRS will forward you a copy. If you agree with the figures, you can sign it. If you don't agree, you will be given an opportunity to dispute it with your own figures or to file a tax return. Or, the IRS will issue a Notice of Deficiency giving you 90 days to contest the IRS report in tax court. (See Chapter 5 for more on going to tax court.)

Other Reasons for Audits

Besides getting picked by the IRS computer, other ways you can get into the audit soup are described below.

Local projects. Local IRS offices can initiate special audit projects based on their perceptions of abuses by individuals and groups in the community. Recent projects include gamblers, people who claim excessive earned income credits, ex-spouses who deduct or receive alimony, and people whose mortgage loan applications show different incomes from those reported on their tax returns.

Compliance initiative projects. Every year, the IRS national office decides that certain businesses and occupations merit audit attention. Past favorites have included airline pilots and flight attendants, physicians, and morticians. Perennial targets are operators of cash businesses, such as bars and laundromats, food servers, cabdrivers, and owners and employees of gambling establishments. This program is being phased into the MSSP audit, described above.

The IRS receives several clues to your occupation. W-2 and 1099 forms filed by others might indicate it. You are required to state it on your tax return. If you are self-employed, you must list a six-digit business identification code. Some people have tried creativity here, such as the prostitute whose return stated "public relations." She was fined by the IRS and could have been criminally prosecuted when the auditor learned the exact nature of those relations. Misstating the source of your income is illegal, even if you report all of it.

Prior and related audits. Audit lightning does strike twice. Previous IRS audits often beget new ones—if they produced tax bills of at least several thousand dollars. But this is not a sure thing. I have seen people audited and hit with an enormous tax bill who never hear from the IRS again. If you are a partner, limited liability company member, or shareholder, and the business entity or any others in it are audited, you may not be far behind.

Criminal activity. Like grapes, trouble usually comes in bunches. If you are investigated for a drug crime or crime involving a lot of money, the IRS may be tipped off by the law enforcement agency and decide to audit. The tax code is morally neutral—it requires that all income, from sources legal or otherwise, be reported. The IRS doesn't care if you made the money as a Mafia hit man as long as you declare it.

If you'd prefer not to disclose the source of income, you can file a Fifth Amendment tax return on which you claim your Constitutional right against self-incrimination. You enter the amount of your income on your 1040 form and write Fifth Amendment next to the lines where you list the source and where the form asks for your occupation. While this may keep you out of the criminal investigation division of the IRS, it undoubtedly increases your audit potential.

 CAUTION
Never file a Fifth Amendment tax return without first consulting a tax attorney.

Amended tax returns. You may file an amended tax return any time after you file an original one. The IRS has discretion to reject amended returns, but it usually accepts them. A few people file amended returns and wind up owing more in taxes, but most people amend their tax returns to get a refund. To get a refund, you must file the amended return within three years of the date you filed the original return, or within two years of the date you paid the tax. Because the IRS doesn't like to give back money, it investigates all refund claims, sometimes by auditing. And if you are audited, everything on the return—not just the items amended—are fair game.

Filing an amended tax return doesn't extend the time the IRS has to audit you—normally three years from the original filing date. So, the closer to the end of the three-year period you file the amended return, the less time the IRS has to audit you. But, the IRS has the discretion to reject amended returns and sometimes will accept them only on the condition the taxpayer agrees to extend the three-year audit limit.

Informants' tips. Undoubtedly, you have heard stories about disgruntled ex-spouses, business associates, and former employees turning someone in to the IRS. While an audit could result, it should put your mind at ease to know that fewer than 5% of all audits result from tattletales. IRS sources say that most tips, particularly anonymous ones, are not seriously followed up. The IRS prefers to rely on its computers for audit selection. Historically, the IRS has found that many tips are not provable and are motivated by spite.

Where you live. Everyone knows that Kansas gets tornadoes, Florida gets hurricanes, and California gets earthquakes. Similarly, some locales get more than their fair share of audits. The audit rate is 150% higher than the national average in Nevada, but 150% lower than that average in Wisconsin. Other high-audit states are Alaska, California, and Colorado. Low-audit states include Illinois, Indiana, Iowa, Maryland, Massachusetts, Michigan, New York (excluding Manhattan), Ohio, Pennsylvania, and West Virginia. The second lowest audit rate locale is the District of Columbia.

What's more, how you come out of an audit depends on where you call home, too. Your chance of getting away without owing a nickel are more than twice as good in Las Vegas (32%) than in Manhattan (15%).

Random selection. The IRS selects some audit victims at random under its new National Research Program (NRP). These Compliance Research Exams are reminiscent of the dreaded TCMP (Taxpayer Compliance Measurement Program) audits that were discontinued in the 1990s. The stated purpose of NRP audits is to gather data to update the statistical models used to score individual tax returns. Nevertheless, these are very "real" audits—in fact, they are much more intensive than ordinary audits.

Frivolous tax return. Claiming that your income is not subject to federal taxes is a surefire way to get on the audit list.

Political selection. It is a crime for a non-IRS employee to request that the IRS conduct or terminate an audit of a taxpayer. An IRS employee must report such a request to his superiors. (Internal Revenue Code § 7217.)

When the IRS Increases Your Tax Bill Without an Audit

The IRS increasingly relies on computer-generated tax bills that are technically not audits. This means your tax return still could be examined in the future.

The IRS is authorized to make changes to your tax account without a formal audit in some cases. (Internal Revenue Code § 6213(g)(2).) The IRS has programs (described below) that often exceed Congressional intent of the law, which was to let the IRS correct minor taxpayer errors. Instead, the IRS effectively performs one-sided mail audits. Many poor souls pay up without question when they receive one of these:

- **Correction notices.** The IRS says there is a math error or a similar obvious problem with your tax return. For instance, you claimed four dependents but only listed the names of three on your return. The IRS corrects your return—and bills you.
- **Penalty assessment notices.** Typically, a penalty notice and bill will be sent if you didn't meet a filing or payment deadline. The IRS may be wrong for any number of reasons, or it might be right but you may have a reason to have the penalty abated, or canceled. Chapter 12 has information on dealing with a penalty notice.
- **Interest assessment notices.** If you did not pay a tax bill on time, you will always be charged interest. Sometimes, the IRS computation of interest is incorrect; occasionally, you can get it waived even if it is correct. Again, see Chapter 12.
- **Underreporter program notices.** The IRS initiates an underreporter case when its computer finds a discrepancy between two data sources. Usually the two sources are your tax return and information reported to the IRS on a 1099 or W-2 form. You will get either a CP-2501 notice—a letter asking you to explain (CP means computer paragraph)—or a CP-2000 notice proposing additional tax, penalties, and interest. In either case, you'll be given 30 days to respond. According to the IRS, the most common underreporter issues are:
  - IRA distributions rolled over but not properly reported (Form 1099R)
  - income reported on the return that does not match IRS data on a Form 1099 or Form K-1
  - mortgage interest deductions that don't match the financial institution's report to the IRS (Form 1098), and
  - wages and/or tax withholding that doesn't match W-2 forms.

Underreporting notices are the most common of the four programs.

Dealing With IRS Automated Adjustment Notices

The most common automated adjustment notice is the CP-2000 (see sample below). Look at the top right-hand corner of the first page of the notice for the code. The problem with CP-2000 notices is that many are totally or partly wrong. *Money Magazine* estimates that at least 25% are in error.

A common IRS mistake is failing to see that the income was reported elsewhere on the form than where the computer looked. For instance, one year I reported earnings in a money market fund as interest instead of dividends, and the IRS computer spit out a CP-2000 notice stating that I did not report $450 of income and billed me for additional tax, and penalties and interest.

If so many of these notices are wrong, why does the IRS keep sending them? The *Money Magazine* article reported that most people who were billed for $589 or less simply paid it. The magazine estimates that IRS collects $7 billion a year it is not entitled to.

Can you fight an automated adjustment notice? Absolutely. If you receive one of these notices, just do the following:

Step 1. Call the IRS. Call the number on the notice (or 800-829-1040) to start. Ask for a full explanation even if you suspect the IRS may be right, but you aren't sure. Ask for an abatement if you believe the IRS is, or probably is, wrong—abatement is the IRS word for canceling a bill. Tell the IRS person why the notice is wrong or that your records are different from the IRS's and promise to send the proof. You probably won't settle this during the telephone call, but you want the fact that you are disputing the notice entered into the IRS computer.

Step 2. Contest in writing. Don't rely on a telephone call to straighten out an IRS problem. The tax code provides that if you don't object to an automated adjustment notice within 60 days, it becomes final.

Mail back the CP 2000 notice after filling in and signing the last page. Place your checkmark for either (a) "total agreement," or (b) "partial agreement," or (c) "total disagreement" with the proposed tax changes. Enclose an explanatory letter (see sample below) unless you totally agree. Make the letter brief and to the point. IRS people have short attention spans and won't struggle through long-winded explanations or unclear handwriting. Staple a copy, not the original, of the IRS notice to the front of your letter. Mail it certified, return receipt requested. Use the IRS bar-coded return envelope that was included with your notice to speed up processing.

When writing the IRS, always make several photocopies of whatever you send. If the IRS misplaces your correspondence, you can send it again—and again, if necessary.

Sample CP-2000 Notice—Page 1

```
DEPARTMENT OF THE TREASURY          TYPE OF NOTICE: CP-2000
INTERNAL REVENUE SERVICE-UR         DATE OF THIS NOTICE: 02/19/
FRESNO  CA   93888                  SOCIAL SECURITY NUMBER:
                                    TAX FORM: 1040     TAX YEAR: 19

    |..III.I.II.I.I.I..III.II..IIIII.I.I.I.II..III..IIIII.I
                                    PLEASE RESPOND TO THIS NOTICE
                                    BY COMPLETING THE LAST PAGE
                                    AND SENDING IT TO US IN THE
                                    ENVELOPE PROVIDED.


                                    FOR GENERAL INFORMATION
                                    PLEASE CALL US AT:

                                    839-1040 LOCAL SF/OAKLAND
                                    1-800-829-1040  ST. OF CA
```

NOTICE OF PROPOSED CHANGES TO YOUR   TAX RETURN

WE ARE PROPOSING CHANGES TO YOUR   TAX RETURN BECAUSE THE INFORMATION ON YOUR TAX
RETURN IS NOT THE SAME AS THE INFORMATION REPORTED TO US BY YOUR EMPLOYERS, BANKS, AND
OTHER PAYERS.

PLEASE READ THIS NOTICE CAREFULLY. IT EXPLAINS WHAT YOU SHOULD DO IF YOU AGREE OR
DISAGREE WITH OUR PROPOSED CHANGES. PAGE 2 SHOWS THE PROPOSED CHANGES TO YOUR
ACCOUNT. WE PROPOSE TO INCREASE YOUR TAX. IF YOU AGREE WITH THIS CHANGE, YOU WILL
OWE US $316.

PLEASE COMPARE YOUR RECORDS WITH THE PAYER INFORMATION SHOWN ON PAGE 3 OF THIS NOTICE.
IF YOU AGREE WITH THE PROPOSED CHANGES ON PAGE 2:
- CHECK BOX A ON THE LAST PAGE OF THIS NOTICE,
- SIGN AND DATE THE CONSENT TO THE TAX INCREASE,
- ENCLOSE YOUR PAYMENT IN FULL, IF POSSIBLE, AND MAKE YOUR CHECK OR MONEY ORDER
  PAYABLE TO THE INTERNAL REVENUE SERVICE, AND
- RETURN THE LAST PAGE OF THIS NOTICE ALONG WITH YOUR PAYMENT IN THE ENCLOSED
  ENVELOPE.

IF YOU DO NOT AGREE WITH THE PROPOSED CHANGES ON PAGE 2:
- CHECK BOX B OR C ON THE LAST PAGE OF THIS NOTICE,
- ENCLOSE A SIGNED STATEMENT EXPLAINING WHY YOU DISAGREE,
- INCLUDE ANY SUPPORTING DOCUMENTS YOU WISH US TO CONSIDER, AND
- USE THE ENVELOPE ENCLOSED TO RETURN THE LAST PAGE OF THIS NOTICE WITH YOUR
  STATEMENT AND DOCUMENTS. PLEASE INCLUDE A TELEPHONE NUMBER, INCLUDING AN AREA
  CODE, AND THE BEST TIME TO CALL YOU.

IT IS IMPORTANT THAT WE RECEIVE YOUR COMPLETED RESPONSE WITHIN 30 DAYS FROM THE DATE
OF THIS NOTICE. YOU HAVE 60 DAYS IF YOU LIVE OUTSIDE OF THE UNITED STATES. IF WE
DO NOT RECEIVE YOUR RESPONSE WITHIN THIS PERIOD, WE WILL ISSUE A NOTICE OF DEFICIENCY
TO YOU FOLLOWED BY A FINAL BILL FOR THE PROPOSED AMOUNT SHOWN ON PAGE 2. YOU MAY
CONTEST THE NOTICE OF DEFICIENCY IN COURT IF YOU BELIEVE YOU DO NOT OWE THE ADDITIONAL
TAX.

PLEASE RESPOND TO US EVEN IF YOU DO NOT UNDERSTAND OUR COMPUTATION OR CANNOT PAY THE
PROPOSED TAX DUE. IF YOU DELAY YOUR RESPONSE, INTEREST ON ANY AMOUNT YOU OWE WILL
INCREASE. INTEREST STOPS ONLY WHEN YOU PAY THE TOTAL AMOUNT YOU OWE. IF YOU SIGN THE
CONSENT TO TAX INCREASE, FULL PAYMENT IS DUE WITHIN 15 DAYS AFTER WE RECEIVE YOUR
SIGNED CONSENT. IF WE DO NOT RECEIVE YOUR PAYMENT BY THEN, WE WILL SEND YOU A BILL.
THIS BILL WILL INCLUDE YOUR TAX, ANY PENALTIES, AND ADDITIONAL INTEREST.

IF YOU AGREE WITH THE CHANGES WE PROPOSE, YOU DO NOT HAVE TO FILE AN AMENDED TAX
RETURN. HOWEVER, YOU SHOULD REVIEW YOUR RECORDS AND RETURNS FILED AFTER THE YEAR
IDENTIFIED IN THIS NOTICE, TO MAKE SURE YOU REPORTED ALL INCOME CORRECTLY.

IF YOU DID NOT REPORT ALL YOUR INCOME CORRECTLY, YOU SHOULD FILE AN AMENDED TAX RETURN
(FORM 1040X) FOR EACH YEAR, AND PAY ANY ADDITIONAL TAX AND INTEREST YOU OWE. IT IS TO
YOUR ADVANTAGE TO CORRECT YOUR TAX RETURNS AND PAY ANY ADDITIONAL TAX AND INTEREST
AS SOON AS POSSIBLE TO AVOID PENALTIES AND ADDITIONAL INTEREST.

THE ENCLOSED PUBLICATION 1383 CONTAINS DETAILED INFORMATION ABOUT HOW TO RESPOND TO
THIS NOTICE. PLEASE KEEP THIS NOTICE FOR YOUR RECORDS. THANK YOU FOR YOUR COOPERATION.

NOTE: WE SEND INFORMATION TO YOUR STATE AND LOCAL TAX AGENCIES ABOUT ANY INCREASE
OR DECREASE IN YOUR TAX AS A RESULT OF THIS NOTICE.

                                                              00001966

                                             CP-2000 (REV. 7/91)

Sample CP-2000 Notice—Page 2

```
FRESNO SERVICE CENTER                                        DO 94 02/19/

               OUR PROPOSED CHANGES TO YOUR      INCOME TAX
          (DETAILED INFORMATION FOR THESE CHANGES BEGINS ON PAGE 3)


CHANGED ITEM(S)                   SHOWN ON      REPORTED TO      INCREASE OR
                                   RETURN      IRS BY PAYERS     DECREASE
TAXABLE WAGES                  $    91,875    $    92,788     $      913.00


PROPOSED CHANGES IN ADJUSTED GROSS INCOME
                                   SHOWN ON      PROPOSED       INCREASE OR
                                    RETURN        AMOUNT         DECREASE
MISCELLANEOUS DEDUCTION        $     2,330    $     2,312     $       18.00
____  TOTAL INCREASE                                         $      931.00

____  PROPOSED CHANGES IN TAX COMPUTATION
                                   SHOWN ON      PROPOSED       INCREASE OR
                                    RETURN        AMOUNT         DECREASE
    1.  TAXABLE INCOME         $    61,648.00 $    62,579.00  $      931.00
    2.  TAX                         13,238.00      13,499.00         261.00
    3.  TOTAL TAXES                 13,238.00      13,499.00         261.00
    4.  NET TAX INCREASE................................................       261.00
    5.  INCOME TAX WITHHELD         16,521.00      16,521.00           0.00
    6.  INTEREST FROM 4/15/   TO 15 DAYS AFTER THE DATE OF THIS NOTICE.......    55.00
    7.  PROPOSED AMOUNT YOU OWE IRS........................................$    316.00











                                  PAGE   2

                                                                CP-2000
```

Sample CP-2000 Notice—Page 3

```
FRESNO SERVICE CENTER                                      DO 94 02/19/


AMOUNTS REPORTED TO IRS BUT NOT IDENTIFIED, FULLY REPORTED, OR CORRECTLY DEDUCTED ON
YOUR INCOME TAX RETURN FOR        .


    1. CHARLES SCHWAB & CO. INC.         ISSUED FORM W-2
                                         FOR TAXABLE WAGES           $      913
                                           SOCIAL SECURITY WITHHELD         68
       ACCOUNT NUMBER                      SOCIAL SECURITY WAGES           913
       EIN 94-1737782
                                                                         0002


                        EXPLANATION OF CHANGES


DISCLOSURE AUTHORIZATION STATEMENT

    IF YOU WISH TO AUTHORIZE SOMEONE, IN ADDITION TO YOU, TO DISCUSS THIS NOTICE
    WITH US, PLEASE SIGN AND DATE THE AUTHORIZATION STATEMENT ON THE LAST PAGE OF THIS
    NOTICE.  ALSO INCLUDE THE NAME AND ADDRESS OF THE PERSON YOU AUTHORIZE.

    THE PERSON YOU CHOOSE MAY ONLY GIVE AND RECEIVE INFORMATION ABOUT THE TAX YEAR IN THIS
    NOTICE.  HE OR SHE CANNOT SIGN FOR YOU, OR REPRESENT YOU IN AN INTERVIEW OR IN
    U.S. TAX COURT.  IF WE NEED MORE INFORMATION, WE WILL ASK FOR IT THROUGH THE PERSON
    YOU CHOSE.  PLEASE HAVE THAT PERSON:
        - WRITE TO US AT THE ADDRESS SHOWN ON THIS NOTICE,
        - SEND ANY SUPPORTING DOCUMENTS TO US, AND
        - GIVE US A TELEPHONE NUMBER, INCLUDING AN AREA CODE, AND THE BEST TIME TO CALL.

    YOU MAY CHANGE OR CANCEL YOUR AUTHORIZATION BY SENDING A SIGNED STATEMENT TO THE RETURN
    ADDRESS ON THIS NOTICE.  PLEASE STATE THE TAX YEAR FOR WHICH YOU WISH TO CHANGE OR
    CANCEL YOUR DISCLOSURE AUTHORIZATION.

    YOUR STATEMENT SHOULD INCLUDE THE NAME, ADDRESS, AND TELEPHONE NUMBER OF THE PERSON WHO
    WILL NO LONGER BE AUTHORIZED TO DISCUSS THIS NOTICE AND THE NAME, ADDRESS, AND TELEPHONE
    NUMBER OF ANY NEW PERSON YOU ARE AUTHORIZING.


MISIDENTIFIED INCOME

    IF ANY OF THE INCOME SHOWN ON THIS NOTICE IS NOT YOURS:
    - SEND US THE NAME, ADDRESS, AND SOCIAL SECURITY NUMBER OF THE PERSON WHO RECEIVED THE
      INCOME, OR SEND US A COPY OF THE INCOME TAX RETURN WHERE THE INCOME WAS REPORTED,
      IF YOU HAVE IT,
    - CHECK BOX B OR C ON THE LAST PAGE OF THIS NOTICE,
    - RETURN YOUR SUPPORTING DOCUMENTS AND THE LAST PAGE OF THIS NOTICE IN THE ENCLOSED
      ENVELOPE.


CHILDREN'S INCOME

    IF THE INCOME BELONGS TO YOUR MINOR CHILD AND THE LAW DOES NOT REQUIRE YOUR CHILD TO
    FILE AN INCOME TAX RETURN:
    - SEND A SIGNED STATEMENT TO US EXPLAINING THIS, AND
    - NOTIFY THE PAYERS TO CORRECT THEIR RECORDS TO SHOW THE NAME AND SOCIAL SECURITY NUMBER
      OF THE PERSON WHO ACTUALLY RECEIVED THE INCOME, SO THAT FUTURE REPORTS TO US ARE
      ACCURATE.


INTEREST PERIOD

    INTEREST HAS BEEN FIGURED FROM APRIL 15,    TO 15 DAYS AFTER THE DATE OF THIS NOTICE
    ON THIS PROPOSED CHANGE ONLY.  IF A FULL PAYMENT WAS RECEIVED, INTEREST IS FIGURED FROM
    APRIL 15,    , TO THE DATE OF THE PAYMENT.  WE ARE REQUIRED TO CHARGE INTEREST AS
    PROVIDED BY LAW, ON THE UNPAID TAX FROM THE DUE DATE OF THE RETURN, TO THE DATE THE TAX
    IS PAID.


MISCELLANEOUS DEDUCTIONS PERCENTAGE LIMITATION

    YOU CAN ONLY CLAIM YOUR MISCELLANEOUS DEDUCTIONS THAT ARE OVER 2% OF YOUR ADJUSTED
    GROSS INCOME ON LINE 31 OF YOUR TAX RETURN.  WE REFIGURED YOUR MISCELLANEOUS
    DEDUCTIONS BECAUSE WHEN YOUR ADJUSTED GROSS INCOME CHANGED, YOUR 2% LIMIT CHANGED.



                        PAGE    3

                                                           CP-2000
```

Sample CP-2000 Notice—Page 4

```
FRESNO SERVICE CENTER                            DO 94              02/19/
                                           FSC
290*00261/806*    /764*      0*    /170*   /310*  /IN  ,0055/680*   /   *   /
               RESPONSE TO OUR PROPOSED CHANGES TO YOUR       INCOME TAX

        PLEASE COMPLETE THE SECTION BELOW THAT APPLIES TO YOU AND RETURN THE ENTIRE PAGE
     IN THE ENVELOPE WE ENCLOSED.  BE SURE THE INTERNAL REVENUE SERVICE ADDRESS SHOWS
     THROUGH THE WINDOW.  IF YOU ARE MAKING A PAYMENT WITH THIS NOTICE, WRITE THE AMOUNT
     OF YOUR PAYMENT ON THIS LINE $_____.  PLEASE MAKE YOUR CHECK OR MONEY ORDER
     PAYABLE TO THE INTERNAL REVENUE SERVICE.

                              CHECK ONE

     A) []    TOTAL AGREEMENT, CONSENT TO TAX INCREASE - I CONSENT TO THE IMMEDIATE ASSESSMENT
              AND COLLECTION OF THE INCREASE IN TAX AND PENALTIES SHOWN ON THIS NOTICE, PLUS
              INTEREST.  I UNDERSTAND THAT BY SIGNING THIS WAIVER, I WILL NOT BE ABLE TO
              CONTEST THESE CHANGES IN THE U.S. TAX COURT FOR THE TAX YEAR SHOWN ON THIS
              NOTICE UNLESS ADDITIONAL TAX IS DETERMINED TO BE DUE FOR THIS YEAR.


     SIGNATURE                           DATE        SPOUSE'S SIGNATURE
                                                     (REQUIRED IF YOU FILED A JOINT RETURN)



     B) []    PARTIAL AGREEMENT WITH PROPOSED CHANGES - I AGREE TO A PORTION OF THE PROPOSED
              CHANGES TO MY INCOME, DEDUCTIONS, TAXES AND/OR CREDITS SHOWN ON THIS NOTICE.
              I HAVE ATTACHED A SIGNED STATEMENT EXPLAINING WHICH ITEMS I DISAGREE WITH AND
              WHY I DISAGREE, ALONG WITH MY SUPPORTING DOCUMENTS.



     C) []    TOTAL DISAGREEMENT WITH PROPOSED CHANGES - I DISAGREE WITH ALL OF THE PROPOSED
              CHANGES ON THIS NOTICE.  FOR EACH PROPOSED CHANGE, I HAVE ATTACHED A SIGNED
              STATEMENT AND SUPPORTING DOCUMENTS EXPLAINING WHY I DISAGREE.



                              AUTHORIZATION STATEMENT
     IF YOU WISH TO AUTHORIZE SOMEONE, IN ADDITION TO YOU, TO DISCUSS THIS NOTICE WITH THE
     INTERNAL REVENUE SERVICE, PLEASE SIGN BELOW.
     I AUTHORIZE_____
                      NAME                   ADDRESS
     TO GIVE AND RECEIVE INFORMATION FROM THE INTERNAL REVENUE SERVICE ABOUT THIS NOTICE.


          SIGNATURE OF TAXPAYER                                  DATE
                                                                        CP-2000
.........................................................................................
                         PLEASE DO NOT DETACH

           PLEASE BE SURE OUR ADDRESS SHOWS THROUGH THE WINDOW




     123283928 XY ALEX 30 0 8912 640 00000031600


         |...|III.I.II..I.I.II.II..IIIII.I.I.I.II.II....IIII.I|


         INTERNAL REVENUE SERVICE
         FRESNO SERVICE CENTER
         FRESNO  CA   93888




                              PAGE   4


                                                        CP-2000
```

Letter to Dispute an IRS Tax Adjustment

Married couples—
use the first
spouse's number on
your tax return

Hamilton and Jill O'Brien
SSN: 123-45-6789
123 Elm St.
Ukiah, CA 90000
June 16, 20xx

IRS ADJUSTMENTS/CORRESPONDENCE
IRS Campus
Fresno, CA 93888

Choose 1, 2, or 3
below followed by
your explanation.
If none fits your
situation, explain in
your own words.

REQUEST FOR ADJUSTMENT

Re: IRS Notice Dated 6/2/xx

To Whom It May Concern:

I am responding to your notice of 6/2/xx, a copy of which
is attached.

1. Math errors

The notice is wrong. I did not make any math errors in my
tax return. Here is how I made the calculations:
$10,432 − $3,190 = $7,242.

2. Matching error
(CP-2000 notice)

The 1099 form filed by Apex Industries was wrong and the
company has prepared a letter stating the correct amount,
which is attached to this letter.

The W-2 form filed by my former employer is incorrect in
that I made $42,815 in 20xx, not $49,815.

3. Partially corrected
errors

I responded to your notice of 5/2/xx but you did not fully
correct your error. Enclosed is a copy of my letter of 5/9/xx
with a full explanation.

In your letter to me of 5/2/xx you said that the tax bill of
$666 was corrected to $222 (copy enclosed), but I just got
a notice dated 6/2/xx for the $666 again.

Letter to Dispute an IRS Tax Adjustment (continued)

Please abate the taxes, penalties, and interest in the amount of $ 1,612.

We can be reached at 707-555-0562 anytime.

Sincerely,

Hamilton O'Brien

Jill O'Brien

Hamilton and Jill O'Brien

Enclosed: Copies of IRS notices, prior correspondence

Step 3. Go to tax court. If you fail to respond to a CP-2000 notice, or if you do respond but the IRS ignores or disagrees with your explanation, the IRS will issue a Notice of Deficiency. You will know when it comes because these notices—also called 90-Day Letters—are sent by certified mail and labeled Notice of Deficiency. If you get one, your only recourse is to file a petition in U.S. Tax Court within 90 days after the date of the letter. This is not a difficult thing to do, but does cost $60. See Chapter 5 for instructions.

Be Patient If You Don't Hear From the IRS Immediately

Don't be surprised if you keep getting bills in spite of your letters contesting an automated adjustment notice. It takes a month or more to get your response into the system to stop the computerized cycle. Simply respond to later IRS notices with a photocopy of your earlier letter. Never ignore IRS letters, and never send originals. If notices ignoring your letters keep coming after 90 days, call the Taxpayer Advocate Service at 800-829-4059. Tell the taxpayer advocate that the IRS has not answered your letters and ask for help.

Consider calling a tax professional for advice, although it is seldom cost-effective to hire one for this type of problem. Many tax professionals will talk to you on the phone free of charge. If the erroneous IRS bill is a biggie, consult with a tax professional first or have them contact the IRS on your behalf.

Even if the IRS eventually proves to be correct, by sending letters, requesting help from the taxpayer advocate, or filing a petition in tax court you will have greatly delayed the final tax bill. This gives you extra time to get the payment together or to figure out another way to deal with the tax bill (see Chapter 6 for alternatives in dealing with a tax debt).

Types of IRS Audits

There are three types of IRS audits: *correspondence, office,* and *field.*

The way the IRS goes about auditing you can produce very different results. A few years back, office audits resulted in additional tax and penalties averaging $1,965 per individual return, correspondence audits $3,817, and field audits a whopping $16,248. For those taxpayers who made more than $100,000 per year, field audits resulted in added taxes, penalties, and interest averaging $35,295! In a recent year, the IRS performed 1.7 million audits

Correspondence Audits—Please, Mr. Postman

The correspondence audit is by far the IRS's preferred method of attack. Seventy-eight percent of all IRS audits are by mail. Like it sounds, a correspondence audit comes by first-class mail. The IRS never notifies by telephone or email of the beginning of a correspondence audit. The IRS requests that you mail information or documents instead of meeting with you. This method of auditing is used to verify such things as stock market transactions, real estate sales, and itemized deductions. Amended tax returns are often audited by mail. These audits often result from a mismatch of a third-party payment report on a Form 1099 or W-2.

You should almost always cooperate with an audit by mail and be thankful that you weren't chosen for a field or an office audit. Unless the documents requested are lost or nonexistent, promptly send copies. Don't send originals—you won't get them back. It's possible to call the auditor to discuss your case. Or, write and ask the auditor to call you. A name and telephone number should be listed in the IRS notice you received. As a precaution, send document copies by certified mail, return receipt requested. Always keep photocopies of everything you send to the IRS.

If you have a problem with the correspondence auditor—for example, he or she is not satisfied with your supporting receipts and canceled checks— you can request that your file be transferred to your local IRS office for a face-to-face meeting. Just making this request may cause the IRS to reconsider. And sometimes, mail audits forwarded to local IRS offices are closed with no adjustments—without even contacting you. If you're given a meeting with an auditor at the local office, consider it a second chance.

Office Audits—Heigh-Ho, Heigh-Ho, It's Off to the IRS We Go

The office audit is announced by an IRS letter sent to your last known address either setting a time or requesting you to call for an appointment. The letter tells you the year being audited and often specifies documents you are requested to bring with you, such as receipts and canceled checks. It may also list up to four specific areas the IRS wants to examine—such as rental property income, deducted interest expenses, deducted unreimbursed business expenses, and charitable contributions.

Thankfully, the IRS doesn't expect auditors to examine every item on a tax return. Remember—only significant items are selected by classifiers, although IRS examination group managers may modify the list before the audit appointment.

> **TIP**
>
> **You don't have to respond to everything immediately.** If you are questioned about unlisted items and you don't want to answer, just say that you are not prepared to discuss those issues. The auditor will probably drop it, or give you more time to get prepared and set a second meeting date.

Review the Audit Notice Carefully

By law, the IRS normally has three years to audit you after you file a tax return. So, if the year on your notice is more than three years ago, either the IRS made a mistake or the IRS suspects you of fraud or of substantially understating your income. If you believe it's a mistake, call the number on the notice and ask that the audit be canceled. If you're told it is no mistake, then head straight for a tax professional's office.

If you were audited in either of the two previous years and the IRS made a small, $100 or so, adjustment—or issued a no change report—you may be able to get the audit canceled under the no repetitive audit rule discussed above. Explain the prior audit and the outcome to the clerk; if he or she seems not to know what you are talking about, ask to speak to a manager. This defense has only limited application, however, and probably won't work if you report any self-employment income.

Call the IRS to Schedule the Office Audit

After you get over the shock of reading "We have selected your federal income tax return for examination," call the IRS phone number on the letter. However, the IRS does not award gold stars for calling as soon as you get the notice and waiting up to 30 days won't hurt.

Even if you don't want to delay, when you call the IRS for an appointment or to reschedule a date set by the IRS, ask for the furthest date available so you have sufficient time to get your records in order. A month or two is common. If you are turned down, ask to speak to a supervisor. The Taxpayer Bill of Rights requires that you be given a say in the appointment process. However, the IRS doesn't audit at night or on weekends.

Also, some tax professionals advise getting an appointment on the last day of the week toward the end of the month, in late morning—just before the auditor's lunch break—or late afternoon. Friday afternoons are perfect, especially if a three-day weekend is coming up. Auditors do not get paid overtime and look forward to going home as much as you do.

Consequently, the auditor may race through your audit without digging too deep. Much like car dealers, IRS offices track monthly case closings. If you come in near the end of the month, an auditor who hasn't kept pace may need to finish your case or else suffer a bad performance review from his or her manager.

Your Rights During an Audit

IRS Publication 1, *Your Rights as a Taxpayer,* should be included with your audit notice. (A copy is in Chapter 15.) It very clearly explains the Taxpayer Bill of Rights. The most important audit rights are to:

- be treated fairly by IRS personnel. If you find someone who is not professional, prompt, and courteous, you have a right to speak to a supervisor.
- have a representative handle your audit. He or she must be qualified to practice before the IRS and have your written power of attorney. With a few exceptions, the IRS can't force you to appear or even contact you if you send a representative in your place.
- sound record the audit, although this isn't recommended. Taping an audit would most likely only cause the auditor to be unfriendly and work harder.
- not have to submit to repeat audits. If you were audited within the last two years, and the IRS made few or no tax adjustments, you can't be audited for the same items again. The IRS can, however, examine different items in your return. If you believe you're being audited again for the same items, complain to the IRS appointment clerk or auditor. The no-repeat audit policy does not apply to examinations of business-related items on an individual's return.
- have proposed adjustments explained. Audit reports are vague, so you are entitled to get a detailed explanation if you ask for it. You can do this by phone or in person. If the auditor refuses, talk to her or his manager.
- not be forced to incriminate yourself. You always have this Constitutionally guaranteed right when dealing with the government, even the IRS. For example, if you earn your living by robbing banks, the IRS can't demand that you give details, as long as you report the income. You cannot, however, lie to the IRS about the source of your income. In this case, you should state on your tax return or during an audit that you are claiming the Fifth Amendment—but see a tax or criminal attorney before doing so.
- appeal your audit. See Chapter 4.

Why and How to Delay an Audit

In general, the words to live by are, "Don't hurry, be happy," and "An audit delayed is an audit well played." The more time an audit drags on, the better the result in most cases. This is because auditors are under pressure to close files, and they want your cooperation to do it. The later it gets, the greater the pressure. The main drawback with prolonging an audit is that interest and penalties are growing—but this may be insignificant next to the damage caused by a large audit bill.

There are two ways to delay an office audit:

- Make the appointment as far into the future as possible. Then, call a day or two before and postpone the audit. You can get one, or possibly two, postponements for almost any reason. Valid excuses include having to order copies of vital documents, such as canceled checks from the bank, your accountant going out of town, and the old standby of having been ill.

- On the day of the audit, leave some records at home. Then ask for time to furnish them later. Auditors have come to expect missing records and will routinely allow taxpayers two weeks or more to get them. If you want to push it to the limit, call right before the deadline and ask for a further extension.

CAUTION

Don't answer an auditor's questions on the phone. The auditor might try to speak to you over the phone about the facts of your case prior to your appointment. It's better to say that you aren't prepared to talk at that time than to give off-the-cuff answers which could come back to haunt you later.

If you can't go to the IRS offices without great hardship—you are disabled or aren't capable of transporting large amounts of records—you may request that a tax auditor come to your home or business. This goes against my general advice of keeping the auditor as far away from your stomping grounds as possible.

You might turn an office audit into a mail audit. If there's a good reason as to why you can't travel—illness or disability, lack of transportation, or whatever—when you call to schedule your audit, request a correspondence audit.

Meet the Office Auditor

Many office auditors are fresh out of school, and some have limited English skills. Make sure you specifically explain your deductions or exemptions. If you are a small business owner or self-employed, you may have to carefully explain how your particular enterprise functions to an auditor without business experience.

Office auditors start with some easy questions to make sure you are the person under audit (you don't have to show any identification)—questions like "Are you married?" or "Where do you live?" Ordinarily, these background questions won't cause you any problem.

Before meeting an auditor on your own, review IRS Form 4700 *Supplement* and, if you operate a business, Form 4700 *Business Supplement*. Both forms are reproduced at the end of this chapter. These internal IRS forms are used as checklists by auditors and contain the questions you should expect. If any question might be difficult, see a tax professional before the audit or consider hiring one to attend the audit in your place.

What an IRS Office Auditor Looks For

After the background questions, the audit will start in earnest. IRS office auditors don't waste time in idle chitchat. Every question has a reason, even if it is not obvious to you. The Internal Revenue training manual instructs office auditors to conduct the initial taxpayer interview as follows. (My comments follow in the brackets.)

(1) [T]he initial interview is the most important part of the audit process. The first few minutes should be spent making the taxpayer comfortable and explaining the examination process … [Read that first sentence again; first impressions are vital.]

(3) sufficient information should be developed to reach informed judgments as to:

(a) financial history and standard of living. [See the next section for a lengthy discussion of new IRS lifestyle auditing.]

(b) nature of employment to determine relationship to other entities. [This means that the auditor may want to look at your partnership or corporation tax returns, too, and look for the possibility of any bartering.]

(c) money or property received … determined to be … not taxable … [For instance, did you get loans or inheritances or sell assets during the year?]

(d) potential for moonlighting income. [For example, are you a firefighter who does odd jobs on your days off?]

(4) if warranted … [If, in covering the above areas, the auditor gets responses or sees things on the return that cause suspicion, he or she should go on to find out more about these areas.]

(a) … property owned, including bank accounts, stocks and bonds, real estate, automobiles, etc., in this country and abroad [Asking these kinds of questions used to be optional; it has become common in most audits.]

(b) … purchases, sales, transfers, contributions or exchanges of … assets [Did you buy or sell anything worth in the thousands of dollars?]

(c) the correctness of exemptions and dependents claimed. [If you claimed a large number of dependents, be prepared to explain, especially if any of the dependents are not members of your immediate family.]

(5) remember, the taxpayer is being examined and not just the return. [I can't overemphasize the importance of this one sentence—it is what an audit is really about.]

Common Audit Issues

Expect the following topics to be covered at an office audit. Not all will apply, but be prepared for the ones that do.

Income. The IRS claims that it loses infinitely more tax dollars from unreported income than from overstated deductions. Once the preliminary questions are over, the auditor will ask point blank if you reported all your income for the year or years under audit.

Auditors are taught to probe for side income—moonlighting electricians and homemakers who do child care. They are concerned with income not reported to the IRS by the person who paid you or income from which no taxes were withheld, such as tips or rent from an in-law unit in your home.

Auditors will probe further into living expenses once omitted income is suspected. For example, the auditor may want to see your insurance policies to see if you have covered expensive items like jewelry, furs, art, and other such assets. Auditors seldom go to this trouble, however.

Exemptions. Were you entitled to claim everyone listed on your return as a dependent? For instance, if you support elderly parents, take documents showing their expenses and sources of limited income. If you are a divorced parent and claim your child as an exemption, have proof of court-ordered child support payments or costs you paid directly for the child's benefit. Also, get a copy of your ex-spouse's Form 8332 filed with his or her return to show that the exemption wasn't claimed. If, however, you both claimed the exemption, produce your divorce papers showing that you are entitled to it.

Theft and casualty losses. Were you legally entitled to claim losses? Produce a list of items lost plus documentation that the loss occurred—copies of police reports and insurance claim forms are good ways to prove losses to the IRS.

Charitable deductions. Can you verify charitable deductions—particularly if the total exceeded $250? For example, if you dropped $40 into the collection plate every Sunday, you will need more evidence than your own statement. Prove it by getting a letter from your church secretary attesting to your regular attendance and copies of automatic teller withdrawal slips made on Sunday mornings.

Employee business expenses. If you are a wage earner, can you verify any unreimbursed employee business expenses claimed on your return—especially for car, travel, entertainment, and home office? At a minimum, you will need a letter from your employer describing its reimbursement policy—that it pays you back for some expenses, but not for other items or beyond certain limits. Keep receipts and a calendar. If you don't have a business diary, you can create one after the fact, but you should tell the IRS that it is a reconstruction. Note that the IRS is very picky in the employee expense area.

Itemized deductions. Can you verify large itemized deductions on your Schedule A—such as mortgage interest or medical expenses? You should have mortgage lender statements on IRS Form 1098 and medical bills or canceled checks and bank statements.

Previous audits. IRS records of previous audits are spotty. Your prior audit history may or may not be noted in the auditor's file. Thus, you will be asked if you've been audited and how it came out. Unless you came out clean, tell the auditor that you were audited, but don't recall the details. If the auditor really wants to dig out the prior report, he or she might do it. Don't make it easy by showing a copy—which might point out issues to probe in the new audit.

Other years' tax returns. Auditors usually ask to see copies of your tax returns for the year before and after the audit year. The reason is obvious—to see if any adjustments are appropriate in those years.

Don't Be Too Eager to Help the Auditor

Auditors frequently ask you for information not related to the year or areas listed on the audit notice. Sadly, most audit victims blindly provide whatever is asked for, often needlessly providing the rope to be hung with.

The IRS cannot require you to furnish data unless it is directly related to the year under audit. If the auditor asks for something you don't think pertains, ask for an explanation of how it specifically relates to the audit year. If you are given *written* notice that the audit has been expanded to other years, however, then you must submit information for those years.

Sometimes data on other years' tax returns—such as loss carryovers or depreciation of assets—does relate to the tax year under audit. In this case, show the auditor only the portion of the other year's tax return in question (such as a schedule of depreciation) not the whole return. Similarly, avoid letting the auditor photocopy your records unless you are certain there is nothing harmful in them. Tell the auditor that you don't see why he or she needs copies and the person will probably back down.

If you are asked if you filed all other years' tax returns and you haven't, reply that you will check your records and get back, or simply shrug your shoulders. Don't lie. If you want to avoid this question altogether, hire a tax professional to go to the audit in your place. Unless you have told your tax pro otherwise, the tax pro should answer that as far as he or she knows, you filed all tax returns when due. An auditor who has no reason to believe otherwise almost always just moves on.

> **TIP**
> **Don't bring other returns to the audit.** Simply say you didn't bring them with you or couldn't find them—even if they are on the list of items to bring with you. Make a vague offer to look for them; an auditor cannot force you to provide past returns.

Don't worry about making the auditor mad by not supplying other years' tax returns. Auditors know you never have to provide a copy of a tax return to the IRS once it has been filed. The only exception is if the IRS auditor says that no return is on record. Then you can give the auditor a signed copy for filing. But, in the normal audit situation when the IRS requests a copy of your return, it is not because the auditor is denying that you filed it—it's because the auditor doesn't have it in his or her file.

Even in this electronic age, the IRS doesn't scan copies of paper tax returns in its computers. Old tax returns are buried in warehouses across the country for ten years and are then destroyed. Yours may be in Box 147963a-7 in the middle of Kansas. Unless you filed electronically, it will take weeks or months to find it—and there is no guarantee that it hasn't been misplaced. Usually, if you don't come up with a copy of your tax return which is on record as filed, the auditor just forgets it.

How Long Does an Office Appointment Last?

Expect to spend from one to four hours with the office auditor. In most IRS offices, two audits per day are set for taxpayers with small businesses and four audits where there is no self-employment income. Auditors must write up their findings between appointments, so they must keep moving and can't scrutinize every piece of paper. An auditor wants to zip through your audit and get you out the door every bit as much as you want to leave.

If You Didn't Bring Everything to the Audit

It is okay not to resolve all audit issues at one meeting. Auditors often ask for something you didn't bring. No problem. Just ask for a reasonable amount of time to submit it (15 to 30 days) and mail it in with a letter to jog the auditor's memory explaining how it helps your audit. To be sure the auditor got what you sent, call four or five days later and ask. If he or she wants voluminous records or you are concerned that the auditor may not understand what you send, request another face-to-face meeting.

If you don't want the auditor to see a particular item, you can vaguely promise to send it in but conveniently forget to—the auditor may forget it, too. If not, you will probably not lose any more than you would have had you cooperated.

Field Audits—Look Out, Here Comes the IRS

If you get a letter notifying you of an audit and asking to meet at your home or business, you have been picked for a field audit.

> **TIP**
>
> **If you get a phone call from the IRS.** Before getting notice by mail, you might get a call from someone at the IRS saying the IRS wants to audit you. Politely tell the caller you want notification in writing to make sure it really is the IRS. Refuse to discuss anything until you get a notice in the mail. Don't worry about upsetting the person; you are within your rights. Some agents like to catch you off guard, in the hope you'll say something revealing.

Field audits are the big leagues, whereas correspondence and office audits are the minors. The IRS puts its best auditors here and expects them to pay their keep. In fact, field audit tax bills are more than four times higher than those from other types of audits.

Local IRS audit managers make the final decision as to who gets field audited. Normally, it is the self-employed, owners of real estate rental properties, or people with high incomes or complex tax returns. Also, corporation, partnership, estate, gift, and trust tax returns are always field, not office, audited.

Revenue agents who conduct field audits must have college degrees in accounting or a minimum of 24 semester hours of college-level accounting courses. At IRS audit training, they are taught techniques similar to detectives—looking for clues to see if your tax reporting matches the home you live in, your business and investments. If you live in a $700,000 home, drive a Range Rover, and report only $20,000 income from your dental practice, they will dig deep.

Do Auditors Have Quotas?

IRS auditors will tell you they are overworked. Because the IRS doesn't pay bonuses or overtime, there is little incentive for them to break their backs on particular cases. Job performance is judged on how many files are closed each month. The Taxpayer Bill of Rights forbids the IRS to evaluate auditors on the dollars produced from their audits. Judging auditors on the number of files closed, however, probably produces much the same result, and there is evidence that IRS managers give bonuses. Prior to 1998, auditors were evaluated by their yield—the total dollar amount of the tax adjustment on an audit, divided by the number of hours the auditor spent on the examination. For example, in the Northern California District, an auditor had to produce $1,000 in taxes for each hour the auditor devoted to a case. Hopefully, these days are gone.

A heavy caseload can work to your advantage. Auditors don't have the time to go over every tax return with a fine-tooth comb. Auditors often miss taxpayer errors that could have resulted in large adjustments in the IRS's favor.

Responding to a Field Audit Letter

The initial notice you get will probably be signed by a revenue agent. The letter will either set a date for the audit or ask you to call to arrange it. An attachment will list items the IRS wants you to produce at the meeting. However, the list should not be taken as inclusive—*everything* is fair game in a field audit. A revenue agent can probe into any area of your tax return as well as your financial or personal life. Remember that *you*, not just your tax return, are under the IRS microscope.

 TIP

Carefully consider when and where you want the audit to be held. The Taxpayer Bill of Rights (see Chapter 15) gives you the right to have a say in when an audit is to be scheduled. You should be given sufficient time to prepare and a convenient date. The IRS doesn't start before 7:30 a.m. and won't go beyond 5 p.m., weekdays only. Field audits last a minimum of four hours and may go into dozens of meetings extending over a year's time.

Agents prefer to come to wherever your records are kept. Ordinarily this is at your business, if you are self-employed. So if you work at home, the IRS will want to come there. If a representative will handle the audit for you, the agent can go to that person's office if requested.

What to Expect at a Field Audit

Be sure to read "What an IRS Office Auditor Looks For" and "Common Audit Issues," above; that information applies here as well. This section covers other issues likely to come up at a field audit.

Revenue agents' primary focus is to find unreported income and personal expenses claimed as business deductions. Field audits typically zero in on the following areas of your work and personal lives.

Unreported income. *This is the auditor's number one concern.* An agent is particularly suspicious if your small business or profession has a lot of cash transactions. This is why so many restaurant, bar, liquor store, laundromat, and grocery store owners are audited. The IRS is always looking for the skimming of cash off the gross receipts of the business.

To ferret out unreported income, the IRS uses indirect methods of detection, unless you furnish direct evidence, such as confessing to the auditor that you didn't report everything.

There are four common methods the IRS uses to probe for income. All four methods have been challenged in federal court; all four methods have survived the challenge. Each one is explained below, with possible defenses you can raise:

- **Net worth method.** Using this method, the IRS attributes any increase in your net worth during the year in question to taxable income—unless you offer a reasonable explanation. The IRS tries to establish your net worth—your total assets less your liabilities—at the beginning of the year and then again at the end. Then it compares the two figures to see if your net worth increased over the year. Assets like real estate and stock are valued at their original cost, so appreciation won't enter into the computation. Typically, the IRS asks for financial statements that may have been prepared for your business or in a loan application. Any increase in your net worth over a prior year will be compared to the income reported on your tax return. If your net worth has increased but your income has not, the IRS will assume you're not reporting all your income.

Defense. Show that the IRS's calculations are wrong or that your net worth increased due to nontaxable factors. For example, you may have inherited money or assets or have a cash hoard accumulated in prior years. The law then shifts the burden to the IRS to negate any explanation you offer before making an audit adjustment.

- **Expenditures method.** The IRS totals up all of your known and estimated expenditures for the year and compares the result with your reported income. If you spent more than you claim you earned, the IRS will attribute the difference to unreported income.

  Defense. Show that the IRS didn't add and subtract correctly or that money you spent was from nontaxable sources, such as loans, gifts, inheritances or prior accumulations.

- **Bank deposit method.** This is the IRS's favorite indirect method of proving unreported income and is always used by field auditors. The IRS simply tallies up the deposits made in all of your bank accounts and compares the total with your reported income. If you have deposited more than you claim you earned, the IRS will attribute the difference to unreported income.

  Some business owners take great pains to skim receipts, but then stupidly put that money into their bank accounts. Financial records can easily be obtained by the IRS from your bank or stock broker if you don't produce them voluntarily. Revenue agents almost always perform a bank deposit analysis early on in a field audit.

> **TIP**
> **Do your own bank deposit analysis before the audit.** Make notes on your bank statements that explain the source of the deposits. There can be any number of explanations when deposits exceed taxable income—loans, redeposits of bad checks, transfers between accounts, inheritances and gifts received, sales of assets, and the like.

Defense. Check the IRS's math for mistakes. And, again, the funds may have been from nontaxable sources or from cash on hand from income from prior years. Also, if you have several accounts, chances are some of the deposits reflect transfers of money between accounts. Adding up deposits leads to double counting, a common mistake.

- **Mark-up method.** If you are in a retail or wholesale goods business, the agent may look at your sales, cost of goods sold, and net profits. If these numbers are much lower than for similar businesses, the IRS will fill in the gap by asserting unreported income.

  Defense. Ask the agent for the source of statistics used by the IRS. She may be comparing you to a completely different type of business—perhaps yours is a computer wholesale operation and the agent is relying on figures from home electronics retailing. If this is not the case, explain why your business underperformed compared to similar businesses: It is a new business or was closed several months due to a fire, your major customer or supplier went bankrupt, or any of a thousand other reasons.

Business expense verification. Agents typically ask you to verify at least the major business expenses you claimed (for sole proprietors on Schedule C). The agent is on the lookout for disguised personal expenses—particularly auto, travel, and entertainment. The tax law specifically requires strict record keeping in these three areas. Bringing a business diary will help immensely. If you didn't keep one, you can create one for the audit, but you should tell the auditor it is a reconstruction.

Asset sales. Can you document your gains and losses from sales of property—particularly stocks and real estate? This can sometimes be a problem, as you may have owned the stocks or property for many years. Show the original documents from when you purchased the asset. You'll also need receipts for improvements of real estate during your ownership and annual statements showing reinvested dividends for stocks and mutual funds.

Tax Basis of an Asset

An auditor may ask you to verify your tax basis in an asset used in your business or sold by you. "Basis" is the figure from which the IRS calculates how much depreciation you get or profit or loss you've made on the sale of an asset. Essentially, tax basis starts with the amount you paid. To this figure, add the cost of improvements and tax benefits, such as rollover of gains from property exchanges, and subtract costs such as the depreciation taken on equipment or rental property. If you received a gift, the tax basis is figured from the date of the original purchase. For property you inherit, the basis is the property's value on the date of the death. A detailed explanation of tax basis is in *Tax Savvy for Small Business*, by Frederick W. Daily (Nolo).

Real estate rental. Can you verify rental property expenses you claimed on Schedule E of your tax return? Can you also show that each expense was for that particular property? Auditors are on the lookout for landlords deducting items that were used at their personal residences. If you are a landlord, you should have records of all income and expenses. If not, you must reconstruct records from canceled checks, deposits, receipts, and notes. Photos of major expense items (like remodeling) are especially persuasive.

Independent contractors versus employees. A frequent audit issue is whether businesses have properly classified people working for them as independent contractors or employees. This issue is covered in Chapter 11.

Keeping the Auditor Away From Your Home or Business

Avoid holding an audit at your home or business, even if you have nothing to hide. Maybe you really earn only $20,000, but appear to live much better. It could be that you inherited a $700,000 house from your aunt, rebuilt your BMW from junkyard parts, and made a few good investments. Assuming you have paperwork to prove all this, you should have no problems with the IRS, right? Well, maybe not. These are the kinds of things that can cause auditors to dig deeper until they find something to justify their efforts.

Here are some tips on how to keep the IRS auditor away from your home or business.

Taxpayer Bill of Rights. The Taxpayer Bill of Rights gives small business owners the right to refuse an audit on their business premises if an audit would virtually shut the business down. In this case, request the audit to be held at the IRS office or at your tax professional's place. If denied, complain to the agent's manager and then, if necessary, to the Taxpayer Advocate Service. (See Chapter 8.)

Tax professionals. If you give a qualified representative a signed Form 2848, *Power of Attorney*, he can insist that the audit be at his office, not yours. (See Chapter 13.) The representative must be the audited tax return's preparer, or an enrolled agent, CPA or attorney and must be in possession of your business records.

If the IRS Comes to Your Business

If the IRS holds the audit at your place, don't make it too comfortable. This doesn't mean that you should stick the agent in an unheated storeroom, but you don't have to give up your personal office, either.

Even if the audit is held at your tax professional's or an IRS office, however, agents have the right to observe your business premises. They may want to verify tax return items by spot checking your inventory or seeing that you use equipment you tax deducted. Remember—auditors are trained to be nosy and routinely want to eyeball business operations.

Before the IRS shows up, remove any items that might cause suspicion, like the picture of your Chris-Craft, Lear jet, or alpine ski cabin. If the agent wants to tour your business, try to schedule it at a time when employees or customers aren't present. This keeps the agent from talking to your employees and tipping them off that you're being audited. An employee's innocent remark could do a lot of harm, and a vengeful one could stab you in the back. Don't let the agent wander around on his or her own—stay nearby.

If the agent asks to see any records during an observation, say that they are not readily available, are at home, or are at your tax professional's office. The agent won't start opening your file cabinets to verify the truthfulness of your assertions.

An auditor does not have the right to enter your home to see your home office or for any other reason. If you don't let the person inside, however, he or she may legitimately retaliate by disallowing a home office deduction.

How an Auditor Approaches an Examination

The tax code gives the auditor wide latitude and authority to pry into your financial affairs. The basic tools in the auditor's kit are the interview, summons, IRS and other government files, and contacts with third parties, like your bank, who have knowledge of your finances.

Information Document Request. Along with your audit notice may come a separate form called an Information Document Request, or IDR. An auditor commonly issues multiple IDRs if the audit, usually a field audit, continues beyond one meeting. An IDR is a written solicitation of records or other papers either in your possession or accessible to you. Typically, bank statements and canceled checks are listed on an IDR. The IRS knows the truth of the words of a former U.S. Supreme Court justice that "a person can be defined by the checks he writes." Ordinarily, you will be given until a follow-up audit appointment or a few weeks to mail these things to the auditor. A sample IDR follows.

TIP

Just because the IRS issues an IDR doesn't mean that you have to produce the items requested. You may decline unless the items are really relevant to your audit. For instance, the IRS commonly uses IDRs to request copies of other years' tax returns—which normally you don't have to supply. If in doubt, don't furnish the item on the IDR and see if the auditor pursues it. If he or she does, ask how it relates to the year selected for audit. If you believe the auditor is crossing the line, just say no. An IDR is merely an informal administrative request—it does not carry any legal force. If what is being requested may seriously hurt or even incriminate you, see a tax attorney before responding.

Summons. If the IRS doesn't get information from you voluntarily—through an IDR—it may issue a summons. (Internal Revenue Code §§ 7602(a) and 7604(b).) A summons is a legally enforceable order and is not to be taken lightly. It orders you to appear before the auditor to answer questions and to bring certain documents. You can raise legal objections to a summons, including:

- self-incrimination—a Constitutional right not to give something to the government that would incriminate you

Sample Information Document Request

Form **4564** (Rev. June 1988)	Department of the Treasury — Internal Revenue Service **Information Document Request**	Request number One

To: *(Name of Taxpayer and Company Division or Branch)* Niles W. Crain & Daphne L. Crain 888 Rain Lane Seattle, WA 99999 *Please return Part 2 with listed documents to requester identified below*	Subject Examination—2009—Form 1040

SAIN number	Submitted to: Taxpayers
Dates of previous requests	N/A

Description of documents requested

1. All personal and business bank statements for 1/1/09 to 12/31/09

2. Copies of individual income tax returns Form 1040 for years 2008 and 2009

3. Credit card statements for 1/1/09 to 12/31/09

4. Office expenses

    a. Accounting records detailing expenses deducted

    b. Receipts and cancelled checks to verify expenses deducted

5. Meals and entertainment

Accounting records detailing expenses deducted. The records should establish pertinent names, business relationship, and the purpose of the expenses deducted.

Information due by	4/2/12	At next appointment ☐	Mail in [X]

From:	Name and title of requester Mortimer J. Snerd, Revenue Agent	Employee ID number 77-07-07	Date 2/15/12
	Office location 110 44th St., Seattle, WA. 88888		Telephone number (555) 555-5555

Catalog No. 23145K

Form **4564** (Rev. 6-1988)

- the summons is vague, overbroad, or unduly burdensome—if you've been asked to produce an overwhelming amount of documents, or
- certain items are protected by a legal privilege—such as the attorney-client privilege.

In the rather unlikely event you get a summons, contact a tax lawyer. If you don't comply, the IRS may bring you before a federal court judge in a summons enforcement proceeding. The judge can order you to produce the documents listed in the summons or face a heavy fine or even a jail sentence. It should give you comfort to know that the IRS rarely goes to this trouble, preferring to compromise or back down.

If You Don't Give Auditors What They Ask For

When you don't give the auditor information that has been requested, the auditor has three choices:

- **Drop it.** You'd be surprised how many auditors back off or are forgetful. They are working on many other cases. If they have most of the information requested from you, they may let it slide.
- **Go further without your cooperation.** Auditors call, write, or issue summonses to third parties, such as your bank, for records of your transactions. Auditors can, but rarely do, summons (order) you to appear before them and provide information.
- **Issue an examination report anyway.** The auditor can issue the report based on the information in hand and estimates for the missing income or expense data. By far, this is the most likely consequence of your not cooperating with an auditor.

Third-party summons. An auditor can issue a summons to get information from banks, employers, business associates, and anyone else. Auditors routinely summons records from others when you don't cooperate, or when verification of information you have given is needed. You must be notified in writing when a third-party summons is issued and you have a right to object. Practically speaking, however, you can't stop a third-party summons.

> CAUTION
> **Never tell another person not to comply with an IRS summons.** That is illegal and could get you both into serious trouble.

IRS files. Your previous tax returns, audit reports, and tax account history can be accessed by auditors. The auditor might first ask you for this information. As discussed above, you don't always have to give everything requested to an auditor. Because a lot of IRS information on you is not accessible by computer, it isn't all that easy for an auditor to get older IRS records. Recovering paper from IRS record storage facilities could take months. As a rule, auditors don't go to this trouble unless they mistrust you or feel that a large adjustment—tax bill against you—will result.

Other government and public records. Auditors have direct computer access to the Treasury Enforcement Communication Systems, or TECS, computer, which has all kinds of data on you. TECS is not public, so you can't be sure what is in the files. The auditor can also access your Social Security Administration, passport office, and postal service records. Auditors can view local and state public records showing ownership of vehicles, boats, airplanes, real estate, and business entities you might be involved in. Private databases, such as LexisNexis and credit reporting agency files, contain a wealth of personal data about all of us and are accessible to auditors. As a rule, office auditors don't make these types of searches, but field agents, who conduct audits at homes or businesses, often do.

Third-party contacts. Auditors can send letters or call or visit businesses and people who have dealt with you, such as the secretary of a church where you claimed a charitable contribution. First, they must give you Notice 1219A, *Notice of Potential Third Party Contact*. You can legally object to these contacts, at least in theory. If the auditor reveals personal or financial information about you to the third party, you can file a complaint with the IRS that your right to privacy has been violated by an unauthorized disclosure.

Preparing for an Audit

In preparing for an audit, begin by doing the following:

Step 1. Review the tax return being audited. If it was professionally prepared, go over it with the preparer. If you did it yourself, review it with a tax professional to see if he or she foresees any problems. Remember, it is always up to you to show the auditor where the data on the return came from. You may decide to hire the pro to represent you depending on your pocketbook and overall comfort level. A seasoned tax professional may be able to offer an educated guess as to why you are being audited.

> **TIP**
> **Mention business losses to the auditor.** If you are in business for yourself and had a net operating loss for a year following the year being audited, point this out to the auditor. This may discourage him or her from spending a lot of time on your audit, because any tax adjustment would be reduced by the loss you were entitled to in the subsequent year. If this might be your case, discuss it with a tax professional.

Step 2. Find all the records you used to prepare the return. Organize records logically and clearly according to the deduction category. Run adding machine tapes on totals of receipts for each classification, such as rent, travel, and utilities. If the totals don't correspond to the numbers on your tax return, be ready to explain why. I cannot overemphasize the importance of well-organized records in an audit.

Step 3. Research tax law if you are unsure whether you were entitled to a deduction or another tax benefit claimed on your tax return. For instance, did you meet all the requirements for a home office deduction? This is another point you should research or cover with a tax professional if you aren't sure.

Step 4. Look for relevant Audit Technique Guides (ATGs). The IRS has issued guides in its Market Segment Specialization Program (MSSP) telling its auditors what to look for when auditing certain businesses and occupations—real estate agents, entertainers, attorneys, fishermen, and others. Also, ATGs cover items that draw special audit attention, such as lawsuit awards, passive losses, and executive compensation. If there's a guide covering your line of work (see the IRS website at www.irs.gov; do a site search for MSSP or Audit Technique Guides), you'll want to read it. It will tell you what the auditor will be looking for beyond the normal audit routine, and you can prepare accordingly.

Not Cooperating in an Audit—When You Have Something to Hide

If you have some "dirty laundry," it may be in your best interest not to cooperate in, or even go to, an audit appointment. Before taking this drastic step, see a tax pro (preferably a tax attorney). For example, if your bank records show deposits in great excess of your reported income or you claimed phony deductions, it may be wiser to suffer the consequences of skipping an audit appointment. Blurting something out could earn you a visit from the Criminal Investigation Division, or CID. Never say "I guess you caught me, ha, ha," or "I didn't think you would find that account." On hearing such things, auditors are instructed to stop an audit and refer the case to CID. (See Chapter 10.)

When you don't show up, the IRS will take one of three actions:

Conduct the audit without you. The IRS may also examine tax years not covered by the initial audit. The auditor may look at all open years—returns due and filed within the past three years. And if the auditor suspects serious misdeeds, he or she may go back as far as six years. At the conclusion, the IRS will issue a report disallowing all items listed as questionable. A month or so later you'll receive a bill. Depending on the circumstances, you may want to accept the bill and move on with your life.

Contact you again. You may be contacted by the auditor and asked why you are not cooperating. Mum's the word. Eventually, the auditor will give up and issue a report, finding unreported income or disallowing most of your deductions and exemptions. A tax bill will follow.

Serve a summons and order you to appear. A summons is a legally enforceable order and you could be held in contempt of court—and even jailed—if you ignore it. See a tax attorney before making your next move.

Your Audit Goals

You have two goals in the audit:

- **To minimize the financial damage.** Because the odds are great that your audit will end with a tax bill, your goal should be damage control—keeping your liability as low as possible. But, don't go in with a defeatist attitude. If you owe no money, try to prove it. Just don't have unrealistic expectations. In a recent year, audits resulted in $19 billion in additional taxes and penalties, and about $600 million in refunds—a ratio of 32 to 1 against you.

- **To prevent expansion.** *Office* audits are initially limited to the items listed on the audit notice. If auditors see other problems, however, they will pursue them. This often happens when you show an auditor a document that you weren't obligated to show, or you make a slip of the tongue. As a rule, never show the auditor anything not specifically related to the tax year in the audit notice. For example, before showing your check register or business diary, edit out the portions that relate to personal matters or that overlap into other years.

Audits may be expanded into other tax years. An auditor may get permission from his or her manager to examine any open tax year if it is likely to be fruitful. Open years are those within three years of when a return was filed, or six years if the IRS finds serious underreporting.

> EXAMPLE: In November 2011, Noreen is audited for 2009. The auditor could expand the examination to 2008 and 2010; Noreen filed those tax returns timely. Without finding evidence of serious problems, the auditor could not expand the audit any farther back, as Noreen filed her 2007 tax return on April 15, 2008, more than three years before the audit date.

TIP

Don't show the auditor copies of tax returns for years other than the one in the audit notice. If the IRS expands the audit, you should demand an official written notice from the auditor.

What Not to Bring to an Audit

Don't bring anything not directly related to the year being audited. The auditor's fishing license is restricted to the year being audited, but he or she can look at materials from other years—and make adjustments—if these items are presented.

Your audit letter includes a list of things to bring. Don't take anything else—*unless* it supports a deduction you missed when you filed your tax return. For example, if your checking account statements overlap two years—January's statement has checks for December—then remove the checks for the year that isn't being audited. Leave at home checks and receipts for personal expenses not claimed as deductions on your tax return. Again, don't bring tax returns for any years other than the one being audited, even if requested by the auditor.

Who Should Attend the Audit?

If you are handling the audit yourself, you can bring someone else to the meeting. The auditor may ask you to sign a form waiving your right of privacy. This person can assist, but cannot represent you, however, unless he or she is the tax return preparer or an enrolled agent, a CPA, or an attorney. Chapter 13 contains tips on selecting a tax professional. It may make sense to bring any of the following people to the audit:

- an employee—your bookkeeper, the accounts payable supervisor, or a similar employee who has knowledge of your business records and can help you explain them
- your spouse—only one spouse needs to attend an audit when a joint tax return is being audited. Both should go if they both have financial knowledge, provided different information on the return, or can substantiate that information. If only one of you is being audited, the other can attend to offer emotional support. Or,
- another family member or friend—to offer moral support, translate if your English isn't very good, wipe your eyes with a handkerchief, or do whatever would help you get through the examination.

 TIP

Even if you skip the audit, you can contest the outcome by going to tax court. (See Chapter 5.) The strategy is to skip the audit so as to keep the auditor from looking into your records. By going to court, you pick the items to contest and can stay away from the problem areas. Before taking this approach, however, check with a tax attorney or tax professional.

How to Act at an Audit

The *Internal Revenue Manual* tells auditors that the initial taxpayer interview is the most important phase of an audit. *You, the taxpayer—not just your tax return—are under examination.* Your actions and behavior are being observed. Does it look like you are being evasive—trying to hide something? Do you become visibly shaken when some items are being discussed?

Dress Like Yourself

Dress according to your occupation and station in life. Anything else may make you uncomfortable and an audit is uncomfortable enough already. Use your common sense. Don't wear expensive clothes and jewelry if you work at Burger King, and don't dress like a fry cook if you are a dentist. If you are a bus driver coming from work, wear your uniform. Don't try to look like someone you are not. It's simple, really. Be yourself.

Mum's the Word

IRS encounters are inherently stressful, and people under stress often talk too much. The IRS knows this principle of human behavior, so auditors are trained to listen and to create silence. They examine records without speaking, with the hope that you will jabber away. Take this advice seriously: Don't talk. Auditors get damaging information from taxpayers who blurt out answers to questions that weren't asked. For example, one clueless soul volunteered that he always deducted clothing expenses because he had to come to work dressed. The auditor then made a disallowance of this expense in two other years.

The six best responses to a question posed by an auditor are:
- Yes.
- No.
- I don't recall.
- I'll have to check on that.
- What specific items do you want to see?
- Why do you want that?

Again, don't say more unless absolutely necessary. As a rule, you can't hurt yourself when your mouth is shut.

> **CAUTION**
>
> **Don't lie to, or mislead, an auditor.** IRS examiners are trained to ask for information they already have to test your credibility. A favorite question is to ask if you have investments when the IRS computer shows you earned interest and dividends. Or, the IRS may ask you about vehicles you own when the auditor has a printout from your state motor vehicles department.

Don't Offer Any Favors to the Auditor

Auditors are trained to watch out for, and report, all offers of favors of any kind. Some taxpayers are from countries where bribing government officials is the norm. IRS employees are closely watched and are among the cleanest of all officials anywhere. Some auditors will accept a cup of coffee, but that's as far as it goes. An offer of a favor, say tickets to a ball game, may be ignored. But any suggestion of an outright bribe will get you a visit from the Criminal Investigation Division and a very thorough audit. Don't try it.

Try to Get Along With the Auditor

When you meet an auditor, be polite and offer some chitchat about the weather, traffic, or sports to break the ice. Office auditors are under time pressures and may want to get right down to business. Field auditors, on the other hand, are encouraged to get to know you; they will chat.

It doesn't hurt to show an interest in the auditor as a person. Ask friendly questions—How long have you been with the IRS? How does someone get to be an auditor? How long have you worked in this area? Everyone likes to talk about their favorite subject—themselves. If the auditor responds, it may get him or her to like you, or at least it will reduce the amount of time the person spends examining your return.

In short, don't go in with an anti-IRS attitude. You are not happy to be there, but make the best of it. Remember what Grandma told you about catching more flies with honey than with vinegar.

What about turning this advice on its head and taking a defiant, aggressive attitude into an audit? This is not my style, but it might work with auditors who are timid or so unused to being challenged that they will give in to get rid of you. One tax professional suggests that you continually ask the auditor why he or she wants to know whenever you are asked a question. Obnoxious or peculiar behavior, or even bad B.O., may work. Similarly, some taxpayers give an agent a poorly lighted, noisy, and cramped space to conduct a field audit. If the offensive approach works, let me know.

When the Auditor Is Unreasonable

You may run into an auditor intent on giving you a hard time. The person may be impolite, hostile, or rude. Worse, he or she may disallow your deductions unless you produce ironclad documentation in triplicate. Perhaps you did something to upset the person, or he or she is having a bad day.

The important thing to understand is that you don't have to take guff from an auditor. Ask the person politely to lighten up. If that doesn't work, say you are too upset to continue and want to recess the audit to another day. If the auditor balks, tell him or her that you want to consult a tax professional before continuing. Legally, you must be granted your request. You don't have to consult the tax professional, but the audit is finished for the day.

Threatening to leave—or demanding a recess—can have positive results. Auditors do change their tune sometimes and try to be more accommodating. Auditors don't want to have to see people again if they can help it, as they already have a backlog of cases. Because their performance is judged by how many files they close, they won't want anything to delay them. In the end, they are looking for your agreement to close the case. If you have a second meeting, the auditor may be in a better mood. Auditors also know that a tax professional won't put up with their lack of professionalism. And it's even possible that your file will be transferred to another auditor for the next meeting. Remember, you never know what is going on in an auditor's life. If someone seems unhappy, it might not have anything to do with you. The person may be ill or in the process of quitting, getting fired, or transferring to another IRS department.

Asking for a New Auditor

If the recess didn't help and the auditor continues to abuse you, demand to see his or her manager. Tell the manager that you are not being treated respectfully, and that you want a different auditor. While chances are slim that you'll be granted your request, the auditor you have should start treating you more civilly.

Have You Seen This Auditor Before?

The *Internal Revenue Manual* discourages an examination by an auditor who has examined your tax return within the previous three years, if that audit was concluded and your case was closed. If you recognize the auditor from your recent past (this might happen if your local office has only a few auditors) and you don't want to deal with the same person, complain to the manager.

When a New Auditor Appears on the Scene

Field audits commonly drag on for months or even years. Your original auditor may suddenly vanish. It is usually for some perfectly understandable reason, like a job transfer, promotion, maternity leave, training, resignation, or firing. For some reason, the IRS treats this as some kind of national security secret and doesn't like to tell you what happened.

The first auditor may call you or send you an examination report prior to moving on. The motive here is to try to close your file by asking you to agree to certain adjustments. Maybe you are agreeable, but before taking the bait, read "Negotiating With an Auditor," below. For now, just realize you may have some leverage if this happens.

A second way to benefit from a change in auditors is by understanding that the new person will not want to do any more work on a half-done audit than is necessary. Few people like to clean up another person's mess. For example, no two people document their work the same way, and few people write in a way to be easily understood by others. The newcomer will probably jump at a chance to close the file as soon as possible. The following example, taken from real life, shows how a change of auditors can be a godsend.

EXAMPLE: Laura had mistakenly claimed a large and improper business deduction for three years running, totaling $120,000. Auditor One raised this issue, and Laura stalled by asking for time to contact her tax professional and do further investigation and research. To her dismay, Laura found out that she was dead in the water and could only be saved by a miracle. She got one when Auditor One was replaced by Auditor Two. The new guy was either too lazy to read the file or didn't understand it, and completely missed this issue. He quickly closed the case after finding another and much smaller adjustment, and Laura cheerfully signed the examination report.

Protest if asked to produce records twice. A new auditor is not always a positive development. The person may be determined to replow old ground. You or your representative may be asked questions you've already answered or to produce documents you showed the first auditor.

If you have produced records once during an audit, it is reasonable to object to doing so again. The longer the audit has been going on, the louder you should complain. Argue that the change of auditors isn't your fault and you shouldn't be punished. Get indignant; take control of the situation by telling the new auditor what the records show and maybe produce a few items to back up what you say. If appropriate, propose a few small adjustments and an immediate settlement.

If the new auditor persists in traveling over old terrain, demand to speak to the person's manager and renew your complaint. The manager might agree or suggest a compromise just to get rid of you. If you don't get anywhere and have a serious basis for objecting (the records are voluminous and have taken a lot of your time), ask for the head person, the examination branch chief. Even if everyone turns you down, by squeaking your wheels you have shown yourself to be someone unlikely to accept an examination report.

Standing Up to the Auditor

As your audit progresses, the auditor will be continually making notes and filling in workpapers, seldom telling you what he or she is writing or thinking. Typically, the more an auditor writes, the more adjustments you can expect. To keep an auditor from running amok, I suggest that immediately after finishing with your documents for one group of items (say, business travel expenses) ask point blank, "Did you find any problems?" If the auditor says yes, don't go onto another area without having the person explain what the problem is.

This approach identifies you as someone who will not meekly take whatever the auditor dishes out without justifying the actions to your face. You are perfectly within your rights to politely ask questions during the audit. If the adjustment is because your records are missing, ask the auditor for at least 15 days to give you time to get the missing records. And if the auditor claims you don't have a legal right to the deduction—for instance, because your business is really just a nondeductible hobby—ask for the specific legal authority for that theory. Say you want to research the matter or talk to a tax professional, and ask that the adjustment not be made until you get back to him or her.

If you continually challenge the auditor to justify any decisions, the person will likely grow weary and think longer and harder about making more waves. This isn't surprising. It's basic human nature to want to avoid conflict. This tack softens the auditor up for negotiation. I know people who have refused to leave the IRS office until the auditor gives in on at least one point! Many auditors don't like to have to justify their actions, as they would prefer to hide behind a mailed examination report rather than give you the bad news to your face.

Don't presume that standing up for yourself will get you a tougher audit— just the opposite is usually true. The more you make the auditor work, the more she or he will want to get rid of you and go on to easier marks.

Proving Your Deductions

You must show that your tax return was prepared properly to win your audit; the IRS is not legally required to prove that you are wrong. Ideally, your proof should be in writing, but auditors have some discretion to accept oral explanations as well.

If you deducted business expenses or expenses that helped you produce income, the expenses must be reasonable and necessary as well as verifiable. This means that even if your expenses are legally allowable, if they are unreasonably large or extravagant, they won't pass muster. For example, Elmer owned a hot dog stand and claimed $20,000 in entertainment

Documents to Bring to the Audit

The audit notice includes a list of documents you are supposed to bring to the audit. You may want to bring additional documents you need to explain or reconstruct missing records. IRS Publication 552, *Recordkeeping for Individuals*, shows how the IRS wants you to keep your records. Don't worry if you haven't followed all the IRS suggestions. You just need to be able to show income and expenses to the auditor in some understandable manner. Listed here are specific documents to bring.

Canceled checks and receipts. Take only the checks and receipts relating to the areas listed in the audit notice. Don't let the auditor rummage through all your checks and receipts. If it appears you are spending more money than you are reporting, the auditor may become suspicious. You can bring a credit card or bank account statement instead of a canceled check. (IRS Revenue Procedure 92-71.)

Books and records, if you operated a business. You aren't required to have a formal set of books as long as the auditor believes your records reflect your true income and expenses. A check register may take the place of a set of books, if it's backed up by canceled checks and receipts.

If your business has no records, you can be fined for failure to keep adequate records. The auditor can make up missing records by guesswork. For example, the auditor may double your gross receipts based on published industry or government statistics.

Appointment books or business diaries. If you claimed travel or entertainment expenses, you will need a writing showing dates and times the expenses were incurred, their business purpose, and who was visited or entertained. If you have no diary, you can write one up for the audit, but tell the auditor it is a reconstruction if you are asked.

Auto logs. Auto logs aren't required by law—despite what some auditors say—but they will help you prove business auto expenses. Again, you can create one after the fact, but be up-front about it. Repair and maintenance receipts should have odometer mileage written on them, and your diary may have notations of trips and expenses.

Escrow papers. These are necessary if you claim rental property depreciation deductions to show how much of a deduction you are entitled to. They are also required if you sold the property.

expenses. The auditor would disallow this amount as unreasonable, even if Elmer could substantiate it. Size or reasonableness of a deduction, however, is not usually grounds for disallowance.

TIP
Never give or mail your original documents to an IRS agent. If an auditor wants a copy, he or she can make it. Don't leave the auditor's office without your originals. IRS offices are black holes when it comes to misplacing things. If the IRS claims not to have received something, it's your word against the IRS's and guess who wins? Courts have said that you can't rely on "the IRS lost it" (or "the dog ate it") excuse. The burden of proof as to whatever the auditor is challenging on your tax return is always on you, and you may have to prove it more than once.

If You Don't Have Documentation

MYTH: If you can't prove a deduction in writing, it won't be allowed by an auditor because you are required to keep records.

FACT: Courts have repeatedly told the IRS that taxpayers can't be expected to keep flawless records. Tax regulations allow taxpayers, within limits, to offer oral explanations, use approximations for some expenses, claim expenses under $75 without receipts, and reconstruct records when the originals are missing.

Despite what an auditor may tell you, here are the *real* audit rules on missing records taken from Income Tax Regulations and court cases.

Substantial Compliance

Begin by claiming that you are in substantial compliance with the tax laws. Substantial compliance means that you have enough proof that you obeyed the tax reporting law even though your evidence is less than complete.

> EXAMPLE: The auditor agrees that Rufus is entitled to deduct a portion of his maintenance expenses as a home office expense. But the auditor finds that four months of bills that were paid in cash are missing. Rufus asserts that he is in substantial compliance and the auditor should accept the average of the other eight months of receipts to approximate the missing four and allow this much as a deduction.

This example shows the wisdom of going through your files long before the audit appointment. If you can't find bills, credit card statements, or canceled checks, order them from the companies and banks. Expect a delay in getting copies. Few businesses keep sales receipts beyond a year or two, and most do not give a priority to getting copies to you. If getting records in time looks like it will be a problem, ask the IRS for a postponement or request that your auditor allow you more time. Most businesses don't charge for copies of invoices or receipts, but banks charge as much as $3 per canceled check. So, you may want to order copies of major expense checks only.

Oral Explanations

Tell the auditor you are entitled to the deduction. Your spoken justification of why you can't produce a record must be given some weight by an auditor, as long as it is reasonable. If your records were lost along with your furniture and other belongings in a move from Iowa to New Mexico, your explanation should pass the believability test. But "burglars stole them when I was asleep" or "aliens with ray guns vaporized them" won't, even if the auditor is an "X Files" fan.

This is a good time to repeat the First Commandment of winning your audit: Establish and maintain credibility with the auditor. Once an auditor catches you in one lie, no matter how small, he or she will have a hard time believing anything else you say.

Business Expenses Under $75 Each

You can claim business deductions for expenses without substantiation (such as a receipt) up to $75 per item. Lodging expenses, however, require receipts, no matter the amount.

Before you rush out to throw away all traces of these lesser expenses, keep in mind that you always need a record. This means a business calendar notation, log, or diary showing the amount, who it was paid to, the time and place of the expense, the business purpose, and relationship of the person you spent the money on.

While this regulation purports to cover only travel and entertainment, many auditors will allow other business deductions under $75 without receipts as well. If you have small expenses without receipts and the auditor wants to disallow them, explain that you thought you didn't need a receipt for items under $75. It might work, and the worst thing the auditor can do is say no.

Reconstruction of Records

Gaps due to missing documents may be filled by reconstruction—a process by which you rebuild lost or destroyed records. As long as the newly minted records appear to be reasonable, the auditor must consider them. This is a judgment call, however, and different auditors apply different standards. The advice that follows is necessarily general.

Courts have given some guidance on what it takes to successfully reconstruct records. If you can establish that at one time you possessed adequate records and that you no longer have them due to circumstances beyond your control, you are allowed to reconstruct them. (Internal Revenue Regulation 1.274-5(c)(5); see also *Gizzi v. Commissioner of Internal Revenue*, 65 T.C. 342 (1975).) You also must explain why they are missing. For instance, if your documents were destroyed when the town river flooded your basement, add a photo of your flooded basement or newspaper clipping of the flood in your area.

Documenting the expense is a little different. Let's say you spent $1,200 cash in fixing up a rented office but lost the file with the receipts for materials. You could reconstruct your expenses with a letter from your landlord attesting to the improvements or a statement from one of your clients who saw you doing the work. Typically, if you think hard enough about reconstructing paperwork to verify an expense, you can do it. Be creative.

If you can't come up with any kind of paper showing an expense, create your own document. For example, you spent $700 cash on carpeting your building and Karpet King has since gone out of business. Write up your own receipt showing the name of store, amount, and date of purchase, or as close as you can get. But, be up-front with the auditor; say you prepared the receipt as reconstruction because it was not possible to document it in any other way.

Cohan **Rule.** An old, well-known tax case has saved many an audit victim with missing records. George M. "I'm a Yankee Doodle Dandy" Cohan was nailed for not having receipts in a 1920s IRS audit. He fought the IRS to a U.S. Court of Appeals, which held that a taxpayer may approximate expenditures for tax purposes, as long as the person can reasonably show that some amount was spent. (*Cohan v. Commissioner of Internal Revenue*, 349 F.2d 540 (2nd Cir. 1930).)

The *Cohan* Rule has its limits. First, you must make some showing of why the records are not available. They may have been lost or destroyed or be in such small amounts and from transactions in which receipts are not normally given, such as cab fares or tips. And the rule can't be applied to approximate travel and entertainment, as mentioned above.

In reality, the *Cohan* Rule is useful as a bargaining chip to use with the auditor. If you are told "no deduction without documentation," cry the *Cohan* Rule. Eyebrows will likely raise in surprise, and the auditor may back down, at least part of the way.

Adjustments in Your Favor—Taking the Offensive

Auditors must make any adjustments in your favor whenever they are found during an audit. Even the most hard-nosed auditor knows that taxpayers occasionally make mistakes that hurt them, not the IRS, or overlook claiming tax benefits on their returns. This is another good reason to see a tax professional before meeting with an auditor: to find out if you missed any deductions or can find anything else in your favor to show the auditor. (In Chapter 13, I suggest some publications that might help you identify deductions you may have missed. Or, if you are self-employed, see *Tax Savvy for Small Business*, by Frederick W. Daily (Nolo).)

If you or your preparer were overly conservative—for example, you decided not to take a certain expense as a deduction because you had no receipt—then claim it at the audit. It just might be accepted by the auditor, and nothing ventured, nothing gained.

Don't, however, bring up any favorable items until the auditor has completed the review and decided on any changes for the IRS. Then present your positive adjustments. If you show them earlier, the auditor might counter by looking harder for some offsetting adjustments. After the auditor is locked into a position, things can only get better if he or she accepts any of your new, positive change items.

Negotiating With an Auditor

Auditors have no power to change your tax return. They can only *propose* tax changes to you. Auditors fully realize that if you don't go along with their proposals, you may appeal in most instances (Chapter 4) or go to tax court (Chapter 5) in all cases. In fact, the IRS's guiding principle for auditors is to close examinations with your consent to keep you from clogging up the appeals office and tax court. Because auditors' performance is judged on their closing ratio—how many examination reports are accepted by taxpayers—you are in a perfect position to negotiate.

Oddly, however, auditors aren't officially supposed to negotiate. They are told to discover the facts of a case and apply the tax law to those facts. In reality, if you can show an auditor that the facts are not black or white, you can reach a compromise. Let me emphasize—you can compromise based on the facts; you cannot wheel and deal just because you cannot afford the tax bill. For instance, never offer an auditor 50¢ on the dollar; instead ask for a 50% allowance of a questioned deduction. You can negotiate specific adjustments on particular items using this principle. Here are two examples:

Missing documentation. If your documentation is lacking, you have what the IRS calls a substantiation or verification problem. Suppose you claimed a storage rental expense of $50 per week, paid in cash, and lost your receipts. The auditor disallows the $2,600 item for lack of verification. The former manager of the storage facility writes a letter attesting to your regular payments, but the storage building has been torn down and replaced by a mall. Try proposing a compromise: suggest a disallowance of 25% to get the audit over with. If the auditor agrees, or offers a 50% disallowance, you have just negotiated a fairly decent settlement and you've learned a lesson about keeping your records.

Questionable legal ground. You may have perfect records, but a shaky legal position. For instance, suppose you spent $5,000 to replace a deck and $5,000 for a new roof on rental property you own. On your tax return, you deducted both items as repairs. The auditor claims that these are capital improvements that must be deducted, or amortized, over the life of the improvements. Assuming the auditor is right, and each has a ten-year estimated life, you would be limited to deducting only one-tenth of the cost ($1,000), for each of the next ten years.

To propose a compromise, you can suggest that one item is an improvement, perhaps the deck, but the other is a repair—the roof, which was leaking like a sieve. You could then deduct all $5,000 for the roof and $500 for the deck. While you wanted to deduct $10,000, deducting $5,500 is much better than the IRS's initial position that you deduct only $1,000. You can still take deductions for the balance ($4,500) over the next nine years.

Ending the Audit

Although it never hurts to delay the start of an audit, once it begins you may want to rush it along. For instance, if a problem lurks that the auditor has not yet found, the longer he or she looks, the greater the chance of discovery. If the auditor hasn't yet seen your bank statements and found the mysterious $10,000 deposits, you want out of there before having to explain them. Also, having the IRS in your life is just plain stressful.

A field auditor may be maneuvered into closing a file, depending on the personality type involved.

Bored, lazy, or unexcited. As soon as the audit begins, tell the auditor that you have heard that audits usually produce adjustments. Say that you would appreciate it if it is over with quickly so you can go about your business. If the auditor gets the idea that you won't fight (at least small adjustments) he or she might take you up on your offer. This is especially true if you point out any obvious errors in your return or records (such as 6 + 6 = 13) that will likely be found anyway. Many auditors have a personal tax adjustment level, which they know will satisfy their manager. Conversely, the more time the agent puts into your case, the more he or she expects to find—and will.

> EXAMPLE: Alison took a questionable tax position on a $2,000 deduction for her business. Nearing the end of a full day of an audit, the auditor hadn't yet reached the item. Alison volunteered that there was a $350 deduction that should not have been taken the year before. The auditor had already found $1,200 in other items to disallow, and Alison thought he might be satisfied with one more adjustment. She was right. The auditor said that another day would not be necessary. Even if she had not kept the auditor away from the $2,000 item, by volunteering the $350 item, Alison came across as reasonable. Such

good deeds are often rewarded later by an auditor, such as by giving you the benefit of the doubt when documents are missing.

Overly conscientious. Some auditors (usually the younger ones straight from IRS basic training) come on strong, looking at every little thing and laying down the law like a Marine drill instructor. When this happens, drop the nice guy approach, get your back up and argue over every item that he or she looks at, even when you know you are wrong. Let the person know two can play the game and that you won't be steamrolled. If you know serious problems are ahead due to questionable items or missing documents, demand an end to the audit for that day. Say that you want to consult a tax professional. The auditor won't like being slowed down, but knows your request must be granted.

At your next meeting, the auditor should at least be more reasonable, if not anxious to conclude the audit. If not, threaten to call in the auditor's manager. This usually causes the auditor to adjust his or her attitude. Often, auditors will figure they can better use their time working on other files where the taxpayer does not stand up to them instead of putting more time into your case.

IRS Pressure on an Auditor to Finish— Extending the Audit Time Limit

The IRS does not have forever to audit you. The deadline is normally three years after your return is due (usually April 15) or actually filed, whichever is later. If the IRS suspects serious fraud or underreporting of income by at least 25%, the period is extended to six years or indefinitely. But audits started beyond the normal three-year limit are rare.

The *Internal Revenue Manual* directs an auditor to issue an audit report within 28 months after the date you filed the return. If an auditor hasn't completed the work by then, you will be asked to extend the deadline by signing IRS Form 872, *Consent to Extend the Time to Assess Tax*. When asked, you have three options:

- Sign the consent form.
- Don't sign.
- Negotiate the terms of the extension.

I recommend the second or third approach in most cases.

The auditor wants you to sign an open-ended extension agreement, meaning that an audit adjustment can be made on any item, at any time in the future. Don't do it; you have the right to refuse to sign. Instead, ask that the form be limited to specific items—those on which the auditor has more work to do. Also, agree to an extension for no longer than six months. These perfectly reasonable limitations on the auditor narrow your risk of further IRS fishing into your affairs.

If you don't negotiate or sign the Form 872 extension, one of two things will happen:

- The auditor will issue the examination report, and a notice of deficiency simultaneously. This means that you cannot appeal the report within the IRS, but you can go to court. (See Chapter 5.) This is not so bad, as it isn't that difficult to take the IRS to tax court.

- The auditor may slip up and let the three-year audit deadline pass— meaning that no assessment can ever be made. This does not happen very often. The IRS gets very upset with auditors who blow the deadline. But when it does happen, it's like winning the lottery.

Finishing Audits

Toward the end of every meeting with the auditor, ask what adjustments will be made. While some auditors may not be willing to commit without running it by their managers, they may have some idea. Try to pin the person down. If you disagree, argue your case on the spot or ask for time to get more documents together. Offer to pay any balance in full, if you get a concession. It may not work, but it's always worth a try.

If the IRS Loses Your Audit File

Audit files sometimes get lost in the IRS bureaucratic maze for many months. When found, an unfinished audit file could be assigned to a new auditor who will not want to work on a half-done case and will look for a quick way to close out the file. Even better, the normal three-year deadline for auditing your return may expire before the file resurfaces. This means that the IRS forever loses its right to make adjustments, and you are in the clear.

Receiving the Examination Report

When the auditor completes the work, you will be handed or mailed IRS Form 4549, an examination report. It shows changes proposed to your tax liability for the years under audit, and for any other open years if the auditor expanded the examination. The report also provides a brief explanation for each change, such as "You did not prove the amount shown was a rental expense."

From your point of view, the examination report falls into one of three categories:

Win. Instead of a report, you will receive a "no change" or even a refund letter. These require no explanation. You've won.

Lose. The report makes changes—you owe more taxes, plus interest and maybe penalties. This means you didn't have good documentation or what you had was not accepted. Or, perhaps the auditor didn't buy your legal entitlement to the tax benefits claimed.

Draw. A mixed bag. Some of your documents and explanations were accepted, but others weren't. Or maybe your legal position was shaky on one or two items but strong on another.

Don't worry if it seems to take forever for the IRS to send you the final report. Three to four weeks is standard, but I have waited six months. Don't take a long delay to mean that the IRS is giving your case special attention. More likely, your case has a low priority and is sitting on someone's desk for routine processing.

Understanding the Examination Report

The total amount of taxes, penalties, and interest added by the audit is shown on your report. Each change is listed, the tax code section cited, and a general explanation given. As stated, most explanations are vague. You are usually not specifically told how you failed to prove your case. If you don't know, call the auditor and ask. An auditor must tell you where you failed. (See the sample examination report on the following pages.)

Sample Examination Report

Internal Revenue Service

Department of the Treasury

Date: 8/10/12

Tax Year Ended: 2011

Person to Contact:

Contact Telephone Number:

Contact Address:

Dear Ms. McMillian:

Enclosed are two copies of our report explaining why we believe adjustments should be made in the amount of your tax. Please look this report over and let us know whether you agree with our findings.

If you accept our findings, please sign the consent to assessment and collection portion at the bottom of the report and mail one copy to this office within 30 days from the date of this letter. If additional tax is due, you may want to pay it now and limit the interest charge; otherwise, we will bill you. (See enclosed Publication 5 for payment details.)

If you do not accept our findings, you have 30 days from the date of this letter to do one of the following:

1. Mail us any additional evidence or information you would like us to consider.

2. Request a discussion of our findings with the examiner who conducted the examination. At that time, you may submit any additional evidence or information you would like us to consider. If you plan to come in for a discussion, please phone or write us in advance so that we can arrange a convenient time and place.

3. Discuss your position with the group manager or a senior examiner (designated by the group manager), if an examination has been held and you have been unable to reach an agreement with the examiner.

If you do not accept our findings and do not want to take any of the above actions, you may write us at the address shown above or call us at the telephone number shown above within 30 days from the date of this letter to request a conference with an Appeals Officer. You must provide all pertinent documentation and facts concerning disputed issues to the examiner before your case is forwarded to the Appeals Office.

(over)

Los Angeles District

Letter 915(D)

Sample Examination Report (continued)

If your examination was conducted entirely by mail, we would appreciate your first discussing our findings with one our examiners.

The Appeals Office is independent of the District Director. The Appeals Officer, who has not examined your return previously, will take a fresh look at your case. Most disputes considered by Appeals are resolved informally and promptly. By going to Appeals, you may avoid court costs (such as the United States Tax Court filing fee of $60), clear up this matter sooner, and prevent interest from mounting. An Appeals Officer will promptly telephone you and, if necessary, arrange an appointment. If you decide to bypass Appeals and petition the Tax Court, your case will normally be assigned for settlement to an Appeals Office before the Tax Court hears the case.

Under Internal Revenue Code Section 6673, the Tax Court is authorized to award damages of up to $5,000 to the United States when a taxpayer unreasonably fails to pursue available administrative remedies. Damages could be awarded under this provision, for example, if the Court concludes that it was unreasonable for a taxpayer to bypass Appeals and then file a petition in the Tax Court. The Tax Court will make that determination based upon the facts and circumstances of each case. Generally, the Service will not ask the Court to award damages under this provision if you make a good faith effort to meet with Appeals and to settle your case before petitioning the Tax Court.

The enclosed Publication 5 explains your appeal rights.

If we do not hear from you within 30 days, we will have to process your case on the basis of the adjustments shown in the examination report. If you write us about your case, please write to the person whose name and address are shown in the heading of this letter and refer to the symbols in the upper right corner of the enclosed report. An envelope is enclosed for your convenience. Please include your telephone number, area code, and the most convenient time for us to call, in case we find it necessary to contact you for further information.

If you prefer, you may call the person at the telephone number shown in the heading of this letter. This person will be able to answer any questions you may have. Thank you for your cooperation.

Sincerely yours,

Mort Meyer

Los Angeles District   **Letter 915(D)**

Sample Examination Report (continued)

Report of Individual Income Tax Examination Changes

Department of the Treasury
Internal Revenue Service

Name of Taxpayer	Year	Form	Filing Status	In Reply Refer To:
Ruth McMillian	2011	**1040**	Single	OOO IRS 222

Authorized Representative	Date of Report	Social Security Number	Examining District
	11/18/12	123-456-7890	000-00

Income and Deduction Amounts Adjusted

Explanation Number (See attached)	Item Changed	Amount Shown on Return or as Previously Adjusted	Corrected Amount of Income or Deduction	Adjustment Increase (Decrease)
6102	Net Operating Loss	23226	0	23226
5605	Sch-C Rentals Loss	13757	0	13757
5605	Sch-C Acting Loss	17246	0	17246
0101	Gross Receipts Rentals	_ _ _	_ _ _	_ _ _
0101	Gross Receipts Acting	_ _ _	_ _ _	_ _ _
8203	S.E. Tax	_ _ _	_ _ _	_ _ _
8138	Negligence	_ _ _	_ _ _	_ _ _
8120	Substantial Understatement	_ _ _	_ _ _	_ _ _

A. Adjustment in income and deductions - increase (decrease) (See explanation of adjustments attached.) — 54,229

B. Adjusted gross or taxable income shown on return or as previously adjusted — 17,660

C. Corrected adjusted gross or taxable income — 71,889

D. Corrected tax (From: ☐ Tax Table, ☐ Tax Rate Schedules, ☐ Form 8615 or ☐ Other) — 16,261

E. Tax credits (general business, child and dependent care, foreign, etc.) (If adjusted, see explanation attached.) — ____

F. Other tax (self-employment, alternative minimum, tax from recapture of Investment credit, etc.) (If adjusted, see explanation attached.) S.E. Tax — 667

G. Total corrected tax (line D less line E plus line F) — 16,928

H. Tax shown on return or as previously adjusted — 4,197

I. Adjustments to EIC/Fuels credit - increase (decrease) (If adjusted, see explanation attached.)

J. Deficiency - Increase in tax or (Overassessment - Decrease in tax) (Line G adjusted by Lines H and I) — 12,731

K. Adjustments to prepayment credits - increase (decrease)

L. Balance due or (Overpayment) - Excluding interest and penalties (Line J adjusted by line K) — 12,731

M. Penalties (See explanation attached)
(1) Negligence § 6652(a)(1) — 636.55
(2) Substantial Understatement § 6661 — 3,182.86
(3)

Consent to Assessment and Collection - I do not wish to exercise my appeal rights with the Internal Revenue Service or to contest in the United States Tax Court the findings in this report. Therefore, I give my consent to the immediate assessment and collection of any increase in tax and penalties, and accept any decrease in tax and penalties above, plus any interest as provided by law.

Although this report is subject to review, you may consider it as your notice that your case is closed if you are not notified of an exception to these findings within 45 days after a signed copy of the report or a signed waiver, Form 870, is received by the District Director.

Ruth McMillian   11/18/12

Your signature	Date	Spouse's signature (IF A JOINT RETURN, BOTH MUST SIGN)	Date

By ____   Title ____   Date ____

Cat. No. 21270C   (See notices on the back)   Form **1902-B** (Rev. 1-91)

Sample Examination Report (continued)

FORM 886-A	**EXPLANATION OF ITEMS**	SCHEDULE NO. OR EXHIBIT A
Ruth McMillian		YEAR/PERIOD ENDED 2011

6102   You did not sustain a net operating loss in the tax year

within the meaning of Section 172 of the Internal Revenue Code

because your loss was attributable solely to nonbusiness

expenses. Therefore, there is no net operating loss carry-back

or carry-over, and your deduction claimed is disallowed.

Taxable income is increased accordingly.

0101   Although not adjusted, gross receipts are an open audit issue.

8203   We have adjusted your self-employment tax due to a change in

your net profit from this self-employment.

5605   Since you did not establish that the business expense shown

on your tax return was paid or incurred during the taxable

year and that the expense was ordinary and necessary to your

business, we have disallowed the amount shown.

DEPARTMENT OF THE TREASURY-INTERNAL REVENUE SERVICE   **FORM 886-A**

Page _____

Sample Examination Report (continued)

FORM 886-A	EXPLANATION OF ITEMS	SCHEDULE NO. OR EXHIBIT A
Ruth McMillian		YEAR/PERIOD ENDED 2011

8138   Since all or part of the underpayment of tax you were

required to show on your return is due to negligence or

intentional disregard of rules and regulations, you are being

charged a penalty under Internal Revenue Code Section 6653(a).

For tax returns due, without regard to extensions, after

December 31, 1994, this penalty is 5% of the underpayment.

The interest on the penalty is calculated according to Internal

Revenue Code Section 6601(e)(2)(B) from the due date of the

return (including extension) until the additional tax is paid.

8120   Since there is a substantial understatement of income tax,

you are liable for a penalty of 25% of the amount of any

underpayment attributable to such understatement. This

applies to tax not assessed prior to October 21, 1992. In

addition, interest is figured on the penalty from the due date

of the return without regard to extensions. See Internal

Revenue Code Sections 6661 and 6601(e)(2).

Your Options After Getting the Examination Report

You have three choices after you receive the examination report.

Agree. The IRS hopes you will sign, date, and return a copy of the report along with IRS Form 870, *Consent to Proposed Tax Adjustment.* This is referred to by the IRS as an agreed case.

By signing Form 870, you agree to the immediate assessment of the tax deficiency found, plus any penalties and interest listed on the examination report. You give up your right to appeal or go to tax court. Theoretically, you could pay, change your mind, and sue the IRS for a refund in court, but this seldom makes sense. Although most tax lawsuits are filed in U.S. Tax Court, a refund case must be brought in a U.S. Federal District Court or the U.S. Court of Claims. (See Chapter 5.)

A report, even if signed by you, is not final until approved by the auditor's manager. Occasionally, a report you signed will be kicked back to the auditor for correction of obvious errors or to further develop issues. If this happens, the auditor may contact you once more. It may seem unfair, but, you can't complain about being audited twice. The first audit was not officially concluded.

Signing doesn't mean you have to pay when you sign the report. Paying, however, may seal the deal. Auditors can offer a payment plan if you owe less than $10,000. You have up to three years to pay on a monthly basis. Interest and late payment penalties still accrue on the unpaid balance. Interest and penalties on late tax payments get added on. For bills over $10,000 (see Chapter 6), you may have to reveal your finances and living expenses to get a payment plan.

> **TIP**
>
> **It is okay to tell the auditor that you will just wait until a bill comes from the IRS campus center computer and then decide how to pay.** Sometimes, the bill is less than the audit report figure because a penalty was dropped or a computation error was made or corrected. If the bill is more than the amount on the report, complain; if it is less, let your conscience be your guide. If you pay the lesser amount, no one may ever notice. Don't be surprised, however, if you are later billed for the difference.

Disagree. Examination reports are not cast in stone until you sign off. If you want to fight the report, call the auditor. Tell the person what findings you disagree with. Ask what additional proof it would take to get the report changed. Request 30 days to get a missing document or reconstruct a record. Most auditors will hold off until you mail the proof to them. Pushing for another appointment may be better. It forces them to face you again, and shows that you are serious about contesting the report's findings. If the auditor is not cooperative, ask to speak to a manager. If you are ultimately successful, you'll be sent an amended examination report to sign.

TIP

If your new documentation doesn't help, ask for a copy of the auditor's workpapers. These are the notes the IRS requires an auditor put in a file. Workpapers should explain and justify any changes made to a tax return. If the auditor shows you his or her notes, ask for a full explanation (and the conclusions) if it isn't obvious. Don't be surprised if the auditor refuses to show you the workpapers. If you are refused, say that you know you are entitled to see them under the Freedom of Information Act and you will make a formal request for them. (Chapter 4 explains how to make a Freedom of Information Act request.)

If you don't get anywhere with the auditor, ask to meet with a manager. Generally, the manager will speak with you. I call this an informal appeal. Managers don't always back their auditors. They have a strong motive to close files handled by their group with an "agreed" notation, so they may appease you.

If you talk to or meet with the manager, don't criticize the auditor. The manager may then concentrate on defending his or her employee instead of considering your position. Instead, talk about the adjustments you don't agree with and suggest a compromise. Even if this doesn't get you anywhere, the manager's explanations may make the IRS's position clearer to you or point out the weaknesses in your case. As a last resort, if the manager won't budge, calmly say that you are disappointed and that you don't want to appeal, but you don't know what else to do. Again, keep in mind that the IRS doesn't like appeals, and this subtle threat may get you what you want.

Team managers may delegate audit disputes to senior agents who are more experienced and may know how to smooth things over. Remember, auditors are instructed to get you to agree to the audit report, if possible. The senior agent may already be familiar with your case, especially if your auditor is fairly new at the IRS. If your auditor ever asked for time during your audit, ostensibly to make copies or check on something, he or she may have been asking a senior auditor what to do.

If you explain your position to the senior manager and still need help, you can insist on talking to the real manager. The IRS, like most other organizations, doesn't like to be bothered by squeaking wheels—you may eventually get greased. If you want to go further up the ladder, ask to speak to a territory manager.

Do nothing. You don't have to respond to a proposed examination report at all. If you ignore it, the auditor may call, or in a month or two you will receive something called a 30-day letter. This is your formal notice that your case is considered "unagreed" and that you have 30 days to start an appeal or the findings become final. The appeals process is covered in Chapter 4, and is also described in IRS Publication 5, *Appeal Rights and Preparation of Protests for Unagreed Cases*. You should receive a copy of Publication 5 with your examination report.

The IRS does not have to grant you an administrative appeal; it is discretionary. However, the IRS must eventually send you a so-called 90-day letter, before the audit can become final. This letter may not arrive for months after the audit was completed. The IRS must send it by certified mail. To contest the audit results now, you must file a petition in the U.S. Tax Court within 90 days. (See Chapter 5.) If you don't, the examination report becomes final and your right to contest the audit without first making full payment has ended.

You can also contest by paying the tax bill and filing a claim with the IRS for a refund. Refund claims are always denied. You can then file a refund suit in U.S. District Court or the court of claims. (See Chapter 5.)

Eventually, if you do nothing, you will get a Notice of Tax Due. This is the beginning of the IRS collection effort. (See Chapter 6.)

Case History of an Informal Audit Appeal

Mr. Ky, a Vietnamese immigrant and San Francisco restaurant owner, was audited. When he received the examination report, Ky was so distraught he considered jumping off the Golden Gate Bridge. Ky had fallen victim to a dishonest tax return preparer who guaranteed his clients they would never have IRS problems. His clients almost always got tax refunds, and he charged a percentage of the refund received.

One day, the office of the bogus tax adviser was raided and his records seized by the IRS. All of his clients got audit notices. Ky was understandably suspicious of anyone calling himself a tax expert, so he decided to handle the audit himself. He wanted to come clean knowing he would have to pay some additional taxes.

The auditor knew Ky was selected as part of a special IRS project involving the crooked tax preparer. At the meeting, things went from bad to worse. Ky spoke broken English and produced records written in his native language. The auditor became irritated and impatient. The examination report came quickly, disallowing most of Ky's business deductions and finding a great deal of unreported income. The resulting taxes, with heavy fraud penalties and interest added, came to $79,500. To pay meant Ky would have had to sell his business and lose everything he had worked for in the ten years he had been in America.

Ky finally sought a tax professional. During their meeting, the tax professional became convinced that Ky should not owe anywhere near $79,500. The tax professional called the auditor's manager and made an appointment to meet her in two weeks. He then found a Vietnamese-American accountant to convert Ky's records and notes into a more conventional set of books. The accountant acted as an interpreter and helped the tax professional take sworn statements from Vietnamese people who had worked in the restaurant. These books and statements created a true financial picture of the business, in clear English.

When the tax professional met with the auditor's manager, he presented the statements and records. In less than an hour they had agreed on a total tax of $13,000 and no harsh fraud penalty. After the tax bill came, Ky negotiated an installment payment agreement with the IRS Collection Division. Ky did not jump off the Golden Gate or any other bridge. His family now owns two restaurants in San Francisco.

Opening a Closed Audit

There is a procedure for reopening a closed audit, called assessment reconsideration, initiated either by you or the IRS. Fortunately, the IRS rarely reopens closed audits. If it does, see a tax pro to find out if the IRS is acting properly, or do a little legal research yourself. (See Chapter 13; the relevant laws are Internal Revenue Code § 7605(b); IRS Regulation 601.105; Revenue Procedure 85-13; and IRS Policy Statement P-4-3.)

Serious Audit Problems

While everyone considers being audited a problem, a few uncommon, yet serious, audit issues merit special discussion.

The Auditor Suspects You of Fraud

Tax fraud is covered in Chapter 10.

You're Billed for an Audit You Didn't Know About

Many taxpayers receive bills from examinations they didn't know about—phantom audits. Yes, the IRS is required to notify you in writing of an audit. Theoretically, if the IRS doesn't let you know about an audit, your return can't be audited. In reality, however, the IRS is only required to mail a letter to your *last known address*. It is not required to verify that you actually receive the notice.

The tax court says the IRS must update its files regularly and send notices to the address on your most recent tax return or newer address that you have provided. (*Abeles v. Commissioner of Internal Revenue*, 91 U.S.T.C. 1019 (1991).) The IRS is allowed three months to update its records on a change of address after it receives notification.

If you don't answer an audit letter and it is not returned to the IRS by the post office, auditors can treat you as a "no show." Exemptions and deductions are disallowed in whatever manner the auditor wishes and an audit bill is issued. It is not a pretty picture.

 TIP

To make sure you get all IRS notices, file IRS Form 8822, *Change of Address***, whenever you move.** (A copy is available at the IRS website www.irs.gov.) Do not just rely on a post office change of address form.

The unfairness of the IRS's charging ahead when you don't get the audit notice is underscored by what happens next. The IRS usually sends an audit report and a letter informing you of the appeal process to your old address. Or, the IRS may send a *Notice of Deficiency* giving you 90 days to object in tax court. This notice comes by certified mail. But, again, the law does not require that you actually receive the letter, only that the IRS send it. The IRS doesn't seem to care if you get any of these notices. Legally, as long as the notices are sent to your address in the IRS records, the audit was legitimate. Hardly fair, but you can fight back.

There are three ways to fight a phantom audit.

Assessment reconsideration. (Formerly called audit reconsideration.) If you receive a mysterious tax bill, immediately write or call the IRS office that sent it. Tell them you never received notice of the audit and you are request-ing an *assessment reconsideration*. Or, call the Taxpayer Advocate Service. (See Chapter 8.) Make an appointment or send the notices by fax or mail. Ask the advocate to help you get an assessment reconsideration meeting with an auditor. See IRS Publication 3598 for details on making a request.

You do not have a right to an assessment reconsideration; it is discretionary with the IRS. Usually, however, requests are granted. The IRS also has an audit reexamination procedure, which differs from an assessment reconsideration. A reexamination can open up your entire file for audit — and not just the items that were charged in the phantom audit.

Petition the tax court. If your assessment reconsideration is denied, file a petition in tax court, stating that a notice of deficiency was not sent to your last known address as required by law. (See Chapter 5.)

Offer in Compromise. In addition to audit reconsideration and tax court, you can challenge a phantom audit by making an Offer in Compromise, based on a doubt as to your liability for the tax bill. (See Chapter 6.) Unlike most Offers in Compromise, which are made to settle an undisputed tax bill, with an Offer in Compromise based on doubt as to liability, you do not offer any money to the IRS. The IRS may treat your offer as it would treat an assessment reconsideration and reopen your case.

Jeopardy Assessments

The IRS has a "shoot first, ask questions later" power to make quick tax assessments without an audit. This is called the jeopardy assessment. Normally there must be a formal assessment of taxes against you before the IRS can legally collect. The jeopardy assessment process allows the IRS to immediately grab your assets without prior notice. You have a right to a hearing, but not until after the seizure.

Thankfully, jeopardy assessments are authorized only if the IRS believes its right to collect taxes will be harmed, and that:

- You appear to be planning to hide out in or depart the United States.
- You are concealing, dissipating, or removing property from the country or transferring it to other persons.
- Your financial solvency is endangered.

Jeopardy assessments are most frequently made against foreign companies or foreigners operating businesses in the United States, or persons arrested with large amounts of cash, especially suspected drug dealers. If you are ever faced with a jeopardy assessment, see a tax lawyer right away.

Form 4700 Examination Workpapers

Form 4700. Examination Workpapers.

Examination Workpapers

Taxpayer's name, address, SSN *(Use pre-addressed label or show changes)*	Date		Year(s)	
	Examiner			Grade
	Taxpayer(s)	Home Phone		Work Phone
	Reviewer			

A

Initial Interview

1. Examination technique: ☐ Correspondence
   ☐ Undeliverable mail ☐ No show
   ☐ Interview with:

   _____

2. Receipt of Publication 1 ☐
3. Appeal rights and Privacy Act explained ☐
4. Continue on Form 4700-A, B or C

B

Representative - Power of Attorney   ☐ Yes   ☐ No
Name   Phone

Closed No Change

Issue: ☐ Letter 590   ☐ Letter 1156   ☐ Other

Examiner

C

Examination Reminders

1. Proforma Worksheets utilized where applicable
2. Alternative minimum tax
3. Inspection of prior and subsequent year return, IRM 4215
4. Probe for unreported deductions and credits
5. Scope of Examination, IRM 4253.2
6. Automatic adjustments resulting from AGI change(s)

Case Processing Reminders

1. Claim Case - Forms 2297 and 3363
2. Information Reports (IRM 4219) - Form 5346
3. FICA, Self-Employment or Tip Income Adjustments
   Forms 885-E, 885-F, and 885-T
4. Inequities, Abuses, Loopholes - Form 3558
5. Inadequate Records Notice (IRM 4271)
6. Special Handling Notice 3198

D

(Items to be considered, explored, verified)	Year	Per Return	Corrected	Adjustment	Workpapers Index

E

	Year	Per Return	Corrected	Adjustment	Workpapers Index

Form **4700** (Rev. 2-80)   Department of the Treasury — Internal Revenue Service

Form 4700-A Supplement

Form 4700-A. Form 4700 Supplement.

| **Form 4700 Supplement** | | Taxpayer | | Year(s) | |
| | | Examiner | | Date | |

		Yes	No	Comments	
1. Preparer Information	A. Was return prepared for Compensation? (If Yes, complete remaining items)				
	B. Identification Penalties required?				
	C. Did preparer negotiate refund?				
	D. Did taxpayer receive a copy of return?				

2. Prior IRS Contacts or Prior Audits

☐ None   ☐ Yes — Year(s)   Do Repetitive Audit Procedures apply? ☐ Yes ☐ No

Issues/Reasons: Was Amended Return(s) filed? ☐ Yes ☐ No

3. All Due Returns Filed?		Yes	No	N/A	Comments
	Individual				
	Household help				
	Employment				
	Excise				

4. Income Probe

If reported or received none, enter (√) in block. If received but not reported, enter (X) in block and comment below.

Interest (S&L) Banks, 2nd Mortgage)	Alimony	Gifts, Inheritance
Dividends	Partnerships	Scholarship, Fellowship, Grant
Sale of assets	Sick Pay	Loans
Other jobs	Child support	Social Security
Investments	Prizes, awards, bonuses	Welfare
Tips	Gambling/Lotteries	Unemployment compensation
Commission	Insurance	VA benefits
Hobbies	Estate/Trusts	Military allowance
Rent/Royalty	State/Local Tax Refund	Foreign Bank Accounts
	Employer Reimbursement	Pensions, Annuities, Profit-Sharing
		IRA/Keogh Distributions

Comments should indicate nature and extent of income probe

5. Bartering			
	Exchange of personal services or merchandise?	Yes	No
	Belong to any bartering clubs or organizations?	Yes	No
	If Yes, explain fully		

6. Foreign Accounts and Foreign Trusts	Is the Foreign Accounts and Foreign Trusts question appearing on the tax return answered correctly? If No, explain fully.	Yes	No	☐ N/A

7. Exemptions	Name	Age	Relationship	Other Information

Form 4700-A (Rev. 9-84)   *(over please)*   Department of the Treasury — Internal Revenue Service

Form 4700-A Supplement (continued)

Form 4700-A. Form 4700 Supplement. (cont'd)

			Complete Remaining Items After Examination
8. Solicit Payment			Payment solicited: Payment received — Include Interest Computation
			Payment solicited: Taxpayer desires to be billed

9. Prior/Subsequent Year Return

Prior/subsequent year audit recommended?

☐ Yes — Date of AIMS Request _____ Date Information Report Submitted _____

☐ No — State reason:

10. Penalties Recommended For Taxpayer

Type	Asserted	Reason
Negligence	☐ Yes	Indicate issue(s) on which 50% interest is applicable.
	☐ No	
Delinquency	☐ Yes	
	☐ No	
Fraud	☐ Yes	Indicate issue(s) on which 50% interest is applicable.
	☐ No	
Other (State penalty)	☐ Yes	
	☐ No	

11. Preparer Conduct Penalties

Any indications of preparer negligence or fraud?	Yes	No

If Yes, explain:

12. Unagreed Case

Group Manager Involvement in Unagreed Case:

☐ Taxpayer Offered Conference with Group Manager. Date _____

Form **4700-A** (Rev. 9-84)   GPO : 1986 0 - 161-268   Department of the Treasury — Internal Revenue Service

Form 4700-B Business Supplement

Form 4700-B. Form 4700 Business Supplement.

Form 4700 Business Supplement	Taxpayer	Year
	Examiner	Date

1. Brief Discription of Day-to-Day Business Operation

2. Business History

How long in business

Number of employees	Full-Time	Part-Time

3. Accounting Method

☐ Cash   ☐ Accrual   ☐ Hybrid

Who keeps the books?

4. Cash on Hand

	Beginning of Year	End of Year
Home	$	$
Business	$	$
Elsewhere	$	$

5. Where do You Maintain Your Bank Account(s)?

Business	Account Number	Personal	Account Numt

6. Banking Practices

Were all business and personal expenses kept separately?

Were all business receipts deposited? To which account?

How are business expenses paid?

7. Safety Deposit Box

Location	Contents

8. Purchases

Any withdrawals of purchases for personal use?

9. Related Transactions

Any transactions between you and relative or related parties? If so, explain.

10. Gross Receipts

How were gross receipts calculated?

Workpaper Index _____

Form 4700-B (Rev. 8-83)   Department of the Treasury — Internal Revenue Service

Form 4700-B Business Supplement (continued)

Form 4700-B. Form 4700 Business Supplement. (cont'd)

	Are inventories material? ☐ Yes ☐ No			
11. Inventories	a. Did beginning and ending balances agree with prior/subsequent returns?		Yes	No
	b. Were there any changes in method of valuing inventories?		Yes	No
	c. When taken:			
	How:			
	d. Include year-end purchases?		Yes	No
	e. Any write-offs or write downs?		Yes	No

12.	Loans, notes, mortgages payable:	AMOUNT	Per	Bus.	PAGE, EXHIBIT, SCHEDULE

13.	Capital items sold:	AMOUNT	PURCHASER	PAGE, EXHIBIT, SCHEDULE

14.	Capital items purchased:		SELLER	

Form **4700-B** (Rev. 8-83)   U S GOVERNMENT PRINTING OFFICE 1983 - 381-341/3424   Department of the Treasury — Internal Revenue Service

Form 1902-B Report of Individual Income Tax Examination Changes

Report of Individual Income Tax Examination Changes				Department of the Treasury Internal Revenue Service	
Name of Taxpayer		Year	Form 1040	Filing Status	In Reply Refer To:
Authorized Representative		Date of Report		Social Security Number	Examining District

Income and Deduction Amounts Adjusted

Explanation Number (See attached)	Item Changed	Amount Shown on Return or as Previously Adjusted	Corrected Amount of Income or Deduction	Adjustment Increase (Decrease)

A. Adjustment in income and deductions - increase (decrease) (See explanation of adjustments attached.)

B. Adjusted gross or taxable income shown on return or as previously adjusted

C. Corrected adjusted gross or taxable income

D. Corrected tax (From: ☐ Tax Table, ☐ Tax Rate Schedules, ☐ Form 8615 or ☐ Other)

E. Tax credits (general business, child and dependent care, foreign, etc.) (If adjusted, see explanation attached.)

F. Other tax (self-employment, alternative minimum, tax from recapture of Investment credit, etc.) (If adjusted, see explanation attached.)

G. Total corrected tax (line D less line E plus line F)

H. Tax shown on return or as previously adjusted

I. Adjustments to EIC/Fuels credit - increase (decrease) (If adjusted, see explanation attached.)

J. Deficiency - Increase in tax or (Overassessment - Decrease in tax) (Line G adjusted by Lines H and I)

K. Adjustments to prepayment credits - increase (decrease)

L. Balance due or (Overpayment) - Excluding interest and penalties (Line J adjusted by line K)

M. Penalties (See explanation attached)   (1)

(2)

(3)

Consent to Assessment and Collection - I do not wish to exercise my appeal rights with the Internal Revenue Service or to contest in the United States Tax Court the findings in this report. Therefore, I give my consent to the immediate assessment and collection of any increase in tax and penalties, and accept any decrease in tax and penalties above, plus any interest as provided by law.

Although this report is subject to review, you may consider it as your notice that your case is closed if you are not notified of an exception to these findings within 45 days after a signed copy of the report or a signed waiver, Form 870, is received by the District Director.

Your signature _____   Date _____   Spouse's signature _____   Date _____
(IF A JOINT RETURN, BOTH MUST SIGN)

By _____   Title _____   Date _____

Cat. No. 21270C   (See notices on the back)   Form **1902-B** (Rev. 1-91)

Chapter Highlights

- In an audit, the IRS wants to find out if you reported all of your income and were entitled to all credits, deductions, and exemptions claimed on your tax return.
- Keep the IRS from holding the audit at your business or home. Instead, go to the IRS office or hire a tax professional to meet the IRS agent at the tax professional's office.
- Give auditors no more information than they are entitled to, and don't talk any more during the audit than is absolutely necessary.
- Don't expect to come out of the audit without owing something. The odds are against you.
- The IRS must complete an audit within three years of the time your tax return is filed, unless the IRS finds tax fraud or a significant underreporting of income (which extends the deadline).
- If the audit is not going well, demand a recess to consult a tax professional or collect your thoughts.
- Speak to the auditor's manager if you think the auditor is treating you unfairly.
- If you are missing receipts or other documents, you are allowed to reconstruct records (in most cases).
- When you get the audit report, call the auditor if you don't understand or agree with it. Meet with the auditor's manager to see if you can reach a compromise if it looks bad.
- If you can't live with an audit result, you may appeal within the IRS or go on to tax court.

Appealing Your Audit Within the IRS

Y ou tried to get the auditor to be reasonable but the person just wouldn't see things your way. In fact, you received a costly examination report. You spoke to the auditor's manager in an effort to win an informal appeal. Again, you didn't have any luck. You are not ready to give up, though. What's next?

A formal appeal, that's what. The IRS has an administrative procedure for appealing unagreed examination reports to an IRS appeals office. The appeals office has nearly 2,000 employees scattered throughout the United States. Take advantage of this procedure, which is described in IRS Publication 5, *Appeal Rights and Preparation of Protests for Unagreed Cases.*

Fewer than one in ten audited taxpayers appeal. Many more taxpayers should. Appealing is neither difficult nor time-consuming, and your chance of achieving at least some tax reduction is excellent. You rarely need to hire a tax professional to file an appeal. Despite this, however, most taxpayers are either too discouraged or intimidated to appeal. That's too bad.

The official IRS position on the appeals process is this:

> *The appeals mission is to resolve tax controversies, without litigation, on a basis which is fair and impartial to both the government and the taxpayer and in a manner that will enhance voluntary compliance and public confidence in the integrity and efficiency of the [IRS].* (Internal Revenue Manual § 8631.)

The Odds of Winning an Appeal

Most auditors privately refer to the appeals office as the IRS's gift shop. There is even an IRS in-joke that appeals officers work on the 50% rule—they like to cut auditors' adjustments by half.

IRS statistics show that the auditors are exaggerating—but not by much. The average appeal results in a 40% decrease in taxes, penalties, and interest imposed by the auditor. So, even the IRS confirms that it pays to appeal. The only mystery is why more audit victims don't.

According to the IRS, in a recent year, over 100,000 appeals were taken by taxpayers and over 80% were resolved in a manner acceptable to both sides.

Appeals of other IRS actions. In addition to audits, many other IRS decisions may be appealed, such as tax liens and levies.

Pros and Cons of Appealing an Audit

There are three solid reasons for appealing an audit and two relatively insignificant reasons not to.

Pros

- Appealing is simple and costs nothing unless you use a tax professional, which is not usually necessary for success.
- Appealing, in the majority of cases, results in some savings, although rarely a total victory.
- Appealing delays your audit tax bill for months, buying you time to consider payment options.

Cons

- The appeals officer can raise issues the auditor missed—but this almost never happens. Nevertheless, if you are afraid that a missed item will be discovered and you'll owe a lot more in taxes, you can skip the appeal altogether. In this case, you can go directly to tax court, where new issues can't be raised. (See Chapter 5.)
- Interest (and sometimes penalties) on the tax bill continue to run while you are appealing. This is typically a small item as compared with the likely tax savings resulting from most appeals.

The IRS Does Not Have to Offer an Appeal

The IRS is not legally required to let you have an administrative appeal after an audit—and sometimes it doesn't. Instead of a 30-day letter offering an appeal, you may get a 90-day letter. This means the only way to challenge the audit without paying the additional tax the IRS claims you owe is to file a petition in tax court. (See Chapter 5.)

Here's something odd: If you don't get an appeals hearing and do file a tax court petition, your case will be sent to the Appeals Office anyway. You will now probably be offered an appeal hearing, or you can request one. If you don't settle in the appeals office, your file will be sent to an IRS lawyer.

How to Appeal an Audit

After the audit, the IRS sends an examination report with proposed adjustments—additional taxes, penalties, and interest. If you don't sign and return a copy of the report within a few weeks, the IRS usually sends a letter (the 30-Day Letter) and an explanation of how to appeal the report.

Time Limit for an Appeal

"Protest" is the official term for formally appealing an IRS determination. You must protest within 30 days of the date on the appeal notice letter—not the date you received it. As discussed in Chapter 3, you can also informally appeal to the auditor's manager.

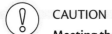 CAUTION
Meeting the manager does not extend the 30-day deadline to file a formal appeal. Make sure you file a written protest, too.

Can't file your protest in time? Request an extension for another 30 to 60 days to appeal. Requests to auditors or managers are usually granted, but don't rely on an oral promise. Send a confirming letter stating the terms of the extension and the name of the person granting it.

How to Get Your Audit to the Appeals Office

There are three ways to get your audit to the IRS Appeals Office. Which one to choose depends on your preference and how much the IRS auditor says you owe:

- **If you owe less than $2,500:** You can simply ask the auditor for an appeal—technically, your oral request is sufficient. But, to make sure you are not forgotten, either write a protest letter in your own words and write at the top "Small Case Request" (following the instructions and sample below) or use IRS Form 12203, *Request for Appeals Review.*
- **If you owe between $2,500 and $25,000:** Either write a protest letter and write at the top "Small Case Request" (following the instructions and sample below) or use IRS Form 12203. I recommend using the form.

- **If you owe more than $25,000:** Write a protest letter. The IRS doesn't have a form for contesting tax debts over this amount. (See below and sample letter.)

IRS Form for Appeals Under $25,000 (Small Case)

To appeal an audit in which the IRS claims you owe $25,000 or less in extra taxes, penalties, and interest, you may use IRS Form 12203, *Request for Appeals Review.* As you'll see from the sample below, this is a simple, one-page form that lets you list the items on the IRS examination report with which you disagree and briefly explain your position. Download the form from the IRS website (www.irs.gov). You can use the Adobe "fill-in" feature or type or handwrite on a printed copy of the form. If the space on the form is insufficient, add a separate page or pages. (Be sure to put your name and taxpayer identification number at the top of any extra pages.)

Where the form asks for "Taxpayer Identification Number(s)," use your Social Security number if you're an individual and your employer identification number (EIN) if you're representing a business or trust. Also, if you're appealing on behalf of your business, the line "Tax period(s) ended" can be answered with quarters of tax years—for example, 4th quarter, 2008—rather than a whole year figure.

Send the completed form to the IRS office that issued the audit report—by certified mail, return receipt requested.

Protest Letter for Appeals Over $25,000 (Large Case)

To contest an audit debt of more than $25,000, you must file a formal protest, which is a letter, not a form (see the sample below). The letter must contain the following:

- your name (or names, if husband and wife) and Social Security number(s)
- a statement that you are appealing an examination report
- the findings in the report that you disagree with, including penalties and interest
- a brief explanation of why the report is wrong; although not required, you can attach copies of any documents supporting your explanation

Sample Request for Appeals Review

Request for Appeals Review

Please complete the information in the spaces below, including your signature and the date.

Taxpayer name(s)	Taxpayer Identification Number(s)
Rick Vallalobos Villalba	555-55-5555

Mailing address	Tax form number
111 Elm Street	1040

City	Tax period(s) ended
Bloomington	2008, 2009

State	ZIP Code	
Indiana	47000	

Identify the item(s) (for example: filing status, exemptions, interest or dividends) you disagree with in the proposed change or assessment report you received with the enclosed letter. Tell us why you disagree. You can add more pages if this is not enough space.

Disagreed item	Reason why you disagree
Disallowance of business expense deductions of $12,999 and penalties and interest of $848	The deductions I took were legitimate expenses of my music business, and I was trying to make a profit.

Disagreed item	Reason why you disagree

Disagreed item	Reason why you disagree

Disagreed item	Reason why you disagree

Signature of Taxpayer(s)	Date
Rick Vallalobos Villalba	4/15/xx
	Date

Name and signature of authorized representative (**If a representative is signing this form, please attach a copy of your completed Form 2848, Power of Attorney and Declaration of Representative.**)

Name	
Signature	Date
Your telephone number	Best time to call

Form **12203** (Rev. 4-2004)   Cat. No. 27136N   www.irs.gov   Department of the Treasury - Internal Revenue Service

- your signature(s) and date under a penalty-of-perjury clause, and
- copies of the 30-Day Letter and examination report.

Make the protest letter short and sweet. Stick to the facts and don't criticize the auditor or the IRS—whether justified or not. Blowing off steam may make you feel better, but it only detracts from an otherwise valid appeal.

Below is a sample protest letter. This sample is a skeleton type of protest letter, giving only the bare bones of why you are appealing. Some tax professionals recommend very detailed protests with copies of all documents you want to be considered. This can be difficult to do if you are not a tax expert, so go with the minimal approach. This gives you time to either send in supporting documents to the appeals officer later or bring them to the hearing.

For details, see IRS Publication 5, *Your Appeals Rights and How to Prepare a Protest if You Don't Agree.*

 TIP

Consult a tax professional if you are unsure about preparing your protest. You can also get advice on preparing for the appeals hearing. An experienced professional can tell you what evidence—documents and statements—the appeals officer will look for. (See Chapter 13.)

Send your letter to the IRS office that issued the report—by certified mail, return receipt requested. Also send or give a copy to the auditor.

Requesting the Auditor's File

Under the federal Freedom of Information Act, or FOIA, you are entitled to a copy of almost everything in your IRS auditor's file. Most important are the notes and workpapers showing how the auditor arrived at the conclusions.

There may be nothing new in the file, but you may mine a gold nugget using the FOIA. For instance, once I got a file with a report transmittal form showing fraud suspected by the auditor. This matter can legally be edited out of your copy, but if it is, it may be apparent or you may be told that something has been kept from you.

Certain things, notably the DIF score—the computer score that probably caused the audit in the first place—are protected from disclosure by law.

Sample Protest (Appeal) Letter

August 15, 20xx

Internal Revenue Service
P.O. Box 44687 (Stop 11)
Indianapolis, IN 46244

VIA CERTIFIED MAIL—RETURN RECEIPT REQUESTED

PROTEST OF MICK RODRIGUEZ
SSN: 555-55-5555

111 Elm Street
Bloomington, IN 47000

Dear Sir/Madam:

I wish to appeal the examination report of 8/1/xx, a copy of which is attached. I request a hearing. The tax years protested are 2005 and 2006.

The adjustments that I disagree with are [*fill in something like "the disallowance of business expense deductions shown on my Schedule C of $12,999, and penalties and interest in the total amount of $848"*].

The adjustments were [*again, fill in your explanation, like "incorrect because the deductions I took were legitimate expenses of my music business, and I was trying to make a profit"*].

Under penalty of perjury, I declare that the facts presented in this protest and in any accompanying documents are, to the best of my knowledge and belief, true, correct, and complete.

Sincerely,

Mick Rodriguez
Mick Rodriguez

Copy to Auditor

Enclosed: Copy of 30-Day Letter and Copy of Examination Report

This is no big deal, as the DIF number won't mean anything to you anyway. (DIF scores are covered in Chapter 3.)

To get your IRS file, you must send a separate letter to the FOIA disclosure officer at your local IRS office. (See sample below.) Specifically ask for a copy of your audit file by year audited and offer to pay for copying charges. Hand deliver your letter or send it by certified mail, return receipt requested. Enclose a photocopy of your driver's license or birth certificate with your letter.

Sample FOIA Letter

August 15, 20xx

Internal Revenue Service
P.O. Box 44687 (Stop 11)
Indianapolis, IN 46244

VIA CERTIFIED MAIL—RETURN RECEIPT REQUESTED

PROTEST OF MICK RODRIGUEZ
SSN: 555-55-5555

111 Elm Street
Bloomington, IN 47000

Dear Sir/Madam:

Under the Privacy Act of 1974, 5 U.S.C. 552A, and the Freedom of Information Act, 5 U.S.C. 552, I request a copy of all files relevant to the audit of my tax return for years 2010 and 2011.

I agree to pay reasonable charges for copying the requested documents, up to $25. If the charges exceed this amount, please contact me for further authorization.

If you determine that any portion of these files is exempt, please identify the portion claimed exempt and the specific exemption that justifies your refusal to release it.

Sincerely,

Mick Rodriguez

Mick Rodriguez

Allow four weeks or more for a response. If you don't hear from the disclosure office, start calling. Technically, the IRS does not have to make copies for you, although it usually will. Instead, you might be told you have to come into the disclosure office to look at the file. If the date of the appeals hearing is approaching and you haven't yet received or had a chance to review your file, ask for a postponement from the appeals officer. Send a return letter confirming the postponement.

How the Appeals Office Works

The IRS Appeals Office is a separate division from the local IRS office that handled your audit. It may not even be in the same city.

Cases are viewed by appeals officers from a fresh perspective—most of the time. Some officers just rely on work done by auditors, but most review files anew. Your auditor plays no part in the process, other than the fact that his or her file is before the appeals officer. Auditors' files often lack detail or notes, however, which can raise questions in the mind of the appeals officer. Appeals officers may contact the auditor to fill in the gaps and clarify the IRS's position on a particular issue. If you submit new data to the appeals officer, he or she may ask the auditor to review it, but not make the final decision on its acceptability.

An appeals officer is aware of the law on recurring issues, like what kinds of documentation are legally sufficient to verify travel and entertainment or home office expenses. So, unless your case is very unusual, the appeals officer will almost surely have considered the same legal issues in the past.

Since appeals officers already know the law, they usually want to learn the facts of your situation—especially anything which might cause a judge to rule for you if you went to court. In short, appeals officers have a motivation to settle with you if, after considering the facts and applying the law, they believe you have some chance of winning in court—no matter how small.

Unlike IRS auditors, appeals officers have discretion to weigh the hazards of litigation. They often settle cases because they do not want the courts to set any precedents unfavorable to the IRS. Decisions against the IRS could be relied on by other taxpayers and cost the government much more in the long run than giving in on your case would.

> ### Appeals Officers Are Negotiators
>
> IRS appeals officers are senior IRS employees with accounting or legal backgrounds. Many have been promoted up from the ranks of auditors. Appeals officers have only one job—to settle cases. You might think that their work involves raising more money for the U.S. Treasury, but that's not the case.
>
> Appeals officers are trained to be flexible and are given discretion in dealing with taxpayers that auditors don't have. Proof of this lies in IRS statistics showing 70% of appeals cases are settled. Appeals officers' job performance is judged by their success in compromising with taxpayers—not how often they uphold IRS auditors!

Appeals officers are realists and know from IRS statistics that about 50% of all taxpayers win at least partial victories in court. Appeals officers don't have authority to settle a case based purely on its nuisance value, however. In other words, they are forbidden to settle just to avoid the expense of going to court. If you supply a justification for a deal though, you may get one.

Besides the fear of losing in court, the appeals officer has another motivation to make deals: The IRS's resources are *not* unlimited. Most of the funding to the IRS in the last decade has gone into computerization and hiring of more collectors—not appeals officers.

No one wants your small potatoes case to use up any more of the government's time than is absolutely necessary. After all, the same court that will try your case if it isn't settled also must hear tax disputes with IBM, Exxon, and GE, where the government has hundreds of millions of dollars at risk.

Preparing for an Appeals Hearing

After requesting your appeal, you will have at least 60 days to prepare for your hearing. When you will be heard depends on how backlogged your IRS Appeals Office is. Use this time to analyze and review everything you presented to the auditor.

Get a copy of the auditor's work papers by making your Freedom of Information Act request. Read it to see if the auditor misrepresented or just plain missed something. Check out any tax law cited by the auditor in the report to see if it really supports his or her position.

If you don't get a copy of the auditor's file before the appeals hearing, ask the appeals officer to show it to you.

Organizing and Presenting Documents

Audits are frequently lost because the taxpayer did not cogently present his or her case to the auditor. If you provided a jumble of papers or messy files, the auditor may have refused to consider them out of frustration. So, ask yourself if there are better ways to organize and present your supporting materials to the appeals officer. For instance, run adding machine tapes of payments for each category of deductions and make up schedules of these items.

Try some creativity. For example, you aren't limited to printed documents. A part-time jazz artist whose musical business was deemed a hobby by an auditor, and his deductions disallowed, brought a demo tape and player to an appeals hearing. Charts, graphs, and drawings can often more effectively make points than words can. And remember the saying about a picture being worth a thousand words. A photo of your professional-looking home office or a group picture at your business's employee picnic may win the deduction. Everyone seems to prefer looking at pictures to reading a description or listening to an explanation. Appeals officers are no different.

If neatness, typing, preparing schedules, or just plain getting paperwork together is not something you're good at, find a bookkeeper or friend to do it for you.

Filling in the Gaps

If you were missing records at the audit, try harder to find them. Make renewed attempts to get copies of checks from banks and duplicate receipts from businesses and people with whom you dealt. Recreate items when original documents can't be found. (See Chapter 3.)

Focusing on Challenged Items

Make a separate file or folder for each item the auditor challenged on your tax return with which you disagree. Write a simple statement next to each explaining why the auditor was wrong.

Collect your documents—canceled checks, receipts, and whatever else—and group them with or attach them to each statement. I use a three-ring binder with dividers for each challenged item. Then I make a second complete copy of the binder. While I give my presentation at the hearing, the appeals officer can follow along. If I lose the appeal, the binder serves me well if I proceed to tax court.

Get written statements from people with knowledge about your disallowed expenses (if you didn't already do so for your audit). For example, you hired a handyperson to make repairs on your rental property who insisted on being paid in cash and has since left town. You can't find the receipts for the labor and materials. Prove the work was done through a statement from a tenant, like the following:

Sample Witness Statement

Declaration of Clara Burton

I, Clara Burton, declare that for most of 2010, I was a tenant in an apartment owned by Alexander Woolf, located at 123 Hannah Road, Appleton, Wisconsin.

Early in the spring of 2010, we had a bad storm. The rain caused plaster to fall from the ceiling in my apartment and ruin the carpet. All the damage was repaired by Joe Williams, who did a good job.

I moved out to be closer to my job in November of 2011. I now live at 456 Dover in Appleton, Wisconsin. My phone number is 555-1290.

Under penalty of perjury, I declare that the statements of fact contained in this declaration are, to the best of my knowledge and belief, true, correct, and complete.

Dated: 6/20/2012   *Clara Burton*
                          Signature

Meeting the Appeals Officer

Appeals officers rarely leave their offices—you will go there for the hearing. You will be shown into a small office or meeting room. Seldom will anyone else be present from the IRS. It is theoretically possible for the auditor to attend, but it virtually never happens.

An appeal is rather informal. It is not like a court, where testimony is taken under oath or where technical rules of evidence apply. The IRS won't tape record the hearing. You have a right to, as long as you inform the appeals officer several days in advance—but I don't recommend it. It would likely make the appeals officer speak less candidly than he or she would otherwise and reduce your chance of reaching any settlement. Even if the appeals officer says something in your favor but you don't reach a settlement, the statement would probably not help you if you go to court.

Speak freely at the hearing. Theoretically, statements made by you could be deemed admissions against interest and used by the government in a court case. But I have never seen the IRS ask an appeals officer to testify as to what was said at an appeals hearing.

A Formal Appeals Hearing May Not Be Necessary to Make a Deal

One of the larger cases I ever settled on appeal I did without ever meeting the appeals officer. We had trouble arranging our schedules, so I sent him my research and documentation. After several lengthy telephone conversations, we compromised a $250,000 audit bill for zero taxes owed.

The appeals officer conceded that my client was correct and agreed that it would not be in the IRS's best interest to go to tax court, where an unfavorable precedent might be set. If it is very difficult for you to meet with an appeals officer, ask if you can have your appeal handled by mail and telephone. If the nearest appeals office is hundreds of miles away, it's worth a try.

Presenting a Case to an Appeals Officer

Before the meeting, write down what you are going to say to the appeals officer—an outline of the points you want to make. List the documents and other evidence you want to present. Then try it out by explaining your case to your friends or family. Ask if they understand it clearly. Their responses may direct you to weaknesses that you can work on before the hearing.

Some appeals officers sit back and wait for you to present your case, while others run the show by asking questions. Unless the appeals officer directs otherwise, start with a brief statement outlining your case. Here's an example:

> *I believe that the auditor was incorrect in finding that I was not entitled to claim a part of my apartment as a home office deduction for my part-time sales business on my tax return in 2001.*
>
> *I can show that my home office deduction is legitimate by my testimony and with the following documents:*
> - *floor plan of my apartment showing the space used exclusively for my home office*
> - *business diary showing that I spent more than 50% of my working hours in the business at my home office, and*
> - *bills and canceled checks for the expenses I incurred in running my home office.*

TIP

Point out to the appeals officer the auditor's errors but don't make it personal. For instance, did the auditor overlook facts or documents? Did the auditor misstate something that you said? Don't bring up the auditor's lack of intelligence or mean-spiritedness; instead characterize the errors as misunderstandings or oversights. After all, the appeals officer may take offense at IRS bashing.

If you and the auditor disagreed on a legal issue—such as whether your enterprise is a legitimate business or a nondeductible hobby—then renew the argument to the appeals officer. He or she will be more knowledgeable about the intricacies of tax law than are auditors. If you did research or consulted a tax professional and came up with something favorable, show it to the appeals officer, who will probably comment on it, one way or the other. If there's no comment, ask if he or she agrees with your research. If not, ask why not.

An appeals officer who doesn't understand something in the auditor's report may call the auditor, but usually not in your presence. This doesn't mean the auditor's words will be automatically taken over yours.

You may not finish up with the appeals officer at the end of the meeting. He or she may want to research an issue before rendering a decision. And if you request it, you will usually be given time to send more documents or do further legal research. Ask for a month to get things in. Appeals officers seem to work at a more leisurely pace than the rest of the IRS, so you may get even a longer time.

The officer may ask you to sign a waiver extending the normal three-year limit the IRS has for assessing a tax liability. It is usually okay to sign this waiver at the appeals level, although this is contrary to my advice when you are requested by an auditor to sign the same waiver.

Negotiating a Settlement

The Internal Revenue Manual states that:

> *A settlement may either resolve each issue on the basis of the probable result in litigation or involve mutual concessions of issues based upon the relative strength of the opposing positions where there is substantial uncertainty of the outcome in litigation.*

In other words, the appeals officer wants to avoid the possibility of an IRS loss in court.

Your first request should be for the IRS to drop any penalties recommended by the auditor. This is the easiest item for appeals officers to give in on, as long as they believe that you or your tax preparer made an honest mistake and weren't trying to cheat the government.

Unless you believe the auditor was completely wrong on everything—be truly objective—then let the appeals officer know that you may agree to some of the adjustments. This breaks the ice, but don't get specific. Just saying this will show the officer that you can be reasoned with—unlike

Case History of an Appeal

Mick was a telephone company executive by day and a rock musician by Saturday nights. For 20 years, he played in local bands. He had his dreams, but never got close to the Big Time. Mick enjoyed performing and was happy—at least until the IRS entered his life.

In recent years, raises and bonuses allowed Mick to buy new musical gear and a Ford van to haul it. He became more enthusiastic about his music, formed his own group, and hired an agent. Following his accountant's advice, Mick reported his musical income and expenses on his tax returns as a sideline business. Mick's business showed net losses in two years. These losses were used to offset Mick's income from his regular job on his tax returns, thereby lowering his total tax bill.

Sideline Business and the Tax Code

A sideline business loss can produce a tax write-off for Mick as long as the IRS believes that he is trying to make a profit. The tax code provides one test for determining if a profit motive exists—if a business does not make money in at least three of the five past years, it is presumed to be not for a profit and is considered a hobby. Hobby losses cannot be deducted for tax purposes. As it turned out, Mick had made a small profit in two of the last four years he had been reporting musical activities on his tax returns.

While this three-of-five-years legal presumption is not final, it puts the burden on Mick to show he was trying to make a profit. The issue would never arise unless Mick was audited.

Guess What?

Mick was audited. IRS audit classifiers are on the lookout for businesses that show losses. This is especially true if business losses offset income from another job—in effect creating a tax shelter. The IRS hunts tax shelters like wolves pursue sheep.

The consequence of an auditor not finding that a business was really run to make a profit is a disallowance of all expenses in excess of income. For example, if your Amway distributorship brought in $1,000 and you claimed $3,000 in expenses, the IRS could disallow your $2,000 tax loss—unless it was convinced that you were seriously trying to make a profit. In this type of case, the IRS has frequently said that the real motive in this type of business was social—entertaining friends and getting home products for personal use. Dabbling in a side business is not good enough.

Case History of an Appeal (continued)

In the year audited, Mick's music income was only $300 but he claimed $12,300 in business expenses. Small wonder he was picked for audit. His largest expenses were the new van and music gear. Under the hobby loss rules, the auditor decided Mick's music expenses were primarily for his personal pleasure, and only incidentally for profit. (Internal Revenue Code § 183.) She disallowed the $12,000 tax loss. This meant added taxes, penalties, and interest of $4,500. To make matters worse, she then said she was going to audit two more years and make the same adjustment.

Mick argued that he had worked hard to make a musical career, that he had been getting local jobs, that his band's reputation was on the rise, and that one hit record would make him millions and the IRS plenty of taxes. The auditor, apparently not a music fan, was unmoved. A meeting, an informal appeal, with her manager did not change things.

Mick got the examination report and then a 30-Day Letter to appeal. He decided to appeal; he had clearly been trying to make money in music, even though his efforts had been largely unsuccessful. Mick knew he had enough to show an appeals officer a justification for compromising the audit result.

The legal principle in Mick's favor is that the profit motive, not the actual result, distinguishes a business from a hobby. The intention to make a profit is sufficient under the tax law, even if the probability of financial success is small or remote. (*Dreicer v. Commissioner of Internal Revenue*, 78 U.S.T.C. 642 (1982); see also *Cornfield v. U.S.*, 797 F.2d 1049 (D.C. Cir. 1986).) At least Mick had some income.

Research for Mick's Appeal

The IRS disallowed Mick's deduction of his music equipment as a business loss. The examination report said only that the business expense was not established. Mick called the auditor to ask what tax code section she relied on to reach her decision. The answer was IRC § 183.

Mick looked at the *Master Federal Tax Manual* index under Section 183 and found the subhead "Business." It directed him to a page that defined a business as "a pursuit or occupation carried on for profit, whether or not profit actually results." The guide has an excerpt from a tax court case which stated that an activity may be for profit although the investment is not expected to generate

Case History of an Appeal (continued)

profits for several years under the current level of activity. This meant that Mick's musical activities are not disqualified as a business just because he lost money. Mick photocopied this page.

Next he opened J.K. Lasser's *Your Income Tax* and found more specific information. The index lists Hobby as a Sideline Business, which leads to the following: "If you show a profit in three or more years the law presumes you are in an activity for profit. The presumption does not necessarily mean that losses will be automatically allowed; the IRS may rebut the presumption." Reading further, Mick saw this as significant because it mentioned tax code Section 183 on which the auditor based her decision. Mick made another photocopy.

In two years of his tax returns since claiming his music business, Mick was still using his old equipment. And he did not claim any vehicle expense on his return. The tax result was in Year One he showed a profit of $100, and in Year Two, a $200 profit. In Year Three, however, Mick bought the van and the new equipment. These purchases caused sizeable losses in Years Three and Four. The appeals hearing took place in Year Five, for which a tax return was not yet due. So Mick cannot rely on the three-year presumption of profit rule. Mick had only two profitable years.

If Mick's appeal hearing was held after he filed a tax return for Year Five, it could be prepared in such a way as to show a profit—for example, by not taking some expense deductions. In this case, he could go into the hearing with the benefit of the three-year presumption of profit rule—that is, Mick made money in three of the last five years. This fact would put him in a position that could be strong enough to give him an outright win.

Mick's Appeal Hearing

After Mick filed his protest requesting an appeal, the IRS set a conference date. Several months later, Mick and an appeals officer met at the appeals office. No one else was present. Mick went directly to the most favorable facts of his case. He showed a contract from a talent booking agent who, in two years, had gotten his group one job. He also presented a flyer and an event calendar showing the group had performed in public twice during the audited year. He omitted the fact that one appearance was at a charity benefit where no performers were paid. He also gave the appeals officer a publicity photo and his diary showing band rehearsals.

Case History of an Appeal (continued)

The documents were not strong enough evidence to win his case, but they got Mick in the door. The goal was to give the officer justification for compromising, not to win outright. In a half hour, Mick finished presenting the evidence and said, "Let's settle the case. I will accept a 25% disallowance of my losses." In other words, Mick was offering to let the IRS reduce his losses from the $12,000 adjustment the auditor made to $3,000.

The appeals officer replied that he was thinking more like a 75% disallowance, from $12,000 to $9,000. Mick was in! The officer had accepted the possibility that a court might find that Mick was trying to make a profit. They took a break.

After the break, Mick commented on the photo of the Little Leaguer on the officer's desk. He had a similar picture at home, and Mick and the appeals officer talked about their kids awhile. The officer seemed relieved not to talk taxes for a bit. At 4:30, near IRS quitting time, Mick said that he'd agree to split the difference, and accept a 50% disallowance from $12,000 to $6,000 of his losses and no penalties.

He also requested the appeals officer not to recommend the other two open years for audit. The officer agreed. While this did not guarantee those years would not be audited—appeals officers don't have this authority—their recommendations carry great weight and their reports are routinely approved. Several weeks later, Mick received a settlement letter.

Mick's case is typical of how IRS appeals are handled—and settled. If Mick hadn't appealed, he would have owed the IRS $4,500, plus he would have been audited for two other years. The potential tax disaster was over $13,000. The settlement made with the appeals officer cost Mick about $2,000.

Epilogue

Mick's appeal didn't require great knowledge of tax law. It did involve several hours of preparation as well as a basic understanding of the IRS appeals process. Evidence of Mick's profit intent was shown; a settlement was proposed and negotiated. The great majority of appeal issues—be they home office deductions, entertainment expenses, or business auto usage—can be handled successfully in this same manner.

some of the irrational and irate taxpayers who come through the door. If the officer doesn't warm to you, he or she may at least breathe a sigh of relief. This is good psychology any way you slice it.

Speak the appeals officer's lingo. Don't talk in terms of dollars. Use the word "adjustments" or "disallowances" instead.

> EXAMPLE: An auditor disallowed 80% of Monika's business entertainment expenses because she couldn't provide complete records of the business purpose of the entertainment. Monika acknowledges to the appeals officer that her records were weak, but emphasizes that they do show that she paid the expenses and that she was in a legitimate business. Monika offered to accept a 20% disallowance of these expenses; the appeals officer responded by meeting her halfway and allowing 50% of the deduction. They finally agree on 35%—a far cry from the auditor disallowing 80%. Monika and the appeals officer never spoke in terms of dollars, only percentages.

The example demonstrates that negotiation is an art, not a science. A successful negotiation is where both sides come out with less than what they wanted but each gets something.

Appeal settlements are usually reached orally and then put in writing on an IRS form. You won't be asked to prepare the settlement document— the appeals officer will. Most settlements are formalized on IRS Form 870, *Consent to Proposed Tax Adjustment*, mailed to you after the hearing. Don't expect the settlement papers right away; it may take several months, as a settlement goes through several levels of approval before leaving the IRS office.

To make sure the settlement contains no surprises or misunderstandings, make careful notes of what was agreed to at the hearing. If the settlement papers don't match up, call the officer and hash it out. If you have some questions about the terms of the settlement document, run it by a tax professional before you sign. He or she can check computations and explain the details to you.

CAUTION

Don't sign a Form 870 settlement unless you are absolutely certain that you understand it. Once you sign it, you are barred from going to tax court if you find an error or change your mind.

In limited situations, the appeals officer is prohibited from negotiating a settlement. If the appeals officer mentions any of the following, your only option is to take the IRS to court:

- Your audit was part of a large group of similar taxpayers and the IRS must be sure that everyone in the group is treated equally.
- A court case or an IRS revenue ruling directly on point and supporting the IRS's position exists. As a practical matter, this is unlikely to happen, because rarely are two cases ever exactly alike or will a revenue ruling prevent you from dealing with an appeals officer.
- Your case has tax crime potential.
- You are a part of a group of investors who are claiming tax benefits from investment losses—tax shelters—that the IRS concludes were not legitimate business deals, but were solely tax dodges.

Should You Hire a Tax Professional for Your Appeal?

The pros and cons of working with tax professionals are outlined in Chapter 13. Here are a few other suggestions.

Most appeals officers respect an experienced tax representative. Appeals officers and tax professionals often know each other. Tax professionals know what appeals officers are looking for and can make their job easier by getting straight to points.

Hiring a tax professional is largely an economic decision. It may not make sense to hire one if you are contesting less than $5,000 in taxes. An attorney or CPA will charge upwards of $2,500 for an uncomplicated appeal, although an enrolled agent may do it for less. If you hire a tax professional, ask how much IRS appeals experience the person has and how the appeals came out. Listen carefully to the responses.

Bringing in a tax professional also depends on the intricacy of the case and how comfortable you are at arguing and negotiating. For example, if you lost your audit because of inadequate records and you have since located or reconstructed them, there's no need to hire a tax professional. If your case, however, turns on a point of law, such as whether or not your business's workers are employees or independent contractors, bringing in a professional could make the difference.

TIP

A preappeals consultation with a tax professional is a good idea—even if you do the appeal yourself. An hour or two of professional time should not cost more than several hundred dollars.

Types of Cases Appeals Officers Won't Hear

IRS appeals officers are prohibited from hearing certain issues under IRS policy, for example, taxpayer refusals to comply with the tax laws based on moral, political, constitutional, religious, and similar grounds. The issues are often raised by what the IRS terms tax resisters or protestors. A word to the wise: If you fit into this category, think long and hard about what you are doing. Get good professional advice before taking on the federal government.

If You Don't Settle on Appeal

If you and the appeals officer haven't reached a settlement by the end of your conference, ask what else you can provide to change things. Chances are it's further documentation or supporting legal precedent. Then, ask for time to get this material to him or her, before any decision becomes final. If in doubt how to follow through, see a tax professional.

If you don't settle, you will be mailed a letter denying your appeal. With the letter comes a Notice of Deficiency advising you of your right to go to tax court. If you ignore the notice, after 90 days, the taxes, penalties, and interest become final. A tax bill from the IRS will arrive several months later.

If you want to keep up the fight, see Chapter 5 on going to tax court.

Chapter Highlights

- You can appeal most audits to the IRS Appeals Office.
- Appeals often reduce your tax bill, but seldom are auditors totally reversed.
- Many appeal issues are simple enough for you to handle without hiring a tax professional, but a consultation with one is a good idea.
- The IRS Appeals Office is independent from the IRS audit division and wants to settle to keep you from going to court.
- Prepare for an appeals hearing by careful record organization and basic tax law research. Consult a tax professional if in doubt.
- If you don't appeal or don't win your appeal, you can always go to tax court.

Going to Tax Court: No Lawyer Necessary

Y ou lost your audit and did not reach a settlement with the IRS on appeal. What's next? You have two choices: You can accept your fate or you can go to court.

In one recent year, more than 30,000 taxpayers filed petitions in tax court after losing their audits and appeals. (There are three other federal courts in which you can contest your tax liability, but only in tax court can you contest without first paying.) Taking your case on to tax court is usually not difficult and in many cases can be done without a lawyer. And your chance of winning—at least partially reducing an audit bill—is excellent. Once you file a petition in tax court, the IRS knows you mean business and will often settle for less than the tax claimed due. Over 90% of tax court cases filed settle before trial.

While it is not necessary to have appealed within the IRS before going to tax court, it's a good idea. Remember—the job of the appeals office is to settle. You can also contest an automated mail adjustment notice you receive from the IRS in tax court. (See Chapter 3.) And tax court can be used to challenge IRS decisions in several other situations—for instance, when the IRS reclassifies a worker in your business from an independent contractor to an employee (see Chapter 11) or if you are denied innocent spouse relief (see Chapter 9).

And even if the IRS doesn't settle before your trial, you have a good chance of having your tax liability reduced once you talk to a judge. More than 50% of all petitions filed in tax court bring some tax reduction. In cases under $50,000 (called small cases), 47% of all taxpayers win at least partial victories. In cases involving $50,000 or more (called regular cases), 60% come out ahead. Tax court isn't a total panacea—the chance of a complete victory over the IRS is only 5%.

> **TIP**
>
> **Filing a petition in tax court buys time.** Just filing will delay an audit bill for at least a year. You can use this time to get your finances in order without worrying that the tax collector will seize your assets. But interest is running.

When Not to Go to Tax Court

You can be fined for filing a petition to tax court without legal grounds. This is not normally something to worry about, however. There is always legitimate reason for disagreeing with an audit report. Only by filing a petition that is clearly frivolous or done for the sole purpose of delay do you risk a fine.

Don't file a tax protestor type of petition; you may get coded into the IRS computer system in the same category as dangerous and potentially violent taxpayers. In IRS computerese, these people are called PDTs. People who use the court to protest government policy or because they don't believe the tax system is constitutional are typically fined up to $5,000 for filing frivolous petitions.

So don't let the fear of a fine keep you from going to tax court unless you are a tax protestor or are being foolish—like the man who deducted the costs of keeping a mistress as a business expense on the theory that she made him more productive.

Tax Court Facts

In the most populous states, tax court hearings are held monthly throughout the year, except summer, in major cities. In smaller states, the tax court may meet only once a year for a week or two, usually in the state's largest city. Sessions are usually held at the local federal building.

The president appoints tax court judges for 15-year terms. Judges are lawyers and come from senior IRS legal staffs or from private law firms. Special temporary judges also regularly serve as small-case judges. Although many tax court judges are ex-IRS employees, they are not especially pro-IRS. Judges do not like to see the IRS cut corners in audits or mistreat taxpayers. Tax court is completely independent from the IRS. You will get as fair and impartial a hearing in tax court as you would in any other federal court.

After you file your petition, it will be at least six months until you are called for trial. While most small cases (see immediately below) are decided within one year, regular cases take much longer.

A minor drawback of tax court is that interest continues to run on your tax bill if the court decides you owe the IRS.

Technically, you can't pay a proposed tax bill and then go to tax court. You can, however, stop the interest accrual before suing in tax court by making a payment and labeling it a deposit or cash bond. Send a check to the IRS with the words "deposit/cash bond" written in the lower left-hand corner of the check and send a cover letter with the payment. This stops the interest accrual. But if you win, you don't get interest back from the IRS for the time the government had your money.

Strict 90-Day Limit for Filing In Tax Court

Once the IRS issues a letter called a Notice of Deficiency, you have only 90 days to file a petition in tax court. The deadline for filing must be stated clearly in the letter. The 90-day period begins on the date in the letter, not on the date you receive it. If you are out of the United States when the letter is sent, you have 150 days. *The law does not require that you actually receive the notice, only that the IRS mail it to your last known address.*

Because of the 90-day deadline, you will want to act quickly. Don't wait until day 83 to contact the court clerk and get the current forms. If you don't have time to get the current forms, see a tax professional. The tax court may accept an out-of-date petition form, but the IRS will object to a late filing and the court will dismiss your case.

This 90-day deadline is one good reason to let the IRS know of your new address whenever you move. Use IRS Form 8822, *Change of Address* (available on the IRS's website at www.irs.gov). If you miss the deadline, you can file in another federal court, but you will have to pay the tax first and sue the government for a refund.

Small Tax Cases—People's Court

There is a small-case division of the tax court for audits in which the IRS claims the taxes and penalties owed for any one tax year are $50,000 or less.

For example, if you've been audited for three years and the amount the IRS claims you owe for each year is $30,000—meaning the total is $90,000—your case will still qualify as a small case. This small claims court-type case is called an S case.

S-case election is made on the tax court petition form by checking a box (see the filled-in sample form below).

The filing fee is $60, and normally you'll have no further court costs.

No jury trials are allowed in tax court. Judges can rule on the spot, although they usually mail their decisions to you a month or so after the hearing. You cannot appeal the decision in an S case.

With S cases, tax court operates much like your local small claims court. You tell the judge your story, show your evidence, and are not expected to know legal procedures. Even if you lose, you have the satisfaction of having had your day in court.

If you're going to court on your own, it's highly recommended that you file a small case. Otherwise, get an attorney to represent you.

Preparing and Filing a Small-Case Petition

You will need a petition, a *Request for Place of Trial*, and a *Statement of Taxpayer Identification Number*. The forms and instructions are available online from the U.S. Tax Court website at www.ustaxcourt.gov. Contact the clerk of the U.S. Tax Court, 400 Second Street, NW, Washington, DC 20217, 202-521-0700, and ask for a petition kit. Unlike many other government agencies, the tax court office is very responsive and efficient. There is no charge for these items, which will be sent promptly.

Completing the Tax Court Forms

First, read *Information About Filing a Case in the United States Tax Court*. This is the first page of the petition kit. You can fill in the forms online or print them out and fill in the hard copy.

Look at the completed sample forms and line-by-line instructions below. The *Request for Place of Trial* and *Statement of Taxpayer Identification Number* forms are self-explanatory and not reproduced here. Don't worry about typos or minor errors—the tax court will usually overlook them.

Sample Tax Court Petition

UNITED STATES TAX COURT
www.ustaxcourt.gov

(FIRST)   (MIDDLE)   (LAST)

ADAM X. & EVE Y. CROMOZONE
(PLEASE TYPE OR PRINT)   Petitioner(s)

v.   Docket No.

COMMISSIONER OF INTERNAL REVENUE,

Respondent

PETITION

1. Please check the appropriate box(es) to show which IRS NOTICE(s) you dispute:

☑ Notice of Deficiency   ☐ Notice of Determination Concerning Your Request for Relief From Joint and Several Liability. (If you requested relief from joint and several liability but the IRS has not made a determination, please see the Information for Persons Representing Themselves Before the U.S. Tax Court booklet or the Tax Court's Web site.)

☐ Notice of Determination
Concerning Collection Action   ☐ Notice of Determination Concerning Worker Classification

2. Provide the date(s) the IRS issued the NOTICE(s) checked above and the city and State of the IRS office(s) issuing the NOTICE(S): _October 27, 2010 Austin, Texas_

3. Provide the year(s) of period(s) for which the NOTICE(S) was/were issued: _2008, 2009_

4. SELECT ONE OF THE FOLLOWING:

If you want your case conducted under small tax case procedures, check here: ☒   **(CHECK**
If you want your case conducted under regular tax case procedures, check here: ☐   **ONE BOX)**

    NOTE: A decision in a "small tax case" cannot be appealed to a Court of Appeals by the taxpayer or the IRS. If you do not check either box, the Court will file your case as a regular tax case.

5. Explain why you disagree with the IRS determination in this case (please list each point separately):

(a) For tax year 2008, we disagree with the IRS disallowance of $3,710 in expenses claimed for Adams royalty

income on Schedule E, as they were ordinary and necessary expenses.

For tax year 2009, (b) we disagree with the disallowance of our charitable deduction of $3,250 to the Church of

What's Happening Now on Schedule A as this is a legitimate charitable deduction.

(c) We disagree with the disallowance of $666 in expenses claimed on Schedule C for the business "Eve's Apples"

as this was a business carried on with a profit intent.

T.C. FORM 2 (REV. 5/11)

Sample Tax Court Petition (continued)

6. State the facts upon which you rely (please list each point separately):

(a) The expenses were incurred on a trip to Jerusalem to research a new book "The Baloney Code." Adam is a

published author and although the book is not yet completed, it may become a best seller.

(b) The deduction for the charitable contribution should be allowed because the organization has been granted

IRC 501(c)(3) status as a nonprofit entity.

(c) The expenses for "Eve's Apples were for advertising for the sales of apples from the family orchard, and the

business subsequently failed to produce any income because a tornado carried all the apples away before they

could be picked.

You may use additional pages to explain why you disagree with the IRS determination or to state additional facts. <u>Please do not submit tax forms, receipts, or other types of evidence with this petition.</u>

ENCLOSURES: Please check the appropriate boxes to show that you have enclosed the following items with this petition:

☑ A copy of the Determination or Notice the IRS issued to you

☑ Statement of Taxpayer Identification Number (Form 4) (See PRIVACY NOTICE below)

☑ The Request for Place of Trial (Form 5)   ☑ The filing fee

PRIVACY NOTICE: Form 4 (Statement of Taxpayer Identification Number) will <u>not</u> be part of the Court's public files. All other documents filed with the Court, including this Petition and any IRS Notice that you enclose with this Petition, will become part of the Court's public files. To protect your privacy, you are <u>strongly</u> encouraged to omit or remove from this Petition, from any enclosed IRS Notice, and from any other document (other than Form 4) your taxpayer identification number (e.g., your Social Security number) and certain other confidential information as specified in the Tax Court's "Notice Regarding Privacy and Public Access to Case Files", available at <u>www.ustaxcourt.gov</u>.

Adam X. Cromozone	12/05/2011	001	010-0101
SIGNATURE OF PETITIONER	DATE	(AREA CODE)	TELEPHONE NO.

848 Eden Road	Paradise, Texas 77777
MAILING ADDRESS	CITY, STATE, ZIP CODE

State of legal residence (if different from the mailing address): _____

Eve Y. Cromozone	12/05/2011	001	010-0101
SIGNATURE OF ADDITIONAL PETITIONER (e.g.,SPOUSE) DATE		(AREA CODE)	TELEPHONE NO.

848 Eden Road	Paradise, Texas 77777
MAILING ADDRESS	CITY, STATE, ZIP CODE

State of legal residence (if different from the mailing address): _____

SIGNATURE OF COUNSEL, IF RETAINED BY PETITIONER(S)	NAME OF COUNSEL	TAX COURT BAR NO.

MAILING ADDRESS, CITY, STATE, ZIP CODE	DATE	(AREA CODE) TELEPHONE NO.

Complete the form. Type or print your name. If a joint tax return was audited, type in your name and your spouse's name exactly as they appear on the tax return.

Check the box for "Notice of a Deficiency" (for appealing an audit).

In the next blank space, type in the date of the IRS-issued notice and the city and state of the IRS office that issued the notice. Next, write the year or years for which the notice was issued. Next, check the box for either "small tax case" or "regular tax case." In the next section, explain briefly why you disagree with the IRS. Finally, state the facts on which you rely.

> **TIP**
>
> **The tax court doesn't expect you to sound like a tax lawyer.** Just make sure your point is clear. For example, "I disagree with the $1,200 deduction disallowed by the IRS. I incurred this expense as the rent I pay on the portion of my apartment I use for my home office."

Sign and date the petition. After completing the petition, check the box of the nearest city from the list of cities in which tax court trials take place. Type your name and your spouse's if a joint tax return was audited. Then sign and date the form. Again, both spouses must sign if a joint return was audited.

Filing the Tax Court Forms

To file your petition, follow these steps (after making sure the filing requirements haven't changed; see the warning below):

1. Make *three* copies (or five if it's a regular case) of your:
   - completed petition
   - *Statement of Taxpayer Identification Number*
   - completed *Request for Place of Trial*
   - Notice of Deficiency—90-day letter—that you received from the IRS.
2. Keep one copy of the petition, *Request for Place of Trial*, and the Notice of Deficiency for your records.

3. Attach the original Notice of Deficiency to the original petition, and attach the remaining copies of the Notice of Deficiency to the remaining copies of the petition.

4. Make out a personal check or money order for $60 payable to Clerk, U.S. Tax Court.

5. Enclose the original and copies of the petition and the Notice of Deficiency, the original and copies of the *Request for Place of Trial, Statement of Taxpayer Identification Number,* and your check or money order in a large envelope. Send to Clerk, U.S. Tax Court, 400 Second Street, NW, Washington, DC 20217, by U.S. mail—certified and return receipt requested.

To timely and legally file your petition to the tax court, the envelope must bear a U.S. mail postmark dated within 90 calendar days of the date on the Notice of Deficiency. Or you can use Federal Express, DHL, or Airborne Express. Currently, you cannot file electronically in tax court. If it arrives after Day 90, that's okay as long as the postmark is within 90 days. And bear in mind that 90 days does *not* mean three calendar months.

CAUTION

Check for any changes to the filing requirements. Call 202-521-0700 or check online at the U.S. Tax Court's website at www.ustaxcourt.gov.

Within seven days of receiving your petition, the tax court will send you a confirmation of receipt and assign you a case number. If you ever write to or call the IRS or the tax court about your case, you will have to refer to your case number.

You don't need to file anything else, unless the IRS files a written response, called an answer, stating that you committed fraud. In this highly unlikely event, you must file a legal paper called a reply. You should consult a tax attorney before filing a reply.

A Tax Professional on the Sidelines

If you file a tax court case yourself, consider using a tax professional as a coach or an adviser. The tax professional can work in the background or go with you to meetings with an appeals officer or IRS attorney. The IRS will usually welcome your bringing in a tax professional if it may help reach a settlement and keep your case from going to trial. The tax professional doesn't have to be admitted to practice before the tax court, which is usually limited to attorneys, as long as he or she doesn't actually sign papers in the case on your behalf.

Meeting With IRS Appeals Officers and Attorneys Before the Trial

After you file your tax court petition, your case will probably be sent from the IRS's lawyers (district counsel) to the nearest IRS appeals office—often in the same building. The Appeals Office considers your file if you didn't appeal before. If you did appeal, but went on to tax court, your case may be reviewed again by the Appeals Office if the IRS lawyer thinks settlement is possible.

Small cases—under $50,000—usually sit in an Appeals Office for about six months—shorter if your trial is set for an earlier date. If you don't settle with an appeals officer, IRS lawyers prepare the case for trial.

Within 30 days before the trial date, the IRS attorney may ask that you meet at the IRS office. The purpose is to discuss the documents and other evidence—both yours and the IRS's—in the case. The attorney will explain how the documents, called exhibits, will be labeled and you both will exchange the names and addresses of any witnesses you plan to call.

The IRS attorney will also ask you to agree in writing to certain undisputed facts about your case. These are forms called Stipulations of Facts. Tax court rules require both sides to agree, or stipulate, to as many facts as possible before coming to court. The purpose is to save the judge's time. Any facts not agreed to in a written stipulation must be proven in court. Judges get upset if you have refused to agree to obvious facts, like "Is this your signature?"

Written stipulations cover routine things like identifying your tax return, that receipts and various documents are yours, and that bank records are genuine and accurately reflect your deposits and withdrawals.

CAUTION

Read carefully before signing a stipulation of fact. Ordinarily, you should sign a stipulation just to keep on the judge's good side. Occasionally, however, the IRS attorney may try to slip something by you. If there are items in the stipulation that you don't agree with, ask the IRS lawyer to revise them accordingly. Or see a tax professional for advice before you sign.

Don't over-worry about anything going wrong at this meeting. The attorney shouldn't raise new issues, make threats, or try to trap you into saying something harmful to your case. If you ask—and you should—he or she will tell you what witnesses are expected to say at the trial.

The IRS attorney may not say it, but the best outcome is to settle the case, not go to trial. This meeting is another chance for you to make a deal rather gamble on the outcome in court. Review Chapter 4 before going to the meeting. Present your case as you did with the auditor or appeals officer. Bring up any new documents, witnesses, or information supporting your case. You and the IRS lawyer can settle the case at any time—even after you have been in front of the judge—as long as the court has not issued a decision.

Settlement Before Trial Is Likely

Well over 90% of all cases settle without a trial. An IRS lawyer may initially turn down your settlement offer and later accept it. A review of the case may make the lawyer decide you have a better chance to win than first thought. Or a government witness may not be available or an IRS document may have been lost, so that the IRS case is weaker than first believed.

If you agree to a settlement, the IRS district counsel's office will prepare a document called a Stipulated Tax Court Decision. This paper is signed by you, the IRS attorney, and the judge. Signing means you usually don't have to appear in court. This is a brief, but sometimes fairly technical, document. Ask to have it explained, or have it reviewed by a tax professional before you sign it. Once you have signed a Stipulated Tax Court Decision, it's nearly impossible to back out.

Notices From the Court Before Your Trial

Approximately four to ten months after you file your tax court petition, you will receive the following items:

Notice Setting Case for Trial. This is a form letter from the tax court setting the place, date, and time of your trial. It also orders you to cooperate with the IRS in certain matters before the trial and warns that if you don't show up for the trial, your case will be dismissed.

Standing Pretrial Order. This is a writing from the judge assigned to your case. It orders you and the IRS to discuss settlement, and if you can't settle, to prepare written stipulations. The order warns that getting a continuance, or postponement, of the trial date is not favored. You and the IRS must exchange lists of witnesses who may testify at least 15 days before the trial date.

Trial Memorandum. You must fill out and send this form to the tax court at least 15 days before the trial. State the issues to be decided by the court, the names of witnesses you will have at the trial, a brief summary of what they will say, and an estimate of how long the trial will last. Most small cases can be tried in two to four hours, so you can put something in this range. Don't worry about precision when filling out this form. The judge knows you aren't an attorney.

Preparing Your Case for Trial

By now, you should have the facts of your case down cold. You may have already told your story to an auditor, a manager, the appeals officer, and the IRS lawyer. But tax court is a whole new ballgame. You are not limited by what went on with the IRS before you came to court. You are given a de novo, or brand new, hearing before a judge who has not seen the IRS file.

Begin preparing several months before your trial date. Make an outline of what you want to tell the judge and list your documents and witnesses backing up each point. You must convince the judge that the IRS is wrong—the IRS doesn't have to prove it is right.

Your Trial Notebook

Arrange your materials the way lawyers do, with a trial notebook—a three-ring binder or a folder with a series of files. Use it to practice your presentation in front of family or friends. Make sure your points are clear and your documents are understandable. Rehearsing gives you confidence in court.

Your trial notebook should contain the items listed below.

Opening statement. The first item should be an opening statement, which you will make at the beginning of the trial. This is your summary of what the case is about and an outline of what you intend to show the judge to prove that the IRS is wrong. It should be brief—five to ten minutes—and to the point. Tell it to the judge as if you were speaking to a friend. Here are two samples:

> *Your Honor, the IRS auditor found that I was not serious about making money in my side business of a Scamway home products distributorship in 2010. She said that the presentations I made in my home were really social gatherings, so she disallowed my $2,492 in business losses. I will show the court that I always had a profit motive and that I operated in a businesslike manner, even though my business showed a loss that year.*

> *Your Honor, the examination report is incorrect in finding that I was not entitled to take my two children, Tammy and Jimmy, as exemptions on my 2010 tax return.*
>
> *I will testify that the children lived with me for the greater part of 2010. I will show the court copies of school records showing that the children were in school next door to my home, and that my address was their home address. I will present canceled checks showing that I paid most of their clothing, medical care, and other needs in 2010. My next door neighbor, Corrine Busybody, will testify that the children were living with me.*

Your testimony. Anytime you speak to the judge, you will be testifying. Before going to court, write down the testimony so you won't forget any points. For example, in proving that you tried to make a profit with your Scamway distribution, you might write as follows:

I first started selling Scamway products in 2010. In the first two years, I made small profits. In my home presentations, I strictly followed the guidelines given to me by Scamway. Although the business lost money, I did make sales at the February, May, June, and October presentations.

Evidence. Luckily for you, formal rules of evidence don't apply in small cases. You can forget all about the TV lawyers who are forever objecting on the grounds of hearsay, relevancy, and other similar legalese. Small-case judges want to get to the bottom of the dispute and will generally consider anything you want to show them.

Arrange your papers in your trial notebook in the order you want to show them to the judge. Keep the originals and make two sets of copies, one to give the judge and one for the IRS attorney.

The most common evidence is canceled checks, receipts, bills, photographs, tax returns, and witness statements. (A sample witness statement is in Chapter 4.) But be creative. Bring anything that helps tell your story. For example, continuing with the Scamway dealership, to show your profit motive, you might bring to tax court the following items:

- Schedule C, *Profit or Loss From Business*, of your 2009 and 2010 tax returns showing your profit for those years
- the Scamway home presentation guidelines
- a videotape of one of your presentations, and
- guest lists of the people attending the presentations.

Witnesses. Many small cases involve oral testimony of only one person, you. Written witness statements—declarations or affidavits—are usually satisfactory to the judge instead of live witnesses. In some cases, however, live witnesses are more effective. If you bring people to court to testify, list them in your trial notebook and summarize what each will say.

Before the trial, review with each witness what the person plans to tell the judge. For example, to bolster your claim that you tried to make a profit in your Scamway side business, ask your neighbor Scarlet to testify. Scarlet could state that she attended Scamway parties at your home, that they were businesslike with only slight social overtones, that she bought some products and saw your Scamway inventory stored in your house.

Written Statements or Live Witnesses?

In deciding whether to use live witnesses or their written statements, consider the following factors.

Persuasiveness. A person whose testimony will be extremely supportive of your position—such as a stranger who attended your Scamway presentation and thus has no motive to lie—should testify in person if possible. The testimony will be much more persuasive in person than on paper.

Convenience. Don't seriously inconvenience a witness and expect him or her to be helpful in court. For instance, if someone who attended your Scamway presentation is an airline pilot who is scheduled to be 40,000 feet above ground when your case is heard, a written statement will be sufficient.

Cost. Expert witnesses must be paid for their time in court. For example, suppose your trial is about work done on rental property you own and deducted as a repair. The IRS disallowed the deduction, saying that it was an improvement that has to be deducted pro rata over its expected useful life of five years. You would subpoena the contractor who did the work, and have the person testify that your rental property was in need of urgent repair. You must pay an expert witness fee typically by the hour. If the hourly rate is high, and there is a long wait, the fee will add up. Consider bringing a statement in declaration or affidavit form.

Harm. If you're concerned that your witness is a loose cannon—might say something harmful to your case—then just bring a written statement. Remember, the IRS attorney and judge get to ask questions in court, too.

If you are not sure a witness will show up, or the witness needs an official court paper to get off from work, you can get an order for the person's appearance—called a subpoena. You must request a subpoena form from the tax court clerk in Washington, DC. Get it at least two weeks before the trial. You can also get a subpoena at the last minute from the local tax court clerk if the court is sitting in your city.

The subpoena must be served on—meaning given to—the witness. Because there are strict rules of what constitutes proper service, this is best done by the U.S. Marshal's office. However, anyone over 18 and not a party to the case can legally serve the subpoena. You can't—you're a party to the case. Neither can your spouse. You must also pay a witness fee in advance, and mileage for the distance from his or her house to the tax court. Ask the clerk for the current witness fee and mileage rate when you request the subpoena.

Legal authority. If legal research is necessary to prove your case, include in your trial notebook copies of cases or other legal authority you or your tax professional found. (See Chapter 13 for information on doing legal research.) Most tax court cases are factual, rather than legal, disputes, so legal research isn't always necessary. If in doubt, ask a tax professional.

Closing statement. The last item for your trial notebook is your closing statement. This is the summing-up presentation you will make to the judge at the end of the trial. Like the opening statement, it should be brief and to the point. Here's a sample:

> *Your Honor, you have heard the evidence and can understand why I disagree with the IRS. I do not believe I owe the government any amount of money as a result of the audit of my tax returns for 2012.*
>
> *I explained how I have tried to make money in the music business for many years. I showed the court my receipts and canceled checks for all of my music expenses. I showed flyers I had printed to promote my appearances. I presented the declaration of my booking agent, Irving R. Clark, stating that he made valiant efforts to get me into more nightclubs.*
>
> *It should be clear to your honor that I always had a profit motive. I operated in a businesslike manner and not as a hobby, as the IRS contends. Therefore, my business losses should have been allowed by the auditor, and I should owe no additional taxes for 2012.*
>
> *Thank you for hearing my case.*

 TIP

Show your trial notebook to the IRS attorney if you meet before trial. If it is well organized and shows that you are serious, there is a good chance the IRS attorney may be impressed and agree to a settlement.

Should You Bring a Tax Professional to Court

If you get cold feet at the last minute, you can always bring a tax professional to court with you. The best choice is a lawyer—but you can also bring an enrolled agent or a CPA if he or she is admitted to practice before the tax court. (See Chapter 13.) Even if your tax professional is not allowed to practice in tax court, he or she may still sit with and advise you during the trial with the permission of the judge.

Again, representatives are not necessary in most small tax cases, although it's wise to consult with one before trial.

Your First Day in Court

On the date that you're scheduled for court, show up on time. Expect to see lots of other folks on the same trial calendar in the courtroom. The court clerk will take roll call.

The clerk or judge will likely assign you another date and time to come back for your actual court trial, usually later that week or in the next one. Or you may be put on telephone notice—told to call in or expect to receive a phone message giving you the precise date and time of your hearing. If the date is impossible for you or your witnesses, ask for a change. Your request may or may not be granted, but most judges are understanding.

If you live far from the tax court, call the court clerk or IRS lawyer in the week prior to your scheduled court date. Ask for permission not to appear until the day your case will actually be heard. This can save you a trip if the judge allows it.

Your Trial Day

For your court date, don't put on fancy clothes or airs. Be yourself. Come early and watch another small-case trial, if possible. You probably won't learn anything helpful to your case, but the preview should put you at ease. If you and your spouse were both audited, only one of you is required to attend the trial. It makes a better impression when both of you show up, however.

Courtroom Tips

- Stand when you speak, unless you are sitting at a conference table with the judge close by or the judge tells you to remain seated.
- Avoid reading aloud to the judge; it's boring. Just speak in your own words.
- Be as brief as possible, but fully explain your case, as if you were talking to a friend.
- Be polite. Never interrupt the judge or disparage the IRS or its lawyer.
- Be well organized. Don't fumble with your papers or otherwise waste the judge's time.

Tax court meets during normal business hours—no evenings or weekends. Most court sessions are held at a local federal building. Because the tax court has only a few permanent locations outside Washington, DC, the facility won't necessarily be a courtroom.

The judge will sit in the elevated area, called the bench, or at the end of a conference table. It's hard to generalize about tax court judges—each is an individual. Most are patient and will give you all the time you need to present your case. Judges are assigned randomly and there is no way you can pick a particular judge, or request a different one once an assignment has been made. It's doubtful you'd ever know a tax court judge, anyway. Address the judge as "your honor" or "judge."

Also present will be the judge's clerk, a court reporter, and the IRS lawyer. When the clerk calls your case, answer that you are present and ready for trial. If you're not ready, ask that your case be continued, or postponed. You must have a very, very good reason, such as a serious illness, death in the family, or that a crucial witness can't come to court that day. The judge came all the way from Washington, DC, to hear your case, and may insist that it go forward.

Once the trial starts, you will be summoned forward to sit at a table in front of the judge or at a large conference table. The IRS lawyer will probably already be ensconced at another table across from you.

Bring your trial notebook and all papers with you. If you have witnesses, ask them to sit nearby. When the case begins, tell the judge that these people will be testifying.

Although tax court trials are open to the public, few spectators attend. You can bring friends and loved ones for support, but they cannot sit at your table without permission from the judge. Rarely are tax court trials reported in the news.

The judge will not know the facts of your case before your trial begins. The judge's file contains only your petition, the IRS's answer, and any stipulation of facts. The judge doesn't work for the IRS and won't have IRS files or anything that you submitted to the auditor or appeals officer. Your slate is clear—start from scratch in educating the judge about your case.

To begin the trial, the judge will ask if you and your witnesses swear or affirm to tell the truth. The judge will then ask you to present your case.

Ask permission to give a brief opening statement. It's rare that the judge will deny your request. The opening statement is the preview and should be the first item in your trial notebook. Don't read it word for word—that's stiff and artificial.

Next, tell the judge your full story and show your evidence to back up each issue. As you present each document, give a copy to the judge and a copy to the IRS attorney. You won't get these documents back, so don't give away your originals. The judge may want to see the originals to compare them to the copies, however. So bring the originals to court. Give the judge copies of any legal authority you have found as you discuss each item.

As you give your documents and legal authority to the judge, you may call witnesses to testify. Ask permission to call each witness to the witness stand. To get their story, you must ask them questions. In the example of the Scamway distributor whose losses were not allowed by the IRS, here are sample questions to ask Scarlet, the neighbor and friend:

> *Are you familiar with my Scamway business?*
>
> *Did you come to my home for presentations?*
>
> *Please describe the sales presentations.*
>
> *How many other people were present?*
>
> *Were you a customer in 2010?*
>
> *How many times have you bought Scamway products from me?*
>
> *Did other people buy products at the presentations you attended?*
>
> *Have you seen where the products are stored in my house?*
>
> *Do you know if I have a home office?*

The IRS attorney may cross-examine each witness and call his or her own witnesses and present evidence.

After you and the IRS have presented your documents, testimony, and witnesses, ask permission to sum up your case. Now is the time to present your closing statement, the last item in your trial notebook.

The typical small-case trial lasts an hour or two, although you will be given more time if you need it. Try not to be nervous. The judge doesn't expect you to be a lawyer or tax law expert.

The Burden of Proof

In our legal system, the "burden of proof" is a rule that says that in order to win a civil lawsuit, you must present more evidence in court than the other side. But keep in mind that courtrooms aren't laboratories in which evidence can be scientifically weighed.

In 1998, Congress amended the tax code to allow courts to shift the burden of proof from the taxpayer to the IRS, but only when the taxpayer and the IRS are in court (not at an audit), and then only under certain conditions.

For example, if a taxpayer did not comply with all reasonable requests by IRS auditors for information, or did not keep good records, the court can place the burden of proof on the taxpayer. Also, a corporation, trust, or partnership with a net worth exceeding $7 million that sues the IRS in court is not entitled to the shift of the burden of proof. And the burden shifts only as to factual issues—the taxpayer still has the burden of proof in contesting legal issues. If this is too confusing, see a tax attorney for an analysis of how it might apply to your situation.

Awaiting the Judge's Decision in a Small Case

While the judge may announce a decision at the end of your trial, don't count on it. Usually, you'll get a ruling in the mail about a month or two later. Judges don't like to announce decisions in court to avoid debates with sore losers.

Judges' rulings in small cases seldom give explanations as to why you won or lost. Futhermore, the decision won't compute the exact amount you owe. This comes in a later bill from the IRS campus center computer.

The Tax Bill

Assuming you still owe some taxes, you will get a bill from the IRS within about two months of the judge's decision. This bill is always higher than indicated in the decision because the court's order will state the tax and any penalties, but not any interest or late payment penalties due. By law, the IRS must charge interest from the date the tax was originally due.

You don't need to pay right away, but interest continues to accrue on the balance until you do. (See Chapter 6 for options in dealing with a tax bill.)

Regular Tax Court Cases—Over $50,000

If the taxes and penalties from an audit total more than $50,000 for any one audited year, your case is called a "regular tax court case." This means you won't qualify for the simplified small-case procedures. But unlike a small case, you may appeal a regular-case decision to a higher court if you lose.

Most people hire a lawyer for cases over $50,000, but about 40% of all regular-case petitions are filed by taxpayers without lawyers. Most of these cases settle before ever reaching a judge, without any legal expenses being incurred other than the court filing fee.

Like a small case, there is no jury, and one judge hears the case. Tax court judges are not as patient with taxpayers representing themselves on a regular case as they are with small-case people. The rules are much more formal.

For a regular case, you and the IRS's attorney may be required to submit formal legal briefs within a few months after your day in court. A legal brief is a highly technical document and anything but brief. You must recite and comment on the evidence produced at trial, supporting legal theories, and tax law precedents. A tax professional—most likely an expensive tax attorney—is required for writing a decent brief.

There are no free, government-appointed attorneys in tax court. But you might check with a nearby law school to see if it has a free or low-cost legal clinic.

In two situations, it makes economic sense for you to handle a regular case dispute without an attorney: One is by asking for a bench decision; the other is by dropping down to the small-case category.

Bench Decisions

An alternative to the complicated post-trial brief writing is to ask the judge for a bench decision at the conclusion of the trial. If the IRS agrees, the judge can dispense with legal briefs. The judge may go along if he or she is satisfied that the facts and law are clear-cut—either for or against you.

If your request is rejected and you don't submit an adequate legal brief, you will lose. You will have delayed the final tax bill, but you will incur extra interest. If buying time is enough of a victory for you, then congratulations.

Not Contesting Amounts Over $50,000

If your audit bill for any single year is over the $50,000 threshold, you may still be able to utilize the simplified S case procedures. The catch is that you must give up your right to contest amounts over $50,000 in taxes and penalties for any one tax year.

> EXAMPLE: Ronnie gets an audit report claiming he owes $62,000 for 2008 and $9,500 for 2009. Ronnie can proceed as a small case in tax court if he contests only $50,000 for 2008, agreeing he owes the $12,000 overage. Of course, he can contest all of the $9,500 for 2009. The total amount contested is $59,500, and this is still a small case under tax court rules.

Other Federal Courts—Paying First Is Required

Instead of going to tax court, you can proceed to one of two other federal courts: a U.S. District Court, located throughout the country, or the U.S. Court of Federal Claims. (If you're in bankruptcy, there's a third option, discussed below.) District courts follow strict rules of procedure—meaning you will need a tax lawyer from start to finish. The court of federal claims is more like the tax court in that its judges travel throughout the country to hear cases, and its rules and hearings are less formal than in district court.

Unlike tax court, where some CPAs and enrolled agents are allowed to represent taxpayers, only a lawyer can represent you in other federal courts—and the legal fees can be staggeringly high. If you win, however, you may be able to persuade the judge to order the IRS pay your attorney's fees. (See "Can You Get the IRS to Pay Your Attorney's Fees?" below.)

Only 5% of all tax disputes for regular cases go to a district court or the court of claims instead of tax court. Usually, these cases involve large corporations. The unpopular feature of these two forums is that you must first pay the tax bill before filing your lawsuit. Technically, you are bringing a refund lawsuit against Uncle Sam for the taxes you contend were overpaid. Before suing, you must file IRS Form 843, *Claim for Refund*, and either have it rejected (available on the IRS's website at www.irs.gov) or wait until at least six months passes without the IRS taking any action on your refund claim.

TIP
Sometimes other federal courts are better than tax court. If the IRS claims you owe a lot—$50,000 or more—and you disagree and can pay first, see a tax attorney. Consider filing in a district court or the court of federal claims. You might have a better chance in these two courts than in tax court, depending on the tax issues involved.

The advantage of these alternative courts lies in our sometimes inconsistent judicial system. The tax court, district courts, and the court of federal claims, as well as some bankruptcy courts, all have the power to decide tax cases, but sometimes decide the same tax issue differently. Because their decisions are published online and in casebooks found in law libraries, it is no secret how each court has ruled in the past.

Although judges can change their minds, and the makeup of courts changes over time, courts seldom go against their own precedents. This means you can choose the court that has been most kind to your tax situation in the past. Perhaps of greater importance is that you can request a jury trial in a district court. If a jury is upset with the IRS or the tax law, it can give you a break.

Can You Get the IRS to Pay Your Attorney's Fees?

If you hire an attorney to represent you, it is possible, but difficult, to get the IRS to pay your attorney's fees. (IRC § 7430.) Not only must you win, but also you must show that the IRS's position was not "substantially justified." This means proving that the IRS knew or should have known that it was wrong on either the facts or the law. This is hard.

Although there is no maximum amount of legal fees you can collect, you are limited to recovering $125 per hour for the attorney's time unless you can show the case was unusually difficult and your attorney normally charges more. The second part will be simple—most tax attorneys charge from $150 to $400 per hour.

> **EXAMPLE:** Thomas lost his audit after supplying documents which were ignored by the IRS. He brought the same records to his trial before a tax court judge and won his case. The tax court awarded Thomas $17,000 in legal expenses incurred in fighting the unreasonable tax assessment. (*Tinsley v. Commissioner of Internal Revenue*, TC Memo 1992-195 (1992).)

If you don't hire an attorney, you are not entitled to compensation for your time in fighting the case—even if you are a lawyer.

There is another reason why some people sue in a court other than tax court. The district court and court of federal claims lawyers do not work for the IRS and are often more reasonable in settling cases than are the IRS's tax court lawyers. The primary disadvantage of going to these other courts is the legal expenses.

Bankruptcy Court

Bankruptcy judges also have the power to decide IRS disputes. I have seen some very favorable tax decisions made in bankruptcy court adversary proceedings. Of course, you must file bankruptcy first to get your IRS dispute heard. If bankruptcy is a serious option for you, see both a bankruptcy and a tax lawyer, or one who works in both areas.

RESOURCE

For an overview of taxes and bankruptcy, see Chapter 6. Also, detailed information, including the forms and instructions for filing for bankruptcy, can be found in *How to File for Chapter 7 Bankruptcy*, by Stephen Elias, Albin Renauer, and Robin Leonard (Nolo); *Chapter 13 Bankruptcy: Keep Your Property & Repay Debts Over Time*, by Stephen Elias and Robin Leonard (Nolo); and *The New Bankruptcy: Will It Work For You?* by Stephen Elias (Nolo).

Appealing to Higher Courts

Small cases (under $50,000) heard in tax court are final and cannot be appealed. All other cases—regular cases heard in tax court, as well as cases brought in a district court, the court of federal claims or bankruptcy court—can be appealed to a U.S. Circuit Court of Appeals. A lawyer is needed to handle this highly technical process, and you can expect legal fees starting at $10,000. Your statistical chance of winning is about 10%. If you lose, you can ask the U.S. Supreme Court to hear your case, but your odds are better for winning your state's lottery.

RESOURCE

The tax court's address is U.S. Tax Court, 400 Second Street, NW, Washington, DC, 20217, telephone number 202-521-0700. The court also has a helpful website at www.ustaxcourt.gov, where you can find all of its decisions as far back as 1995.

Chapter Highlights

- The tax court hears disputes between taxpayers and the IRS.
- It's often easy and inexpensive to go to tax court without a lawyer.
- IRS lawyers settle most cases without ever going to court by reducing an individual's or a business's tax bill.

When You Owe the IRS:
Keeping the Tax Collector at Bay

According to the IRS, 15% of all taxpayers owe back taxes. And this figure includes only people who have actually filed tax returns. As mentioned in Chapter 2, many people required to file tax returns haven't.

There are several possible reasons you might owe the IRS back taxes:

- You didn't file a tax return; the IRS prepared a return for you and sent you a bill.
- You didn't pay your income taxes in full when you filed your tax return.
- You believed you paid your taxes in full when you filed your return, but you later received an automated adjustment notice from the IRS. This probably means you forgot to report some item of income.
- After an audit, the IRS found that you owed additional taxes; you signed the audit report in agreement.
- After an audit, the IRS found that you owed additional taxes; you didn't sign the audit report, but you neither appealed nor filed a petition in tax court.
- After an audit, the IRS found that you owed additional taxes; you appealed and lost and did not file a petition in tax court. The tax bill became final.
- After an audit, the IRS found that you owed additional taxes; you filed a petition in tax court and came out still owing something.

No matter which of these categories you fit into, one thing is clear—you have a problem with the IRS. Let me tell you what passes for humor there: An auditor recently told me (with a straight face) that the IRS now requires a basic humanity test for all applicants. Those who flunk are hired by the collection division.

He may have been joking, but you won't laugh if an IRS collector calls. This will probably be the toughest bill collector you'll ever face, with the possible exception of Louie Loanshark's boys.

Unlike other creditors, the IRS has no legal obligation to take you to court before seizing your car or paycheck. You can lose your business, your bank accounts, and even your pension. As far as the IRS is concerned, your tax obligation takes priority over all other debts. If the IRS records a notice of tax lien, your credit rating may be ruined for years.

Luckily, this doesn't have to happen to you. If you deal with the IRS—in particular, if you intelligently respond to the IRS collector—chances are good that you'll keep your property and survive the worst of what the IRS throws at you.

The IRS goal is to collect the maximum amount of taxes from you with the minimum amount of effort. The IRS starts by sending you computer-generated notices. Next, the IRS Automated Collection System, or ACS, kicks in, calling and sending you more threatening notices. Finally, if the IRS still doesn't get its money, it assigns a human being from its collection division—a revenue officer—to get up close and personal with you.

How Long Does the IRS Have to Collect?

There is a little mercy in the tax code—it's called the statute of limitations on the collection of a tax debt. In general, the IRS has ten years to collect from the date of assessment, called the "23C" date by the IRS. (Internal Revenue Code § 6502.) After ten years, the debt is wiped out. There are a number of ways the ten-year period can be extended:

- The ten-year period does not start to run until you file your return and the IRS officially assesses the tax against you. Not filing a return and hiding for ten years accomplishes nothing.
- The IRS can extend the ten-year period by suing you in federal court. The IRS rarely does this. If it's getting close to the ten-year period and you don't owe millions, the IRS usually lets the statute of limitations run out, and you're off the hook forever.
- Certain actions on your part can extend the ten years. For example, if you file an Offer in Compromise, are out of the United States, are in litigation with the IRS, file for bankruptcy, request a Taxpayer Assistance Order, sign a waiver form agreeing to extend, or request a Collection Due Process hearing, the ten-year period is extended until these circumstances are resolved.

These various rules are more complicated than this summary. See an experienced tax professional for more information.

Dealing With an IRS Tax Bill You Owe

You have six ways to deal with a tax bill you unquestionably owe:
- pay in full
- pay in monthly installments, by agreement with the IRS
- reduce, eliminate, or pay the debt through bankruptcy
- reduce the debt and pay it through an IRS Offer in Compromise
- have the IRS determine that you are temporarily unable to pay and suspend collection, or
- wait for the statute of limitations on collection to expire.

All of these options are covered in this chapter.

While reducing your bill through an Offer in Compromise, going into bankruptcy, or having the IRS determine you are temporarily unable to pay may be the most attractive options, they are the most difficult to get. Paying in full is the only alternative for most working people with homes and other assets. For many taxpayers, however, paying in installments is the only way they can do it. Recently, more than 2.6 million taxpayers were on installment plans, paying collectively in excess of $4.5 billion.

In 2005, Congress radically changed the bankruptcy laws, making it harder to use this alternative for dealing with tax bills.

Don't jump to the conclusion that paying your IRS debt over time (or paying it at all) is your best option. Read this entire section before making your decision on how to deal with the tax collector.

First, do you really owe all the IRS says you owe?

Before you agree to pay any amount to the IRS, make sure the bill is correct. You are entitled to a full explanation of why you owe any IRS bill. Here are some suggestions for making sure your bill is correct—or for possibly reducing it:

- Review your tax returns or have a tax professional look at them to see if you may have missed any deductions, losses or carryovers, or similar items. If you find any, you can amend your tax return and reduce your bill.
- Review the bill to make sure you have been credited with all payments, including any wage or bank levies and any refunds taken. It is

common for the IRS to miss or incorrectly apply payments and credits to your account.

Find out how the IRS calculated your bill and credited your account by requesting an account for the period in question. Call 800-829-1040 or your local IRS office. These printouts are not always easy to understand. If you need an explanation, call 800-829-1040, go to your local IRS office, or ask a tax professional for help. Compare your canceled checks, prior tax notices, tax refunds withheld, and bank and wage levies with the IRS printout. If it doesn't match up—perhaps the IRS missed some credits you were due—immediately bring this to the attention of the IRS. Send copies of your proof of payment or other supporting documentation.

Almost all old tax bills include penalties and interest. It may be possible to have some or all of these unwanted additions canceled (or abated). See Chapter 12 to determine whether or not you qualify and how to go about asking the IRS for an abatement.

The Tax Gap

Despite its fierce image and extraordinary powers, the IRS, by its own admission, is a lousy bill collector. Recently, the amount of income taxes reported owed but uncollected exceeded $345 billion! The IRS collects only 85.5% of what it says it is owed by taxpayers. Add to that amount the taxes the IRS estimates are owed on unfiled returns and the total is even higher. The government calls this the tax gap.

The IRS claims it has neither the personnel nor the computer power to do better. Congress has responded with increased funding. When the IRS systems have been fully modernized, the IRS will be able to track down tax delinquents and seize their bank accounts and wages more quickly than it can now.

When You Can't Pay Your Tax Return

If you are coming up on a tax return filing date and owe a balance you can't pay, file anyway. This avoids the hefty late-filing penalty (but not the smaller late payment penalty).

Send in as much as you can. If you can pay over time, enclose a completed Form 9465, *Installment Agreement Request*. (This one-page form can be filled in and submitted online at the IRS website. You can get a copy of the form at the IRS website at www.irs.gov or by calling 800-829-FORM.) If you're sending in a hard copy of the form, include a copy of your tax return showing the balance due.

On Form 9465, tell the IRS how much you can pay monthly on the balance. The IRS should reply in 30 to 60 days to let you know if a plan has been approved, or to request more financial information from you before making the decision. During the rush of tax season (February to May), it will probably take longer for the IRS to reply. You may even receive a bill. Don't assume that the IRS lost your installment request form. Chances are the IRS simply hasn't processed it yet. Respond by sending in another copy of your completed Form 9465 along with the IRS bill.

If you owe less than $25,000, your request should be granted. The IRS might bump up the amount required to be paid every month, however. If you are turned down, or you and the IRS cannot agree on an amount, you'll have to furnish financial data and negotiate over the phone, via letter, or in person.

The IRS charges interest and a late payment penalty for each month you carry a tax balance. The initial late payment penalty is ½% per month, reduced to ¼% if you get a payment plan. The interest rate changes quarterly. Figure an additional 6%–8% average per year to the balance to get the full cost of owing the IRS. The IRS accepts payment by major credit card, but there is a hefty charge. Call 800-829-1040 for details.

Getting Time to Pay After the Tax Bill Comes

If you didn't pay your taxes or submit Form 9465—or it was ignored or rejected—call the IRS after you receive a tax bill. Request an extension of time to pay a bill or a payment plan. You can do this without talking to IRS personnel. Call 800-829-7650 on a touch-tone phone. It should work if you owe less than $25,000 (including interest and penalties), are an individual or couple (not a business), and have no other balances due to the IRS.

You can get either an extension of up to 120 days to pay in full or a monthly payment plan. If you choose the payment plan, you'll be asked how much you want to pay each month. Be sure to think about this before you call. If you need just a little time, request a 45-day extension. If you can't pay at the end of the 45 days, you can request a payment plan or another extension.

If you don't want to interact with an IRS computer, you can mail in a request for more time or another Form 9465 or call an IRS customer service representative at 800-829-1040.

IRS Tax Billing Process

The IRS mission is to collect the tax using the least amount of human effort possible. This accounts for the reams of computer-generated tax bill notices you will get long before ever hearing from a human being. No person is likely to even look at your account until your bill is at least six months overdue—often more like a year. And if you owe less than $1,000, no one may ever look at your account. You simply become a number in the IRS computer and get billed in the mail.

Once a balance due from a tax return has been posted to your account, a Computer Paragraph, or CP, notice is automatically mailed out. Your file is termed a tax delinquency account, or TDA. The first letter is a nonthreatening CP-14 *Balance Due.*

If you don't pay up within 30 days, you will receive a series of computer-generated notices. If you have other outstanding tax bills, the IRS may speed up the notices. By checking below for the number or type of notice you've received, you can figure out how close the IRS is to taking serious action.

Individual income taxes. About five weeks after sending the friendly bill, the IRS computer usually sends three "500 series" notices, identified by the number following the date in the upper right-hand corner: CP-501, *Reminder Notice—Balance Due,* CP-504, *Urgent Notice—Intent to Levy,* and CP-503, *Immediate Action Is Required.* In four to eight months, you will get CP-207, *Final Notice—Intent to Levy.*

CP-207 usually means your case is going to another IRS department. So don't panic just yet.

The total cycle, from the first notice to the last computer-generated letter, averages four to six months. This is the cushion before the IRS horror stories start coming true. At some point, the IRS will also send you Publication 594, *The Collection Process* (available on the IRS's website at www.irs.gov). It describes what the IRS can legally do to collect from you—which is plenty. Read it.

Payroll taxes. If you owe business or payroll taxes, collection on your account may be accelerated. The IRS often shortens the notice cycle to as few as eight weeks, depending on the size of the delinquency.

Special circumstances. If you did not file a return or owe $100,000 or more, the IRS may go straight from the CP-501, *Reminder Notice—Balance Due*, to the CP-504, *Notice—Intent to Levy*. Or, the IRS may stop the notices if it determines that your account is currently uncollectible, or that you are deceased, filing for bankruptcy, or incarcerated.

Delaying the Computerized Notice Cycle

If your goal is simply to buy more time, respond in writing to each IRS notice. Send a letter with the bill saying that you can't pay right now. You don't need to give an excuse; just ask for 45 more days to pay. This is the maximum time period that can be entered into the IRS computer to suspend the collection notice cycle. When the next CP notice comes, try responding by requesting another 45 days. If you are able, send a small payment with each of your request letters to show that you are trying. This should buy you an unofficial short-term payment plan, which might be all you need.

Sometimes, making 45-day delay requests throws a monkey wrench into the system. Taxpayers have been known not to hear from the IRS again for as long as a year. It all depends on the efficiency of your particular IRS campus and the priority your account is given.

Automatic Refund, Asset, and Wage Seizures

Even if you ignore the first few notices, you can buy some time by responding to the CP series notices. After the IRS sends the CP-504 notice, it is required to send you a final notice, designated Letter 1058, before it can take any assets. This letter explains your rights to a hearing and requests an immediate response.

It you don't respond, the IRS computer may send levy notices to any financial institution suspected of holding funds under your Social Security number or name or to any employer or contractor who filed a W-2 or 1099 form showing they have paid you in the past. Levy notice recipients must then freeze your account or pay the IRS a portion of your wages or money owed to you. (Liens and levies are covered in Chapter 7.) As discussed later in this chapter, you are entitled to appeal an IRS levy. The IRS could also issue Form CP-49, *Overpaid Tax Applied to Other Taxes You Owe*, and seize tax refunds that you are owed.

IRS Automated Collection System

As mentioned above, if you don't pay during the IRS campus computerized notice series, your file will be sent to the IRS Automated Collection System, or ACS. The ACS has the authority to collect most overdue tax bills, solicit tax returns from people who haven't filed, and levy (seize) assets and wages.

The ACS is a staffed telecommunications system for collecting seriously delinquent accounts. The ACS operates by mail and phone only.

The ACS computer automatically analyzes accounts that require telephone contact and dials and redials your phone number automatically if the IRS gets no answer or a busy signal.

The ACS is the IRS's primary mail dunning and telephone harassment apparatus. I have visited ACS facilities, although they are not open to the public, and have found 150 or more clerks sitting in front of computer monitors, wearing telephone headsets. They follow scripts demanding payment from tax debtors and respond to calls or faxes requesting payment plans or more time to pay. The ACS mails collection letters and issues levies to third parties such as banks and employers.

ACS computer data is often inaccurate. For example, the ACS frequently requests tax returns from women who have filed under a new name after getting married or from deceased taxpayers.

How Long Your File Stays With the ACS

Unless your case has enough "points" to be assigned to a field collector—under a secret IRS scoring system—it can stay with the ACS for as long as the IRS still has to collect (generally ten years from the date the tax was first assessed). The chief factor is the amount you owe—most importantly, whether it's over or under $25,000. Other point factors are your past history of tax delinquencies and the number of years of taxes you owe.

As your case gets near the end of the ten-year statute of limitations for collection, even small balances may be sent to the local office for handling by a revenue officer.

Delaying the ACS Collector

If you want to slow down the ACS, ask for more time to pay. To suspend the computerized collection process, a collector must enter an appropriate freeze code into the computer. There are many freeze codes, but the precise details—such as the code designations, the exact number of codes, and when they can be used by ACS collectors—are not public information. Requesting more time to pay, filing for bankruptcy, or asking for a suspension of collection due to a hardship all have different freeze codes.

When a freeze code is entered into the computer, collection activity on your account is put on hold for the time specified for that code number— up to one year or even longer. No action will be taken on your case during that period, but you may still get tax bills. And, any tax refunds you are owed will be held by the IRS. After the time period elapses, the computer automatically pulls the case back up for further review and contact by the IRS.

Short-term hold. You can get a short-term hold—up to 45 or more days— usually by just asking for it. First, make your request over the telephone. Also, follow up with a written response to the ACS. Just photocopy the notice you were sent, write on it that you need up to 45 days to get the money to pay, and send the notice back—a separate letter is not necessary.

Long-term hold. If you really can't afford any monthly payment amount, ask the collector to classify your account as "currently not collectible" or a "significant hardship case" and to suspend collection activities for 12 months or more. You must convince the collector you are truly down and out—no assets, no job, or very meager income and you survive mostly through welfare or the kindness of others. If you keep giving excuses, you may come up with one that convinces the collector to enter a long-term hold code. But, ACS collectors are on short leashes and not known for being sympathetic.

Other Ways to Stop the ACS Collector

If asking for a hold doesn't delay the tax collector for long, you can try one of these tactics:

- **Question the accuracy of the tax bill.** Because tax bills are difficult to decipher, you don't need to say anything other than it doesn't look right. If you raise a doubt in an IRS collector's mind, he or she must exercise reasonable forbearance—that is, no further steps to collect can be taken until the bill's accuracy is verified. This could take several days or several months. If your request is refused, ask to talk to a manager. If this doesn't work, call the Taxpayer Advocate Service. (See Chapter 8.) If anyone questions your right, refer them to the *Internal Revenue Manual* 0018; IRS Policy Statement P-5-16.
- **Submit an Offer in Compromise.** The IRS usually suspends all collection activities while the offer is pending, often a period of several months or as long as two years.
- **File for bankruptcy.** This immediately stops all IRS collection activities.

Calling the IRS and Arranging Installment Payments

If you owe less than $25,000, you can usually get a payment plan for up to 60 months by asking for it. You can be denied a payment plan if you have unfiled tax returns. If you owe more than $25,000, you may have to negotiate with the IRS.

Before talking to the IRS, have a plan of action. If the IRS calls you and you're not prepared, give a polite excuse, such as you're late for a doctor's appointment, the baby is playing with matches, or you work nights and are sleeping now, and promise to call back. Don't answer any questions, other than your name, until you are ready with your facts and figures.

Make a comprehensive list of your assets, debts, income, and—most importantly—your living expenses. The collector will be looking for information similar to that requested on IRS Form 433-A, *Collection Information Statement for Wage Earners and Self-Employed Individuals*, Form 433-F, a shorter version of Form 433-A, or Form 433-B, *Collection Information Statement for Businesses*. Use the appropriate form to organize the information, especially your expenses. Your goal is usually to convince the collector to give you time to pay your taxes. The collector's goal, however, is getting you to pay the full tax bill as soon as possible.

Checklist If You Contact the IRS Collector by Telephone

If you are committed to making payment arrangements with the IRS over the telephone, be prepared to provide the following information:

- alimony or child support paid or received
- employer information, including work telephone number
- investment income
- life insurance policies with cash value
- information about individuals living in your household
- out-of-pocket medical expenses
- pension and Social Security income
- profit and loss statement if self-employed
- rental income
- secured loans
- substantiation of court-ordered payments
- three months of current bank statements (all accounts)
- three months of current pay stubs
- value of retirement accounts
- value of all property and available equity, and
- vehicle information: year, make, value, amount owed, and monthly payments.

Once you've compiled your financial data, call the IRS. Have a notepad, pencil, the tax bill, and your Form 433-A or 433-F, or 433-B information. IRS offices are open from the early morning to the late evening. Of course, getting through may be a different story. The best times seem to be Tuesdays, Wednesdays, and Thursdays, early morning or lunchtime. Expect to be put on hold, and be prepared for a long wait—set aside snacks, the remote control, reading material, or your knitting.

When a collector finally comes on the phone, write down the person's name and ID number. You may get only a first name or a pseudonym. The collectors often do not give their real names out of fear of retaliation. This person may be on an IRS collection team of five to seven members. Make notes of important points throughout the conversation. If you ever have to call back, you probably will not be able to talk to the same person—the system is nationwide, with thousands of employees. The IRS claims that you will get the same result no matter who you speak to, but don't believe it. If you don't like a particular collector, politely end the call and try back the next day. You will likely get a different, and hopefully more reasonable, collector.

IRS collectors sit all day long listening to every excuse in the book—and some that aren't. They hear so many lies that they become cynical and unsympathetic. Without lying, accent the negative—how hard your life is, your large expenses and low income, and the like. If the collector becomes rude or bullying, ask to speak to the person's supervisor. If all else fails, try begging or crying. You may be assigned another collector, or the supervisor may personally handle your case.

The telephone collector's purpose is to identify assets, called levy sources, that the IRS can seize if you do not voluntarily pay the tax bill. Don't lie—about your assets or anything else. If you're asked a question you don't want to get into with the collector, such as whether or not you have any sideline income, gracefully end the conversation—use a prepared excuse, such as you are running late for work. Call back later. You may not be asked the question again.

The IRS telephone collector will also ask about bank balances and equity in your home or other real estate. You may be asked about your cash borrowing power, but you can't be forced to take out a loan. Remember—

the goal is to get you to pay the full tax bill at once. If the collector thinks that you can pay, he or she will demand payment immediately.

If the collector concludes that you can't pay now, you will be asked questions to see if you qualify for a monthly payment plan, called an installment agreement, or IA. You will be asked about your family's size, income, and living expenses.

Then, you may be asked to send substantiating documentation, such as rent receipts or pay stubs. The collector may demand that you fill out an IRS financial statement form. Follow the instructions below for advice on completing the form, called a Collection Information Statement.

TIP
Be prepared to negotiate a monthly payment. State the amount you can afford. Start low, as the collector may well ask for a higher amount. The collector may insist that you cut back on some of your expenses. Be firm if the expenses are really necessary to your survival, and not luxuries.

> **EXAMPLE:** The IRS collector questioned Yung's assertion that his family's monthly grocery bill totaled $600, saying it was beyond IRS allowances for a family of four. Yung explained that his two children were lactose-intolerant diabetics on special costly diets.

If you verbally agree to a payment plan, the IRS will send monthly statements and payment vouchers. Start making payments on the date you and the collector agreed you would start. If you haven't yet received the IRS monthly billing, send in a payment, enclose a letter stating that you are paying "per a telephone conversation with Carol, ID# 123456, on 12/29/xx, in which I agreed to pay $350 per month beginning 1/15/xx." Send your payment to the billing address on your notice. Write your Social Security number or federal ID number and tax period on the check or money order.

Interest and late payment penalties are running while you are in an installment plan.

If you are ever unable to make a monthly payment when it is due, see "Installment Payment Plan," below.

Requesting That Your File Be Sent to the Local Office

If you can't get anywhere with the IRS by phone, or you don't want to deal with them—for example, the bill is wrong—request that your file be transferred to your local IRS office. There, your case will be handled by a revenue officer. There are several other reasons why you might want your file transferred from the ACS:

- Once ACS collectors know where you live, work, or bank, the IRS computer may garnish your wages or seize (levy) your bank accounts. (See Chapter 7.) This is less likely to happen when a person has been assigned to your case.
- Revenue officers can grant longer-term payment plans and suggest more alternatives than can collectors. You will, however, have to disclose more details of your financial life to a revenue officer than to an ACS collector.

How do you get your case out of the ACS? ACS collectors do not grant transfer requests without a good reason. Just asking probably won't do it. Reasons that may work include telling the ACS collector that you don't agree with the tax the IRS claims you owe and that you want to meet with the IRS to discuss it. Very few of us understand tax notices, so you won't be lying. ACS staff are supposed to transfer a file whenever a taxpayer questions the correctness of taxes on a notice.

If the collector refuses to send your file to your local IRS office, ask for a supervisor. Unless your complaint is clearly phony, you should get your way. Keep asking for a transfer if you don't first succeed. The more you owe, the easier it will be to get a transfer—that is, the ACS will grant transfers to people owing $50,000 more readily than to those owing $5,000.

Make the same transfer request in writing in response to the notices you receive in the mail. Write that you don't understand how the tax bill was computed and therefore don't agree with it. Ask to meet with someone from your local IRS office for an explanation and to discuss payment.

Revenue Officers—Frontline Collectors of the IRS

If you owe more than $25,000 and the IRS notices have failed to get you to pay, or if you've requested that your file be transferred to your local IRS office, your case will end up with a revenue officer. These tax collectors follow a four-step process.

1. They may make a surprise visit or telephone call to your home or work.

2. They either ask you questions on the spot or set up an interview at their office or by telephone.

3. Revenue officers may record your financial information—income, assets, liabilities, and living expenses—on detailed IRS 433 forms, which you'll be asked to verify and sign.

4. Revenue officers try to collect—in one or more of the following ways—by:
   - demanding immediate payment
   - requesting that you obtain a bank loan
   - requesting that you sell assets
   - proposing an installment payment agreement
   - suggesting an Offer in Compromise
   - beginning enforced collection—seizing your wages, bank accounts, and other assets, or
   - reporting your case as currently uncollectible.

These steps are all discussed in detail below.

The First Visit

Some revenue officers try to catch delinquent taxpayers off guard by what I call the ambush. The officer simply comes to your home or work, usually between 8 a.m. and 6 p.m. If you aren't there, the person will leave a card requesting that you call back within a few days.

If the officer finds you at home or work, or if you call back, he or she will start asking financial questions or set a time for you to be interviewed at the IRS office. Don't lie, but avoid giving financial information unless you are completely prepared. Say that you have to check your records. Then you'll be asked if you've filed your tax returns. If you have, no problem. If you haven't, don't lie. Say you need to check your records or with a tax professional, but don't say yes if you haven't filed.

Assuming you clearly owe the IRS, begin your first conversation with a revenue officer by acknowledging your responsibility and stating that you have every intention of cooperating. You don't have to offer details on how you plan to pay. Don't launch into the problems of your life, complain about the unfairness of the tax law, or be generally defensive. Being positive—even if you have to grit your teeth the entire time—will send a signal that you are not unreasonable. Considering how much discretion collectors have to make your life miserable, this is a wise approach.

The revenue officer will set an in-person or telephone appointment for a collection interview. He or she may, however, want to talk to you in person or on the phone before the interview. Before giving any information, ask if you will be expected to supply financial data at the meeting.

After the officer says yes—and he or she will say yes because that is the purpose of the meeting—request that you be sent a copy of the collection form. It will be Form 433-A or 433-F, *Collection Information Statement.* You will go over the form together during the interview. (For the most current form, check the IRS website at www.irs.gov.)

By requesting the IRS form before the interview, you can delay the collection process a bit. Explain that you want the form ahead of time so that you can be as accurate as possible during the interview. The officer can't argue with that. Fill in the form before you go to the meeting.

The Collection Interview—Meeting the Revenue Officer

According to the *Internal Revenue Manual,* the first taxpayer interview is the most important event in the IRS's collection process. The revenue officer plays detective and is trained to first act sympathetic to gain your confidence and cooperation. But after the honey often comes the vinegar.

Legally, you can't be forced to answer any questions. But if you don't, you risk rapid "enforced collection" action—seizure of your assets and wages. What you say at the collection interview often will determine how successful you will be in resolving your problem. Be on your best behavior.

If You Refuse to Divulge Financial Information

In general, you don't have to give the IRS financial information about yourself. While lying to a collector is a crime, refusing to give information is not. (Internal Revenue Code § 7206.) If you don't cooperate or you only partially cooperate, the IRS has three options:

- Seize known assets and/or levy your wages and other income—the most likely outcome of your lack of cooperation. Revenue officers can check public real property and motor vehicle records, and contact financial institutions. The IRS has a hard time finding out-of-state deposit accounts and real estate, however.
- Back off and go after other tax delinquents—you should be so lucky.
- Issue a summons for you. A summons is a legal order to appear and bring records or give information. The IRS doesn't often use this power because of the paperwork and trouble. If you get a summons and aren't sure what to do, see a tax attorney. If you ignore a summons, you risk a court hearing and jail.

CAUTION

Never lie to the IRS. If the IRS catches you trying to conceal assets or outright lie about them, at best it will cause the auditor to probe harder; at worst, you'll get a referral to the IRS Criminal Investigation Division. (See Chapter 10.)

The IRS purpose for the interview is to gather information for the Collection Information Statement, which details your finances.

The IRS has several versions for its financial statement:

- Form 433-A, *Collection Information Statement for Wage Earners and Self-Employed Individuals*
- Form 433-B, *Collection Information Statement for Business Entities* (partnerships, corporations, and LLCs), and
- Form 433-F, *Collection Information Statement*, which is a shorter version of Form 433-A.

To negotiate with a revenue officer, all individual and self-employed persons must complete Form 433-A or 433-F. Business entities, such as corporations, or those who owe payroll taxes for their employees must submit Form 433-B.

A revenue officer will push hard to get all questions on the 433 forms answered. All 433 forms are divided into two main parts—assets and liabilities, and income and expenses. You will probably know the figures for your assets, debts, and income. The expense part is where problems usually arise. Most of us know exactly how much our car and house payments are, but not how much we spend on other living expenses. The IRS expects you to know these costs when it comes time to fill out the forms.

After the interview, the revenue officer will ask you to immediately sign the financial disclosure forms. Don't be coerced into signing, even if you are desperate to get out of the IRS office. If you haven't prepared your figures ahead of time, you will probably underestimate your living expenses by 10% to 40%. (Precise instructions for completing this form are given below.) In turn, this gives the IRS the false impression that you have a lot of money left over after paying your monthly expenses. Then the revenue officer will demand you pay the IRS all of this leftover money plus whatever amount he or she deems as "unnecessary" living expenses listed on your 433-A or 433-F.

TIP

Don't rush it. Tell the revenue officer you want to go over the forms in your home or office with your records at hand. Make this request even if you got the forms in advance and filled them out before the meeting—if nothing else, you can buy a little time. This is far less nerve-wracking than coming up with figures at the IRS office. If the officer gives you a hard time or asks what part is incorrect, say that you want to go over your records or talk with your tax adviser first. If he or she still balks, ask to discuss the matter with a supervisor. He or she probably will relent without calling in the boss.

If it's too late—you've already signed the 433 form without the chance to review your expenses—you may still be able to revise it. Tell the revenue officer that some of your original figures were incorrect and you have further information to make them right. Then provide the correct numbers.

Defending Your Expenses to the Revenue Officer

The IRS allows only "reasonable necessary and proven living expenses for a tax debtor and his dependent family members." Be prepared to defend your expenses to a tax collector. Bring your canceled checks, rent, or mortgage receipts, apartment leases, repair bills, insurance notices, medical bills, and paid receipts to the interview. The 433-F form is similar so the following applies to both versions

Filling in IRS Collection Forms

The key parts of 433 forms are assets and monthly expenses. Let's go over these. Also, thumb a few pages ahead to view the sample filled-in Form 433-A. The 433-F form is similar so the following applies to both.

Assets

The form asks you to reveal your assets and their values. The IRS wants this information to determine your ability to pay and to seize your assets or request you to sell them or borrow against them. Some assets are easy to value, like bank accounts and stocks. Other asset values can be estimated, like your home, furniture, boats, and banjos. The lower the value you place on your property, the less interested the IRS will be in seizing it or requiring you to sell or borrow on it.

TIP
Consider prepaying some expenses. Because the tax collector may pressure you to pay the IRS from any existing liquid assets revealed on a Form 433—like cash, stocks, or CDs—you can beat the IRS to the punch by prepaying some of your future expenses—like your mortgage, rent, or insurance. This will reduce your collectible assets and make sure you have a roof over your head. Or, use your liquid assets to pay past-due debts. Wouldn't you rather repay your best friend the $10,000 loan made three years ago than give that money to the IRS?

Here are some suggestions for valuing specific items.

Vehicles (Questions 18, 19). List and value your vehicles, whether owned or leased. Start with the lowest wholesale value shown in the *Kelley Blue Book*, which the IRS follows. This book is at your local library, at car dealerships, and online at www.kbb.com. Reduce the book value accordingly if the car has a lot of miles on it or needs work.

> **EXAMPLE:** Marcia drives her Honda to work. It has a *Blue Book* value of $10,000. She enters that in the first column. She owes her credit union $9,000, which goes into Column 2. But the car needs $700 of transmission work. The amount for Column 3, equity in asset, would be $300. Add a note to the form that the car needs work.

Market value		$ 10,000
Loan	–	9,000
Repairs needed	–	700
Equity	=	$ 300

The IRS would not seize Marcia's car under these circumstances. First, the $300 equity would be wiped out by the costs of seizure and sale. Second, IRS policy discourages seizing vehicles needed for work transportation.

Real estate (Question 17). Call several real estate agents. They'll be happy to tell you the fair market value of your property if they think there is any chance you might list it for sale. Check real estate websites and ads in the paper for similar properties. Discount that value by 20% and list it on Forms 433-A or 433-B. This 20% reduction is realistic, as you would have to pay closing costs, sales commissions, fix-up fees, and other expenses if you were forced to sell the property. Beware: Real estate agents tend to be overly optimistic in their valuations, hoping you will list the property for sale with them.

Personal items (Question 19). Value your appliances, furniture, and fixtures at garage sale or thrift shop prices, which are extremely low. A sofa you bought five years ago for $1,000, for instance, would probably be worth only $100 or less today. On the form, you can group items. For example, furniture—$250 total is sufficient.

The IRS rarely verifies the values you list for personal items like household goods or wearing apparel. And the IRS can't get into your home to see these items unless you invite them in—which you don't have to do.

Necessary Living Expenses (433-A, Page 4)

If you have trouble getting a fair installment agreement from the IRS, the problem is likely to be over what constitutes your necessary living expenses.

Most tax debtors owing more than $25,000 are put on a budget if they want an IRS payment plan. In effect, the IRS dictates how much you can spend to live. Collectors follow specific IRS national, regional, and local published guidelines on how much money they believe is necessary to sustain a family. The IRS uses these stingy guidelines regardless of your actual living expenses.

National Standards

The *Internal Revenue Manual* establishes national standards for living expenses in six IRS-established categories:
- actual cost of health insurance plan
- out-of-pocket health care, including medical services, prescription drugs, and eyeglasses (not cosmetic surgery)
- housekeeping supplies, apparel, and services,
- personal care products and services, such as hair cuts and toothpaste
- food, and
- miscellaneous expenses.

Except for the miscellaneous expenses, the standards are derived from the annual Bureau of Labor Statistics Consumer Expenditure Survey. The dollar maximum allowances are updated periodically and can be found at the IRS website (www.irs.gov). The allowances depend on the size of your family. It is no surprise that the IRS figures used are always a year behind and don't reflect reality. Tax debtors usually must provide documentation that their actual expenses are higher than the national standards.

Local Standards

The IRS also establishes local expense allowances for:
- housing and utilities—includes mortgage or rent, property taxes, maintenance, trash pickup, utilities, and telephone expenses (and depends on the size of your family), and
- transportation—includes car payments, insurance, gasoline, registration, parking, tolls, and maintenance or public transport, such as buses or cabs.

The allowances for transportation expenses do not take into account the size of your family (unlike the national standards above). Whether you are single and childless or married with ten kids, the IRS allows you the same amount for transportation.

Also, local housing standards don't take into account disparities in living expenses within the same locale. If you live in a better part of town, you probably spend more than the IRS local standard.

Court-ordered child support and alimony may be deducted as living expenses in addition to the above items.

Conditional Expenses

The IRS considers many types of expenses conditional, meaning they aren't absolutely necessary for your well-being. The general rules are:

- You will be allowed to claim conditional expenses only if you can pay your taxes in full within three years. Otherwise, you will be expected to pay anything spent on conditional expenses to the IRS in your payment plan.
- You have a grace period of *one year* to eliminate conditional expenses from your budget if your payment plan won't pay your tax debt in full within three years. The effect of this rule, for example, is that if you spend more than the IRS standards for housing and utilities, you'd better be moving to a cheaper place within 12 months.

In addition to expenses that exceed the national and local allowances described above, the following are examples of conditional expenses:

- charitable contributions
- educational expenses, including college costs, and
- unsecured debts.

Conditional expenses are usually not allowed when you submit an Offer in Compromise or try to get your tax debt declared to be currently not collectible.

The standards are tough but not chiseled in stone. The *Internal Revenue Manual* lets the IRS allow greater expenses when it is convinced that the additional amounts are necessary for your family's health and welfare, or are needed to produce income. Revenue officers are reluctant to permit greater expenses, however, because they must justify their actions to their managers. You may have a fight on your hands, so be prepared with good reasons and documents.

Living Expense Checklist

The expense checklist below gives a far truer picture of your monthly living expenses than does Form 433-A or F. Go through this list and then transfer the information to the form. If a particular item doesn't fit on the IRS form, use a separate sheet of paper. Everyone's expenses are different; don't feel confined by this list in making yours. Remember to add up expenses that don't recur monthly (such as a doctor's visit or auto repair) and divide by 12 to get a monthly average amount.

Housing & Utilities

Rent or mortgage payment $ _____

Second mortgage payment _____

Home equity loan payment _____

Repairs and upkeep _____

Electricity and gas _____

Water and sewer _____

Telephone _____

Garbage _____

Food

Groceries _____

Meals out _____

School lunches _____

Clothing _____

Replacement and mending _____

Laundry and cleaning _____

Medical

Doctors and dentists _____

Medications _____

Hospital bills _____

Transportation

Public transportation _____

Gas _____

Registration _____

Maintenance _____

Parking and tolls _____

Insurance

Homeowners' or renters' $ _____

Motor vehicle _____

Health _____

Life (term only) _____

Disability or other _____

Taxes (not deducted from wages)

Property _____

Income—federal _____

Income—state _____

Other (such as back taxes) _____

Retirement plan*
(voluntary contribution) _____

Installment payments

Motor vehicle _____

Credit cards*

_____ _____

_____ _____

_____ _____

_____ _____

_____ _____

Department stores*

_____ _____

_____ _____

_____ _____

_____ _____

* Items marked with an asterisk are not generally allowed by the IRS unless you can prove they are necessary for the health and welfare of your family or for the production of income.

Living Expense Checklist (continued)

Installment payments (continued)		**Other**	
Student loan	$_____	Payments to help dependents	
Personal loan*	_____	outside immediate family*	$_____
Other installment payments*	_____	Personal items	_____
Family expenses	_____	Charitable contributions*	_____
Child support (court ordered)	_____	Entertainment*	_____
Alimony (court ordered)	_____	Recreation*	_____
Child care	_____	Subscriptions*	_____
Other (such as back taxes)	_____	Miscellaneous*	_____
Private school, college*	_____	**Total Monthly Expenses**	$_____
Bills for professional services	_____		
Accountant	_____		
Attorney	_____		
Tax professional	_____		
Other	_____		

* Items marked with an asterisk are not generally allowed by the IRS unless you can prove they are necessary for the health and welfare of your family or for the production of income.

Collection Information Statement for Individuals (Form 433-A)—Page 1

Form **433-A**

Form **433-A**
(Rev. January 2008)
Department of the Treasury
Internal Revenue Service

Collection Information Statement for Wage Earners and Self-Employed Individuals

Wage Earners Complete Sections 1, 2, 3, and 4, including signature line on page 4. *Answer all questions or write N/A.*
Self-Employed Individuals Complete Sections 1, 2, 3, 4, 5 and 6 and signature line on page 4. *Answer all questions or write N/A.*
For Additional Information, refer to Publication 1854, "How To Prepare a Collection Information Statement"
Include attachments if additional space is needed to respond completely to any question.

Name on Internal Revenue Service (IRS) Account	Social Security Number *SSN* on IRS Account	Employer Identification Number *EIN*
John Q. Taxpayer	444-44-4444	

Section 1: Personal Information

1a Full Name of Taxpayer and Spouse (if applicable) John Q. Taxpayer and Wanda P. Taxpayer	**1c** Home Phone (666) 666-6666	**1d** Cell Phone ( )
1b Address *(Street, City, State, ZIP code) (County of Residence)* 101 Debtor Way, Gamblin, Nevada 89590	**1e** Business Phone (999) 999-9999	**1f** Business Cell Phone ( )
	2b Name, Age, and Relationship of dependent(s) Ulysses S. Taxpayer, two, son Zena W. Taxpayer, one, daughter	

2a Marital Status: ☑Married   ☐Unmarried *(Single, Divorced, Widowed)*

	Social Security No. (SSN)	Date of Birth *(mmddyyyy)*	Driver's License Number and State
3a Taxpayer	444-44-4444	8/10/1975	NV00000000X
3b Spouse	777-77-7777	12/12/1972	NV00000000Y

Section 2: Employment Information

If the taxpayer or spouse is self-employed or has self-employment income, also complete Business Information in Sections 5 and 6.

Taxpayer		Spouse	
4a Taxpayer's Employer Name Willy Wonka Chocolate Factory		**5a** Spouse's Employer Name Self	
4b Address *(Street, City, State, ZIP code)* 86 Hershey Hwy Sweettooth, NV 89590		**5b** Address *(Street, City, State, ZIP code)* 101 Debtor Way Gamblin, NV 89590	
4c Work Telephone Number (999) 999-9999	**4d** Does employer allow contact at work ☐ Yes ☑ No	**5c** Work Telephone Number (666) 666-6666	**5d** Does employer allow contact at work ☑ Yes ☐ No
4e How long with this employer 2 *(years)* 1 *(months)*	**4f** Occupation Elf Director	**5e** How long with this employer 1 *(years)* 6 *(months)*	**5f** Occupation Dog Collar Seller
4g Number of exemptions claimed on Form W-4 4	**4h** Pay Period: ☐ Weekly ☐ Bi-weekly ☑ Monthly ☐ Other	**5g** Number of exemptions claimed on Form W-4 N/A	**5h** Pay Period: ☐ Weekly ☐ Bi-weekly ☐ Monthly ☑ Other

Section 3: Other Financial Information *(Attach copies of applicable documentation.)*

6 Is the individual or sole proprietorship party to a lawsuit (If yes, answer the following)			Yes ☐ No ☑
☐ Plaintiff ☐ Defendant	Location of Filing	Represented by	Docket/Case No.
Amount of Suit $	Possible Completion Date *(mmddyyyy)*	Subject of Suit	

7 Has the individual or sole proprietorship ever filed bankruptcy (If yes, answer the following)			Yes ☐ No ☑
Date Filed *(mmddyyyy)*	Date Dismissed or Discharged *(mmddyyyy)*	Petition No.	Location

8 Any increase/decrease in income anticipated **(business or personal)** (If yes, answer the following)		Yes ☐ No ☑
Explain. *(Use attachment if needed)*	How much will it increase/decrease $	When will it increase/decrease

9 Is the individual or sole proprietorship a beneficiary of a trust, estate, or life insurance policy *(If yes, answer the following)*		Yes ☐ No ☑
Place where recorded:	EIN:	
Name of the trust, estate, or policy	Anticipated amount to be received $	When will the amount be received

10 In the past 10 years, has the individual resided outside of the United States for periods of 6 months or longer *(If yes, answer the following)*		Yes ☐ No ☑
Dates lived abroad: *from (mmddyyyy)*		To *(mmddyyyy)*

Collection Information Statement for Individuals (Form 433-A)—Page 2

Form 433-A (Rev. 1-2008)				Page **2**

Section 4: Personal Asset Information for All Individuals

11 Cash on Hand. Include cash that is not in a bank.   **Total Cash on Hand** $ 112.39

Personal Bank Accounts. Include all checking, online bank accounts, money market accounts, savings accounts, stored value cards (e.g., payroll cards, government benefit cards, etc.) List safe deposit boxes including location and contents.

Type of Account	Full Name & Address *(Street, City, State, ZIP code)* of Bank, Savings & Loan, Credit Union, or Financial Institution.	Account Number	Account Balance As of 01/10/2009 mmddyyyy
12a Checking	Enron Bank & Trust 711 Stagecoach Luckless, NV 89999	M123456789	$ 432.07
12b			$

12c Total Cash *(Add lines 12a, 12b, and amounts from any attachments)* $ 432.07

Investments. Include stocks, bonds, mutual funds, stock options, certificates of deposit, and retirement assets such as IRAs, Keogh, and 401(k) plans. **Include all corporations, partnerships, limited liability companies or other business entities in which the individual is an officer, director, owner, member, or otherwise has a financial interest.**

Type of Investment or Financial Interest	Full Name & Address *(Street, City, State, ZIP code)* of Company	Current Value	Loan Balance (if applicable) As of _____ mmddyyyy	Equity Value Minus Loan
13a stock	Blackhole Mining & Pizza Company 666 Area 51 Road Roswell, New Mexico 77777 Phone unknown	$ 10	$	$ 10
13b	Phone	$	$	$
13c	Phone	$	$	$

13d Total Equity *(Add lines 13a through 13c and amounts from any attachments)* $ 10

Available Credit. List bank issued credit cards with available credit. Full Name & Address *(Street, City, State, ZIP code)* of Credit Institution	Credit Limit	Amount Owed As of 01/01/2009 mmddyyyy	Available Credit As of _____ mmddyyyy
14a MasterFullCard 15 Pitiless Street Forlorn, Nebraska 55555 Acct No.: 6667777888	$ 5000	$ 5000	$ 0
14b Acct No.:	$	$	$

14c Total Available Credit *(Add lines 14a, 14b and amounts from any attachments)* $ 0

15a Life Insurance. Does the individual have life insurance with a cash value (Term Life insurance does not have a cash value.)
☐ Yes ☑ No   If **Yes** complete blocks 15b through 15f for each policy:

15b Name and Address of Insurance Company(ies):			
15c Policy Number(s)			
15d Owner of Policy			
15e Current Cash Value	$	$	$
15f Outstanding Loan Balance	$	$	$

15g Total Available Cash. *(Subtract amounts on line 15f from line 15e and include amounts from any attachments)* $ 0

Form **433-A** (Rev. 1-2008)

Collection Information Statement for Individuals (Form 433-A)—Page 3

Form 433-A (Rev. 1-2008)   Page 3

16 In the past 10 years, have any assets been transferred by the individual for less than full value
(If yes, answer the following. If no, skip to 17a)   Yes ☐   No ☑

List Asset	Value at Time of Transfer	Date Transferred *(mmddyyyy)*	To Whom or Where was it Transferred
	$		

Real Property Owned, Rented, and Leased. Include all real property and land contracts.

	Purchase/Lease Date *(mmddyyyy)*	Current Fair Market Value (FMV)	Current Loan Balance	Amount of Monthly Payment	Date of Final Payment *(mmddyyyy)*	Equity FMV Minus Loan
17a Property Description	05/05/2005	$ 175,000	$ 186,000	$ 847.08	2025	$ 0
Location *(Street, City, State, ZIP code)* and County 101 Debtor Way, Gamblin, NV 89510			Lender/Lessor/Landlord Name, Address, *(Street, City, State, ZIP code)* and Phone **Loanshark Mortgage 1204 Bellyup Blvd Fatcat, IL. 33333 (555) 444-3333**			
17b Property Description		$	$	$		$
Location *(Street, City, State, ZIP code)* and County			Lender/Lessor/Landlord Name, Address, *(Street, City, State, ZIP code)* and Phone			

17c Total Equity *(Add lines 17a, 17b and amounts from any attachments)* $ 0

Personal Vehicles Leased and Purchased. Include boats, RVs, motorcycles, trailers, etc.

Description *(Year, Mileage, Make, Model)*	Purchase/Lease Date *(mmddyyyy)*	Current Fair Market Value (FMV)	Current Loan Balance	Amount of Monthly Payment	Date of Final Payment *(mmddyyyy)*	Equity FMV Minus Loan
18a Year 2001 Mileage 142,000	2/15/2006	$ 1700	$ 1000	$ 120		$ 700
Make Yugo Model Nogo	Lender/Lessor Name, Address, *(Street, City, State, ZIP code)* and Phone **Vegas Bob's Barely Used Heaps 333 Crooked Street Galump, NV 88877 (702) 166-8800**					
18b Year Mileage		$	$	$		$
Make Model	Lender/Lessor Name, Address, *(Street, City, State, ZIP code)* and Phone					

18c Total Equity *(Add lines 18a, 18b and amounts from any attachments)* $ 700

Personal Assets. Include all furniture, personal effects, artwork, jewelry, collections *(coins, guns, etc.)*, antiques or other assets.

	Purchase/Lease Date *(mmddyyyy)*	Current Fair Market Value (FMV)	Current Loan Balance	Amount of Monthly Payment	Date of Final Payment *(mmddyyyy)*	Equity FMV Minus Loan
19a Property Description Furniture	05/05/2005	$ 4800	$ 4200	$ 240	10/10/2010	$ 600
Location *(Street, City, State, ZIP code)* and County 101 Debtor Lane, Gamblin, NV 89450			Lender/Lessor Name, Address, *(Street, City, State, ZIP code)* and Phone **Love-Itz Furniture 370 Stickway Rocky, N.C. 11111 (800) 800-8000**			
19b Property Description		$	$	$		$
Location *(Street, City, State, ZIP code)* and County			Lender/Lessor Name, Address, *(Street, City, State, ZIP code)* and Phone			

19c Total Equity *(Add lines 19a, 19b and amounts from any attachments)* $ 600

Form **433-A** (Rev. 1-2008)

Collection Information Statement for Individuals (Form 433-A)—Page 4

Form 433-A (Rev. 1-2008)   Page **4**

If the taxpayer is self-employed, sections 5 and 6 must be completed before continuing.

Monthly Income/Expense Statement *(For additional information, refer to Publication 1854.)*

	Total Income			Total Living Expenses		IRS USE ONLY
	Source	Gross Monthly		Expense Items [5]	Actual Monthly	Allowable Expenses
20	Wages *(Taxpayer)* [1]	$ 3030	33	Food, Clothing, and Misc. [6]	$ 800	
21	Wages *(Spouse)* [1]	$ 0	34	Housing and Utilities [7]	$ 740	
22	Interest - Dividends	$ 0	35	Vehicle Ownership Costs [8]	$ 120	
23	Net Business Income [2]	$ 300	36	Vehicle Operating Costs [9]	$ 100	
24	Net Rental Income [3]	$ 0	37	Public Transportation [10]	$	
25	Distributions [4]	$ 0	38	Health Insurance	$ 340	
26	Pension/Social Security *(Taxpayer)*	$ 0	39	Out of Pocket Health Care Costs [11]	$ 50	
27	Pension/Social Security *(Spouse)*	$ 0	40	Court Ordered Payments	$	
28	Child Support	$ 0	41	Child/Dependent Care	$	
29	Alimony	$ 0	42	Life insurance	$	
30	Other (Rent subsidy, Oil credit, etc.)	$ 0	43	Taxes *(Income and FICA)*	$ 770	
31	Other	$ 0	44	Other Secured Debts (Attach list)	$	
32	**Total Income** *(add lines 20-31)*	$ 3330	45	**Total Living Expenses** *(add lines 33-44)*	$ 2920	

1   **Wages, salaries, pensions, and social security:** Enter gross monthly wages and/or salaries. Do not deduct withholding or allotments taken out of pay, such as insurance payments, credit union deductions, car payments, etc. To calculate the gross monthly wages and/or salaries:
    If paid weekly - multiply weekly gross wages by 4.3. Example: $425.89 x 4.3 = $1,831.33
    If paid biweekly (every 2 weeks) - multiply biweekly gross wages by 2.17. Example: $972.45 x 2.17 = $2,110.22
    If paid semimonthly (twice each month) - multiply semimonthly gross wages by 2. Example: $856.23 x 2 = $1,712.46
2   **Net Income from Business:** Enter monthly net business income. This is the amount earned after ordinary and necessary monthly business expenses are paid. **This figure is the amount from page 6, line 82.** If the net business income is a loss, enter "0". Do not enter a negative number. If this amount is more or less than previous years, attach an explanation.
3   **Net Rental Income:** Enter monthly net rental income. This is the amount earned after ordinary and necessary monthly rental expenses are paid. Do not include deductions for depreciation or depletion. If the net rental income is a loss, enter "0". Do not enter a negative number.
4   **Distributions:** Enter the total distributions from partnerships and subchapter S corporations reported on Schedule K-1, and from limited liability companies reported on Form 1040, Schedule C, D or E.
5   **Expenses not generally allowed:** We generally do not allow tuition for private schools, public or private college expenses, charitable contributions, voluntary retirement contributions, payments on unsecured debts such as credit card bills, cable television and other similar expenses. However, we may allow these expenses if it is proven that they are necessary for the health and welfare of the individual or family or for the production of income.
6   **Food, Clothing, and Misc.:** Total of clothing, food, housekeeping supplies, and personal care products for one month.
7   **Housing and Utilities:** For principal residence: Total of rent or mortgage payment. Add the average monthly expenses for the following: property taxes, home owner's or renter's insurance, maintenance, dues, fees, and utilities. Utilities include gas, electricity, water, fuel, oil, other fuels, trash collection, telephone, and cell phone.
8   **Vehicle Ownership Costs:** Total of monthly lease or purchase/loan payments.
9   **Vehicle Operating Costs:** Total of maintenance, repairs, insurance, fuel, registrations, licenses, inspections, parking, and tolls for one month.
10 **Public Transportation:** Total of monthly fares for mass transit (e.g., bus, train, ferry, taxi, etc.)
11 **Out of Pocket Health Care Costs:** Monthly total of medical services, prescription drugs and medical supplies (e.g., eyeglasses, hearing aids, etc.)

Certification: *Under penalties of perjury, I declare that to the best of my knowledge and belief this statement of assets, liabilities, and other information is true, correct, and complete.*

Taxpayer's Signature	Spouse's Signature	Date

Attachments Required for Wage Earners and Self-Employed Individuals:
Copies of the following items for the last 3 months from the date this form is submitted (check all attached items):

☑ Income - Earnings statements, pay stubs, etc. from each employer, pension/social security/other income, self employment income (commissions, invoices, sales records, etc.).

☑ Banks, Investments, and Life Insurance - Statements for all money market, brokerage, checking and savings accounts, certificates of deposit, IRA, stocks/bonds, and life insurance policies with a cash value.

☑ Assets - Statements from lenders on loans, monthly payments, payoffs, and balances for all personal and business assets. Include copies of UCC financing statements and accountant's depreciation schedules.

☑ Expenses - Bills or statements for monthly recurring expenses of utilities, rent, insurance, property taxes, phone and cell phone, insurance premiums, court orders requiring payments (child support, alimony, etc.), other out of pocket expenses.

☑ Other - credit card statements, profit and loss statements, all loan payoffs, etc.

☑ A copy of last year's Form 1040 with all attachments. Include all Schedules K-1 from Form 1120S or Form 1065, as applicable.

Form **433-A** (Rev. 1-2008)

Collection Information Statement for Individuals (Form 433-A)—Page 5

Form 433-A (Rev. 1-2008)   Page **5**

Sections 5 and 6 must be completed only if the taxpayer is SELF-EMPLOYED.

Section 5: Business Information

46 Is the business a sole proprietorship (filing Schedule C) ☑ Yes, Continue with Sections 5 and 6. ☐ No, Complete Form 433-B.
All other business entities, including limited liability companies, partnerships or corporations, must complete Form 433-B.

47 Business Name	**48** Employer Identification Number	**49** Type of Business
Wanda's World of Dog Collars	66-666-6666	**Retail sales** Federal Contractor ☐ Yes ☑ No

50 Business Website	**51** Total Number of Employees	**52a** Average Gross Monthly Payroll
www.wwdc.com	none	none **52b** Frequency of Tax Deposits

53 Does the business engage in e-Commerce (Internet sales) ☐ Yes ☑ No

Payment Processor (e.g., PayPal, Authorize.net, Google Checkout, etc.) Name & Address *(Street, City, State, ZIP code)*	Payment Processor Account Number
54a ZPal, 401 Banana Leaf, Thirsty, AZ 78910	XYZ000ABC
54b	

Credit Cards Accepted by the Business.

Credit Card	Merchant Account Number	Merchant Account Provider, Name & Address *(Street, City, State, ZIP code)*
55a WISA	RUKDing404	WISA, 1313 Usury Road, Raton, FL 3333
55b		
55c		

56 **Business Cash on Hand.** Include cash that is not in a bank.   Total Cash on Hand $

Business Bank Accounts. Include checking accounts, online bank accounts, money market accounts, savings accounts, and stored value cards (e.g. payroll cards, government benefit cards, etc.) *Report Personal Accounts in Section 4.*

Type of Account	Full name & Address *(Street, City, State, ZIP code)* of Bank, Savings & Loan, Credit Union or Financial Institution.	Account Number	Account Balance As of **01/03/2009** *mmddyyyy*
57a checking	RastaBank, 17 Mon, Bongo, N.M. 98765 ☑	00001111333	$ 110
57b			$

57c **Total Cash in Banks** *(Add lines 57a, 57b and amounts from any attachments)* $ 110

Accounts/Notes Receivable. Include e-payment accounts receivable and factoring companies, and any bartering or online auction accounts. *(List all contracts separately, including contracts awarded, but not started.)* **Include Federal Government Contracts.**

Accounts/Notes Receivable & Address *(Street, City, State, ZIP code)*	Status *(e.g., age, factored, other)*	Date Due *(mmddyyyy)*	Invoice Number or Federal Government Contract Number	Amount Due
58a				$
58b				$
58c				$
58d				$

58e **Total Outstanding Balance** *(Add lines 58a through 58d and amounts from any attachments)* $

Form **433-A** (Rev. 1-2008)

Collection Information Statement for Individuals (Form 433-A)—Page 6

Form 433-A (Rev. 1-2008)   Page **6**

Business Assets. Include all tools, books, machinery, equipment, inventory or other assets used in trade or business. Include Uniform Commercial Code (UCC) filings. Include Vehicles and Real Property owned/leased/rented by the business, if not shown in Section 4.

	Purchase/Lease/Rental Date (mmddyyyy)	Current Fair Market Value (FMV)	Current Loan Balance	Amount of Monthly Payment	Date of Final Payment (mmddyyyy)	Equity FMV Minus Loan
59a Property Description Dog Collars	various	$ 888	$ 0	$ 0	0	$ 888
Location (Street, City, State, ZIP code) and County 101 Debtor Way, Gamblin, NV 89450			Lender/Lessor/Landlord Name, Address (Street, City, State, ZIP code) and Phone			
59b Property Description		$	$	$		$
Location (Street, City, State, ZIP code) and County			Lender/Lessor/Landlord Name, Address (Street, City, State, ZIP code) and Phone			

59c Total Equity (Add lines 59a, 59b and amounts from any attachments) $ 888

Section 6 should be completed only if the taxpayer is SELF-EMPLOYED

Section 6: Sole Proprietorship Information (lines 60 through 81 should reconcile with business Profit and Loss Statement)

Accounting Method Used: ☑ Cash ☐ Accrual

Income and Expenses during the period (mmddyyyy)   12/01/08   to (mmddyyyy)   1/01/09 .

Total Monthly Business Income			Total Monthly Business Expenses (Use attachments as needed.)		
	Source	Gross Monthly		Expense Items	Actual Monthly
60	Gross Receipts	$ 750	70	Materials Purchased [1]	$
61	Gross Rental Income	$	71	Inventory Purchased [2]	$ 350
62	Interest	$	72	Gross Wages & Salaries	$
63	Dividends	$	73	Rent	$
64	Cash	$	74	Supplies [3]	$ 50
	Other Income (Specify below)		75	Utilities/Telephone [4]	$
65		$	76	Vehicle Gasoline/Oil	$
66		$	77	Repairs & Maintenance	$
67		$	78	Insurance	$
68		$	79	Current Taxes [5]	$
			80	Other Expenses, including installment payments (Specify)	$ postage 50
69	**Total Income** (Add lines 60 through 68)	$ 750	81	**Total Expenses** (Add lines 70 through 80)	$ 450
			82	**Net Business Income** (Line 69 minus 81) [6]	$ 300

Enter the amount from line 82 on line 23, section 4. If line 82 is a loss, enter "0" on line 23, section 4.

Self-employed taxpayers must return to page 4 to sign the certification and include all applicable attachments.

[1] **Materials Purchased:** Materials are items directly related to the production of a product or service.

[2] **Inventory Purchased:** Goods bought for resale.

[3] **Supplies:** Supplies are items used in the business that are consumed or used up within one year. This could be the cost of books, office supplies, professional equipment, etc.

[4] **Utilities/Telephone:** Utilities include gas, electricity, water, oil, other fuels, trash collection, telephone and cell phone.

[5] **Current Taxes:** Real estate, excise, franchise, occupational, personal property, sales and employer's portion of employment taxes.

[6] **Net Business Income:** Net profit from Form 1040, Schedule C may be used if duplicated deductions are eliminated (e.g., expenses for business use of home already included in housing and utility expenses on page 4). Deductions for depreciation and depletion on Schedule C are not cash expenses and must be added back to the net income figure. In addition, interest cannot be deducted if it is already included in any other installment payments allowed.

FINANCIAL ANALYSIS OF COLLECTION POTENTIAL FOR INDIVIDUAL WAGE EARNERS AND SELF-EMPLOYED INDIVIDUALS		(IRS USE ONLY)
Cash Available (Lines 11, 12c, 13d, 14c, 15g, 56, 57c and 58e)	Total Cash	$
Distrainable Asset Summary (Lines 17c, 18c, 19c, and 59c)	Total Equity	$
Monthly Total Positive Income minus Expenses (Line 32 minus Line 45)	Monthly Available Cash	$

Privacy Act: The information requested on this Form is covered under Privacy Acts and Paperwork Reduction Notices which have already been provided to the taxpayer.

Form **433-A** (Rev. 1-2008)

Signing Form 433—Proceed With Caution

If you didn't prepare Form 433-A or 433-F in advance of your IRS interview, don't let the IRS rush you into it at the meeting. Instead, take the forms home and complete them. This gives you time to remember all your expenses. Ask the revenue officer if you can phone it in, mail it back, or bring it to your next meeting.

Protecting Yourself After Making Financial Disclosures to the IRS

You went through a collection interview, telling the IRS everything. Now the IRS collectors know where you work, bank, live, and more. In short, the IRS is in great shape to seize your wages and assets. What can you do to legally protect yourself if you are worried?

TIP

Financial information must be true on the date that you give it, whether orally or on an IRS form. Do not commit to the IRS that you won't change jobs, sell assets, or switch banks the next day. In fact, switching banks is good self-defense if you fear the IRS may levy upon your account. Alternatively, reduce the known bank balances to a minimum. Take the excess funds and open a new account at a different bank. Bank account moving is only a short-term solution to dealing with IRS collectors or IRS computers, which might freeze and seize your accounts.

Contrary to what many people think, banks do not automatically report your account information to the IRS. If you have an interest-bearing account, however, the interest is reported to the IRS annually after the end of each year. If you live in a small town, open the account outside the area or in another state. If you don't, a local bank canvass by a revenue officer might find your account. In large metropolitan areas with many banks, this is not as likely to happen.

Deposit all further income into the new account. If and when you start paying taxes, pay the IRS out of the old account or with money orders. The reason is that whenever you pay the IRS, the agency records your bank account number in its computer. Don't give the IRS your new account number by using the new account.

If the collector requests an updated Form 433-A or 433-B, you must disclose the new accounts. Updates usually aren't requested more than once a year. Then you can begin the account-moving process over again.

Revenue Officers Can Snoop

Don't expect a collector to take your word for anything. It is the collector's job to verify what you said and the information on a 433 form. Revenue officers are alerted for transfers of your assets or assets held by members of your family. In such a situation, a revenue officer will treat you harshly—and may try to get the property back under a law that prohibits fraudulent transfers. The revenue officer will also check public records, such as DMV files and real property recordings, and may ask for past tax returns for clues to stocks, real estate, and businesses you previously owned. You don't have to turn these over, but the officer can retrieve some tax filing data through the IRS computer system.

What the Collector Does Next

After reviewing your financial disclosures on Form 433-A (and possibly Form 433-B), the revenue officer will proceed by doing one or more of the following:

- demanding immediate payment if your forms show your ability to pay right away
- requesting that you obtain a bank loan—the *Internal Revenue Manual* mentions only bank loans, so the collector should not ask you to borrow from a finance company or relative if the bank turns you down
- requesting that you sell unnecessary assets and use the proceeds to pay the IRS
- suggesting that you file an Offer in Compromise
- proposing a monthly installment agreement
- mentioning your bankruptcy options

- beginning enforced collection—seizing (levy) your wages, bank accounts, and other assets, and
- reporting your account as currently not collectible, subject to future review.

Installment Payment Plan

The most widely used method for paying an old IRS debt is the monthly installment agreement, or IA. If you owe $25,000 or less, an IA is usually easy to get. If you owe over $25,000, it is more difficult. As mentioned above, if you have money or assets available beyond the amount of the IRS calculation of your allowable expenses, the IRS isn't required to grant a payment plan, but it may do so.

Don't assume that a payment plan is your best option—there are definite drawbacks. The biggest is that interest and penalties continue to accrue while you pay. The interest rate is adjusted by law quarterly. Combined with late payment penalties, recently the rate has averaged between 6% and 8% per year (less than your credit card). It's possible to pay for years and still owe more than when you started because of the compounding of principal and interest.

> EXAMPLE: Rodney and Rebecca owe the IRS $40,000 in back taxes. They enter into a $300 per month payment plan at a time when interest and penalties total 10% a year, adding $4,000 to their balance. But 12 months' worth of $300 payments add up to only $3,600, and so they will owe $40,400 at the end of the year ($40,000 minus $3,600 paid plus $4,000 in interest).

You can set up an IA by calling the number on the IRS bill, or you can do it online using IRS Form 9465, *Request for Installment Agreement*.

CAUTION
You must be current on your tax filings. If IRS computers show that you haven't filed all past due tax returns, you will not get an IA until you are current. Likewise, if you are self-employed, you must be making your quarterly estimated tax payments for the current year. If you are an employer, you must be current on your payroll tax deposits as well.

The IRS May Ask for Longer to Collect From You

The tax code imposes a ten-year time limit on the IRS to collect taxes. (Internal Revenue Code § 6502.) This period starts on the date the tax was officially assessed. If you were audited, the ten years runs from the date the IRS assessed additional taxes, if any. If you don't file a required tax return, the ten-year limitation on collection doesn't start.

Sometimes, as a condition of granting an IA, the IRS will require that you allow the ten-year period to be extended. You will be asked to sign Form 900, *Tax Collection Waiver*. Generally, the extension period requested is five years beyond the time left on the statute of limitations for collection (normally ten years). When the revenue officer hands you Form 900, say that you want to talk to your tax adviser before signing. This stalling tactic may work. Often the IRS forgets to ask for the form later, and you are home free. If the IRS insists (and doesn't forget), go ahead and sign. The IRS has you over a barrel—no waiver, no installment agreement.

If You Owe More than $25,000

Getting an IA if you owe more than $25,000 means dealing with an IRS collector. It can be done either in person at the local IRS office, or by phone or mail. The IRS makes this choice, not you.

The collector starts by taking information from you for an IRS Collection Information Statement, Form 433-A or 433-F. Based on this data, the collector determines the amount you should pay monthly. If you believe the amount is greater than your ability to pay (almost always the case), then you may be able to negotiate for a lower amount.

Here are some strategies for negotiating an installment plan:

- When you hand the completed Form 433-A or 433-B to the revenue officer, immediately propose a payment plan you can live with.
- You must offer to pay at least the amount shown on the bottom of the last page of Form 433-A—income less necessary living expenses. This is the cash the IRS says you have left over every month after paying for the necessities of life. Don't promise to pay more than you can afford just to get your plan approved. Once an IA is approved, the IRS makes

it difficult for you to renegotiate it unless your circumstances have changed dramatically.

• If your bottom line is $0 or a negative number, consider submitting an Offer in Compromise; asking for a suspension of collection activities; or filing for Chapter 7 bankruptcy.

• Give a first payment when you propose the agreement—and keep making monthly payments even if the IRS hasn't yet approved your IA. If you don't have the funds, the IRS may agree to accept a postdated check. Ask your revenue officer about this. Making voluntary payments demonstrates your good faith and creates a track record. For example, if you pay $200 a month for three months before your IA is approved, the revenue officer may be inclined to believe that this is the right amount.

A collector doesn't have sole authority to grant a payment plan for amounts over $25,000. The collector can only recommend it to his or her manager for approval. Most of the time, approval is given, but not always.

If an IA is verbally agreed upon with the collector, it may take a few weeks for the IRS to notify you in writing that it has been formally approved.

Installment Agreement Set-Up Fee

There's no free lunch with an IRS payment plan. The IRS now charges a "user fee" of $105 to set up an IA. Cut this to $52 if you agree to a direct debit arrangement with your bank to make monthly withdrawals. Or, it can be as low as $43 if your income is below the IRS poverty level. (The IRS looks at your most recent tax return to see if you qualify.) If you miss a payment and the IA is revoked, it will cost you $45 if the IRS agrees to reinstate the payment plan.

Making Payments on the IA

Send payments under your IA to the IRS using the payment vouchers and bar-coded envelopes mailed to you each month. Write your name, Social Security number, type of tax (income, payroll), and tax periods (years or quarters) covered by the IA in the lower left-hand corner of your check, and make a photocopy for your records. If you don't want the IRS to know where you bank, use a money order or cashier's check from another financial institution.

You have two other options for making payments once your IA is approved:

- Request a direct payroll deduction using Form 2159, *Payroll Deduction Agreement*. Your employer must agree to send payments to the IRS each month using the IRS's payment slips.
- Use a direct debit, where your bank automatically debits your checking account each month and sends a payment to the IRS. Request this by filling out the back of Form 433-D, *Installment Agreement*, and returning it to the IRS with a blank voided check from your account. As long as you keep the account open, this is the most foolproof way to make sure you don't miss a payment and risk having the agreement revoked.

If the IRS Says "No" to an IA

Before the IRS will accept an IA, the IRS officer must believe that the information on your 433-F form is truthful, your living expenses are "necessary," and the IRS is getting the maximum amount you can pay.

When the IRS won't agree to installment payments, it is for one of three reasons:

- Your living expenses are not all considered necessary under the IRS standards discussed above. For example, if you have hefty credit card payments, make any charitable contributions, or send your kids to private school, expect the IRS to balk. Although reasonable people would disagree on what is necessary and what is extravagant, the IRS is rather stingy here.
- Information you provided on Form 433-F, *Collection Information Statement*, is incomplete or untruthful. The IRS may think you are hiding property or income. For example, if public records show your name on real estate or motor vehicles that you didn't list, or the IRS received W-2 or 1099 forms showing more income than you listed, be prepared to explain.
- You defaulted on a prior IA. While this doesn't automatically disqualify you from a new IA, it can cause your new proposal to be met with skepticism.

> **TIP**
>
> **If your IA proposal is first rejected, you can keep negotiating. Ask to speak to the revenue officer's manager.** Just making this request is sometimes enough to soften the officer up. But, if you talk to the manager, don't criticize the employee or start yelling. Keep your cool and if the manager believes you are trying to be reasonable, he or she may take over the case or ask the revenue officer to reconsider.

If you get nowhere with the manager, you can go to the IRS Appeals Office (see "If the IRS Records a Tax Lien," in Chapter 7 and Form 9423), or contact a taxpayer advocate (see Chapter 8).

Revoking an Installment Agreement

Once you receive written approval of your IA, you and the IRS are bound by the terms of the agreement, *unless:*

- You fail to file your tax returns or pay taxes that arose after the IA was entered into. Although IRS computers do not continue to review your finances, they do monitor you for filing future returns and making promised payments.
- You miss a payment. Under the terms of all IAs, payments not made in full, and on time, can cause the IA to be revoked. The IRS usually waits 30 to 60 days before revocation—at least on the first missed payment. You are entitled to a warning or a chance to reinstate the agreement.
- Your financial condition changes significantly—either for the better or worse. The IRS usually won't find out about this unless you tell. The IRS may review your situation periodically and require you to submit a new Form 433-F, but this seldom happens.
- The IRS discovers that you provided inaccurate or incomplete information to the collector. For instance, not listing all of your assets or neglecting to mention your moonlighting jobs.

If the IRS intends to revoke your installment agreement, you will receive CP-523, *Notice of Default of Installment Agreement*. You can appeal the revocation of an IA. See Chapter 7 for the procedure. You must use Form 9423.

If You Can't Make an Installment Payment

If you can't make a monthly IA payment, call the taxpayer assistance number at 800-829-1040. If you negotiated with a revenue officer, call that person, too.

Explain your problem. Ask for more time to pay and that collections be suspended. You'll need a good excuse, like losing your job, becoming disabled, or a similar mishap. If you don't get anywhere and the IRS says your IA is in default—meaning the IRS can begin grabbing your property—call the Taxpayer Advocate Service. A taxpayer advocate can keep your agreement from being revoked if it would result in a significant hardship. (See Chapter 8 for information on taxpayer advocates.)

CAUTION
If your IA is revoked and your appeal fails, you can start negotiations over from scratch. The IRS may grant a reinstatement, but don't count on it. Remember, unless you owe less than $10,000, installment agreements are discretionary with the IRS. If the IRS is willing to grant a new IA, you'll need a good excuse for defaulting and likely have to furnish updated documentation of your income and living expenses. And while you are trying to get a new IA, the IRS may start seizing your bank accounts and wages.

Making an IA When You Also Owe State Taxes

Often you will owe both the IRS and your state. If you do, negotiate payment plans with both agencies at the same time. Otherwise, any deal you make with one may not leave you with anything to pacify the other. See Chapter 14 for information on negotiating installment plans with both taxing authorities.

Offers in Compromise—Settling Tax Bills for Pennies on the Dollar

Would you like to wipe your tax slate clean at an enormous discount? The IRS has accepted less than 1% of a tax bill and called it even. There is no legal right to ever have a valid tax bill reduced by the IRS. It is entirely a matter of government discretion whether or not you qualify for an offer in compromise, referred to as an offer or OIC. (Internal Revenue Code § 7122.) In all but a few instances, the IRS must give a properly submitted OIC its fair consideration. You even have the right to take a rejected OIC to the IRS Appeals Office.

The IRS occasionally makes deals—but be aware that there is no "tax debt fire sale" happening in Washington. Nevertheless, fewer than one in four offers in compromise are eventually negotiated with the IRS. This doesn't mean that the IRS accepted the original offer; typically the IRS and the taxpayer do some bargaining.

> **TIP**
>
> **Make sure you qualify.** Read the IRS Form 656 booklet (28 pages) before you decide to make an OIC to the IRS. If you find out early that you don't qualify, you can save yourself a great deal of time and avoid frustration.

Think Twice About Trying an OIC

Submitting an OIC to the IRS is a very formal process—you can't simply call the IRS and say "Let's make a deal." Start by reading carefully the rest of this section.

Along with Form 656, submit Form 433-A and, for certain business owners, Form 433-B. There is an application fee and an initial payment required. The IRS scrutinizes your Forms 433-A and 433-B much more closely when considering an OIC than when you request an installment agreement. If you are married, the IRS may request that your Form 433-A include financial data on your spouse—even if you alone owe the IRS.

Completing Forms 656 and 433-A (and 433-B for business entities) is just the beginning. After receiving your OIC documents, the IRS will ask for rafts of written proof and backup—paystubs, bank records, vehicle registrations, and myriad other items. Expect a long and time-consuming process, unless you are quickly rejected, which happens too.

Are You Eligible for an OIC?

Wanting to make a deal with the IRS is not enough—everyone would like to have his tax bill reduced. To qualify, you must check the right box on Form 656 and show the IRS that one or more of the following conditions exists:

- There is some doubt as to whether the IRS can ever collect the tax bill from you—now or in the foreseeable future. The IRS calls this *doubt as to collectibility*.
- There is some doubt as to whether you owe the tax bill. The IRS calls this *doubt as to liability*. This condition is unusual and should only be claimed after talking to a tax pro.
- You have sufficient assets to pay in full but, due to exceptional circumstances, payment would cause an "economic hardship" or would be "unfair" or "inequitable." The IRS considers offers here under the heading of *effective tax administration*. (See below, "Special Circumstances.")

In addition, you must not be in bankruptcy.

How Much Should You Offer?

The amount of an OIC must be equal to (a) the net realizable value of your assets, plus (b) the present value of the total sum the IRS could collect under a monthly payment plan. For example, if the first number is $7,200 and the second $14,800, the minimum offer must be $22,000. Let's look at how these numbers are calculated by the IRS.

Net realizable value of your assets. The net realizable value of your assets is the amount the IRS could collect if it seized your assets and sold them today—after paying off any debts associated with the property, such as a mortgage. To figure out the net value or equity in real estate, the IRS allows a "quick sale value," or QSV, generally 20% less than the fair market value. In a depressed real estate market, you can argue for a greater discount, perhaps as high as 50% depending on where you live.

> EXAMPLE: Darlene owes the IRS $47,850 for back taxes resulting from the failure of her Beanie Baby Bazaar venture. Darlene has $1,500 in

cash and a house, which has a fair market value of $150,000 and a quick sale value of $120,000. She owes $77,000 on her first mortgage, $33,000 on a home equity loan and $4,000 in back property taxes.

Fair market value (home)	$150,000	
Less 20%	(30,000)	
Quick sale value		$120,000
Less:		
First mortgage	(77,000)	
Home equity loan	(33,000)	
Unpaid property taxes	(4,000)	
Total debt on property		($114,000)
Net realizable value (home)		$6,000
Realizable value (cash)		1,500
Total Net Realizable Value		$ 7,500

When totaling up your assets for an OIC, you can exclude most household property and personal effects, such as clothing, furniture, and appliances, as long as they are not luxurious. List luxury items like your sable coat and Louis XIV dining room set. In the example above, Darlene's stuff was pretty much from Levitz and Wal-Mart, so it didn't have to be figured in.

Retirement plan balances, SEPs, IRAs, and 401(k)s, must be included in the asset calculations for an OIC. But you can discount their values by any income tax and any penalties for early distribution you would owe after cashing them in. Attach a written explanation of how you arrived at the discounted value.

Excluded assets. A list of the relatively few items that may be excluded from your asset calculation is in IRS Publication 594, *The IRS Collection Process*, a copy of which is available on the IRS's website at www.irs.gov. The list is titled "Some property cannot be levied or seized."

Future income less living expenses. This calculation is made by subtracting your necessary living expenses from your total monthly income (see Form 433-A). This is your monthly disposable income which is the amount you could be expected to pay if you were on a monthly payment plan with the IRS.

How much to offer. After you determine the monthly disposable income amount, you must multiply it by a number according to the type of offer you propose. There are two payment options:

- **Payment Option One.** Use the number 48, if you propose to pay the amount of your offer in one or more payments within five months of IRS notification that your offer has been accepted.
- **Payment Option Two.** Use the number of months remaining on the statute of limitations for the collection of the taxes—120 months minus however many months have passed since the date the IRS assessed the taxes—if it is less than 48 or 60. The example below shows how these offers compare.

EXAMPLE: Let's continue with Darlene. Using Form 433-A, she calculates that she could pay a maximum of $150 per month.

1. With Payment Option One, Darlene must offer $7,200 (48 x $150) under the *future income* formula. (Added to the $7,500 under the asset test, her total offer must be at least $14,700.)
2. Under Payment Option Two, if Darlene's tax debt had been assessed seven years (84 months) ago, Darlene would multiply $150 by 36 months (120 − 84), meaning a future income of $5,400 and with her $7,500 in assets a total offer of $12,900. The longer-term offer calculation actually results in a lower offer in this case. This is not the usual result. (The 36 months is the remaining time on the 10-year statute of limitations on collection.)

CAUTION

Be ready for a tax lien. If the IRS accepts either type of periodic payment offer in compromise (for payments over two years or longer), it may record a Notice of Federal Tax Lien showing your tax debt. The lien will remain on the public record until every last penny has been paid or the statute of limitations for collection has expired, whichever occurs first.

Special Circumstances: Effective Tax Administration

What if you calculate the minimum amount required for an OIC and it shows you have too many assets? However, selling those assets would cause an economic hardship to you or your family. For example, full payment would mean losing your retirement account income or your home. IRS personnel have leeway to accept less than required under strict application of the normal rules, under the "effective tax administration" (hardship) condition.

The IRS favors offers from people with bleak financial prospects due to advanced age—over 60 in particular. And the IRS gives special consideration to people with physical or psychological infirmities, including HIV or drug- or alcohol-related problems. The problem could even be related to a family member if it has a detrimental financial effect on you. For medical conditions, get statements from doctors and medical records to prove it. If the medical data doesn't make the point clear, then explain how the condition prevents you from earning much of a living now or in the foreseeable future. As the Rolling Stones sang, "Paint It Black." The best way to bring special circumstances to the IRS's attention is through a letter attached to your Forms 656 and 433. It doesn't have to be formal or fancy, just one or two pages telling your tale of woe.

Do You Need a Tax Professional to Submit an OIC?

If you follow the IRS's OIC instructions in the Form 656 booklet and the suggestions here, your chances of success should be as good as if you had hired a tax professional. My advice though: Run your 656 and 433 completed forms and documents by an offer-experienced tax professional before sending them to the IRS.

Or, if you just can't stomach dealing with the IRS, hire a tax professional to prepare and submit your OIC. Expect to pay between $1,500 and $7,500. While the IRS won't give special consideration to an OIC submitted by a tax professional, that person is much less likely to make a fatal mistake in the process than you are.

Pros and Cons of Making an Offer in Compromise

Making an offer in compromise has its advantages and disadvantages.

Advantages

The obvious advantage is that if your offer in compromise is accepted, you'll save a heap of money. If your offer includes deferred payments, interest continues to accrue, but only on the amount you're paying under the offer in compromise—not on the original amount owed.

Also, even if your offer is ultimately rejected, your stress level will be reduced while the offer is pending. This is because the IRS normally doesn't seize your wages or property during this period.

Finally, once an offer in compromise is accepted and paid in full, the IRS must release tax liens within 30 days. (See Chapter 7.) Your credit rating will improve as soon as a Certificate of Release of Federal Tax Lien is filed on the public record.

Potential Disadvantages to an OIC

There are eight potential disadvantages to an OIC, as follows:

- After your offer in compromise is accepted, you must timely file all future tax returns and make all tax payments in full for the next five years. This includes payroll taxes for your business and estimated tax payments if you're self-employed.
- Just filing an offer gives the IRS extra time to collect from you, whether it is accepted or not. As mentioned, the IRS normally has ten years to collect taxes. If you make an offer, the IRS adds the period that the offer is under consideration, plus time pending in an appeal, if any, plus 30 days to the ten-year statute of limitations period.
- After your offer in compromise is accepted, you give up any tax refunds for the years prior to the offer and for the year in which the offer is accepted.
- After submitting an OIC, you cannot later contest, either in court or to the IRS, any taxes for years listed in the offer, even if your offer is rejected.
- In making an offer in compromise, you must thoroughly disclose your assets. If you don't and the IRS accepts, but later finds out you fibbed, the offer may be revoked.

- While your offer is pending and the IRS is investigating your assets, it may decide to audit you, based on something you revealed or didn't disclose in your offer forms. This is not likely, but it is a possibility.
- If your offer is accepted and you default on any payments due, the original amount owed, plus penalties and interest, may be reinstated in full. And if you fail to file or pay any taxes due for *five years after your offer is accepted,* the same thing happens—the deal may be nullified and your original tax debt reinstated. You are given credit for any payments made under the offer, however.
- You must make a nonrefundable payment of 20% if it's a lump sum offer, or one periodic payment if it's one of the other types of offers. This payment is nonrefundable if your offer is rejected.

The Offer in Compromise Forms

Offers must be presented on Form 656, *Offer in Compromise.* You also must submit a completed Form 433-A and, for certain business owners, a Form 433-B as well.

Make sure your *Offer in Compromise* and 433-A and 433-B forms are the latest versions. Call the IRS at 800-829-1040 or check the IRS website for the correct form (www.irs.gov).

> **TIP**
> **Alert the IRS.** Call the IRS (800-829-1040) to tell them you intend to submit an OIC, and ask that no collection action be taken while you prepare the offer. Your request should be granted, depending on your history of problems with the IRS. Then file your offer within 45 days.

Completing Forms 433 and 656

Suggestions for completing Forms 433-A and 433-B are in "Filling in IRS Collection Forms" and "How Much Should You Offer?" above. See the IRS Form 656 booklet for instructions on submitting an offer (www.irs.gov).

A completed sample of Form 656 is below. Also see the IRS website for a worksheet. Here are some additional tips, by the paragraph numbers on Form 656.

Sample Offer in Compromise (Form 656)—Page 1

Form **656**
(Rev. March 2011)

Department of the Treasury — Internal Revenue Service

Offer in Compromise

Attach Application Fee and Payment *(check or money order)* **here.**

IRS Received Date

Section 1	**Your Contact Information**

Your First Name, Middle Initial, Last Name

Martin Kuhn

If a Joint Offer, Spouse's First Name, Middle Initial, Last Name

Konnie K. Kuhn

Your Physical Home Address *(Street, City, State, ZIP Code)*

49999 Liberty Lane, Ocala, Florida 38888

Mailing Address *(if different from above or Post Office Box number)*

Business Name

Your Business Address *(Street, City, State, ZIP Code)*

Social Security Number (SSN)		Employer Identification Number (EIN)	(EIN not included in offer)
(Primary) 100 – 01 – 0101	(Secondary) 909 – 11 – 9999	–	–

Section 2	**Tax Periods**

To: Commissioner of Internal Revenue Service

In the following agreement, the pronoun "we" may be assumed in place of "I" when there are joint liabilities and both parties are signing this agreement.

I submit this offer to compromise the tax liabilities plus any interest, penalties, additions to tax, and additional amounts required by law for the tax type and period(s) marked below:

[X] 1040 Income Tax-Year(s) 2005, 2006, 2007, 2008

[ ] 1120 Income Tax-Year(s) _____

[ ] 941 Employer's Quarterly Federal Tax Return - Quarterly period(s)_____

[ ] 940 Employer's Annual Federal Unemployment (FUTA) Tax Return - Year(s) _____

[ ] Trust Fund Recovery Penalty as a responsible person of *(enter corporation name)* _____
for failure to pay withholding and Federal Insurance Contributions Act taxes (Social Security taxes), for period(s) ending

[ ] Other Federal Tax(es) [specify type(s) and period(s)] _____

Note: If you need more space, use attachment and title it "Attachment to Form 656 dated _____." Make sure to sign and date the attachment.

Section 3	**Reason for Offer**

[X] **Doubt as to Collectibility** - I have insufficient assets and income to pay the full amount.

[ ] **Exceptional Circumstances (Effective Tax Administration)** - I owe this amount and have sufficient assets to pay the full amount, but due to my exceptional circumstances, requiring full payment would cause an economic hardship or would be unfair and inequitable. I am submitting a written narrative explaining my circumstances.

Catalog Number 16728N

www.irs.gov

Form **656** (Rev. 3-2011)

Sample Offer in Compromise (Form 656)—Page 2

Page 2 of 4

Section 3 — Reason for Offer *(Continued)*

Explanation of Circumstances *(Add additional pages, if needed)*

The IRS understands that there are unplanned events or special circumstances, such as serious illness, where paying the full amount or the minimum offer amount might impair your ability to provide for yourself and your family. If this is the case and you can provide documentation to prove your situation, then your offer may be accepted despite your financial profile. Describe your situation below and attach appropriate documents to this offer application.

Taxpayer, Martin Kuhn, is 62 years old and employed as a part-time janitor (pay stubs attached).

Taxpayer Konnie Kuhn suffered a massive stroke in 2010 and is bedridden. (Medical report attached)

The small business that taxpayers owned, "Perpetual Motion Machines, LLC" failed in 2009 leaving us over $200,000 in business debts and judgments (legal documents attached).

Taxpayers' home burned down in 2011 and the insurance proceeds all went to partially pay the first and second mortgages on the home (documents attached). Taxpayers then signed over the deed to the home under threat of foreclosure. Taxpayers now live in a spare room in their daughter's home.

Section 4 — Low Income Certification *(Individuals Only)*

Do you qualify for Low-Income Certification? You qualify if your gross monthly household income is less than or equal to the amount shown in the chart below based on your family size and where you live. If you qualify, you are not required to submit any payments during the consideration of your offer.

☐ **Check here if you qualify for Low-Income Certification based on the monthly income guidelines below.**

Size of family unit	48 contiguous states and D.C.	Hawaii	Alaska
1	$2,256	$2,596	$2,819
2	$3,035	$3,492	$3,794
3	$3,815	$4,388	$4,769
4	$4,594	$5,283	$5,744
5	$5,373	$6,179	$6,719
6	$6,152	$7,075	$7,694
7	$6,931	$7,971	$8,669
8	$7,710	$8,867	$9,644
For each additional person, add	$ 779	$ 896	$ 975

Section 5 — Payment Terms

Enter the amount of your offer $ 20,000

Check one of the payment options below to indicate how long it will take you to pay your offer in full:

Payment Option 1

☒ **Check here if you will pay your offer in five or fewer payments:**

Enclose a check for 20% of the offer amount (waived if you are an individual and met the requirements for Low-Income certification) and fill in the amount(s) and date(s) of your future payment(s).

20% of the offer amount is $ 4,000 leaving a balance of $ 16,000 to be paid as follows after the acceptance of your offer:

Amount of payment 1 $ 16,000 date one month after acceptance of offer

Amount of payment 2 $ _____ date _____

Amount of payment 3 $ _____ date _____

Amount of payment 4 $ _____ date _____

Amount of payment 5 $ _____ date _____

Payment Option 2

☐ **Check here if you will pay your offer in full in more than five months and pay in monthly installments**

Enclose a check for one month's installment (waived if you are an individual and met the requirements for Low-Income certification)

$ _____ is being submitted with the Form 656 and then $_____ on the _____ (day) of each month thereafter for a total of _____ months. Total payments must equal the total Offer Amount.

You must continue to make these monthly payments while the IRS is considering the offer. Failure to make regular monthly payments will cause your offer to be returned.

Sample Offer in Compromise (Form 656)—Page 3

Section 6	Designation of Down Payment and Deposit *(Optional)*

If you want your payment to be applied to a specific tax year and a specific tax debt, please tell us the tax form _____ and Tax Year/Quarter _____ . If you do not designate a preference, we will apply any money you send in to the governments best interest.

If you are paying more than the required payment when you submit your offer and want any part of that payment treated as a deposit, check the box below and insert the amount.

[X] I am making a deposit of $ __4,000__ with this offer.

Section 7	Source of Funds

Tell us where you will obtain the funds to pay your offer. You may consider borrowing from friends and/or family, taking out a loan, or selling assets.

We are borrowing the funds from taxpayer Konnie Kuhn's aunt Minnie Pearl (letter from Ms. Pearl to taxpayers attached).

Include separate checks for the payment and application fee.
Make payable to the "United States Treasury" and attach to the front of your Form 656, Offer in Compromise. **Do not send cash.** Send a separate application fee with each offer; do not combine it with any other tax payments, as this may delay processing of your offer. Your offer will be returned to you if the application fee and the required payments are not properly remitted, or if your check is returned for insufficient funds.

Section 8	Offer Terms

By submitting this offer, I/we have read, understand and agree to the following terms and conditions:

Terms, Conditions, and Legal Agreement

a) I request that the IRS accept the offer amount listed in this offer application as payment of my outstanding tax debt (including interest, penalties, and any additional amounts required by law) as of the date listed on this form. I authorize the IRS to amend Section 2 on page 1 in the event I failed to list any of my assessed tax debt.

IRS will keep my payments, fees, and some refunds.

b) I voluntarily submit the payments made on this offer and **understand that they are not refundable even if I withdraw the offer or the IRS rejects or returns the offer.** Unless I designated how to apply the required payment (page 3 of this application), the IRS will apply my payment in the best interest of the government, choosing which tax years and tax liabilities to pay off. The IRS will also keep my application fee unless the offer is not accepted for processing.

c) The IRS will keep **any** refund, including interest, that I might be due for tax periods extending through the calendar year in which the IRS accepts my offer. I cannot designate that the refund be applied to estimated tax payments for the following year or the accepted offer amount. If I receive a refund after I submit this offer for any tax period extending through the calendar year in which the IRS accepts my offer, I will return the refund as soon as possible.

d) The IRS will keep any monies it has collected prior to this offer and any payments that I make relating to this offer that I did not designate as a deposit. Only amounts that exceed the mandatory payments can be treated as a deposit. Such a deposit will be refundable if the offer is rejected or returned by the IRS or is withdrawn. I understand that the IRS will not pay interest on any deposit. The IRS may seize ("levy") my assets up to the time that the IRS official signs and accepts my offer as pending.

Pending status of an offer and right to appeal

e) Once an authorized IRS official signs this form, my offer is considered pending as of that signature date and it remains pending until the IRS accepts, rejects, returns, or terminates my offer or I withdraw my offer. An offer will be considered withdrawn when the IRS receives my written notification of withdrawal by personal delivery or certified mail or when I inform the IRS of my withdrawal by other means and the IRS acknowledges in writing my intent to withdraw the offer.

f) I waive the right to an Appeals hearing if I do not request a hearing within 30 days of the date the IRS notifies me of the decision to reject the offer.

I must comply with my future tax obligations and understand I remain liable for the full amount of my tax debt until all terms and conditions of this offer have been met.

g) I will file tax returns and pay required taxes for the five year period beginning with the date of acceptance of this offer, or until my offer is paid in full, whichever is longer. If this is an offer being submitted for joint tax debt, and one of us does not comply with future obligations, only the non-compliant taxpayer will be in default of this agreement.

h) The IRS will not remove the original amount of my tax debt from its records until I have met all the terms and conditions of this offer. Penalty and interest will continue to accrue until all payment terms of the offer have been met. If I file for bankruptcy before the terms are fully met, any claim the IRS files in the bankruptcy proceedings will be a tax claim.

i) Once the IRS accepts my offer in writing, I have no right to contest, in court or otherwise, the amount of the tax debt.

I understand what will happen if I fail to meet the terms of my offer (e.g., default).

j) If I fail to meet any of the terms of this offer, the IRS may levy or sue me to collect any amount ranging from the unpaid balance of the offer to the original amount of the tax debt without further notice of any kind. The IRS will continue to add interest, as Section 6601 of the Internal Revenue Code requires, on the amount the IRS determines is due after default. The IRS will add interest from the date I default until I completely satisfy the amount owed.

I agree to waive time limits provided by law.

k) To have my offer considered, I agree to the extension of the time limit provided by law to assess my tax debt (statutory period of assessment). I agree that the date by which the IRS must assess my tax debt will now be the date by which my debt must currently be assessed plus the period of time my offer is pending plus one additional year if the IRS rejects, returns, or terminates my offer or I withdraw it. (Paragraph (e) of this section defines pending and withdrawal). I understand that I have the right not to waive the statutory period of assessment or to limit the waiver to a certain length or certain periods or issues. I understand, however, that the

Sample Offer in Compromise (Form 656)—Page 4

Page 4 of 4

Section 8 - *(Continued)*

IRS may not consider my offer if I refuse to waive the statutory period of assessment or if I provide only a limited waiver. I also understand that the statutory period for collecting my tax debt will be suspended during the time my offer is pending with the IRS, for 30 days after any rejection of my offer by the IRS, and during the time that any rejection of my offer is being considered by the Appeals Office.

I understand the IRS may file a Notice of Federal Tax Lien on my property.	l) The IRS may file a Notice of Federal Tax Lien during the offer investigation. Generally, the IRS files a Notice of Federal Tax Lien to protect the Government's interest on offers that will be paid over time. This tax lien will be released when the payment terms of the accepted offer have been satisfied.
I authorize the IRS to contact relevant third parties in order to process my offer	m) By authorizing the IRS to contact third parties including credit bureaus, I understand that I will not be notified of which third parties the IRS contacts as part of the offer application process, as stated in section 7602(c) of the Internal Revenue Code.
I am submitting an offer as an individual for a joint liability	n) I understand if the liability sought to be compromised is the joint and individual liability of myself and my co-obligor(s) and I am submitting this offer to compromise my individual liability only, then if this offer is accepted, it does not release or discharge my co-obligor(s) from liability. The United States still reserves all rights of collection against the co-obligor(s).

Section 9 — Signatures

Under penalties of perjury, I declare that I have examined this offer, including accompanying schedules and statements, and to the best of my knowledge and belief, it is true, correct and complete.

Signature of Taxpayer *Martin Kuhn*	Date *(mm/dd/yyyy)* November 28, 2011
Signature of Taxpayer *Konnie K. Kuhn*	Date *(mm/dd/yyyy)* November 29, 2011

Section 10 — Paid Preparer Use Only

Signature of Preparer

Name of Paid Preparer	Date *(mm/dd/yyyy)*	Preparer's CAF no. or PTIN

Firm's Name, Address, and ZIP Code

Include a valid, signed Form 2848 or 8821 with this application, if one is not on file.

Section 11 — Third Party Designee

Do you want to allow another person to discuss this offer with the IRS?   ☐ Yes   ☐ No

If yes, provide designee's name

Telephone Number ( )

IRS Use Only

I accept the waiver of the statutory period of limitations on assessment for the Internal Revenue Service, as described in Section 8 (k).

Signature of Authorized Internal Revenue Service Official	Title	Date *(mm/dd/yyyy)*

Privacy Act Statement

We ask for the information on this form to carry out the internal revenue laws of the United States. Our authority to request this information is Section 7801 of the Internal Revenue Code.

Our purpose for requesting the information is to determine if it is in the best interests of the IRS to accept an offer. You are not required to make an offer; however, if you choose to do so, you must provide all of the taxpayer information requested. Failure to provide all of the information may prevent us from processing your request.

If you are a paid preparer and you prepared the Form 656 for the taxpayer submitting an offer, we request that you complete and sign Section 10 on Form 656, and provide identifying information. Providing this information is voluntary. This information will be used to administer and enforce the internal revenue laws of the United States and may be used to regulate practice before the Internal Revenue Service for those persons subject to Treasury Department Circular No. 230, Regulations Governing the Practice of Attorneys, Certified Public Accountants, Enrolled Agents, Enrolled Actuaries, and Appraisers before the Internal Revenue Service. Information on this form may be disclosed to the Department of Justice for civil and criminal litigation.

We may also disclose this information to cities, states and the District of Columbia for use in administering their tax laws and to combat terrorism. Providing false or fraudulent information on this form may subject you to criminal prosecution and penalties.

Section 2. Check the box or boxes specifically by year and type of tax—such as income, employment, or corporate taxes.

Section 5. Study your options carefully and enter the amount you propose to pay and how you intend to pay it—in a lump sum or a combination of a down payment and installments.

Where To Send OIC Forms

If you live in Alaska, Alabama, Arizona, California, Colorado, Hawaii, Idaho, Kentucky, Louisiana, Mississippi, Montana, Nevada, New Mexico, Oregon, Tennessee, Texas, Utah, Washington, Wisconsin, or Wyoming, send your completed OIC forms and attachments to:

> Memphis IRS Service Center
> COIC Unit
> P.O. Box 30803 AMC
> Memphis, TN 38130-0803

If you live in another state or in a foreign country, send your OIC materials to:

> Brookhaven IRS Service Center
> COIC Unit
> P.O. Box 9007
> Holtsville, NY 11742-9007

When your packet arrives at one of these processing units, it will first get a quick review to make sure you filled in the forms correctly and attached the proper supporting documents. After that, the unit will formally open your case and either contact you directly or assign it to your local IRS office for investigation. The processing unit or a local IRS offer specialist will likely contact you for follow-up information and questioning.

Submitting Documentation

After you have filed your Form 656 *Offer*, the IRS will want evidence supporting the information on your Forms 433-A and 433-B, if applicable. Be prepared to submit copies, (but not the originals) of:

- your income tax returns for the last two years
- deeds and mortgage documents to all real estate you own

- titles to motor vehicles, boats, planes, and the like
- bank statements for all your accounts for the last three months, in whole or in part
- life insurance policies—the IRS may want to see if the policies have cash value that could be borrowed against
- sources of nonwage income, such as unemployment, workers' compensation, a disability policy, or a retirement or pension plan
- unpaid notes, bills, and other evidence of your debts
- evidence of your major living expenses, such as rent receipts, and
- doctors' statements and other evidence of your medical problems.

The IRS is always impressed by paper, so lay it on.

Most Common Mistakes With IRS Offer Forms

According to the IRS, the most common errors taxpayers make when submitting an offer in compromise are:

- **Not including essential information on the OIC form.** Answer all questions; leave nothing blank. Use the most current forms. Call 800-829-1040 for the current forms, or download them from the IRS website.
- **Altering the form.** The IRS will not process an offer if you have altered or deleted any preprinted items.
- **Omitting signatures.** If you and your spouse are submitting an offer, you both must sign the form.

All of these mistakes are easily corrected; you can fix the problem and resubmit your offer. This will cause weeks or months of delays, however.

Bottom Line: Making an Offer the IRS Will Accept

There are no secrets here: Just complete the IRS offer forms with every last detail and pay strict attention to the advice given above in "How Much Should You Offer?" The IRS screens out most offers on technicalities—for not following the rules to a "T." After assisting clients with hundreds of offers over the years, I know just how much work it can be to run the numbers and get all the paperwork together, but there are no shortcuts.

It is very instructive to look at offers from the IRS's standpoint. The IRS weighs your offer against what it calls "reasonable collection potential" or RCP for short. Simply put, this means an amount determined by how much the IRS believes it could reasonably collect from your assets and future earnings. The limit on future earnings is set by the legal period of time left that the IRS has to collect—normally ten years from the date the taxes were assessed against you.

One important implication of the RCP approach—and this surprises many people: There is absolutely no relationship between the amount you owe the IRS and the amount the IRS will accept as an offer. For instance, if you owe $2 million and the IRS determines the RCP is extremely low, it might accept $2,500 and call it square. But if your RCP is very high, you have the assets and a promising earning future, the IRS might turn down a $1.9 million offer.

The Application Fee and Initial Payment

There is an application fee of $150 due with your offer, with one exception: You may request a waiver of the fee by completing Section 4 "Low Income Certification" of Form 656. If your monthly income is below the published standards for your family size, you could save the $150. The section is self-explanatory. Request the waiver by checking the box. If the IRS says "no," just send in the fee. The downside is that this will likely delay the processing of your offer.

Payment Option One—20% Down

If you propose to pay the offer in five payments or fewer within five months or under, you must send in a minimum of 20% of the offer with your forms.

> **EXAMPLE:** Apollo plans to offer $10,000 on his tax debt of $47,000. Apollo must send in $2,000 (20%) with the offer and agree to pay the balance within five months of acceptance of the offer by the IRS.

Payment Option Two—First Installment

If you're going to take longer than five months to pay, you must pay the first installment with the offer. And, you must also make all proposed payments while the offer is pending at the IRS. This could get expensive, considering the many months it takes the IRS to evaluate offers.

> EXAMPLE: Caesaria is making an offer of $12,000 on a $105,000 tax bill. She proposes to pay $500 per month for 24 months. Caesaria must send $500 (1/24 x $12,000) with her offer and pay $500 per month while the offer is being investigated by the IRS.

CAUTION

No refunds for prior payments. All payments to the IRS, including application fees, made before an offer is accepted or rejected by the IRS are non-refundable. However, offer payments (but not application fees) will go toward the tax bill balance.

Awaiting the IRS's Answer

If the IRS finds your offer defective (or nonprocessable, in IRS-speak), it will send your offer paperwork back to you. Simply make the corrections and refile. Don't get discouraged, as this is very common.

If the IRS deems your offer legitimate and processable, it usually takes between four and 18 months to review and investigate it and make a decision. You must continue to make payments under an existing installment agreement unless you get permission from the IRS to stop. When it's time to file your next return, do so or make sure you file an extension, and pay whatever taxes are due. Otherwise, the IRS can reject your OIC. If the IRS doesn't make a decision within 24 months, the offer is automatically accepted.

The IRS works in mysterious ways. Sometimes, offers to pay 5% of the tax bill are accepted, while 80% payment offers are turned down. Consider the following two cases.

> CASE 1: Leroy and Mary were in their late sixties and had filed for Chapter 7 bankruptcy (liquidation) several years before. Their income tax debts did not qualify for discharge, and they still owed the IRS $35,000. They retired and were living modestly on Social Security. The IRS collection notices and threats kept on coming. This was

particularly upsetting to Leroy, who had a bad heart. Their credit was bad and they couldn't get a loan from a bank.

Leroy and Mary submitted an offer in compromise to pay $3,500 cash, with a $700 deposit, which Mary's sister promised to give them. The IRS accepted their offer for processing and assigned it to an offer specialist, who contacted them. The couple emphasized to the offer specialist their frugality and Leroy's health problems. Almost a year later, they received a letter saying that the offer had been accepted. Leroy and Mary paid the IRS and the IRS released its $35,000 tax lien. A very happy ending.

CASE 2: Louis, 42, and Juanita, 39, owed the IRS $51,000 as a result of a failed business venture. Louis worked sporadically in the Merchant Marine and Juanita was a nursing home attendant. Together they earned $42,000 per year. An aggressive IRS revenue officer demanded payments of $1,500 per month. This was clearly impossible, as they had four children.

Louis and Juanita made an offer of $15,000 cash on Form 656. The IRS rejected the offer because Louis and Juanita had $59,000 of equity in a 401(k) plan. However, the IRS considered and agreed to a $400 per month payment plan.

If Your Offer Is Initially Rejected—Keep Trying

The IRS must give a written explanation if your offer is not accepted. The IRS usually rejects an offer in compromise:

- because the offer is too low, or
- for public policy reasons, which typically means that you are a notorious character—for example, you've been convicted of a serious crime.

If the offer is too low, the IRS letter will state what amount would be acceptable.

You should receive a copy of the report in the mail which lists the factors that caused the rejection. If they won't give it to you, make a request under the Freedom of Information Act. (See Chapter 4.)

After finding out why your offer was rejected, you can try again without a new 656 form if you resubmit it within 30 days. Write a letter upping your offer. For example, state that you will increase the cash offered from $10,000 to $15,000, or whatever is appropriate.

To submit a significantly different offer, complete another Form 656. The IRS offer specialist might help write your new offer.

> **TIP**
> **Looking at Offers in Compromise that were accepted might give you an idea of what kinds of proposals the IRS goes for.** Call the IRS at 800-829-1040 for an appointment to see offers that were accepted in your area. These are available to the public for one year, although not all personal details are revealed. You will have to go into an IRS office to view these documents.

Appealing a Rejected Offer in Compromise

If your offer in compromise is turned down, first, call whoever signed the letter and try to get that person to change his or her mind. If this doesn't work, you can formally appeal. (See Chapter 4 for information on how to appeal.) This administrative appeal goes to a division separate from the one that turned down your offer.

An appeal is your last chance; you cannot take the IRS to court for rejecting your offer.

An appeal begins with your letter following a format laid out by the IRS. Follow the letter in Chapter 4, "Protest Letter for Appeals Over $25,000 (Large Case)," but substitute the following for the first three paragraphs.

> *I wish to appeal the rejection of an offer in compromise submitted June 20, 2010, and rejected on January 7, 2011. I request a conference.*

The IRS must receive your appeal within 30 days of the date of the rejection letter. Otherwise, you have to submit a new and "improved" offer and appeal it if it's rejected. The IRS frowns on offers submitted within six months of the first rejection unless there's been a significant change of your circumstances or you offer substantially more.

An appeal will not be seriously considered unless all of the following are true:

- You furnished all of the data requested by the IRS during your offer processing.
- You have filed all past tax returns.
- You are current on your tax filings and payments for the present year. Self-employed people must have made all quarterly estimated tax payments; employers must have made all payroll tax filings and deposits for the current period and for two prior quarters.

My experience with appealing offers has been mixed. Sometimes, instead of forwarding cases to the appeals office, the IRS will reconsider and invite further negotiation. An appeal further delays the collection process—but interest and penalties keep accruing if you don't eventually make a deal.

Using the Bankruptcy Code to Stop the IRS

[The following section was written with the assistance of two bankruptcy experts: John Raymond, J.D., and Alan Rosenthal of the law offices of John Raymond, San Francisco, California.]

Filing a petition under the bankruptcy code can often reduce or erase tax debts. Alternatively, using bankruptcy can buy time and force a repayment plan on the IRS. Bankruptcy might be just the answer to your tax debt prayers.

 RESOURCE

For more information on bankruptcy, including recent changes to bankruptcy law, see Nolo's website at www.nolo.com and *The New Bankruptcy: Will It Work for You?* by Stephen Elias (Nolo); *How to File for Chapter 7 Bankruptcy,* by Stephen Elias, Albin Renauer, and Robin Leonard (Nolo); and *Chapter 13 Bankruptcy: Keep Your Property & Repay Debts Over Time,* by Stephen Elias and Robin Leonard (Nolo).

Types of Bankruptcy

Bankruptcy is a legal procedure for sorting out your debt problems, including your tax debts, by filing a petition in federal bankruptcy court. There are two basic types of bankruptcies:

- **Straight bankruptcy, or Chapter 7.** This is a liquidation of your debts, which can wipe out some or all of your income taxes.
- **Repayment plans, or Chapters 11, 12, or 13.** These allow you to pay your debts, including tax bills, over an extended period of time, often at pennies on the dollar.

The Automatic Stay

One of bankruptcy's most alluring features is a legal refuge called the automatic stay. The moment you file for bankruptcy, the automatic stay stops all creditors and bill collectors—including the taxman—cold.

The only way a creditor can collect while your bankruptcy case is open is to ask the bankruptcy judge to remove, or lift, the stay. The IRS rarely applies to have a stay lifted.

Downsides of Bankruptcy

There are several negatives to consider before deciding to take the plunge into bankruptcy.

Counseling Requirement

Before filing for bankruptcy, you must complete credit counseling with a government-approved agency. This doesn't stop an IRS action to collect.

Additional Time for IRS to Collect

If you go into bankruptcy and emerge still owing the IRS—meaning that not all of your taxes were erased in bankruptcy—the IRS gains extra time to collect the balance.

The IRS normally has *ten years* to collect tax bills, penalties, and interest from you. Once your bankruptcy case is over, the IRS gets whatever time remains on the original ten years to collect, plus the time your bankruptcy case was pending plus another 180 days.

Your Credit Rating and Tax Liens

A bankruptcy filing is a matter of public record and it usually remains on your credit record for ten years.

If the IRS or state taxing authority recorded a tax lien notice, the harm to your credit has already been done. A bankruptcy filing at least shows that you are making a positive effort to deal with your debt problem.

Taxes and Chapter 7 Bankruptcy

Not all tax debts can be wiped out in a Chapter 7 bankruptcy. For example, you must have filed the past four years' tax returns before filing for bankruptcy. You'll need to read some mind-bending rules to determine if bankruptcy can help you with your tax debt. (See the Nolo books listed at the beginning of this section.)

State Income Taxes and Bankruptcy

The bankruptcy code only talks about taxes—not just federal income taxes. But there are three areas of special concern with state taxes and bankruptcy.

First, some states send out interim, not final, notices of tax assessments. In California, for example, the final date for bankruptcy counting is no less than 60 days after the issuance of the proposed additional tax. The result is that the waiting time to discharge California state income taxes is 300 days from assessment, not 240 days.

Second, many states require a taxpayer to file an amended return after an IRS assessment based on audit or examination. The three-year rule is measured from when the original return was due, and the two-year rule from when it was filed.

Finally, state sales taxes are usually not dischargeable in Chapter 7 or Chapter 13, so they must be paid in full. In a few states, however, including Hawaii, California, and Illinois, unpaid sales taxes can be discharged the same as income taxes if they meet the 240-day, three-year, and two-year rules. Again, see a bankruptcy attorney in your state if this might be an issue.

Taxes That Can Be Wiped Out in Chapter 7 Bankruptcy

In Chapter 7 bankruptcy, the court can erase or discharge an individual or a married couple's taxes in certain circumstances.

Federal tax bills can be discharged in a Chapter 7 bankruptcy *only if all of the following are true.*

Taxes must be income taxes. Other taxes, such as most payroll taxes, Trust Fund Recovery Penalty, or fraud penalties, can never be eliminated in bankruptcy.

No fraud or willful evasion. You must not have filed a fraudulent tax return or otherwise willfully attempted to evade paying taxes. This usually applies only if you've been assessed a fraud penalty.

Three-year rule. The taxes were due at least three years before you file for bankruptcy. This usually means three years from April 15 of the year the return was due. But, if you filed a request for an extension, it could be October 15. If the 15th fell on a Saturday or Sunday, your return wasn't due until the following Monday. That is the date you start counting from for this rule.

Two-year rule. You actually filed all tax returns at least two years before filing the bankruptcy. Having the IRS file a substitute return for you doesn't count. If you don't file a tax return, you can never discharge the taxes you owe for that year in bankruptcy. You can, however, include the taxes in a repayment plan.

240-day rule. The income taxes were assessed by the IRS at least 240 days before you file your bankruptcy petition. Normally, this applies only if you've been audited within 240 days before the petition is filed.

If any of the following apply, you will have to add time to the three-year, two-year or 240-day rules for your debts to qualify for discharge in bankruptcy:

- **Prior bankruptcy.** If you filed a previous bankruptcy case, all three time periods—three years, two years, and 240 days—stopped running while you were in the prior bankruptcy case. You must add the length of your case plus 180 days to all three periods.
- **Offer in compromise.** An offer in compromise delays the 240-day rule by the period starting on the date the offer is made until the IRS

rejects it or you withdraw it, plus 30 days, plus any period for which an appeal is pending.

- **Tax court.** If you have a case pending before the U.S. Tax Court, the time rules are extended by 60 days after the case has been decided or dismissed.

 TIP

Before filing bankruptcy for tax debts, call the IRS to obtain a record of your filing dates. This is called an account transcript. Specify each tax year or other period on which you might owe. This free computer printout lists important tax dates—when the returns were filed, when the taxes were assessed, and the various dates of any tolling or time-extending events. Check the dates from the IRS transcript before filing bankruptcy. This is very important, so get it right.

Federal Tax Lien and Chapter 7

If your taxes qualify for discharge in a Chapter 7 bankruptcy case, you still may have a problem. This is because previously recorded tax liens are still on your record. A Chapter 7 discharge will wipe out only your personal obligation to pay the tax. *Any lien recorded before you file for bankruptcy survives the discharge to the extent your property has equity to which the lien can attach.*

After your bankruptcy is over, the IRS can seize many of the assets you owned at the time the bankruptcy was filed. (It may be possible to reduce the amount of the tax lien. See a bankruptcy attorney for more information.) Unless you owned real estate or have an IRA or a pension plan, the IRS lien probably won't harm you.

Taxes and Chapter 13 Bankruptcy

If you or your tax debts do not all qualify for Chapter 7, consider a Chapter 13 repayment plan. This can be the next-best solution to a tax bill problem.

RESOURCE

For more information on bankruptcy see the following resources:

- Nolo's website at www.nolo.com
- *The New Bankruptcy: Will It Work for You?* by Stephen Elias (Nolo)
- *How to File for Chapter 7 Bankruptcy*, by Stephen Elias, Albin Renauer, and Robin Leonard (Nolo), and
- *Chapter 13 Bankruptcy: Keep Your Property & Repay Debts Over Time*, by Stephen Elias and Robin Leonard (Nolo).

Basics of Chapter 13

Chapter 13 is the most widely used bankruptcy option for people with tax debts. In Chapter 13, you propose a payment plan for the bankruptcy court's approval. You make monthly payments to a court-appointed trustee, who divides up the money among your creditors, including the IRS. This repayment plan runs for five years.

Taxes Paid in a Chapter 13 Plan

Secured taxes—those for which a lien was recorded and you own property whose current value is equal to the tax lien—must be paid in full in a Chapter 13 case. Once you pay off your secured taxes in Chapter 13, the tax lien is satisfied. The lien no longer attaches to property you own or may acquire in the future.

Chapter 13 can still be beneficial, for many reasons, including:

- Chapter 13 forces a repayment plan on the IRS. The IRS cannot get anything more than the bankruptcy judge approves. The IRS cannot restart collection activities—seizures of your property or wages—as long as your Chapter 13 plan is underway. Chapter 13 is a way to get around an unreasonable revenue officer who won't agree to a fair installment agreement.
- Interest and penalties stop accruing the moment you file for Chapter 13, except on secured taxes. By contrast, with an IRS installment agreement (IA), the interest and late payment penalties continue to accrue. For example, if you owe $60,000 to the IRS and pay $1,000 a month, you'll still owe about $30,000 after five years under an IA. The same payment in a Chapter 13 plan will pay off the debt in full.

- Tax penalties may be paid at less than 100%. It is within the discretion of the bankruptcy judge.

Qualifying for Chapter 13 Bankruptcy

To file for Chapter 13 bankruptcy, much like Chapter 7, you must complete a rather imposing set of forms disclosing your assets, liabilities, income, and expenses and you must have filed all your tax returns for four years prior to filing. You must also submit a proposed payment plan to the court. See *Chapter 13 Bankruptcy: Keep Your Property & Repay Debts Over Time*, by Stephen Elias and Robin Leonard (Nolo), or consult a bankruptcy attorney before tackling the forms.

If you qualify under these rules, submit a Chapter 13 payment plan to the bankruptcy judge. The judge reviews your petition and appoints a trustee to oversee your case. The trustee holds a hearing in which your creditors can come and object to your plan. The IRS rarely ever contests a Chapter 13 plan—so don't worry.

The judge might make adjustments to the plan, but will normally approve it if the forms are right. You make 60 monthly payments to the trustee, who in turn pays your creditors on a pro rata basis.

Taxes and Chapter 11 Bankruptcy

Chapter 11 bankruptcy is primarily for troubled businesses. It gives businesses protection from their creditors while attempting to make a profit and reorganize their debts. Individuals can file for Chapter 11 bankruptcy, but it is rarely done.

Chapter 11s require the help of a knowledgeable (and expensive) bankruptcy attorney. Fees start upwards of $10,000. Chapter 11 bankruptcies may last many years. Eventually, the business either becomes healthy or fails. If it fails, the bankruptcy may be converted to a Chapter 7.

In a Chapter 11 bankruptcy, the automatic stay stops all IRS collection efforts, but interest continues to accrue. (By contrast, in Chapter 13, interest usually stops accruing on your tax bills.)

Taxes and Chapter 12 Bankruptcy

Chapter 12 bankruptcy is for debts arising from the operation of a family farm. Its rules are similar to Chapter 13 but there are some differences not discussed here.

Protecting Your Assets From the IRS

It is illegal to transfer assets to defeat the IRS once it has started trying to collect a tax debt. It is possible to protect some assets through entities or family members. The key is advance planning and timing the transfers.

Before moving your property beyond the reach of the IRS, consider the following:

- Once you legally transfer ownership, it may be very difficult, if not impossible, to get it back.
- Asset protection strategies are not foolproof—the IRS has legal powers to challenge a transfer and recover the asset.

SEE AN EXPERT

Protect yourself. See an attorney to make sure you do a transfer legally and do not commit fraud on the IRS or any other creditors.

Listed here are a few of the most common ways people *attempt* to protect their assets from their creditors, including the IRS.

Transfer assets to a corporation with a friendly owner. You can also work for a corporation owned by your spouse or child. If you keep the salary low, you may be able to negotiate an IRS installment agreement that you can live with. The IRS could seize corporate assets if it deems the corporation a sham, but it seldom does so.

Put assets into a family limited partnership. See an attorney if this sounds promising. Don't simply put property into joint tenancy with family members—that won't stop the IRS.

Transfer assets to a trust for a spouse or other family members. A children's trust, for example, can own assets used in your business. Again, see an attorney. Putting property into a revocable living trust won't offer any protection, because you maintain control over the asset. And the IRS considers the use of offshore trusts very suspiciously.

Put life insurance policies into an insurance trust. This generally safeguards them from IRS seizures if done in advance of tax problems.

Fully fund your retirement plans and 401(k) accounts. The IRS can legally take non-ERISA qualified plans, but IRS policy discourages it. You can borrow from a 401(k) plan to reduce the amount that could be seized by the IRS. This is your safest bet.

Transfer assets to family members outright. If you are going to leave property to your children on your death, and you fear a future IRS tax bill, this might be a way to save the property from the IRS.

File separate tax returns. Married couples who file jointly and owe the IRS have their refunds automatically grabbed by the IRS. One way to get around this may be to file separate tax returns if only one spouse owes the IRS. If you reside in a community property state, however, this may not work.

Tax Debtors Abroad

How far does the reach of the tax collector extend? Many countries have treaties with the IRS allowing them to collect U.S. taxes due from our taxpayers on their soil. As a practical matter, even our strongest allies don't pursue our tax deadbeats. You may be able to beat the IRS by leaving the country and taking all of your property with you. And you may have to stay away permanently, as the IRS computer is linked to the U.S. Citizenship and Immigration Services computer. And, one more thing: The ten-year statute of limitations on collections is suspended while you're out of the country and for 180 days after your return.

There are also ways to protect your assets by sophisticated estate planning devices. See an attorney if you want to learn more.

Suspending Collection of Your Tax Bill

If your prospects are bleak—no job, little or no money, and pressing creditors—ask an IRS collector to "53" your case. If the collector agrees, he or she recommends that your tax account balance be classified as "currently not collectible."

The collector then fills in IRS Form 53. If approved, it is entered into the IRS computer. Once you're declared a 53, you shouldn't hear from the IRS again for six months or longer. The IRS stops bothering you, but interest (and late payment penalties) still accrue. At the end of your 53 grace period, the computer brings your account back up and the process starts over again.

The IRS doesn't grant 53 status lightly. A collector may agree to 53 your account over the telephone, but first you may be required to submit one or more of the 433 series forms showing your assets, liabilities, income, and expenses. The IRS may want other documentation, too, such as doctors' statements showing you are disabled and cannot work.

Being classified as currently not collectible doesn't solve your IRS problem. It only gives you more time for dealing with it.

> **TIP**
> **The 53 process buys time.** It can be helpful if you're hoping to beat the IRS by filing for bankruptcy or waiting out the ten-year collection statute. Even when your debt is in 53 status, IRS time limits for collecting are running in your favor.

Suing the IRS

A taxpayer may sue the IRS for up to $1 million if an IRS collector willfully disregards the law. For example, the collector seizes your assets after you filed for bankruptcy, or the IRS seizes your home without a court order. Be aware that taxpayers rarely win lawsuits against the IRS, and not many lawyers are willing to take IRS cases on a contingency basis.

> **RESOURCE**
> **For further information, consult the following resources:**
> - IRS Publication 908, *Bankruptcy Tax Guide*
> - IRS Publication 594, *The IRS Collection Process*
> - Taxattorneydaily.com (my website).

Chapter Highlights

- The IRS has far greater powers than any other bill collector. It can take your wages, bank accounts, and other property (with a few exceptions).
- The IRS collection process starts with computerized form letters. If you can't pay, request more time.
- Avoid giving bank account and employment information to the IRS. If you don't want to deal with the IRS over the phone, request that your file be sent to the local IRS office so you can meet with a tax collector.
- Treat a collector with respect, but remember—you have rights. Read IRS Publication 1. (See Chapter 15.)
- Never lie to the IRS about your assets or anything else. It is a crime. Keeping silent is okay.
- Carefully prepare your financial information before speaking with the tax collector. Don't understate your living expenses.
- If you can't pay your taxes all at once, propose a monthly payment plan. Interest and penalties keep accruing until you pay in full.
- It is possible, but never easy, to reduce your tax debts through a formal Offer in Compromise.
- Bankruptcy can wipe out tax debts or allow you to pay over time without interest and penalties mounting.
- If you are in dire financial straits, ask the IRS to temporarily suspend collection for hardship.

IRS Enforced Collection: Liens and Levies

f you don't deal with the IRS using any of the options discussed in Chapter 6, "When You Owe the IRS," you are likely to face IRS enforced collection measures. These are the IRS's awesome lien and levy powers.

The average IRS levy (seizure) brings in about $1,600, mostly from bank accounts or wages. And, just because it happens to you once is no reason to believe it won't happen again—and again—until the debt is paid in full.

Federal Tax Liens

Whenever you owe taxes to the U.S. Treasury and don't pay, a claim against you by the federal government arises by law. (Internal Revenue Code § 6321.) This claim is called a tax lien. The existence of the government's claim is not public information—at least initially—and so it is sometimes called a "secret" or "statutory" or an "automatic" lien.

The tax lien automatically attaches to just about everything you own or have a right in. If you owe interest and penalties on the tax, which is often the case, the lien covers these additions too.

States may also have tax lien rights; those aren't covered in this book.

Notice of Federal Tax Lien

If the IRS sends you a valid tax bill and you don't pay it, you may receive a written demand to pay. This paper is called a CP-501 notice, referring to the IRS number on the right-hand corner. If you don't pay within 30 days and owe at least $10,000, the IRS may file a notice in the public records showing your tax debt. This paper is officially called a Notice of Federal Tax Lien. The IRS typically files over one million notices each year in the county and/ or state public records offices where debtors live, work, or own real estate. Most filed tax liens are for amounts over $25,000. In the few states without county recording systems, the IRS sends the Notice of Federal Tax Lien to the secretary of state's office. The state or county fee for recording the tax lien is paid by the IRS and added to your bill.

The IRS does not check first to see if you actually own anything before recording the lien notice. It has no reason to. Even if you don't own property now, you might later and the IRS gets first dibs on the proceeds from its sale or financing.

EXAMPLE: Joyce owes the IRS and lives in Orange County with her Aunt Mildred. The IRS records a Notice of Federal Tax Lien at the county recorder's office, even though Joyce owns no real estate. Aunt Mildred dies and leaves her home to Joyce. The IRS's lien now attaches to the house. Joyce won't be able to sell the house with a clear title without first paying off the IRS. And Joyce won't get rid of the lien by getting rid of the property. Any buyer takes the property with the IRS lien on it. And the IRS then has two sources of collection—Joyce and the property held by the buyer.

Effect of a Recorded Notice of Federal Tax Lien

Just as a recorded mortgage tells anyone who searches the public records or pulls your credit report that you owe on your home, a Notice of Federal Tax Lien shows the world that you owe the IRS.

A recorded tax lien scares off buyers and potential creditors or lenders, making it difficult for you to refinance or get loans. Tax lien notices are picked up by credit reporting agencies, such as Experian, Equifax, and TransUnion.

RESOURCE

There's a lot of helpful credit information. For information on credit ratings and rebuilding your credit after a financial setback, including owing the IRS and many other debt and credit issues, see *Solve Your Money Troubles: Debt, Credit & Bankruptcy,* or *Credit Repair,* both by Robin Leonard (Nolo).

Neutralizing a Recorded Federal Tax Lien

Keep in mind that the automatic, secret, or statutory tax lien and a recorded Notice of Federal Tax Lien are two distinct things.

You can't escape a valid automatic tax lien without (a) paying the tax, interest, and penalties owed, (b) eliminating it in bankruptcy, (c) reducing and paying it through an offer in compromise, or (d) having the time limit for collections run. An automatic tax lien will not appear in any public record, such as a county recorder's office. Hence, it's sometimes called a silent or secret tax lien.

A recorded Notice of Federal Tax Lien tells the world your secret. The best way to get rid of it is to get an IRS Certificate of Release of Federal Tax Lien. The IRS will issue a Certificate of Release if you fully pay the tax owed, discharge it in bankruptcy, or pay it through an offer in compromise or if the time limit for IRS collections has run out.

The IRS will *not* reduce the original amount shown on a tax lien as you make payments. So, if the lien starts out at $100,000 and you pay it down to $1,000, the lien will show as $100,000 until the last penny is paid. Only then will the IRS issue the Certificate of Release.

When the tax is paid in full, eliminated, or reduced and paid through an offer in compromise or bankruptcy or the time for collections has lapsed, the IRS must issue the Certificate of Release (Form 668Z) within 30 days. Once you get the Certificate of Release, you should record it (if the IRS doesn't) and pay the recording fee in the counties where the IRS filed the lien. Also send a copy to the major credit reporting agencies to make sure it gets into your file.

Unfortunately, the original recorded IRS lien notice is not erased by the lien release. Credit bureaus can and do report the original lien—and the release—as long as ten years after the recording.

New IRS "Fresh Start" Tax Lien Rules

In 2011, the IRS said it was going to file fewer tax liens to make it easier for some tax debtors to maintain their credit ratings and their ability to borrow money. This is somewhat welcome news to struggling small business owners. The highlights include:

- The IRS will no longer file tax liens if the amount owed is less than $10,000.
- The IRS will grant lien withdrawals if the balance owed is less than $25,000 and an installment payment plan is in effect.
- Tax debtors can get up to 24 months to pay installments on debts of $25,000 or less more easily than in the past.

The IRS says the new rules, dubbed "Fresh Start," will reduce tax lien filings by "tens of thousands" but declined to be more specific.

> TIP
> **You can appeal a tax lien filing.** IRS tax lien filings can be contested in the IRS Appeals Office. For details, see the discussion in "Dealing With the IRS Levy Process" and Chapter 4 on appealing IRS decisions.

If the IRS Records a Tax Lien

Legally, the IRS must notify you in writing and give you a chance to pay or try to prevent the lien from being recorded before sending the notice to the public records offices. But if you've moved or the notice is lost in the mail, you may never get the warning and only learn of it when you apply for credit or a loan—and are turned down.

Below is a flowchart from the *Internal Revenue Manual* instructing IRS personnel when to file a Notice of Federal Tax Lien. The IRS does not always file tax lien notices. It's hit or miss.

You can appeal an IRS tax lien notice filing to the IRS Appeals Office. First request a telephone conference with the manager of the IRS unit filing the lien. If the manager turns you down, fax or mail a completed Form 9423, *Collection Appeal Request*, to the collection office. (A copy with instructions is at the IRS website, www.irs.gov.)

The appeal request is usually decided within five business days. The appeals officer looks at whether the collectors followed correct procedures and considers the facts and circumstances of your case. The officer should telephone you, so list your work and home telephone numbers in your letter. Most taxpayers lose.

Avoiding or Eliminating a Tax Lien

A recorded tax lien can be the kiss of death on your credit rating. It may effectively prevent you from selling or refinancing real estate. It won't, however affect your right to sell personal property, such as a motor vehicle, boat, or furnishings.

As discussed in Chapter 6, the best way to deal with a tax lien is to avoid one in the first place.

IRS Personnel Criteria Used in Deciding Whether or Not to File a Notice of Federal Tax Lien

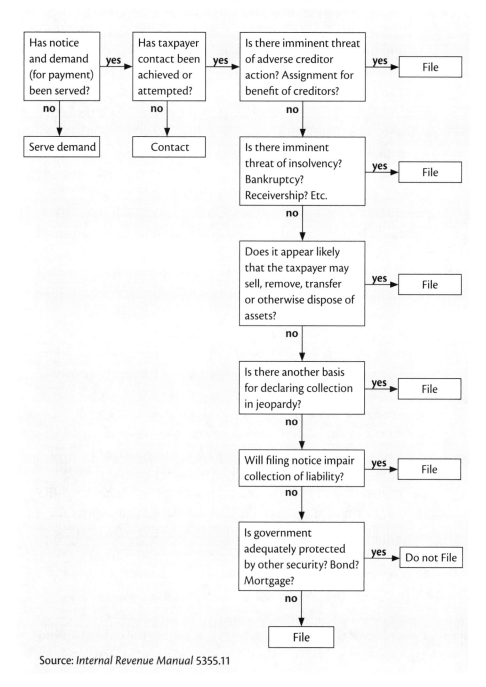

Source: *Internal Revenue Manual* 5355.11

For some, a tax lien is just one more black mark on their credit report and won't make it much worse. You should respond to an IRS letter threatening a lien filing by contacting the IRS at the telephone number on the letter, or calling 800-829-1040, or calling the Taxpayer Advocate Service. Be ready to convince the IRS that you fall into the category "Will filing notice impair collection of the tax liability?" Point out that a tax lien will kill your chance of getting a bank loan, for example.

If you tried but failed to convince the IRS to forgo recording a tax lien, here are your options after the lien notice has been filed:

- **Appeal the lien filing.** The IRS has five business days after filing the lien to provide written notice to the taxpayer. This must include notice of the right to request a hearing within 30 days from the sixth day after the lien filing. If you win the appeal, the lien will be withdrawn; unfortunately, the fact of the lien filing will still appear on your credit report. (Internal Revenue Code § 6320.)

- **Pay in full.** If you don't have the funds, can you borrow from friends or relatives? It is better to owe just about anyone other than the IRS. The IRS must record a release within 30 days of full payment, but often the agency doesn't follow through. Call the IRS Centralized Lien Processing Office at 800-913-6050 to verify the release was filed. Or, obtain a copy of your credit report. If it's still in the report, call the Taxpayer Advocate Service for fastest service. (See Chapter 8.)

- **Request a partial discharge.** If you own several assets that are encumbered by the tax lien and want to use one to pay off the IRS, ask for a discharge from the tax lien. The IRS will likely do this.

- **Direct debit agreement.** If you get an installment plan and the IRS takes payments directly from your bank account, you can ask the IRS to withdraw any filed tax lien. The IRS may not go along with this, but it doesn't hurt to ask. (See Internal Revenue Code § 6320.)

CAUTION

Bankruptcy doesn't wipe out a recorded tax lien. If your tax debts qualify for a discharge under any chapter of bankruptcy, the lien will remain, although your personal liability is wiped out. If you owned any real estate going into bankruptcy, it is still subject to the tax lien. The IRS could seize that property after your bankruptcy is over. Or, the more likely scenario is that the IRS would allow you to pay over the value of the property rather than seizing it. And, in some cases, the IRS never tries to enforce the lien after bankruptcy—it is hit or miss. (See a bankruptcy attorney for an analysis of your situation.)

When the IRS Files a Tax Lien in Error

The IRS occasionally files a tax lien notice in the public records when you don't owe anything. For example, you paid the bill but the IRS did not properly credit your account. Under the Taxpayer Bill of Rights you are entitled to a Certificate of Release stating that the lien was filed in error. Contact the IRS lien center at 800-913-6050 as soon as possible.

Send photocopies of the release to the big three credit bureaus—Experian, TransUnion, and Equifax. Call to find out where to send the copies of the release to minimize the damage to your credit rating caused by the IRS error.

Getting a Tax Lien Withdrawn

The IRS must issue a formal Certificate of Release of Lien within 30 days after either of the following:

- The taxes are fully paid, discharged in bankruptcy, or satisfied through an offer in compromise.
- The lien becomes unenforceable because the statute of limitations for collections has run—usually ten years after the tax was first due (Internal Revenue Code § 6325(a)). See prior section regarding liens filed in error. The lien eventually will become uncollectible after the ten year statute of limitations on collection runs. However, a tax lien on real estate "secured property" never expires.

If 30 days pass and no release has yet been issued (not uncommon), then write or call the IRS Centralized Lien Processing, P.O. Box 145595, Stop 8420G, Cincinnati, Ohio 45250-5595; 800-913-6050. Give the date of your request and your name, Social Security number, employer identification number, address, telephone number with the best time to reach you and tell why the lien should be released (such as the taxes were paid, the lien was filed in error, or the statute of limitations has run). Enclose a copy of the tax lien you want released. If you paid the tax, also enclose a copy of an IRS written acknowledgment of payment, an IRS transcript showing payment, or a canceled check.

For emergencies (such as a mortgage loan closing held up by the tax lien), call the Taxpayer Advocate Service. If there is a balance due and you need quick action, be prepared to pay with a certified check, cashier's check, or money order. Alternatively, the IRS should agree to accept payment out of the proceeds of the real estate escrow.

Suing the IRS for Wrongful Collection Actions

It is possible to sue the IRS in U.S. District Court for damages if it fails to release a tax lien or takes unauthorized collection actions. (Internal Revenue Code § 7430; IRS Regulation 1.7430.) To win in court, you must prove that you suffered direct economic damages from the IRS's actions. Before suing, you must first try to solve the problem using channels within the IRS. Your litigation costs are recoverable, too, but not any costs of fighting the IRS before you filed the suit.

Don't get too excited about suing the IRS. The law makes it tough to prove your case or to recover any big money. And judges are reluctant to award attorneys' fees and costs even when you win. Very few lawyers are willing to take this kind of case on a contingency basis (in which the fee is a percentage of the amount recovered).

Tax Levies

Recorded tax liens are just notices to the world that an individual or a business owes the IRS. No money or other assets are taken by the filing of a Notice of Federal Lien. Instead, the IRS collects by seizing your real or personal property through the *levy* process. Typically, levies are made on financial accounts held for you by others—such as a bank, a stockbroker, or an employer. Although the IRS usually records a tax lien before levying on assets, it does not have to. The IRS makes about four million levies per year.

Significance of a Tax Levy

Most levy notices issued by the IRS are computer generated. Some notices are mistakes and not that hard to straighten out if you contact the IRS quickly. The vast majority of levy notices are issued to tax debtors' financial institutions and employers. The rest are usually for seizures of vehicles, business equipment, and miscellaneous property. With few exceptions, anything you own—wholly, partially, or jointly with others—may be seized and sold to satisfy your tax debts.

The likelihood that the IRS will seize your assets depends on factors such as your previous history of payments—good or bad—and where you live. For some unknown reason, a delinquent taxpayer in Los Angeles is six times more likely to suffer a levy than a similar taxpayer in Chicago. About 3% of all taxes owed to the government are collected by levy. The IRS files about three million notices of levies each year.

Dealing With the IRS Levy Process

The IRS can levy on a person's assets *only* if it follows strict legal rules (Internal Revenue Code §§ 6330 and 6331):

- Before the IRS can seize your money or personal property, it must serve a written *Notice of Intent to Levy.* This is done by certified mail to your last known address in the IRS computer files, or the notice must be left at your home or handed to you.

- The levy notice must be accompanied by a letter explaining your appeal rights. The law provides an opportunity for a IRS Levy Process by an IRS appeals officer before the levy takes place. (See Chapter 4 for the appeals procedure.) This gives you a chance to buy some time. If the Appeals Office turns you down, you may take your case to the tax court or even federal district court. Few folks go the court route because of the legal fees and the small chance of success. However, going to court will delay the levy process for many months. See a tax attorney if this sounds promising.

- The intent to levy notice must be given at least 30 days before any seizure is made with one rare exception, called a "jeopardy levy."

(Internal Revenue Code § 7429.) (See Chapter 3 for more on jeopardy assessments.)

If the IRS doesn't follow the rules, you are entitled to a return of any assets seized. (Internal Revenue Code § 6343).

Assets the IRS Can't or Won't Seize

Not everything you own can or will likely be taken by the IRS levy machine. Some items are exempt by law, and others are protected by IRS policy considerations.

Exempt Assets

It should raise your spirits to find out that the IRS cannot use its levy power to seize everything you own. (Internal Revenue Code § 6334.) Don't get carried away, however, as the list of items the IRS can't take is hardly generous. The exemption list covers tax debtors and their dependents, and subject to annual cost of living adjustment, includes:

- wearing apparel and school books. This doesn't include luxury wear, like a sable jacket, but your cloth coats should be safe.
- fuel, provisions, furniture, and personal effects to $7,700. Livestock is included if you are a farmer.
- books and tools of a trade, business, or profession up to $3,860
- 85% of unemployment benefits
- undelivered mail (no one knows quite what this means)
- Railroad Retirement Act and Congressional Medal of Honor benefits
- workers' compensation benefits
- court-ordered child support
- minimum exemption amount for wages, salary, and other income
- certain service-connected disability payments
- most public assistance payments, such as welfare and SSI, and
- assistance under federal job training partnerships.

Vehicles are generally not considered "personal effects" or "tools of the trade" and are not exempt or partially exempt from levy. However, you can often convince an IRS collector that the vehicle is necessary for your employment and it won't be levied.

Assets of Last Resort That the IRS Can Seize

The IRS can seize anything not listed above; however, IRS policies discourage collectors from taking certain items. Retirement plans and homes are generally off limits. Vehicles needed for work are generally not seized if you can demonstrate there is a necessity for the vehicle.

Retirement Accounts

The IRS can take your Keogh, 401(k), IRA, or SEP. With an ERISA plan, however, the IRS can only grab it if it is vested—that is, if you have the immediate right to take the benefits. In that case, you will be taxed when it's levied by the IRS but do not have to pay any penalty for early withdrawal.

In the case of hardship, the IRS can be stopped from taking retirement plans. Contact the Taxpayer Advocate Service immediately and plead that this will create "a significant and undue economic hardship" on you and your family. You may have to enter into a payment plan with the IRS in order to protect your retirement account from levy.

 CAUTION
Social Security and other federal payments aren't safe. The IRS can legally seize 15% of Social Security payments. First, the IRS must serve a *Notice of Intent to Levy* (form letter IRS CP-91 or CP-298). In extreme circumstances, the IRS is allowed to levy 100% of Social Security benefits, but, thankfully, it rarely does. (Internal Revenue Code § 6331(a).)

Primary Residences

As a last resort for dealing with an uncooperative taxpayer, the IRS can take a personal residence, mobile home, boat, or any other place you call home if you owe more than $5,000. (Internal Revenue Code § 6334.) For married couples, if only one spouse owes the IRS, the other may be able to stop the seizure.

Seizing your primary residence requires a court order. If the IRS threatens to do so, contact the Taxpayer Advocate Service immediately. Offer to make arrangements to pay the taxes owed. A second home or vacation place, however, can be levied without a court order.

If all else fails and you are about to lose your pension plan or house, call your Congressperson. A sympathetic staff person, or even the representative, may persuade the IRS to back off. Again, expect to negotiate a payment arrangement in return for keeping your house or retirement plan.

You and Your Spouse's Income

The tax code allows the IRS to take some—but not all—of your wages or other income. If your income is fairly low or you have several mouths to feed, all of your earnings may be exempt from levy. In most parts of the country, you would be hard pressed to live on the paltry amount the law allows you to keep from the levy.

A portion of each paycheck or independent contractor payment you receive is exempt from IRS levy. The amount you get to keep is determined by the tax code. It is based on the number of exemptions you (and your spouse) can claim on your tax return, plus your standard deduction. (See table in IRS Publication 1494.) The amounts exempt from IRS seizures are subject to annual revisions.

> **EXAMPLE:** In 2012, Ben earns $26,000 as a baker for Acme. He and his wife, Bonnie, owe the IRS $32,000 in back income taxes. If the IRS levies Ben's wages, Ben, Bonnie, and their two kids are allowed $438 per week exempt from IRS wage levy.
>
> All amounts paid to Ben over $438 per week (after income tax and payroll deductions) go to the IRS. If Bonnie also worked, the IRS could take *all* of her net income for their joint tax debt.

Claiming the Wage Exemption

If you claim only yourself—and not a spouse or dependents—you get the one exemption automatically. Otherwise, you must file a claim for additional exemptions for others that you support.

To seize part of your wages, the IRS sends a levy notice to your employer or to anyone the IRS suspects is paying you for services as an independent contractor. The recipient of the notice must immediately give you a copy of the notice by law.

On the back of the notice is a simple form you must complete to claim the exemption amount to which you are entitled. List your spouse and dependents, date and sign the form, and immediately take it to the IRS office that issued it. After three days, your employer or the business that owed you money as an independent contractor must pay the IRS any nonexempt money owed to you. If the employer or business doesn't, it is liable to the IRS for any money paid you above the exemption.

 CAUTION
You only have three days to get the exemption claim form back to the IRS. If you don't, the IRS grants only one exemption, no matter how many you are entitled to by law.

Defending Against a Wage Levy

Once a levy on your income takes effect, it remains in force for as long as *all* of the following are true:
- Any part of the tax debt is unpaid.
- The statute of limitations on collections hasn't run out.
- You still work for the same employer.

How to stop or minimize a wage levy:
- Negotiate with the IRS to release the levy, for example by proposing an installment payment plan or asking for time to sell an asset.
- File an Offer in Compromise. This doesn't automatically stop a wage levy, but the IRS should hold off unless it concludes your offer is just a stalling tactic.
- Change employers or temporarily quit your job. Neither you nor your employer must inform the IRS if you quit. The IRS must hunt you down at your new employment, which could take months. If you quit and are rehired after a month or two, the wage levy is no longer effective as long as your employer notified the IRS that you quit.
- File for bankruptcy. This automatically stops a wage levy, but don't do it without considering all of the ramifications.
- Contact the Taxpayer Advocate Service and ask for hardship relief. See Chapter 8.

- Reduce your income to the exemption amount. A friendly employer, especially if you work in a family business, may let you cut back your hours temporarily. But if you keep working full-time while your boss holds back all wages over the exemption amount, your employer could later be forced to pay it to the IRS.

Jointly Owned Assets

The IRS can legally seize assets owned jointly by a tax debtor and a person who doesn't owe anything. But the nondebtor must be compensated by the IRS, meaning that the co-owner must be paid out of the proceeds of any sale.

If, however, you owe taxes and add a co-owner to an asset—without that person paying you fair consideration—the IRS can ignore the interest of the new owner. This is called a fraudulent transfer.

> EXAMPLE: Rudolph owns a vacant lot worth $25,000. He sells a one-half interest in it to his sister, Wilma, for $10. The IRS could seize the lot and sell it to pay off Rudoph's taxes, ignoring Wilma's ownership because she did not pay a fair price. Wilma might get her $10 back, though.

Avoiding a Levy

There are several ways that you might be able to avoid an IRS seizure of your assets, or at least slow an IRS collector down.

Transfer Your Assets

Under certain circumstances, you may be able to transfer ownership of property or assets—sell, give away, or a combination of the two—and avoid losing it to the IRS.

For the transfer to withstand later IRS attack, you must have conveyed your assets before the IRS issued a Notice of Intent to Levy. However, there are two "gotchas" that can defeat asset transfers, as described below.

Transferee Liability

Tax debtors sometimes try to defeat the IRS by transferring assets to family members or partnerships, trusts, or corporations for free or a bargain price. While this slows the IRS down, it may backfire. The recipient of the assets is called your "nominee." Nominees are not protected from IRS seizure—the tax debt attaches to the asset in their hand.

An IRS attorney determines if the transfer was legitimate. Bottom line: A nominee gives the IRS an additional person to pursue while you remain primarily responsible for the tax debt. Also, the IRS can charge transferors with a crime under certain circumstances. (See Chapter 10 and below.)

> **EXAMPLE:** Hank, who owes the IRS $75,000, gives his $80,000 rental building to his best friend Penn. The IRS can ignore the transfer and seize and sell the property.

The IRS doesn't always discover asset transfers made for less than full value, especially if they are made before the tax was assessed. For instance, someone under audit, fearing that a big bill is coming, might consider getting property out of his or her name.

Joint Ownership

The IRS can, but is less likely to, seize an asset when there is another owner besides the tax debtor. The IRS must compensate the other owner for his or her share—but only if that owner can show that he or she paid full value for that share. Just putting someone else's name as a co-owner of the asset is not enough.

A better alternative to giving an asset away is to sell it for full value to a friend or relative, with no down payment, taking back a promissory note. Secure the note with the property, which gives you the right to reclaim it if full payment is not made. Once the IRS is at bay, you can get the asset back.

> **EXAMPLE:** Hank sells one-half of his rental building to Penn in exchange for a promissory note of $40,000, the fair market value of a 50% interest. Hank owes the IRS back taxes of $75,000. The IRS doesn't like to be in the real estate business and isn't likely to seize the building, especially if Hank agrees to a payment plan or makes

some other financial guarantee. Of course, the IRS can claim any cash proceeds Hank receives from the sale.

⚠ **CAUTION**

Transfers made for no other reason than to deliberately evade IRS collection are fraudulent. Conveyances may be ignored by the IRS or set aside by a federal court. Before transferring assets, see a lawyer Make sure the transfer is legally effective—use a valid deed, for example. If you make a transfer after the levy process has begun, you might be charged with attempting to evade payment of taxes by deliberately placing assets beyond the government's reach. (*U.S. v. Mal*, 942 F. 2d 682 (9th Cir. 1991).)

Convince the IRS That a Levy Would Be Uneconomical

If you can convince the IRS that the levy of a certain item would be uneconomical, the IRS may back off. Show that the expenses of the levy and sale would exceed the fair market value of the item. (Internal Revenue Code §§ 6334(e) and 6331(f).) This is termed a no-equity seizure and is against IRS policy.

> EXAMPLE: Felice owes the IRS $10,000 and her primary asset is a nonrunning vehicle, which she is going to fix when she can afford the parts. Right now, the car is worth no more than $250. It would probably cost the IRS more than $250 to send a wrecker to tow the car, pay for storage, and then advertise the sale in the newspaper. The IRS backs off.

Show That the Levy Would Prevent You From Working

If the item targeted by the IRS for levy is essential for your work or to get to your job, tell the collector that it is exempt property. If the collector doesn't agree, ask for an accelerated appeals process to determine whether or not the asset is exempt. (Internal Revenue Code § 6343(2).)

> EXAMPLE: Arnold, a farmer, owes the IRS $43,000. One of his major assets is his pickup truck, which is absolutely essential for running his farm. Arnold convinces the IRS collector not to take his truck.

Keep Mum About Your Assets

Unless the IRS issues a summons—a legal order to produce documents or appear at an IRS office—you don't have to reveal the existence or location of your assets. It is perfectly legal not to give information to the IRS or to ask to speak with a tax professional before answering any questions. Although the IRS may already know about your local real estate holdings from searching public records, it may not know about property in other states, or in the name of an entity or another person. But remember, it is a felony to lie to the IRS.

Keep Assets Out of Sight

It is illegal to actively conceal assets from an IRS collector. Rarely, however, is an ordinary citizen pursued for keeping a classic '57 Chevy in a friend's garage. Nevertheless, particularly if you are a known tax protestor or crime figure, don't try this without first getting some legal advice.

Keep moveable items away from your home or business premises. The IRS won't know where to look for vehicles, boats, and similar assets if they're not located where the IRS expects them. Similarly, assets located outside the state or country can be quite difficult for the IRS to discover.

Sell Your Assets

If it is inevitable that the IRS is going to grab things, don't wait for the levy. If possible, sell your real estate, your yacht, airplane, or whatever else, yourself. An IRS levy followed by a so-called "forced sale" typically results in a (way) below fair market sale price. Plus the IRS will tack onto your bill various fees and costs of the forced sale

Move Financial Accounts

There is nothing illegal about moving bank accounts whenever you owe a tax bill. In fact, it is an excellent self-protection move. The IRS is not automatically notified of taxpayers' financial accounts—except once a year on interest-bearing accounts when the institution must issue a Form 1099.

Nor are IRS computers linked to financial institutions. (See Chapter 6 for more information on revealing financials to the IRS.)

Rent, Don't Own

If you lease property—real estate, vehicles, furniture, or equipment—you aren't the legal owner. The IRS can't seize items you don't own, unless you have built up equity, or an ownership interest, in a leased asset. For most items, such as a rented auto, you won't have any equity or it will be too small for the IRS to consider. But if you have a lease-purchase option for real estate or business equipment, you may be building up equity—and provide a target for IRS collectors.

Deposit Money Into Retirement Accounts

IRS policy discourages (but doesn't forbid) tax collectors from seizing retirement plan funds. Exceptionally uncooperative taxpayers are the ones at risk. So, if you owe a lot to the IRS and the levy process hasn't yet begun, consider fully funding your retirement plan with unprotected moneys.

File for Bankruptcy

Filing for any type of bankruptcy—Chapter 7, 11, 12, or 13—stops all IRS enforced collection actions. (See Chapter 6.) The relief from the tax collector is often only temporary, so use this time to work things out with the IRS while keeping your assets intact.

Use Safe Deposit Boxes

Banks require your Social Security number to open a safety deposit box. IRS collectors will canvass the banks in your area to see if there's a box in your name. If the box is out of state or in the name of your entity, such as a corporation or an LLC, with its own tax ID number, the IRS may never locate it. To enhance your privacy, open the box at a bank where you have no accounts and pay the annual box rental in cash.

> CAUTION
> **Don't lie to the IRS.** Silence is golden but it is illegal to actively conceal assets from the IRS. If in doubt, consult a tax attorney.

Getting a Tax Levy Released

It is not easy getting anything back from the IRS once it has been seized if you owe taxes. If the property taken is a bank account or another liquid asset, it may be nearly impossible.

Assets such as vehicles or business equipment may be returned when any of the following are true:

- The taxes for which the levy was made have been paid in full or through an Offer in Compromise or discharged in bankruptcy.
- The time limit for collections has expired—normally ten years from the date of assessment (see Chapter 6).
- The IRS believes the release of the levy will facilitate collection of the tax debt.
- You enter into an installment payment agreement.
- The IRS is persuaded that the levy creates a financial hardship on you or your dependents.

(Internal Revenue Code §§ 6331(e) and 6332(c).)

Argue that your situation fits into one of these categories, typically the financial hardship one. For example, you could argue that the seized item, such as an old car, has little value *and* seizing it causes a hardship in your search for employment.

Begin by calling the IRS officer who signed the levy notice. Request an immediate release based on one of the above grounds. If the officer balks, ask for an appointment with his or her manager—within a day or two. To get your property returned, you will probably have to:

- **Pay the IRS in full.** Borrow on credit cards, take a home equity loan, or ask Uncle Mack.
- **Request a short reprieve—some more time to pay in full.** Explain how you expect to raise the money—a bank loan, selling other assets, or whatever. If your plan sounds reasonable, the IRS may go for it. Do your utmost to follow through.

- **Propose an installment agreement.** The IRS will usually agree to one as long as you propose reasonable payments, don't have a past record of defaulting on another installment agreement with the IRS (see Chapter 6), and are current in your tax form filings.
- **Submit an offer in compromise.** If the officer believes you are sincere and that your offer has a shot at being accepted, he or she may release the levy.
- **Cry hardship.** The IRS must release a levy if it would cause economic hardship. But the IRS levy officer initially decides what qualifies. Be ready to show that the levy affects your health or welfare or keeps you from earning a living to keep a roof over your family's head. If your situation is dire and the officer is playing Scrooge, go straight to the manager and then to the Taxpayer Advocate Service. (See Chapter 8.)
- **Show the asset has little value to the IRS.** A valuable asset, such as a truck or business equipment, may have little equity value because chattel mortgages or other liens take priority. Show the IRS all your agreements with the secured creditors. The IRS has a policy against no-equity seizures made just to teach a lesson. If the collector persists, go straight to the manager and then to the Taxpayer Advocate Service.
- **Post a bond with the IRS.** Although this is legally an option, it is so difficult to get a bond that it is not realistic. Essentially, if you meet the qualifications to post a bond, you could pay the taxes owed in full.
- **File for bankruptcy.** A bankruptcy court may order the IRS to return any seized property to you.
- **Appeal.** You can appeal an IRS levy or other collection action. You must first request a telephone conference with the manager of the IRS unit filing the levy. If the manager turns you down, fax or mail a completed Form 9423, *Collection Appeal Request*, to the collection office. You must request the appeal within two days of your conference with the manager. The appeal request is usually decided within five business days. The appeals officer looks at whether the collectors followed correct procedures and considers the facts and circumstances of your case. Don't get too excited, however, as the vast majority of taxpayers lose collection appeals.

An IRS release of levy on an item does not prevent the IRS from levying on the same item sometime in the future. (Internal Revenue Code § 6331(e).)

How Long Does a Levy Last?

The IRS can seize your assets as long as you owe any part of a tax debt and the ten-year statute of limitations on collections has not expired.* Generally, levies are one-shot affairs; the government must prepare and send a new levy notice every time it wants to grab something (unless it's wages or independent contractor payments).

> **EXAMPLE:** The IRS levies Remington's account at Piker Bank on Monday. After a 21-day holding period, the bank must send to the IRS everything in Remington's account on the day of the levy notice. If the balance is $0, then the IRS gets nothing from Piker. If Remington deposits $150,000 on Tuesday, the day after the notice, the IRS can't touch it without sending a new levy notice. If Piker Bank sends the IRS anything from Tuesday's deposit without having received another levy notice, it will have to repay Remington the amount it sends the IRS.

Independent Contractors and Employees: As long as you work for the same employer, it must continuously withhold a portion of each paycheck for the IRS. This rule also now applies to independent contractors. The IRS can intercept funds owed to a self-employed person from a business.

An employer's failure to honor the IRS levy notice can mean severe penalties.

*Tax levies on wages should stop, by law, at the end of the normal ten-year statute of limitations on collections by the IRS. There is an exception to the rule if the IRS has begun a levy on a retirement fund before the end of the ten-year period; it may collect from distributions from the fund for an unlimited period. Hardly seems fair, but it's the law.

IRS Sales of Levied Assets

When the IRS seizes assets other than real estate, it physically takes custody of them—cars, cash, stock, equipment, and other items. For financial assets, the IRS sends a notice to your financial institution ordering it to freeze your account and send the balance after 21 days. For other things, the IRS hires a local mover to drive a truck to your door and empty your home or office of furniture, machinery, and the like. Real estate is handled differently, as explained below.

IRS Sales of Personal Property

Once the IRS has seized your personal (non-real estate) property, it can sell it at an IRS auction. (Internal Revenue Code § 6335(e).) Before the auction, the IRS will set a minimum bid price and send you notice of it. If you believe the price is too low, you have five days to object; present documentation, such as an independent appraisal, that the bid price is unfairly low.

The IRS must determine the fair market value of an asset and then it discounts that value by 25% to 45% to determine the "forced sale" value. Generally, that amount becomes the IRS minimum bid at the auction.

The IRS must also notify you of the time and place of the auction. Up until the auction, you can try to negotiate to stop the sale. If you aren't successful—or don't try—the revenue officer handling the case usually acts as the auctioneer. You will then receive a letter from the IRS after the auction informing you of the outcome.

IRS auctions are usually held on the steps of federal courthouse buildings—very public. You don't have to attend, but go for it, especially if you'd like to try to get the property back from the buyer. Some people make a living out of buying property from the IRS cheap and may offer to sell it back to you or a friend after the auction.

If no one bids the IRS minimum bid figure, the IRS has two options:

- Bid the minimum amount itself and dispose of the property by private sale later.
- Give the property back to you. While this is rare, it does happen. If the local district director decides that keeping the property is not in the best interests of the government, you may get it back with the expense of the levy and attempted sale added to the amount you already owed. The IRS considers the cost of maintaining, repairing, transporting, or safeguarding personal property in deciding whether or not to give your property back. And if the IRS gives the property back to you, the lien remains and it could be levied again in the future.

The winning bidder must give the IRS a bank certified or cashier's check for at least 10% of the bid price and pay the balance within a few days. The IRS won't turn over the levied property until it has been paid in full.

The IRS applies the payment first to your tax bill and then to the costs of the seizure and sale, such as advertising and storage. There is no commission owed to the auctioneer, as he is a government employee. If there is still money left over, send a letter to the revenue officer handling your case asking that it be returned to you. If you don't, the IRS will keep the excess and apply it to your future taxes.

If the proceeds from the sale of your assets don't cover your tax bill, you are still liable to the IRS for the balance.

IRS Sales of Homes and Other Real Estate

If the IRS levies on your home or other real estate, it must post a notice of seizure prominently on the property. If it is your residence, the paper is usually taped on your front door. And if the IRS knows of your whereabouts, it must attempt to hand deliver a copy of the notice to you. If you can't be found or are hiding inside and don't come to the door, the IRS will most likely mail a certified letter with the notice to you. As mentioned above, the IRS must obtain a court order before it can levy your primary residence.

> CAUTION
> **The IRS will not evict you.** You do not have to move out of your home when you receive a levy notice. If IRS personnel ask to enter your home—to inspect the interior or bring in a real estate appraiser—you don't have to let them in unless they have a court order. Rarely will the IRS do this.

The IRS must publish the date, time, and location of the auction in a local newspaper. This information is also posted on a public bulletin board at the nearest federal courthouse or federal office building or in the public area of the local IRS office. The sale is usually set for a date 45 days after the seizure notice is first posted.

Any mortgages, judgment liens, real estate taxes or other liens on your property at the time of the IRS sale remain in place after the IRS auction—as long as they were recorded *before* the IRS recorded its Notice of Federal

Tax Lien. This means that the auction buyer takes the property subject to any liens, such as a mortgage. But any lien recorded *after* the IRS recorded its Notice of Federal Tax Lien is wiped out at the IRS sale—so the buyer gets it free and clear.

A well-off relative or friend can buy your home at the auction and lease or sell it back to you. Obviously, you don't want the property back in your name until the IRS bill has been entirely satisfied, or you risk losing the house again.

Staying in Your Home After the IRS Auction

You do not have to voluntarily move out of your home after the IRS has sold it—no matter what. The high bidder at an IRS auction of real estate receives only an IRS certificate of sale. (Internal Revenue Code § 6335.) This certificate does not give the buyer the full rights of a deed holder. You still are the deed holder although you are now subject to the rights of the certificate holder.

If you are living in the home, the certificate holder cannot enter it against your will or even ask you to leave. He must bring an eviction lawsuit in your local state court. An eviction usually takes time and money, and so you may be able to negotiate a voluntary move-out date or ask for moving expenses in return for vacating right away. You may even be able to rent back the home. Having this right to stay also gives you time to figure out whether you can possibly redeem the property.

Getting Back Real Estate

Even after the auction and the issuance of the certificate of sale, you may be able to get your home or other real property back. (Internal Revenue Code § 6337.) This is called the right of redemption. And you might be able to stop an eviction if you can convince a judge that you intend to exercise your redemption right.

You have 180 days from the date of sale to redeem your real estate from the certificate holder, who *must* let you do so. If you do not redeem within that time period, the IRS will issue a deed to the buyer. Redemption means paying the holder, not the IRS—unless the IRS was the high bidder. Payment must be by cash or by bank-certified or cashier's check for the full bid price plus interest at the rate of 20% per year, prorated to the date of your payment. You must present payment to the certificate holder on or before 180 days from the auction date. If you are a day late, the right is lost.

> **EXAMPLE:** Georgina's house sold for $100,000 at an IRS auction to Charlton, the high bidder. This satisfies Georgina's debt to the IRS in full. The home is worth about $150,000 and Georgina wants to redeem it so she and her three daughters can remain there. She finds a mortgage company willing to lend her $110,000. She will have to pay Charlton $104,932:

Bid price	$100,000
Interest	
Prorated interest rate	
(90 ÷ 365 days x 20%) = 4.932%	
Interest due ($100,000 x 4.932%)	4,932
Total needed for redemption	$104,932

It might be possible to buy the property back from the certificate holder with a promissory note and mortgage if you can't get a loan from a financial institution. It doesn't hurt to ask.

Make sure you communicate and document your intent to exercise your right of redemption. Notify the holder of the certificate of sale in writing by certified mail, and send a copy to the IRS office handling your case. Follow up with telephone calls to the buyer and the IRS employee who handled the auction. If you can't contact the certificate holder or the person states that he or she won't take your payment, ask that the IRS contact the holder and inform the holder of your right to redeem. If the IRS won't, contact a lawyer ASAP.

SEE AN EXPERT

Get professional help when exercising your right to redeem. Many certificate holders will be unhappy about your redemption or unaware of your right to exercise it. Even if the holder is cooperative, you need a quitclaim deed. A lawyer or title or escrow company should perform this service and see that the deed is recorded in the public record.

After the redemption is completed, write a letter with copies of the proof of payment and the quitclaim deed from the buyer to the IRS local office: Hand deliver or send it by certified or registered mail. The letter should simply state that you have exercised your right of redemption and that a deed to the certificate holder should not be issued.

If the IRS was the buyer, then you won't get a quitclaim deed, but instead will get a release of lien document. Once you record this document you will once again have title to the property—except for any mortgages or other recorded liens against the property that existed prior to the IRS lien.

Levies of Business Assets

The IRS has the power to take just about anything if you owe taxes. If you are a partner or a sole proprietor of a business, the IRS can levy on the business's bank accounts for your personal tax debts. The IRS might also intercept your accounts receivable by notifying your customers to make future payments to the IRS instead of to your business. If you're in a partnership, the IRS can go after the business's assets, even if only one partner is having IRS problems.

If your business is incorporated, the IRS can seize your shares of stock in the corporation (but not the assets of the company) for your individual tax debts. If the IRS believes you have created the corporation simply to shield your assets from the IRS, it may levy the corporate assets. If you're faced with this, see an attorney.

Before levying on assets located inside your business, however, the IRS will ask your permission. If you refuse, the IRS can still take property from *public* areas of your business. If you own a restaurant, for example, the IRS can grab the tables and chairs, but not the kitchen equipment. To get the nonpublic area items, the IRS needs a court order, which can take days or weeks. This gives you time to negotiate or raise money to pay your bill.

As a practical matter, the IRS rarely seizes a small business's inventory, equipment, or fixtures. It is usually not worthwhile—auctions for used business equipment and inventory typically bring only pennies on the dollar. The IRS also realizes that if the auction proceeds don't cover the complete tax bill, the chance of collecting the balance is reduced severely if you're put out of business.

Payroll tax exception. The IRS can seize assets and even padlock your doors if your business gets behind in payroll tax deposits. This is doubly true if you are pyramiding employment tax liabilities—you owe past payroll taxes and are not making current payroll tax deposits. The IRS will do its best to put you out of business, just to keep the problem from getting worse. For more information on a business's obligation to pay payroll taxes, see Chapter 11.

Levies of Joint Tax Refunds

If the IRS takes a joint income tax refund when only one spouse owes back taxes, the other spouse can request his or her share of the refund money. File an amended tax return, Form 1040X. Attach an *Injured Spouse Claim and Allocation* (Form 8379), listing the injured spouse's separate income, deductions, exemptions, and credits. The IRS computes the refund and issues a check if the spouse qualifies.

Suing the IRS for a Wrongful Levy

If the IRS erroneously seized your property—for example, you didn't owe anything—you can sue. (Internal Revenue Code §§ 6343(b), (c).) The IRS must return the property or its value together with interest, reasonable attorneys' fees, and related legal costs. See a tax attorney to find out if you have a case. Be warned, however: Successfully suing the IRS won't be easy.

Chapter Highlights

- A tax lien filed in the public records severely damages your credit.
- The IRS has power to levy (seize) most of your worldly goods, with a few important exceptions.
- You can contest a lien or levy within the IRS or in court.

The Taxpayer Advocate: A Friend at the IRS

Y ou've tried to solve your problem with the IRS, but no one seems to want to help—your letters and calls have fallen onto closed ears and the collectors are about to take the shirt off your back. So whom can you call? The IRS Taxpayer Advocate Service (TAS) at 877-777-4778.

Free help is available whenever normal IRS channels have failed. Each state and IRS campus has at least one local taxpayer advocate office. (See IRS Publication 1546, available at the IRS website at www.irs.gov.) Taxpayer advocates have the power—mandated by Congress—to cut through red tape and help you. There are 2,300 employees of the Taxpayer Advocate Service spread across the United States. In a recent year, they received 200,000 cases.

The IRS claims that nearly half of all requests for help from the Taxpayer Advocate Service are resolved satisfactorily to the taxpayer, in under five days. Complex problems take much longer. Sad to say, in recent years, the TAS performance has slipped considerably.

The IRS has a program called Problem Solving Days. These are sessions for taxpayers or their representatives to bring in matters they haven't been able to resolve through normal IRS channels. Senior IRS people there have the power to cut through red tape and get to the bottom of things. You can walk in or, better, make an appointment ahead of time. Call 800-829-1040 to see if the program is offered in your area. Or, check the IRS website at www.irs.gov. Don't expect miracles, but the feedback on this program has been positive. It's worth a shot—and it's free. As of this writing (2011), the Problem Solving Days program at the IRS may be on hold.

Who Qualifies for Help From a Taxpayer Advocate?

Contact the Taxpayer Advocate Service only after first attempting and failing to fix the problem within normal IRS channels. Be ready to provide the taxpayer advocate with copies of previous IRS correspondence and notes indicating dates, times, and summaries of telephone conversations.

Who initially caused the problem—you or the IRS—is immaterial, according to the *Internal Revenue Manual*. So a taxpayer advocate can't beg off by saying that you should have filed your tax return on time, paid your taxes when they were due, or whatever else you did or didn't do wrong.

Goals of the Taxpayer Advocate Program

The IRS acknowledges that taxpayers are often ignored or shuffled among different IRS departments. The Taxpayer Advocate Service's goals are to:

- assist taxpayers facing hardships
- ensure that taxpayers have an independent, monitored system for the resolution of problems that have not been solved through regular IRS channels
- serve as a taxpayer's advocate within the IRS to make sure that the taxpayer has a say in the IRS decision-making process, and
- recommend administrative and legislative changes to Congress.

Problems the Taxpayer Advocate Will Pursue

The taxpayer advocate won't investigate all difficulties you are having with the IRS. Your problem must fall into one of the situations listed below, and you must have first taken the necessary steps for the given situation.

Refunds Not Received

Before the Taxpayer Advocate Service will help, you must have made at least two inquiries into the status of your refund, and at least 90 days must have passed since you filed your tax return (or amended tax return).

> EXAMPLE: Edith filed an amended tax return claiming a refund on July 15, 2011. On October 1, 2011, she called the IRS and was told to expect the refund in three weeks. When she still had no refund on November 1, 2011, she called again. This time the clerk told her to keep waiting. Edith qualifies for taxpayer advocate assistance.

No Response to Your Inquiries

Before the Taxpayer Advocate Service will help, you must have contacted the IRS at least twice before. At least 45 days must have passed since you made your first inquiry. And you must not have received an IRS response by the date promised.

EXAMPLE: Gary wrote to the IRS requesting a copy of his tax account on February 13, 2012. He received an IRS letter promising a copy by April 7, 2012. When that date passed and he still didn't have a copy of his account, he called the IRS. The clerk told him she had no information. Gary qualifies for taxpayer advocate assistance.

IRS Notice Problems

Before the Taxpayer Advocate Service will help you deal with an IRS notice, you must have responded at least twice by requesting some IRS action. And you must not have received any meaningful IRS response.

EXAMPLE: Ooma received two tax bills that were a month apart. She responded to each notice with a letter stating she had paid the amount in question and enclosed copies of canceled checks as proof. When Ooma received a third bill, she qualified for taxpayer advocate assistance.

Emergencies and Other Problems

Even if your problem doesn't fall into one of the above three categories, you still may qualify for taxpayer advocate help—if you believe the IRS mistreated you.

EXAMPLE 1: Peter was informed by his bank that the IRS issued an Intent to Levy Notice for his bank account. Peter never received any notice from the IRS indicating that he owed money. Peter qualifies for taxpayer advocate help.

EXAMPLE 2: A revenue officer (tax collector) showed up at Betty's job. He asked questions about her tax debt in front of her boss and customers. Her complaint to the collector's supervisor went unanswered. Betty is afraid more visits may cause her to lose her job. Betty can call the Taxpayer Advocate Service.

EXAMPLE 3: The IRS recorded a tax lien against Sam. Sam paid off the debt, but two months later the IRS still hadn't filed a Satisfaction of Lien. Sam is trying to buy a car, but the dealer won't arrange financing because of the lien in his credit file. Sam needs immediate help and can call the Taxpayer Advocate Service.

EXAMPLE 4: The IRS recorded an erroneous tax lien against Janice, but it was her husband, not her, who owed the debt. The collection division has exceeded the 30-day limit for filing a Certificate of Release, even after she informed them of the error. Janice qualifies for help from the Taxpayer Advocate Service.

Problems the Taxpayer Advocate Won't Pursue

The Taxpayer Advocate Service won't help you in the following situations:
- You haven't followed an IRS-established administrative procedure, such as requesting an appeal.
- The IRS responded to you, but you don't agree with the answer. (Contacting the taxpayer advocate may be worth a try if, for example, you've requested an installment agreement, the IRS rejected your proposal and is about to seize your bank account.)
- The problem does not directly involve your taxes. For example, the Taxpayer Advocate Service won't take complaints about IRS personnel or about documents you were denied in a Freedom of Information Act request.
- The problem can't be solved by the IRS. If you don't like a particular tax law, for instance, write your congressperson, not the taxpayer advocate. Or your problem may be with another federal agency, such as the Social Security Administration.
- Your case is in the Criminal Investigation Division of the IRS.
- The IRS has classified you as a tax protestor or you have raised a similar issue, such as claiming the tax laws are unconstitutional.
- Your position is that you cannot or will not pay your tax bill under any circumstances.

Contacting the Taxpayer Advocate Service

The Taxpayer Advocate Service is located at many, but not all, IRS offices. (See www.irs.gov for the office nearest to you.) If it's an emergency— for example, your business vehicle is scheduled to be sold by the IRS tomorrow—call, fax, or visit the nearest IRS office and ask for the local taxpayer advocate.

Otherwise, request help by calling 877-777-4778 (toll free). If you don't get through, leave a phone number for a return call. Or if it's not an emergency, write and describe the problem. (A sample letter is below.) Mail or fax your letter to your local Taxpayer Advocate Service office.

If you call first, follow up with a letter concisely reiterating your problem. And because the IRS loves documentation, whether you write first or write as a follow-up, include in your letter:

- your full name and Social Security number, or a Taxpayer Identification number if it is a business issue.
- copies of IRS notices and prior correspondence to and from the IRS—this is very important
- a concise explanation of your problem
- if applicable, clear, legible copies of canceled checks—both front and back—showing payments that were not credited to your account, and
- a daytime telephone number and hours when you can be reached—this is vital for quick action.

Sign and date your letter.

 CAUTION

Tell the truth! The IRS is authorized to contact third parties to verify facts about your claimed hardship.

If you qualify for taxpayer advocate help, your case will be assigned to a specific taxpayer advocate. That person will immediately begin working on your problem or assign it to a staff member.

Below is a sample letter requesting taxpayer advocate assistance.

Control yourself when working with an IRS taxpayer advocate. If you yell, you may be classified as a nut case or as irate, and the advocate may back off from helping you. Remember, the taxpayer advocate may be your last chance.

Emergency Help: Taxpayer Assistance Orders

Taxpayer advocates can quickly intervene on behalf of taxpayers to local IRS officers and IRS campuses. The advocates can order the IRS to cease any action that causes a significant hardship by issuing a Taxpayer Assistance

Sample Taxpayer Advocate Letter

Internal Revenue Service
Taxpayer Advocate Service
P.O. Box 1302 (Stop 1005)
Denver, CO 80201

November 18, 20xx

Re: Benedict Cooper—SSN 555-55-5555

Dear Sir or Madam:

Please help me straighten out a problem that I have been unable to resolve with the IRS.

Enclosed is a copy of a tax notice dated September 1, 20xx in the amount of $892.40. I paid this on July 15, 20xx when I sent in my tax return. Enclosed is a copy of my canceled check, front and back, which shows that the IRS received the money.

I wrote the IRS on September 5, 20xx and sent a copy of this check. On October 5, 20xx, I received another notice (copy enclosed) again requesting payment. On October 10, 20xx, I sent another letter and copy of the check. On November 15, 20xx, I received a third notice for the same amount instead of a response to my two prior letters.

I can be reached during the day at my work, 303-555-1800, from 9 a.m. to 5 p.m. My address is 47 Bear Circle, Littleton, CO 80001.

Sincerely,

Benedict Cooper
Benedict Cooper

Enclosures: Copies of IRS notices and my two responses

Order, or TAO. Or, they will try to work out a solution to your problem without actually issuing a formal TAO, especially in the following situations:

- The IRS has seized or has threatened to seize your bank account, pension plan, or car. You need to pay rent or your family will be thrown out on the street, and you need that car to get to work.
- Your paycheck was garnished by the IRS leaving you too little on which to survive. You are willing to enter into a reasonable payment plan if the wage garnishment is stopped.

What Constitutes a Significant Hardship to the IRS?

The IRS says that a significant hardship means not being able to "provide the necessities of life" for yourself or your dependents. (Publication 1546.) Whether or not a taxpayer advocate will give you emergency assistance depends on his or her view of the seriousness of your hardship. The IRS *Problems Resolution Program Handbook* advises taxpayer advocates as follows:

> *Generally, when deciding the presence of a significant hardship, accept any application unless there is a clear reason not to do so. Any doubt should be resolved in the taxpayer's favor.*

Most taxpayer advocates take this obligation seriously and really try to help, particularly if this is your first time in trouble with the IRS.

To get the taxpayer advocate to act, you must show more than that the IRS has harmed you or is about to do so. For example, an IRS seizure is not, in and of itself, a significant hardship. The IRS's seizure or other drastic action must jeopardize:

- your ability to obtain or keep shelter, food, and clothing for yourself and your family
- your transportation to work
- your employment
- your ability to get medical care for yourself or your family
- your education
- your credit rating, or
- your ability to meet a business payroll or stay out of bankruptcy (the IRS is less likely to help a business than an individual, however).

Taxpayer advocates consider evidence of your being overwhelmed by the enormity of the tax situation. They are instructed to be sensitive to your emotional state, whether it is tears or talk of doing yourself in. Far be it from me to suggest that you have a nervous breakdown in front of a taxpayer advocate, but ….

Under *Internal Revenue Manual* 1279 (10)(70), the IRS cannot hold against you the following:

- the degree to which you were at fault in causing the hardship
- your past history of IRS difficulties, if any
- the type of tax that you owe—income, payroll, or property, and so on, or
- the taxpayer advocate's opinions and values—for instance, if part of your problem stems from a charitable donation you made to the Church of Snake Worshippers, the taxpayer advocate can't consider his or her distaste for snakes in deciding whether to help you.

Getting Hardship Relief—Calling the IRS's 911 Line

For emergency help, request a Taxpayer Assistance Order by calling your local Taxpayer Advocate Service office (the toll-free telephone number is 877-777-4778). Don't expect to get through to a taxpayer advocate immediately. Leave your telephone number for a call back, usually within 24 to 48 hours.

Or, request a Taxpayer Assistance Order in writing by using IRS Form 911, *Application for Taxpayer Assistance Order*. All IRS offices have this form. To order by phone, call 800-829-3676. Or go to the IRS's website at www.irs.gov. The website form can be filled in online if you have the computer capability (the Adobe *Reader* program is available online for no charge).

A completed sample is shown below. Once you've filled in Form 911, mail, fax, or hand deliver it to the IRS at either the local office or an IRS campus. (See Publication 1546.) It is not complicated, so there's no need to hire a tax professional to request a Taxpayer Assistance Order.

Expect a telephone call from the taxpayer advocate within one to two days to let you know if your problem will be handled and the name of the person working on it.

Request for Taxpayer Assistance Service Assistance

OMB No. 1545-1504

Department of the Treasury - Internal Revenue Service

Request for Taxpayer Advocate Service Assistance
(And Application for Taxpayer Assistance Order)

Form **911**
(Rev. 5-2011)

Section I – Taxpayer Information *(See Pages 3 and 4 for Form 911 Filing Requirements and Instructions for Completing this Form.)*

1a. Your name as shown on tax return	1b. Taxpayer Identifying Number (SSN, ITIN, EIN)
Henry Hambone	555-555-5555

2a. Spouse's name as shown on tax return *(if applicable)*	2b. Spouse's Taxpayer Identifying Number (SSN, ITIN)
Loretta Hambone	222-222-2222

3a. Your current street address *(Number, Street, & Apt. Number)*

1234 Haviture Way

3b. City	3c. State *(or Foreign Country)*	3d. ZIP code
Burgertown	Michigan	99999

4. Fax number *(if applicable)*	5. Email address
	hambone@ham.com

6. Tax form(s)	7. Tax period(s)
Form 1040	2010

8. Person to contact	9a. Daytime phone number	9b.
Henry or Loretta Hambone	555-555-3333	☐ Check here if you consent to have confidential information about your tax issue left on your answering machine or voice message at this number.
10. Best time to call	☒ Check if Cell Phone	

11. Indicate the special communication needs you require *(if applicable)*

☐ TTY/TDD Line   ☐ Interpreter - Specify language other than English *(including sign language)*

☐ Other *(please specify)*

12a. Please describe the tax issue you are experiencing and any difficulties it may be creating
(If more space is needed, attach additional sheets.)

The IRS is taking most of my pay and has taken all money out of our checking account. We called Mr. Jones whose name was on the IRS notice and he said that there was nothing he could do about it. We do not have money to pay our rent and the landlord says he will kick us out in 3 days if we don't pay. We have 3 children and Loretta is 8 months pregnant.

12b. Please describe the relief/assistance you are requesting *(If more space is needed, attach additional sheets.)*

I need all my paycheck to take care of bills. We could pay the IRS something monthly on the bill if they would let us.

I understand that Taxpayer Advocate Service employees may contact third parties in order to respond to this request and I authorize such contacts to be made. Further, by authorizing the Taxpayer Advocate Service to contact third parties, I understand that I will not receive notice, pursuant to section 7602(c) of the Internal Revenue Code, of third parties contacted in connection with this request.

13a. Signature of Taxpayer or Corporate Officer, and title, if applicable	13b. Date signed
Henry Hambone	5/20/2010
14a. Signature of spouse	14b. Date signed
Loretta Hambone	5/20/2010

Section II – Representative Information *(Attach Form 2848 if not already on file with the IRS.)*

1. Name of authorized representative	2. Centralized Authorization File (CAF) number

3. Current mailing address	4. Daytime phone number
	☐ Check if Cell Phone
	5. Fax number

6. Signature of representative	7. Date signed

Catalog Number 16965S   www.irs.gov   Form **911** (Rev. 5-2011)

Nationwide, the IRS claims that it helps about half of all taxpayers who apply for Taxpayer Assistance Orders. In most cases, however, the taxpayer advocate won't formally issue an order requiring the IRS to stop certain action. Typically, relief is granted informally, without an official order.

Submit a 911 form to the IRS Taxpayer Advocate Service any time you feel that the IRS is ignoring you or treating you unfairly. It is easy to do, and you have absolutely nothing to lose. Filing the form requires the IRS to act quickly. Request an IRS employee to complete the Form 911 for you if it is an emergency. You can do this in person or over the phone.

Chapter Highlights

- The Taxpayer Advocate Service helps folks with problems they are having with regular IRS channels.
- A taxpayer advocate cuts through IRS red tape and provides emergency relief in special cases.
- Contact the Taxpayer Advocate Service by calling 877-777-4778 (toll free).

Family, Friends, Heirs, and the IRS

The tax laws contain special rules affecting folks related by blood or marriage and people who own property together. A taxpayer's responsibilities don't end at death—his or her family may inherit tax troubles. Maybe the old saying should be changed to "Nothing is certain except death and MORE taxes."

It's a Family Affair

If you are married, divorced, or a parent, familiarize yourself with some special tax rules.

Filing Tax Returns—Joint or Separate?

Married couples always have the option of filing a joint tax return or filing separate tax returns. And, if only one spouse has income, the other doesn't have to file a return—although filing jointly will likely result in a tax savings. The only qualification for filing jointly is that the couple be legally married as of December 31 of that year. Occasionally, it pays, tax-wise, for married couples to file separate returns. However, taxes are higher in most instances, especially in community property states. This is because each spouse is considered to have earned 50% of the other spouse's income for tax purposes. If in doubt how to file, calculate your tax liability both ways each year. Computer tax programs can do this very quickly.

CAUTION

Each spouse is 100% liable for all the taxes owed on a joint return. But only the spouse in whose name a separate return is filed is liable for his or her income taxes. So, another reason some married couples file separate tax returns is to relieve each other of direct financial responsibility if the IRS should audit one of them, or if one can't pay a tax bill.

EXAMPLE 1: Leon and Margaret are married and always file their tax returns jointly. Leon owns a dry cleaning business which reported an operating loss on their tax return. The couple was audited, and the IRS discovered that the business income was understated by $50,000. Leon and Margaret didn't pay the resulting $22,000 bill and the IRS filed a lien against both of them. The IRS may collect on it from any jointly or separately owned property of either Leon or Margaret.

EXAMPLE 2: Now assume that Leon and Margaret file separate tax returns. Leon filed the phony tax return, but Margaret's return showed only her wages as an office manager. Both returns were audited. Margaret's audit resulted in no change. Leon was slapped with a $22,000 bill. The IRS filed a lien, damaging only Leon's credit rating and subjecting only his assets to collection. Margaret is in the clear.

The Innocent Spouse Rule

The innocent spouse rule is the one exception to the law making both currently married or former spouses responsible for an IRS debt. (Internal Revenue Code § 6013(e).) A spouse, or more commonly, an ex-spouse, may be relieved of joint tax debts incurred after July 22, 1998 (the effective date of major changes to the law), as well as joint tax debts incurred before that date but paid afterwards.

Under the current rule, an innocent spouse filing a joint tax return must show all of the following:

- All or part of the tax understatement was due to erroneous items of the other spouse.
- He or she did not know, and had no reason to know, there was an understatement by the other spouse.
- It would be unfair to hold the innocent spouse liable.

Even if a spouse does not qualify, the IRS can grant partial relief by apportioning the tax bill. The IRS will allow the "partially" innocent spouse to recompute his or her separate tax liability (what would be owed under a separate return) and owe just that amount.

The IRS can deny innocent spouse relief if it concludes that the spouse had actual knowledge of the tax misdeed and still voluntarily signed the return. The only hope for the innocent spouse is to show that he or she signed the return under duress.

Prior to July 22, 1998, it was harder for a spouse to avoid liability for joint tax debts. In addition, the IRS couldn't grant proportional liability like it can under the current law—it was all or nothing. Under the old law, a spouse would be relieved of the tax debt only if the tax bill was for unreported income or overstated deductions of at least 25% of the total income originally reported, OR if all of the following are true:

- There was a substantial understatement of tax attributable to grossly erroneous items of only one spouse.
- The couple filed a joint return.
- The spouse claiming to be innocent did not know about the unreported income or overstated deduction, and had no reason to know about it, and did not benefit from it (this benefit rule disqualifies most innocent spouses).
- Holding the innocent spouse responsible would be unfair.

CAUTION

The pre–July 22, 1998 innocent spouse rule is strictly applied. Neither the IRS nor the courts readily accept pleas of innocence under this law. In one case, the tax court denied a wife's claim of innocence, although she had not known of her husband's tax cheating. The court reasoned that she should have known that the income reported on her joint return was way too low to support her family's lifestyle. Perhaps, if the husband had squirreled the nontaxed lucre away and clothed his wife in rags, she would have won.

Usually, innocent spouse claims are made by divorced taxpayers. People who are still married, however, can also use the innocent spouse rule.

EXAMPLE: Francisco and Imelda filed a joint return, were audited, and were found to have substantially underreported Francisco's business income. Francisco had skimmed about $60,000 from his delicatessen. Imelda convinced the IRS that she was an innocent spouse—she knew nothing about the income, had no reason to know about it (she was in the hospital recovering from surgery when Francisco did their taxes), and did not benefit from it (Francisco blew the money gambling)—and so it would be unfair to hold her liable. Francisco changed his ways, and the marriage survived. Imelda went back to work and, using her good credit, bought a home and obtained a mortgage in her name alone. She and Francisco lived there, and he entered into an installment payment plan with the IRS for the taxes.

Avoiding Liability for Your Spouse's Dishonesty With the IRS

The innocent spouse rule isn't the only way to avoid liability for your spouse's underreporting or overdeducting to the IRS. The rules differ, depending on what state you lived in when you filed your return. The rules for community property states, non-community property states, and those that apply to all states—including the innocent spouse rule—are briefly described below.

Community Property States

(Arizona, California, Idaho, Louisiana, Nevada, New Mexico, Texas, Washington, and Wisconsin)

Innocent Spouse Rule:
- You and your spouse did not file a joint income tax return.
- You did not know and did not have reason to know of the unreported income (this means you had no knowledge of the amount of the income, and you had no knowledge of the existence of the item of income itself).
- The income belongs solely to your spouse.
- It would be unfair to include the unreported income in your income.

Abandoned Spouse Rule:
- You and your spouse were married at some time during the calendar year.
- You lived separately and apart during the entire calendar year.
- You did not file a joint return.
- You did not receive any portion of your spouse's income.

Denying Benefit of Community Property Law Rule:
If your spouse acts as if he or she is solely entitled to a portion of community income and does not tell you about that income by the time your tax return is due, your spouse will be solely responsible for reporting the income. This is because even when spouses file separate returns, each must report one-half of the combined community income.

Avoiding Liability for Your Spouse's Dishonesty With the IRS (continued)

Non-Community Property States (the rest)

Innocent Spouse Rule:

- There is a substantial understatement of tax from income and deductions of the other spouse.
- You did not know and did not have reason to know of the dishonesty. This claim presents a problem because a spouse is required to read a joint return before signing it.
- It would be unfair to hold you liable.
- You did not receive any benefit from the unreported income.

All States

Innocent Spouse Rule:

If you had no income and believed that you were not obligated to file a return, you will not be assumed to have authorized your spouse to sign your name on a joint return. You may be able to claim that your spouse forged your name to a joint return.

On the other hand, if you have your own income and do not file separately, the IRS will assume you intended to file jointly, and you cannot claim that your spouse forged your name to a joint return.

Duress Rule:

You must have been unable to resist the demands of your spouse to sign the return, and you would not have signed the return if the pressure had not been applied.

File IRS Form 8857 to request innocent spouse relief. The form is available online at the IRS website (www.irs.gov).

Tax Court for Innocent Spouses

Were you denied innocent spouse relief by the IRS? You can sue the IRS in tax court. (Internal Revenue Code § 6015.) You must file your petition within 90 days of the IRS denial notice date. Until the court decides, the IRS may not take any collection action against you. (See Chapter 5 for details on going to tax court.)

Divorce and the IRS

Alimony—Deductible and Taxable

Several tax issues arise at divorce. Alimony, sometimes called maintenance or spousal support, is one. Payments are tax deductible to the payer and taxable income to the recipient. Alimony must be specifically ordered by a court or in a legally binding written agreement signed by both spouses. Otherwise, payments to a spouse aren't deductible and the other spouse does not have to report them as income.

If you get alimony, you can deduct any attorneys' fees paid to secure or collect it. And professional fees for attorneys, accountants, and financial planners for advice on tax consequences of a divorce are tax deductible to both sides.

Marital Settlement Agreements

Divorcing couples often agree to issues of property division, debt allocation, alimony, and child support in a writing called a marital settlement agreement, dissolution agreement, or separation agreement. One item that should be covered is who pays any joint tax liability—past taxes, taxes currently owed, or any that may be assessed in the future for a period during marriage.

The IRS is not bound by marital settlement agreements with regard to tax debts. The IRS can pursue either spouse, no matter what an agreement says. Of course, if the party liable under the agreement doesn't pay the tax bill and the other one does, the person who paid can sue the other in state court for reimbursement. Good luck.

You might escape joint liability for taxes by claiming innocent spouse relief. You must be divorced, legally separated, or not living in the same household for the last 12 months. You might escape the tax completely, or at least have it reduced to your proportional share.

Parenting and the IRS

The IRS seems to pop up in all areas of our lives, including parenting. Here are the rules on child support and the dependency deduction.

Child Support—Is it Deductible?

No. Unlike alimony, child support is neither deductible for the paying parent, nor reportable as income for the custodial parent. If you pay or receive family support—alimony and child support combined as one payment—you can deduct, or must report as income, only the alimony portion. Make sure your settlement agreement or court order distinguishes between the two—many do not.

Who Gets the Dependency Exemption?

Dependent children are valuable tax exemptions. Divorced, single, and married parents filing separately—including separated but not yet divorced parents—cannot both claim the same children as exemptions. IRS computers cross-check parents' returns for this kind of double dipping.

Without a written agreement to the contrary, the parent with the children the most days gets the exemption. But if the other parent furnishes over 50% of the child's support, he or she is entitled to the exemption. However, the parent must file with his or her tax return IRS Form 8332, *Release of Claim to Exemption for Child of Divorced or Separated Parents*, signed by the other spouse, usually the mother. If the father claims the exemption without filing Form 8332, he may be contacted by the IRS for proof that he furnished over 50% of the support.

Child Support Collecting by the IRS

An effective child support collection device is an IRS interception of the owing parent's tax refund.

If you owe more than $150 in child support and the other parent complains or receives welfare, the local district attorney can request that the IRS send your refund directly to the state. You should first receive an intercept notice allowing you to request a hearing. But judges will intervene only if you can show that the back support has been paid or that the tax refund is greater than you owe. Rarely will a judge listen to a delinquent parent's claim of a desperate need for the funds.

If you are now married to someone other than the custodial parent to whom you owe support, your new spouse can attend the hearing and file a claim for his or her share of the tax refund as an *injured spouse*. The IRS cannot take this portion to satisfy a child support debt of yours. Your current spouse should file Form 8379, *Injured Spouse Claim and Allocation*.

If all or a part of your refund is intercepted wrongly—for example, the IRS took too much, or your current spouse's share was taken—you may be able to get it back. File an amended tax return on Form 1040X.

States with income taxes also intercept tax refunds for child support debts. In Nebraska, for example, court clerks report all child support arrears to the state tax agency. Delinquents are mailed a notice and given a hearing. Your new spouse may have the right to file a claim to have his or her share withheld from what is sent to your child's other parent.

RESOURCE

For extensive information on divorce and taxes, including the innocent spouse rule, see *Divorce & Money: How to Make the Best Financial Decisions During Divorce*, by Violet Woodhouse with Dale Fetherling (Nolo).

Owning Property Jointly

Many people—friends, domestic partners, parents and children, siblings, lovers, and married people who file their taxes separately—own real estate or other assets like bank accounts together. There are three serious tax dangers inherent in co-ownership, however.

Audit Risk. If the joint property is held for investment, an IRS auditor may challenge the co-owners' allocation of their tax liability—how each reported annual income or losses, or the gain or loss on the sale of the asset.

> EXAMPLE: Marcus bought a warehouse with his funds and his daughter, Anita's, separate funds. He put title to the property in his name with Anita. He wanted Anita to inherit his interest in the warehouse when he died. Marcus did substantial repairs and renovations to the building, and the rents that year did not cover the expenses. Consequently, Marcus took a rental property loss on his tax return. He was audited, and the IRS held that as co-owner, he could deduct only one-half of the loss. Anita, a college student, was entitled to deduct the other half of the loss. Anita had no income, however, and so the loss was of no tax benefit to her.

Ownership Risk. If one joint owner owes the IRS, the entire property may become an IRS seizure target. For instance, the IRS can easily grab a joint bank account you hold with your mother, brother, or lover to satisfy either their tax debt or yours.

> EXAMPLE: Let's stick with Marcus and Anita and change the facts a little. Several years after Anita graduates from college, she opens a business. The business folds and she's left owing the IRS $34,000. The IRS issues a seizure notice to take the warehouse because of Anita's name on the deed. Marcus calls the IRS to object to the seizure. If Marcus presents evidence showing that he is the true owner—he paid the deposit and all the mortgage payments and Anita didn't contribute anything—the IRS may hold off from seizing the property to satisfy Anita's tax debt. (See Chapter 7 for more information on seizures, and Chapter 8 for information on contacting a taxpayer advocate.)

Death Risk. At the death of a joint owner, an IRS auditor may allocate 100% ownership to the estate of the deceased to maximize taxes on the estate.

All of the IRS assumptions in the scenarios above can be overcome. Legal precedent allows joint owners to:

- allocate income, losses, and deductions unequally, according to the contributions of the co-owners toward the purchase and maintenance of the property
- keep their share of joint property away from the IRS, and
- prove that true property ownership is not necessarily what is stated on a deed or other title document.

But to convince an auditor, an appeals officer, or a tax court judge, you must provide testimony or other evidence showing that the way title is held does *not* reflect the property's true ownership. If this is your situation, see a tax professional—preferably a tax lawyer.

Death and Taxes

RESOURCE

This is not a book about estate planning, but we will go over some tax basics. There is good information on the subject, including *Plan Your Estate*, by Denis Clifford (Nolo). You can get free information on death-related taxes from the IRS. Visit the IRS's website at www.irs.gov or call 800-829-3676 and ask for Publication 448, *Federal Estate and Gift Taxes*.

IRS problems don't always stop at death—at least for the survivors. Past taxes can be collected from an estate or from its heirs. For instance, a few years back a drug smuggler and his plane went down with narcotics aboard. The IRS presented a tax bill to his estate for the street value of the drugs, which were subsequently destroyed by the police.

Audits begun before death or even after must be defended by your executor. The executor is legally responsible for paying all income or estate taxes from your assets before your heirs get anything.

If you are an heir, executor, or administrator and are concerned about taxes owed on an estate, ask a tax professional, or get IRS Publication 559, *Tax Information for Survivors, Executors and Administrators*.

CAUTION

If estate taxes are due, the IRS holds a tax lien on all estate assets. (Internal Revenue Code § 6324.) The IRS can seize money or property from the heirs and executors if the tax isn't paid, for up to ten years after the estate tax is determined.

Filing a Federal Estate Tax Return

If the gross value of an estate—everything owned at death—exceeds the estate tax-exempt amount ($5 million), the estate's executor must file a federal estate tax return (Form 706). Anything over the exempt allowance for the year of death is taxed—except what is left to a spouse. (Certain other bequests are also tax free.)

If the net worth of an estate is less than the exempt amount, the estate won't owe federal taxes—assuming no taxable gifts were made during the decedent's lifetime. This exception means that you can't avoid the estate tax by making large gifts—if the total given away and remaining in your estate exceeds the exemption granted in the tax code for the year that you die.

> EXAMPLE: Doug died in 2011. He had a money market account of $4 million and two houses. House One has a market value of $800,000, with $700,000 still owing on the mortgage. The market value of House Two is $500,000; the mortgage balance is $100,000.
>
> | Gross Estate | | | Net Estate | | |
> |---|---|---|---|---|---|
> | Money market | | $4,000,000 | Money market | | $4,000,000 |
> | House 1 mkt value | + | 800,000 | House 1 equity | + | 100,000 |
> | House 2 mkt value | + | 500,000 | House 2 equity | + | 400,000 |
> | Gross Estate | | $5,300,000 | Net Estate | | $4,800,000 |
>
> Because Doug's gross estate exceeds the $5 million exempt amount, his executor must file a federal estate tax return. Doug's estate won't owe any federal taxes, however, because the net value of $4.8 million is less than the exemption. It may owe state death taxes, however, depending on the law in the state Doug lived in.

IRS Audits of Estate Tax Returns

The larger the estate shown on the federal estate tax return, the more likely an audit. The IRS figures that there is more incentive to cheat when a lot of money is at stake. The overall audit rate is 15%. While the estate tax audit rate has dropped over the past ten years, the additional tax and penalties collected has more than made up the slack.

When the IRS picks an estate tax return for audit, the auditor will automatically scrutinize the deceased taxpayer's last two income tax returns.

SEE AN EXPERT

Hire a professional if the estate is over the exempt amount. The personal representative of an estate should hire a top-flight tax professional—a CPA or tax attorney—to prepare an estate tax return whenever the estate exceeds the exempt amount ($5 million in 2011).

An estate tax audit is similar to an audit of an income tax return. Both require documentation and explanation of the data on the tax return. (See Chapter 3.) The legal issues are quite different from the audit of a living taxpayer—typically more complex. This is a tax professional's territory.

In contrast to an audit of a live taxpayer, an estate tax auditor does extensive investigation before anyone is notified of the audit. The auditor will likely go to the probate court and copy documents from the file and research legal issues such as marital property rights.

The auditor begins the examination interview by requesting documentation of common items like administration expenses, such as lawyer's fees. Ordinarily, cancelled checks and paid bills will adequately substantiate these deductible expenses.

After covering routine matters, the auditor moves on to thornier issues, such as the value of stock in a family corporation or whether any deathbed gifts were made to cut down the size of the estate. If so, the auditor will want to know if the proper gift tax returns were filed or if the gifts were covered by the gift tax exclusion rule.

Dealing With an Estate Tax Auditor

A personal representative should not handle an estate tax audit without a top-flight tax professional. Estate return audits are usually held at the IRS offices. You or your tax professional may need to research the law or find additional documents. If the auditor wants more records, he or she will schedule another meeting and give you an Information Document Request at the conclusion of the day.

Estate auditors are more likely to intimidate a personal representative than an experienced tax professional. Auditors will negotiate tax issues on which the facts or law are uncertain, if you know how to play the game. Estate auditors want to close out cases without appeals. (See Chapter 3, "Winning Your Audit," for tips on negotiating with an auditor.)

If you aren't happy with the way the estate tax audit comes out, you can appeal (see Chapter 4, "Appealing Your Audit Within the IRS") or go to tax court (see Chapter 5, "Going to Tax Court").

> ⚠ **CAUTION**
>
> **IRS estate tax auditors are the cream of the IRS crop and are usually CPAs or lawyers.** They can spot things like whether the assets listed are consistent with the deceased person's lifestyle, business, or profession. They are always skeptical of the values of assets listed in estate tax returns. That's why you should always bring a tax pro.

What Estate Tax Auditors Look For

Auditors look out for certain red flags on estate tax returns. (*Internal Revenue Manual* § 4350.) Some hot items include the following:

- **Unrealistically low valuations of estate assets.** This is the single most common adjustment made by auditors. Heirs and the personal representative may be tempted to undervalue an estate asset because the estate tax is so heavy. It is easy to value bank accounts and publicly traded stocks and bonds. Family businesses, real estate, art, antiques, and other items, however, all present valuation issues for the IRS to probe.

  The personal representative of the estate should always get written appraisals of all large assets other than cash and listed securities. Many states mandate court-appointed appraisers for estate assets. The IRS is not bound by any appraiser's figures. The IRS may hire its own appraiser if a valuation is questionable or if the estate's value is in the millions of dollars.

- **A discount of an asset's value.** Discounts from fair market value may be taken by appraisers to value the interests in family LLCs, partnerships, or corporations. Discounts must satisfy specific tax rules. For example, the fair market value of Veronica's 40% share of a family limited partnership dry cleaning business is $1,800,000 when she dies. But because there are few buyers for a minority interest in a small business, a discount of 30% to $1,260,000 for estate tax purposes would likely pass muster.

- **Claims against the estate by heirs, for more than what they would otherwise inherit.** For example, Sam's estate tax return shows a $500,000 promissory note from Sam, the deceased parent, to Sam, Jr. Since this claim reduces the taxable estate, an auditor will want details on when and why the loan was made and to see the loan documents.

- **Property in safe deposit boxes** that may not have been shown on the tax return. The personal representative should inventory the box's contents and attach this to the estate tax return.

- **Erroneous or incomplete estate tax returns.** Expect a problem if schedules or documentation that normally accompany an estate tax return are missing. An estate tax return is longer and has more attachments than does an ordinary tax return. Have it prepared by a tax pro or an attorney to reduce IRS audit issues.

- **Any gift tax returns that were filed during the deceased's lifetime.** The auditor will compare past gift tax returns with the estate tax return for consistency. For example, Malia filed a gift tax return five years prior to her death showing that she gave her daughter, Ariana, a home worth $1,500,000. The law requires all large lifetime gifts to be listed on the estate tax return. Also, the auditor will look for occasions when a gift tax return should have been filed but was not.

Are you the executor or personal representative of an estate with heirs other than yourself and with assets worth at least the exemption amount? See an experienced CPA or tax lawyer. (See Chapter 13 for information on finding a CPA or lawyer.) Don't take any chances—you are personally liable to the IRS, as well as to the heirs, if you understate or don't pay all estate taxes due—including those that may be assessed on an estate tax audit. The estate should pay your professional fees for this service.

EXAMPLE: Randolph, an executor, filed a federal estate return for his deceased old friend, Gregory. He listed values of various estate assets, including artwork, according to a list that Gregory prepared shortly before he died. He did not hire any professional appraisers.

Per Gregory's wishes, Randolph distributed the estate's assets to Gregory's son, Isaac, who promptly blew the money in Vegas. The IRS audited the estate tax return two years later and found the estate assets were undervalued by $2,000,000. The estate was hit with a tax bill of almost $800,000 with penalties and interest. "But all of the estate assets are gone," Randolph said. "Too bad," said the IRS. Legally, Randolph, as executor of the estate, was personally liable for the tax!

If Randolph had gotten bona fide appraisals, he could have properly prepared the tax return and defended the valuation of the assets against IRS attack.

> **TIP**
>
> **Reduce your chances of being picked for an IRS estate tax audit.** Attach copies of appraisals and other documents supporting valuations to the federal estate tax return. This is the first thing the IRS looks for in deciding whether or not to audit an estate tax return.

Joint Ownership and Death

Contrary to popular belief, you cannot escape federal estate taxes through joint ownership of assets. The only exception is when the co-owners are legally married to each other. If a joint owner dies, an IRS auditor may reallocate all the ownership shares to the deceased person's estate if the other co-owner didn't contribute equally to acquire the asset.

This issue is a concern only for nonspouse co-owners who hold their property as joint tenants with the right of survivorship—where the survivor(s) automatically inherits the deceased person's share.

EXAMPLE: Hilda (mother) and Gertie (daughter) jointly hold title to an apartment building free and clear with a market value of $5 million. Hilda bought the building many years ago with the proceeds of a life insurance policy she received when her husband died. Gertie made no contributions to the purchase price of the property or for its upkeep. When Gertie reached adulthood, Hilda added her name to the deed so that Gertie would inherit the building without going through probate.

After Hilda died, Gertie filed a federal estate tax return listing the building's value at $2.5 million, thinking that only her mother's one-half ownership portion was taxable. The IRS audited the return and properly reallocated the entire $5 million to Hilda's estate, producing a hefty tax bill. Even though Gertie avoided probate, the joint ownership didn't avoid the estate tax.

Chapter Highlights

- There are special tax rules for folks related by blood or marriage.
- Married couples filing taxes jointly should be aware of negative consequences to one spouse if there is a tax balance due.
- Owning property jointly with another may have some hidden tax traps.
- Death often brings estate tax issues requiring professional help.

Fraud and Tax Crimes:
Do You Really Have to Worry?

t is a crime to cheat on your taxes. In a recent year, however, fewer than 2,200 people were convicted of tax crimes —0.0022% of all taxpayers. This number is astonishingly small, taking into account that the IRS estimates that 15.5% of us are not complying with the tax laws in some way or another. The number of convictions for tax crimes has increased slightly over the most recent five-year period.

The point is that the statistical likelihood of your being convicted of a tax crime is almost nil. Nevertheless, if you are in the unlucky minority of people criminally investigated by the IRS, you need more than this book. Hire the best tax and/or criminal lawyer you can find.

According to the IRS, 75% of the tax cheating is done by individuals—mostly middle- and high-income earners. Most of the rest of the cheating is done by business entities. Cash-intensive businesses and service providers, from self-employed handypeople to doctors, are the worst offenders.

Second on the tax cheaters hit parade are *false claims*. For example, filing multiple tax returns claiming refunds, typically from the Earned Income Credit program, or claiming a bunch of dependents when there aren't any, or falsely seeking a tax refund from an earlier year on an amended tax return.

Third, and somewhat surprising, is the IRS report that exaggerating or claiming outright phony deductions comes far behind income underreporting and false claims on the cheating scale. The IRS says an average of only 6.8% of deductions are disallowed at the typical audit.

Criminal tax investigations are on the rise—big time. In IRS fiscal year 2010-2011, the number doubled from the previous year.

How People Cheat on Their Taxes

Most cheating is from deliberate—actual or willful—underreporting of income. This is called tax evasion—the most commonly charged tax crime. A government study found the most underreporting of income was by self-employed restaurateurs, clothing store owners, and—you'll no doubt be shocked—car dealers. Telemarketers and salespeople came in next, followed by doctors, lawyers (heavens!), accountants (heavens, again!), and hairdressers.

More recently, the IRS criminal investigators are hot on the trail of off-shore tax evasion schemes. Just because your assets are out of the country doesn't mean the IRS won't find out. Just ask the people who were ratted out by their Swiss bankers over the past few years.

If You Are Caught Cheating

Tax crimes are most likely to be first spotted during an audit. If you are caught in a tax lie, an auditor can either slap you with a penalty or refer your case to the IRS's criminal investigation division (CID). In the vast majority of cases, the auditor won't call in the CID.

The IRS Suspects You of Fraud

Auditors are trained to look for "badges" of tax fraud. Tax fraud is defined as a willful act done with the intent to defraud the IRS—that dark area beyond honest mistakes. Badges include a false Social Security number, keeping two sets of financial books, claiming a blind spouse as a dependent when you are single, and transferring all of your assets. While auditors look for fraud, however, they do not routinely suspect it. They know the tax law is complex and expect to find a few careless mistakes in every tax return. They will give you the benefit of the doubt most of the time.

However, if the auditor does not refer suspected fraud to the CID, he or she can impose fines, called civil penalties, if you omitted a chunk of taxable income on your tax return. Overstated or phony deductions and exemptions can also be punished by the fraud civil penalty—for example, claiming exemptions for dependents who have long since left home, died, or were never born. Fraud penalties can also be added for exaggerating deductions, such as adding a zero to $200 making it $2,000, or by claiming a casualty loss for a nonexistent accident.

The *Internal Revenue Manual* directs auditors suspecting serious criminal tax fraud to contact the IRS criminal investigation division, or CID. In reality, auditors make very few criminal referrals. Making a fraud referral is added paperwork. If auditors find a couple of obviously phony receipts, they usually will quietly disallow them and move on. Fraud referrals are more likely in special project examinations. These are targeted audits of particular industries and professions, such as building contractors or chiropractors or nightclub owners.

Fraud or Negligence?

A negligent mistake on your tax return might get you a 20% penalty tacked on to your tax bill. While not good, this sure beats the cost of tax fraud—a 75% civil penalty. The line between negligence and fraud is not always clear, however, even to the IRS and the courts.

Auditors are trained to spot common types of wrongdoing, called "badges of fraud." Examples include a business with two sets of books or without any records at all, freshly made documents, and cancelled checks altered to increase deductions. Altered cancelled checks are easy to spot by comparing written numbers with computer coding on the check or bank statements.

CAUTION

The auditor will not tell you if he or she has made a criminal fraud referral. One indication, however, may be an audit stopping midstream for no apparent reason. But never assume a fraud referral was made just because months pass and you don't hear from the auditor. The person is probably just behind in his or her work.

Indirect Methods of Proving Fraud

Direct proof of fraud by the IRS typically consists of finding unsubstantiated or phony deductions and exemptions. Direct proof is not usually found by the IRS for income underreporting. Instead, the IRS relies on primarily four indirect methods.

Specific items. If you cashed a check received by your business and pocketed the money without entering it in your books, this check is a "specific item." It can be viewed as evidence of fraudulent intent. If the auditor suspects fraud, he or she may talk to your business's customers to compare your bank account deposits and actual payments you received from customers.

The IRS wants more than just one specific item to make a fraud case—unless the item was for many thousands of dollars. While you might argue that one or two items were negligently left off the books (or your computer crashed or you lost your records), 15 or 20 omitted items shows a pattern of fraud.

Bank deposits. This is the IRS's favorite indirect method to prove unreported income, because it is so easy. The IRS simply adds up all deposits in your bank accounts. If the total exceeds your reported income, you may be suspected of fraud.

There may be a perfectly legitimate explanation, such as nontaxable sources of bank deposits—loans, gifts, inheritances, sales of assets, and tax-exempt income, such as municipal bond interest. Also, transfers from one bank account to another appear to be multiple deposits under this simplistic method. Point this out to the suspicious auditor. Or, deposits in your accounts may belong to relatives or friends who did not use their own accounts for some reason.

Expenditures. The IRS calculates your living expenses by totaling up the credit charges you paid, checks you wrote, and adding known or estimated expenses you paid by cash. If the total is greater than your tax-reported income, the IRS will suspect fraud. The IRS has statistical reference books showing average costs of various necessities, such as food and shelter, in your community.

To counter this, explain where you got the money to pay your bills. It could be savings from prior years, selling assets, or receiving loans or gifts. To figure your living expenses, the IRS often asks you to complete IRS Form 4822, *Statement of Annual Living Expenses*.

TIP

Never fill out IRS Form 4822 listing your living expenses. Just say you didn't keep track of every penny you spent for the year and don't want to guess. Or, diplomatically say you will consider it and then throw the form away. The IRS cannot punish you for refusing to fill out this form. If the IRS is intent on proving fraud, it will do it with or without your cooperation.

Net worth. Under this indirect method, the IRS adds up all of your assets and deducts all of your liabilities at the start and end of the tax year under audit. If there was an increase in your net worth—what you own minus what you owe—without an increase in income from the previous tax year, you may be suspected of fraud.

Again, there are many valid explanations as to how your net worth can increase besides unreported income. For example, you may have received nontaxable gifts or loans or inheritances. Or the IRS may have mistakenly included appreciation in its calculations.

Penalties for Civil Tax Fraud

You will probably never face *criminal* fraud penalties. At least 98% of the time, the IRS punishes fraud with *civil* penalties—fines of 75% added to the tax due. For example, if the additional tax due from fraud is $10,000, the penalty is $7,500, for a total of $17,500. Interest is added on to both the tax and the fraud penalty, starting on the date the return was due or filed, whichever is later.

Defending Against Alleged Tax Fraud

The three defenses most often raised against tax fraud allegations are cash hoard, nontaxable income, and honest mistake. Don't expect the IRS to accept any of these defenses at face value. A skilled attorney is better able to persuade the IRS than you are. Combatting tax fraud, like brain surgery, is not a do-it-yourself project.

I lived off my cash hoard. This defense can be raised whenever the IRS uses the bank deposits, expenditures, or net worth methods of proving fraud. There is no law (not yet, anyway) against having cash of any amount buried in your backyard or kept in a safe deposit box. The IRS's only legitimate concerns with your cash holdings are whether or not they were from taxable income, and if you reported them and paid tax on them. The IRS understandably is suspicious of people who hold large amounts of cash rather than putting it in an interest-bearing account.

I lived off a nontaxable source. The receipt of money is not always taxable income, as discussed above. You may innocently acquire tax-free wealth by gift, loans, inheritances, and other ways. This defense can be coupled with the cash hoard defense.

I made an honest mistake. If you make an error on your tax return, it is not necessarily fraud. For example, you didn't report profit from a sale of investment real estate because you believed you had two years to reinvest the proceeds without tax consequences. In reality, the law only allows you 180 days. Because intent to cheat the IRS is required for fraud, your mistaken belief is a valid defense to a tax fraud charge—but you may have to convince a judge or jury that it really was a mistake.

> **CAUTION**
>
> **Don't try to lie your way out of a fraud charge.** If in doubt, keep your mouth closed. Lying to the IRS can make matters worse. The right against self-incrimination is guaranteed by the Fifth Amendment. You have the absolute right to remain silent before the IRS whenever there is a possibility you may be charged with a crime. Lying to an IRS employee can result in a felony conviction with up to three years in prison and a $100,000 fine.

Options When the IRS Finds Fraud

If an IRS auditor believes you've cheated on your taxes, he or she has several options.

Ignore the cheating. If the amount is small, an IRS auditor will overlook it. Typically, an auditor just wants the file closed—particularly if there are other significant adjustments. The auditor will likely leave it at that and never refer your file to the CID.

Impose civil penalties. IRS auditors draw the line at outrageous cheating. Most will add civil, as opposed to criminal, penalties on to your tax bill, especially if your case is deemed too small to send to the CID.

In the case of small mistakes, auditors can add a 20% penalty to your bill if they find that your tax error was "accuracy related." If they conclude you owe an additional $1,500 of taxes, they can add a penalty of $300, bringing the bill to $1,800. The IRS imposes civil penalties about 25 million times each year.

If auditors find more serious misdeeds, however—particularly if an omission or overdeduction was fraudulent—they could add a 75% penalty, bringing your $1,500 tax bill to $2,625. And, interest will be added to both the penalty and the taxes.

Begin a criminal investigation. If the IRS suspects that you have gone too far, the CID can investigate.

The CID usually gets information that leads to an investigation from one of the following sources:

- referrals from other IRS divisions, most often from auditors who discovered unreported income during an examination
- tips from law enforcement agencies; the IRS isn't concerned with the nontax crime itself, often a drug-related offense, but whether or not the illegal income was reported.

> EXAMPLE: When Morgan was arrested for suspected drug trafficking, $150,000 in cash was in his car's trunk. After his arrest, the local police notified the IRS. The CID looked at Morgan's last few tax returns, where he reported only $35,000 of income per year. The CID immediately began a formal investigation.

- tips from citizens; ex-spouses or disgruntled employees and business associates often contact the IRS. These people are called squeals. The CID usually follows up only on well-documented tips. Many allegations are not provable and are motivated by spite, and the CID doesn't waste its time on them. It may refer the case to the examination division, however.
- IRS undercover or sting operations; CID agents often pose as buyers of businesses to find off-the-books income. Unwary sellers who brag about second sets of books and how much cash the business takes in get nailed. Other undercover operations investigate gross discrepancies in reported income and a taxpayer's lifestyle. This is how the U.S. government finally got Al Capone!

> EXAMPLE: Roy owned a rather seedy-looking pawn shop and was featured in a local newspaper article on successful businesspeople. Roy proudly posed for the paper in front of his waterfront home and Rolls Royce. Soon thereafter, Roy was audited. The IRS wanted to know how someone lived so well while reporting only $20,000

a year income. The audit turned into a lengthy CID investigation. Two CID agents pored over six years of Roy's financial records, business and personal. Eighteen months later, Roy was indicted for criminal tax evasion.

At the conclusion of the criminal tax investigation, the CID has two options—drop it forever or recommend that the Justice Department prosecute. The IRS, a part of the Treasury Department, cannot directly prosecute anyone. If the investigation is terminated without prosecution, it doesn't mean you've gotten off completely. Your case will be sent to an auditor, who can impose civil fraud penalties.

You will be pleased to know that in the great majority of investigations, the CID does not recommend prosecution. The Justice Department will prosecute only a select few cases. Therefore, the CID won't waste its time referring (and, in some cases, even seriously investigating) a case unless it feels it has a sure winner.

If the CID does recommend prosecuting and the Justice Department gets a conviction, you can be imprisoned, put on probation, fined, or all three. For example, if you're convicted of failing to file a tax return for three separate years, you can be sent to prison for one year and fined up to $25,000 for each year you didn't file. The total could be three years in prison and $75,000 in fines. You will also have a permanent criminal record.

That's not all. After a criminal conviction, an auditor will slap on civil fraud and other penalties for underpayment of taxes. Combining criminal and civil punishment does not constitute double jeopardy—the constitutional guarantee against being tried, convicted, or sentenced more than once for the same crime.

If you are prosecuted but not convicted, you will nonetheless probably be audited.

IRS Criminal Investigations

The IRS police force is called the Criminal Investigation Division (CID). This branch has 4,400 employees, 2,800 of whom are called special agents. CID agents are spread throughout the United States and abroad. Special agents are not out to audit you or collect a dime of taxes. Their sole purpose is to put tax cheaters in prison. They are armed and have badges but no uniforms. Make no mistake—they are detectives highly trained by the IRS and FBI. If someone identifies himself or herself as an IRS special agent, you or someone you know is under suspicion. Most special agents travel in pairs, for their protection and to corroborate oral evidence gathered during an investigation.

The CID is divided into general and special enforcement sections. Special enforcement targets organized crime, drugs, and unions. General enforcement watches ordinary taxpayers and everything else.

Will You Know If You're Being Investigated?

Unless and until you are formally charged, you may not know that you're being investigated by the CID. The IRS does not have to tell you, but often does. A friend, an employee, your accountant, your tax preparer, your lawyer, or anyone else contacted by the IRS during the investigation might tell you first. The IRS cannot legally swear these people to secrecy.

You might be able to find out indirectly if you are under investigation. When a criminal investigation begins, IRS personnel must complete and file Form 4135, *Criminal Control Notice*. This data is entered into your master file in the IRS computer. Your tax account is frozen, meaning that no refunds can be made or payments credited to your account.

To find out if Form 4135 has been filed, send a token tax payment for a year you believe is under investigation—even if you've paid the tax already. If a freeze is in effect, you may receive notice that your payment is being held in a suspense account. Also request a computer printout of your account for any year in question by calling 800-829-1040 or visiting your local IRS office. The printout may indicate a Form 4135 filing or show that the payment was not credited to your account without explanation.

Alternatively, the IRS may never send your requested statement if it has a criminal investigation freeze code in the computer. If you call on the phone to find out, IRS employees are told to not answer if you ask whether or not a Form 4135 has been filed.

How Special Agents Conduct Investigations

In a recent year, 4,600 individuals were criminally investigated by the CID. Only if the IRS has strong indications of wrongdoing does it send out its elite police. Cases involving less than $20,000 in taxes are rarely investigated. A criminal investigation starts with special agents interviewing the taxpayer's friends, business associates, professional advisers, and anyone else who might have information. Later on the special agents usually invite the targeted individual to speak to them.

CID investigations work in the reverse order of regular detective probes. The TV series "CSI" starts with a dead body—and then figures out whodunnit. Step 1 is the crime; Step 2 is finding the culprit. This is the standard solving-the-mystery approach.

In contrast, IRS investigations begin with an allegation from a source, usually an IRS auditor, a collector, or an informant, that a tax crime may have been committed. Then special agents work at building a case. Step 1 is naming the suspect; Step 2 is finding the crime. Special agents are among the best trained of all federal employees (FBI Academy). And they have the full resources of the federal government behind them.

Contacting Everyone Around the Target

CID investigations are unbelievably thorough, often taking a year or more. The IRS spends more time investigating a criminal tax case than other police departments devote to murder cases. This intensive use of federal resources explains why so few people are charged with tax crimes. The CID recommends prosecution only when it has built a rock solid case.

If you are under investigation, the special agent may talk to your friends, family, neighbors, coworkers, employees, business associates, bankers, insurance agents, and even travel agents and department stores. Even your spouse may be contacted. Your mail may be monitored, in cooperation with the Postal Service. While the IRS can't open mail, it follows leads from return addresses. The CID may get copies of bills from phone and credit card companies, trail suspects, or get a court order authorizing a phone tap.

Special agents subtly intimidate businesspeople and bankers into giving information. Don't expect even your most trusted advisors to protect you if the CID comes calling. Even your accountant can be compelled by the IRS to give criminal evidence against you.

Attorney-Client Privilege

In a criminal matter, the only person who can't be forced to speak about you to the IRS is your lawyer. This is a special relationship given protection under the law—called the attorney-client privilege. Your lawyer cannot disclose to the IRS anything you say that relates to a criminal tax matter. And, if an accountant is employed by your attorney to help render legal advice, the accountant's work also falls under the attorney-client privilege and cannot be disclosed to the IRS in a criminal matter. The limited tax practitioner–client privilege does not extend to criminal tax matters.

When IRS Special Agents Contact Your Associates and Friends

If you're contacted by IRS special agents about another person, be wary. Don't answer any questions if there is any possibility you could be connected to the individual under probe, such as a business partner. And read "connected to" broadly. If you worked as the manager in a shop and the owner is under investigation, you may not yet be a suspect, but there's a chance you will be. Keep quiet until you speak to a lawyer.

In any event, never lie to the CID. The law does not allow you to protect others by withholding information or lying. It is legal, however, to tell someone that the IRS was asking about them.

If someone tells you that he or she has been contacted in an IRS criminal investigation of you and asks you what to say, don't give any suggestions. It is a separate crime to ask someone to lie to the IRS. Also, resist the urge to call the CID and ask what's going on. Instead, call a tax or criminal lawyer fast. Let them call the IRS.

If the CID Contacts You

If the CID is building a case against you, chances are you will be the last person interviewed. By the time the CID agents contact you, they may have looked at thousands of records and spoken to 20 potential witnesses—your banker, ex-spouse, accountant, former employees, and others with knowledge of your financial affairs. If the CID still wants to talk to you, more than likely you are about to be recommended for prosecution. The *only* purpose for the CID questioning you is to get a confession or other damaging admission—the icing on the IRS's cake.

Once you're contacted as the target of an investigation, a special agent must tell you so immediately. He or she must read to you a version of the Miranda rights—the right to remain silent, the right to have an attorney, and the warning that anything you say can be used against you. Believe me, it will be. Answer only the question, "Are you August Fondue?"

It is highly unlikely that you'll be arrested on the spot or even invited to go to the IRS office. Simply state that you want to contact an attorney and that someone will get back to them. Don't call an attorney while the special agents are present, unless they threaten you with immediate arrest, or something similar, if you don't cooperate. Wait until they leave, you have calmed down, and you can speak freely. If you don't know a criminal-tax attorney, see Chapter 13 for tips on finding one.

How about trying to talk the special agents out of pursuing their case against you? Forget it—it's a terrible mistake. It makes no difference to them if your mother is dying, you have money problems, or your marriage is falling apart. Mentioning your problems, only strengthens the IRS's position; giving an excuse often shows that you knew what you did was wrong. Similarly, don't lie. Lying is as serious a crime as tax evasion.

> **CAUTION**
>
> **Keep your mouth shut—take this advice seriously.** If you give the CID agents any opening, you're dead. They'll start with soft background questions, but before you know it, will have trapped you. And many CID questions won't be genuine—that is, the special agents already know the answers and are asking only to see if you will lie or confess.

Questions typically asked by CID agents include:

Have you reported all of your income?

Where are your bank accounts and safe deposit boxes?

Can you tell us about the cars, boats, planes, and real estate that you own?

Do you gamble?

What is the procedure for reporting sales in your business?

Do you keep a lot of cash on hand?

Who are your business associates?

Have you traveled out of the country recently?

Have you or any of your businesses been audited?

Faced with a barrage of questions from two trained agents who show up unannounced, most people fall apart. They either blurt out a confession or a transparent lie within five minutes. This gives the Justice Department the rope to hang them with.

IRS Considerations in Deciding Whether or Not to Recommend Prosecution

The CID's chief considerations in deciding to recommend prosecution is how strong a case it has. If you were caught red-handed or confessed, you can be sure of prosecution. But remember—for any crime, including a tax crime, the government must prove your guilt beyond a reasonable doubt. If you keep your mouth closed, a good criminal-tax lawyer may be able to mount a decent defense. As a general rule, if you have some facts in your favor, the IRS may not recommend prosecution and may impose civil penalties (fines) instead.

The IRS looks closely at the case's publicity value—locally or nationwide. A prominent local doctor or movie star is a juicy plum. The agency firmly believes that front-page headlines make would-be tax cheaters think twice.

The CID also analyzes personality traits of the individual target, including age, physical and mental health, and previous criminal record.

How would a jury react to the person? Leona "Only the Little People Pay Taxes" Helmsley was no doubt selected for prosecution because the IRS guessed she'd be an unsympathetic figure. The judge and jury (and most Americans) obviously agreed.

Finally, the CID looks at the amount you cheated the government out of. The larger your indiscretion, the more likely the agents will recommend prosecution. The typical amount of taxes owed in criminal cases is over $70,000 and covers three or more years of cheating.

The bad news: When the CID recommends prosecution, and the Justice Department accepts the case, the chances of conviction are at least 80%. More than half of the people convicted go to prison even if they have no prior criminal record.

The good news: The government is quite concerned with maintaining this high rate of conviction. For every two people prosecuted, another one person under suspicion is passed by or just tried in a civil proceeding.

Crimes With Which You Can Be Charged

If the CID recommends prosecution, it will turn its evidence over to the Justice Department to decide the special charges. Individuals are typically charged with one or more of three crimes: tax evasion, filing a false return, or not filing a tax return.

Tax evasion or fraud. Tax evasion is defined as "intentional conduct to defeat the income tax laws." Any sort of tax scheme to cheat the government can fall into this broad category. Tax evasion is a felony, the most serious type of crime. The maximum prison sentence is five years; the maximum fine is $100,000. (Internal Revenue Code § 7201.)

Filing a false return. Filing a false return is what it sounds like. Your tax return contained a material misstatement, such as describing your line of work as bricklaying when you are a bookie. More people are charged with filing a false return than with tax evasion because in a filing-a-false-return case, the government does not have to prove an intent to evade the income tax laws—only an intent to file a false return. Filing a false return is a less serious felony than tax evasion and it carries a maximum prison term of three years and a maximum fine of $100,000. (Internal Revenue Code § 7206(1).)

Failure to file a tax return. Not filing a return is the least serious tax crime. It's defined as intentionally failing to file a return when you were obligated to do so. Not everyone must file tax returns. For example, only those people earning above a specified amount must file. The minimum changes from year to year. Not filing a tax return is a misdemeanor. The maximum prison sentence is one year in jail and/or a fine of $25,000 for each year not filed. The vast majority of nonfilers are never prosecuted criminally and are only hit with civil fines.

Money laundering. Although technically not tax crimes, the CID also investigates and can recommend prosecution for money laundering and filing false claims against the IRS. Typically, these crimes are charged in the same case along with tax crimes against the same individual or entity.

If You Are Prosecuted

Once the Justice Department receives a file recommended for criminal prosecution, an assistant U.S. attorney reviews it. If the prosecutor feels that the IRS has a strong felony case, he or she will seek an indictment from a federal grand jury, which usually goes along with the government. You can be criminally charged for a tax misdemeanor—such as not filing a tax return—without a grand jury indictment.

If formally charged, you will either be arrested or, if you are not deemed a flight risk, ordered to report before a federal judge to plead guilty or not guilty. You might be required to post bail or be released on your own recognizance.

If you ever find yourself in this position, find a criminal or tax lawyer immediately. Don't delay, as the government has already completed its investigation. Your lawyer will need time to catch up and learn the government's case. Keep heart; the government's case may be legally defective, or your attorney may recognize defenses to the charges. In any case, don't be your own lawyer.

Should You Plead Not Guilty?

Unless you have made a plea bargain with the government before your first court appearance, your lawyer will have you plead not guilty. Remember:

The IRS recommends for prosecution only those cases in which conviction seems a near certainty. Justice Department weeds these cases out even further. Therefore, it's not surprising that over two-thirds of all defendants eventually change their pleas to guilty without going to trial.

This is called plea bargaining, meaning you plead guilty if the Justice Department agrees to reduce or drop some charges, or both. For example, if you are charged with three years of tax evasion, the government may drop two years for a guilty plea to one year. Sometimes the government will also agree to a favorable sentencing recommendation. However, the final sentence will depend on a presentence investigation report, federal laws governing minimum sentences, and the judge's discretion.

What the Government Must Prove

If you don't plead guilty, you will eventually have a trial. At the trial, the Justice Department and the IRS, working together, must prove you are guilty of the crimes charged. Essentially, the government must show you acted intentionally and that you are guilty beyond a reasonable doubt. You are entitled to a trial by a jury, or you can choose to be tried by the judge alone.

Intent. The primary element of any tax crime is intent. In legalese, this intent is called willfulness. If the government can't prove you acted intentionally, you can't be convicted. Put another way, you can't be convicted of a tax crime if you only made a mistake, even if it was a big mistake. For example, if you didn't file a tax return because you honestly believed that 65-year-olds didn't have to file any longer, you did not act intentionally.

Before you senior citizens get carried away with this example, bear in mind that to succeed, you will have to convince a jury that your mistaken belief was honest. Given that most people remember watching their parents or grandparents fill out returns—and many people, in fact, completed those returns for their elderly relatives—you will have a hard time convincing your 12 peers that your omission was an honest mistake. More believable is a recent immigrant who did not report his or her income from investments made back home, which he or she wrongly thought was tax-exempt.

Beyond a reasonable doubt. All crimes must be proven beyond a reasonable doubt. If a judge or jury has any degree of doubt that you did what you were accused of or acted intentionally, the government's case will fail. For instance, without additional evidence showing an intent to cheat the IRS, a juror may not believe beyond a reasonable doubt that an immigrant who omitted his foreign investment income was filing a false tax return. The reasonable doubt standard is why the Justice Department prosecutes only airtight cases.

Possible Defenses

Not everyone charged with a tax crime is found guilty. For example, keep in mind the story of Dr. Rudy Mays, a former client whose name has been changed.

> EXAMPLE: Dr. Mays worked at an inner city clinic. Over 80% of his income was from Medicare, with the rest paid mostly in cash. He was indicted for income tax evasion when the IRS found that he had reported $240,000 in total income in a year in which his Medicare income alone was $280,000.
>
> Dr. Mays was offered a plea bargain—if he'd plead guilty, the charge would be reduced and he'd receive probation, not a prison term. But this plea bargain meant that Dr. Mays' medical license would be revoked, ending his career. He rejected the offer and went to trial.
>
> Dr. Mays testified that he was a man of medicine, not a businessman. He relied on his bookkeeper and accountant; he signed whatever they put in front of him. The prosecuting attorney scoffed at this defense by telling the jury that everyone bears the responsibility for the accuracy of their tax returns. The jury sympathized with the good doctor and found him not guilty.
>
> P.S. Immediately after the trial, the IRS began an audit. Dr. Mays had to pay thousands of dollars in taxes, interest, and fraud penalties, but at least he stayed out of jail and kept his medical license.

In another case, Mr. Cheek, an airline pilot, was found guilty of tax evasion. The U.S. Supreme Court reversed his conviction. (*United States v. Cheek*, 498 U.S. 192 (1991).) Mr. Cheek claimed that he had formed a belief, based on materials provided by a tax protester group, that certain income tax laws did not apply to him. The trial judge told the jury not to consider this as a defense to tax evasion. The Supreme Court, however, held that his mistaken belief was a valid defense, and ordered Mr. Cheek to be retried. The question in the new trial was whether Mr. Cheek's belief was a good-faith misunderstanding of the tax laws or was a criminal intent to evade paying taxes.

Mr. Cheek wasn't as lucky his second time around in court as he was his first. At his new trial, Mr. Cheek raised the Supreme Court-approved defense, but was convicted by a new jury of several tax crimes, anyway. The judge sentenced him to one year and one day in prison and fined him $62,000. (*Wall Street Journal*, March 25, 1992.)

If You Are Convicted

If you are convicted of a tax crime after putting the government to the trouble of a trial, chances are eight in ten that you will be sent to federal prison. The Federal Sentencing Guidelines and the judge determine how long the sentence will be.

If, however, you reach a plea bargain without a trial, chances are better that you will be fined and/or placed on probation, given home confinement, or sent to a halfway house, rather than sent to jail. Added to the fine may be the costs incurred by the government in prosecuting you.

In general, public figures are most likely to go to jail. Back in the 1930s, President Hoover ordered that our income tax evasion law be used to put away the notorious Al Capone. This is the only charge ever made to stick on Scarface, who found his way to Alcatraz.

Today, instead of landing on the Rock, tax convicts are usually sent to a Club Fed minimum security facility filled with bankers, lawyers, politicians, and Wall Street sharpies. The average length of time served for a tax crime is a little less than two years. If this sounds like a breeze, think twice. Tax alumni of the federal prison system all agree that it was a humiliating and crushing experience. And licensed professionals—lawyers, doctors, stockbrokers, and CPAs—lose their professional licenses after conviction.

Phillip S. Fry, author of *Pay No Income Tax Without Going to Jail*, was apparently unclear on the concept. In 1986, he pleaded guilty to tax fraud and, you guessed it, went to jail. Other tax criminals with whom you are probably familiar and their prison terms include:

- Pete Rose—five months
- Chuck Berry—four months
- Aldo Gucci—one year
- Wesley Snipes—three years, and
- Leona Helmsley—four years.

Richard Hatch failed to pay taxes on the $1,000,000 he won on the show "Survivor," but he didn't survive the IRS police; he was sentenced to 51 months in federal prison.

One of my favorite stars of yesteryear, Sophia Loren, served 17 days in jail in her native Italy for tax evasion. It appears that big stars get off lighter in Italy than in the United States. So if you're thinking of evading taxes, maybe you want to brush up on your Italian and find a job in Venice, Florence, or Rome.

Chapter Highlights

- Tax fraud is more than carelessness or honest mistakes and can be punished by the IRS either civilly or criminally or both.
- The IRS seldom puts tax cheaters in jail but often imposes heavy fines.
- See a criminal or tax attorney if the IRS is investigating you for a tax crime.

Small Business/Self-Employed: When IRS Trouble Comes

f you are in business for yourself, or you work for someone who is, know that the IRS is watching. The three major concerns of the IRS here are:

- Are workers wrongly classified as independent contractors when they are legally employees?
- Is the business making payroll tax deposits?
- Are all transactions—especially large cash transactions—made to the business being reported to the IRS?

 RESOURCE
This chapter provides an overview of the most common small business tax issues. For details, see *Tax Savvy for Small Business*, by Frederick W. Daily (Nolo). In addition, *Working With Independent Contractors*, by Stephen Fishman (Nolo), contains the forms and information needed by employers who do, or plan to, hire independent workers. Finally, I heartily recommend *Legal Guide for Starting & Running a Small Business*, by Fred S. Steingold (Nolo), for general information (including some tax advice) for any small business owner.

Self-Employed—You're a Prime Audit Target

Because the IRS claims that most tax cheats are self-employed, it is not surprising that this group is more closely scrutinized than are wage earners. With 47,000 employees, the IRS's Small Business/Self-Employed Division is the biggest of all. If the IRS chooses to come after you by way of an audit—or worse, a criminal investigation—be aware that it can easily get to your bank and other financial records. So, if you've been foolish enough to deposit unreported income in your bank accounts, the IRS can find it.

If you are audited, the IRS will want to know:

- Did you report all of your business's sales or receipts?
- Did you write off any personal living expenses as business expenses?
- Does your lifestyle apparently exceed the amount of self-employment income reported?
- Did you write off automobile expenses for travel that was not business related?
- Did you claim large business entertainment expenses?

If you are self-employed and audited, be sure to read Chapter 3 and concentrate on the section "Living Beyond Your Means."

Employees or Independent Contractors?

If your business is improperly treating workers as self-employed individuals—that is, as independent contractors—expect trouble if the IRS calls. The IRS has the power to change the classification of any worker, with expensive consequences for the business owner.

By calling workers "independent contractors," business owners avoid burdensome tax reporting, bookkeeping, and withholding taxes from their workers' paychecks. Moreover, entrepreneurs dodge the tax expense of matching employees' FICA contributions and paying the unemployment tax. The tax savings and reduced paperwork of improperly calling employees independent contractors can be significant—unless you get caught. Violators can be penalized up to 35% of the payments made to the wrongly classified worker, plus interest.

In any event, a business must annually report to the IRS amounts paid to true independent contractors as well as employees. Within one month after the end of each calendar year, owners must file Form 1099 for each independent contractor paid more than $600. Owners must also send a copy of Form 1099 to the contractor.

If the IRS finds that you failed to issue a Form 1099, you may be hit with a separate penalty. (Internal Revenue Code § 3509.) Plus, it bolsters the IRS's case that you misclassified the worker.

Misclassification of independent contractors is an IRS priority. The IRS has targeted for audit businesses suspected of wrongly classifying workers, such as building contractors, medical professionals, graphic designers, and neighborhood beauty shops, to name a few.

IRS and state auditors can assess an employer not only the payroll taxes that should have been collected and paid, but also the reclassified employee's unpaid income taxes. And as the penalties and interest mount, businesses can receive audit bills of 50% or more of wages paid. For example, if you paid Millie Ways, an employee, $20,000 as an independent contractor, the

IRS might hit you with $10,000 in taxes, penalties, and interest for the misclassification.

How to Classify a Worker

To determine worker classification from the IRS point of view, see Form SS-8, *Determination of Employee Work Status for Purposes of Federal Employment Taxes and Income Tax Withholding.* (Available at the IRS's website at www.irs.gov.) Here is a summary of the SS-8 factors, gleaned mostly from court decisions.

Factors Tending to Show the Worker Is an Employee

- You require—or can require—the worker to comply with your instructions about when, where, and how to work.
- You train the worker to perform services in a particular manner.
- You integrate the worker's services into your business operations.
- You require the worker to render services personally; the worker can't hire others to do some of the work.
- You hire, supervise, and pay assistants for the worker.
- Your business has a continuing relationship with the worker or work is performed at frequently recurring intervals.
- You establish set hours of work.
- You require the worker to devote the majority of the work week to your business.
- You have the worker do the work on your premises.
- You require the worker to do the work in a sequence that you set.
- You require the worker to submit regular oral or written reports.
- You pay the worker by the hour, week, or month, unless these are installment payments of a lump sum agreed to for a job.
- You pay the worker's business or traveling expenses.
- You furnish significant tools, equipment, and materials.
- You have the right to discharge the worker at will and the worker has the right to quit at will.

Factors Tending to Show the Worker Is an Independent Contractor (IC)

- The worker hires, supervises, and pays his or her assistants.

- The worker is free to work when and for whom he or she chooses.
- The worker does the work at his or her own office or shop.
- The worker is paid by the job or receives a straight commission.
- The worker invests in facilities used in performing services, such as renting an office.
- The worker can realize a profit or suffer a loss from his or her services, such as a worker who is responsible for paying salaries to his or her own employees.
- The worker performs services for several businesses at one time— although sometimes a worker can be an employee of several businesses.
- The worker makes his or her services available to the general public.
- The worker can't be fired so long as he or she meets the contract specifications.

People Who Are Automatically Employees by Law

In most situations, the status of a worker is determined by the above-listed factors. Certain workers fall into special tax categories, and the usual IRS criteria don't apply. Workers who are automatically employees include:
- officers of corporations who provide service to the corporations
- food and laundry drivers
- full-time salespeople who sell goods for resale
- full-time life insurance agents working mainly for one company, and
- at-home workers who are supplied with material and given specifications for work to be performed.

Exempt Employees and Small Business Owners

The tax code states that licensed real estate agents and door-to-door salespeople are tax classified as nonemployees or exempt employees. They may be treated as regular employees for nontax purposes, however, such as liability insurance and workers' compensation.

Sole proprietors or partners in their own business are neither employees nor independent contractors. They pay their own income tax and Social Security/Medicare self-employment tax. But a shareholder in an incorporated business is legally an employee of the corporation in most cases.

How Independent Contractor Rules Are Applied

Let's look at two workers—one an employee and the other an independent contractor—who provide similar services but fall into different tax classification categories.

State Rules May Be Different

IRS classification rules are similar to those of most states for state taxes and unemployment rules, but there are differences. For example, in California, a person working for a licensed contractor who performs services requiring certain state licenses is classified as an employee unless he, too, has a valid contractor's license. If you plan to hire independent contractors, check the law in your state to see if there are special rules in effect.

EXAMPLE 1—EMPLOYEE: Wendy Wordsmith teaches marketing at a community college. Wendy also works part-time for ABC Enterprises writing ads, catalogs, and consumer information leaflets. Wendy works every Wednesday at ABC's offices, receiving a $200 salary each week. Wendy receives direct supervision and instructions from the owner. Wendy occasionally does some work at home when required to by ABC and is not allowed to do this kind of writing for anyone else. Wendy is an employee of both ABC Enterprises and the college.

EXAMPLE 2—INDEPENDENT CONTRACTOR: XYZ Distributors has similar needs for writing on an occasional basis. But when XYZ needs a newspaper ad or catalog produced, it calls upon Frank Freelance. Frank always works out of his home and frequently hires assistants whom he pays directly. Frank pays all his own expenses. Each time he completes a job for XYZ, he sends the company an invoice. Frank is not prohibited from writing ads for other businesses. He clearly is an independent contractor and not an employee of XYZ.

Part-Time Workers

John operates a desktop publishing shop specializing in writing and designing brochures, flyers, and other promotional materials for small businesses. At the start, John does most of the work himself, turning any overload over to others, including Sue, Ted, and Ellen, all working out of their homes. John collects from the customer and pays these people as independent contractors. So far, so good.

But as John's business grows, he brings Sue, Ted, and Ellen into his office to work part-time under his broad supervision, an average of about one or two days per week each. The rest of the time they work for themselves. John continues to treat them as independent contractors. By law, he shouldn't. If he continues along this line, he's tempting fate—and the IRS. John is exercising significant control over these workers and using their services in-house on a regular basis. Under the IRS guidelines, they are all employees, even if they are regularly employed or working as independent contractors elsewhere.

How Business Owners Can Protect Themselves

In order to be able to prove a worker was an independent contractor if you are audited:

- Enter into a written contract with the independent contractor. Spell out the responsibilities of each party and how payment is to be determined for each job. The contract should allow the independent contractor to hire his or her own assistants.
- Require the independent contractor to furnish the tools, equipment, and material needed for the job.
- Have the independent contractor do all or most of the work at his or her own place—not at yours.
- Make it clear that the independent contractor is free to offer services to other businesses besides yours.
- Pay for work by the job rather than by the hour, week, or month. Require the independent contractor to submit invoices for each job before you make payment.

- Require the contractor to show proof of a business license and insurance.
- Require the worker to prove he or she is reporting what you pay on his or her tax return.

The IRS invites businesses or workers to submit Form SS-8 for an IRS analysis of whether or not a particular worker qualifies as an independent contractor. I don't suggest using this form because it will alert the IRS to the issue. Instead, consult a tax professional, or use your own judgment based on what you read here and in other Nolo books.

Payroll Taxes—IRS Dynamite

If you own a business with employees, each payroll period you must hold back from each employee's paycheck:

- federal and maybe state income tax, and
- FICA contributions (Social Security and Medicare).

How much income tax you withhold from each employee's earnings depends on the number of exemptions claimed by the employee on Form W-4 when he or she started working for you. The FICA contribution is a percentage of the employee's gross earnings, which you must fully or partially match.

As an employer, you must turn over withheld taxes to a bank qualified as a depository for federal taxes. Use a federal tax deposit form with your payment. Many states have similar tax withholding forms.

A small business employer must deposit payroll taxes weekly, monthly, or quarterly, depending on the size of the payroll.

All employers must also send the IRS:

- Form 941, *Employer's Quarterly Federal Tax Return*. This form is filed every three months as long as your business has employees. Form 941 reports the amount of your employees' federal income tax and FICA withheld for the previous quarter.
- Form 940, *Employer's Annual Federal Unemployment Tax Return*, or FUTA. Form 940 is filed once a year. On it, you report your total quarterly payroll tax deposit. On this amount, a federal unemployment

tax is calculated. The FUTA tax is paid by your business and is not withheld from your employees' paychecks.

According to the IRS, most businesses are delinquent in filing or paying employment taxes at one time or another. The IRS considers payroll taxes the most serious of all tax debts. The theory of the payroll tax law is that the employer acts as a collector for the government, holding its workers' taxes in trust until paid over to the IRS. Consequently, the IRS views operating a business while owing payroll taxes as illegally borrowing money from the U.S. Treasury.

 CAUTION

IRS collectors are extremely tough if you owe payroll taxes. Review Chapter 6 for how to deal with IRS collections. Keep in mind that revenue officers can seize assets and force you out of business if you owe back payroll taxes.

How Businesses Can Minimize Payroll Tax Trouble

Give top priority to making payroll tax deposits when they are due. Never borrow from your employees' tax funds. Even if you eventually make the payment to the IRS, the penalties and interest can be substantial. Pay Uncle Sam first, not last. If you can't pay, then maybe you shouldn't be in business.

Stay out of trouble by using a bonded payroll tax service to both file and make all payroll tax deposits. Banks and companies like ADP and Safeguard offer this service at reasonable prices. If they goof up and don't get a form or payment in on time, they will pay the late payment penalty.

If your business is able to make only a partial payment of payroll taxes, write on the lower left-hand portion of the check that the payment is designated to the trust fund portion of the tax. Also, enclose a letter stating that you designate the payment to the trust fund portion.

The trust fund portion is the employee's income tax and FICA contributions. The smaller part—the employer's share of the FICA contribution—is not subject to the Trust Fund Recovery Penalty. This reduces the amount that the IRS can assess against responsible persons by around 8% (every little bit helps).

The Dreaded Trust Fund Recovery Penalty

Here's a familiar scenario: Your small business is struggling. You pay the rent and your employees' wages, but not the payroll taxes. You know things will turn around next month, however, when the big order comes in. And Christmas is just around the corner; you are sure you'll pull out of the slump and be able to pay Uncle Sam in full.

Six months go by. Your sales have gone down. Orders stopped coming in and holiday sales were terrible. Your suppliers have sued you and your landlord is threatening to evict. You haven't filed payroll tax forms or deposited payroll taxes for the last four quarters. You shut down and sell your assets to pay off the creditors—although you don't pay the IRS the payroll taxes you owe. You manage to avoid bankruptcy by the skin of your nose.

If you did it this way, woe unto you. You should have paid the IRS first and then, if need be, filed for bankruptcy to handle private creditors. This is because the IRS is the creditor to be most feared.

When payroll taxes haven't been paid, the IRS can review a company's books, speak to employees, and then hold its owners, managers, and bookkeepers personally responsible for the payroll taxes due. The IRS transfers the business payroll tax obligation to individuals—penalizing them for the business's failure to make the payroll tax deposits. This is known as the Trust Fund Recovery Penalty (TFRP). It applies primarily to incorporated businesses. If your small business was an LLC, a partnership, or a sole proprietorship, you can be found directly responsible for payroll taxes without the TFRP provision.

Because the penalty equals the taxes owed, it's also called the 100% Payroll Penalty. (Internal Revenue Code § 6672.) And although in most instances the TFRP is transferred to employees of a defunct business, the IRS can—and will—impose the liability on people working for an ongoing business as well.

The relevant section of Internal Revenue Code § 6672 states:

> *Any person required to collect, truthfully account for, and pay over any tax imposed by this title who willfully fails to collect such tax, or truthfully account for and pay over such tax, or willfully attempts in any manner to evade or*

defeat any such tax or the payment thereof, shall, in addition to other penalties provided by law, be liable for a penalty equal to the total amount of the tax evaded, or not collected, or not accounted for and paid over.

> ⚠ **CAUTION**
> **The IRS makes over 50,000 TFRP assessments each year, averaging $21,000 per responsible person.**

The IRS has three years to assess the TFRP against responsible people after the tax was originally assessed against the business. Once the TFRP is assessed against the responsible people, the IRS has ten years to collect it from them.

How the IRS Determines the Responsible People

On average, the IRS finds 1.6 responsible persons for each defunct business owing payroll taxes. There is no limit, however, and it's not uncommon for six or more people to be declared equally responsible. And all are jointly and severally liable for the entire amount; the penalty is not divided among the group—each person owes *all* of it to Uncle Sam until the penalty is paid in full.

> **EXAMPLE:** Skyrocket Corporation went out of business owing $60,000 in federal payroll taxes. The IRS finds Zoe, Emily, and Robb responsible for the money owed. Each is liable for the whole $60,000, and the IRS will go after the easiest target. The IRS can't collect more than $60,000 total, however. If Zoe pays, Emily and Robb are off the hook. If this happens, Zoe may be able to sue Emily and Robb in state court and get back $40,000.

The TFRP is one of the scariest parts of the tax code. It is directed at business owners, but it can also be assessed against low-level employees with no financial stake in the businesses. IRS investigations of businesses owing payroll taxes are conducted by revenue officers. They begin by putting together a list of people with any authority over business finances:

- Who made the financial decisions in the business?

- Who signed or had authorization to sign on the checking account?
- Who had the power to pay or direct payment of bills?
- Who had the duty of tax reporting?

To get this information, the officer may interview everyone whose name comes up when asking the above four questions. He or she looks at bank and corporate records for the names on bank signature cards and to find out who actually signed checks and who were corporate officers.

IRS Interviews of Potentially Responsible People

In interviewing each potentially responsible person, revenue officers ask the questions on IRS Form 4180, *Report of Interview With Individual Relative to Trust Fund Recovery Penalty or Personal Liability for Excise Tax*. If you are ever called for IRS questioning about a business with which you were associated, study the form ahead of time so that you won't be caught off guard. Depending on how much tax is owed, you might also review the form with a tax attorney before meeting the IRS.

At the interview, you can bring a representative with you—a tax lawyer, a CPA, or an enrolled agent. (See Chapter 13.) And you should, especially if you were the bookkeeper or check writer or had financial dealings in the business and don't believe that you should be held responsible.

Anyone whom the revenue officer believes acted willfully in preventing the IRS from receiving the payroll taxes is found liable. Unfortunately, "willful" does not mean that you intentionally tried to beat the government out of payroll taxes. It means only that you knew about the payroll taxes and knew they weren't being paid. Under this test, the IRS has found $100-per-week bookkeepers liable for enormous sums of money. The reasoning is that if the bookkeeper paid other bills, he or she could have paid the IRS.

Revenue officers often ignore business realities in order to find responsible persons. Most vulnerable are people with check-signing power and with corporate titles, but without any real authority.

Check-signing power. Revenue officers often assume that anyone who had the power to sign checks is guilty. They often ignore IRS rules stating that the TFRP should not be imposed based on check-signing authority alone. (*Internal Revenue Manual* 5632.1(3).) This is in line with court decisions that an employee with no financial interest in a business, but who signed checks under the explicit directions of a boss, is not a responsible person under the TFRP.

Corporate titles. Running a close second to check-signing power is the IRS assumption that anyone with a corporate title—president, secretary, or treasurer—is a responsible person. IRS policy, however, states that this presumption should be made only if the corporate officers do not cooperate in the IRS's investigation. (IRS Policy Statement P-5-60.) In many small corporations, titles bear little relationship to who really runs the business.

An individual may be responsible for the TFRP but not for all the tax periods. You aren't liable for the TFRP for payroll taxes owed before you came onto the scene or after you departed.

Appealing a Trust Fund Recovery Penalty

If you are found to be a responsible person by a revenue officer, you will be sent a preliminary notice and a tax bill. Revenue officers tend to find as many people responsible as is remotely possible. But their decisions can be protested to the appeals division, where many TFRP responsible-person findings are reversed. If you don't think you really were responsible, then you should appeal.

The preliminary notice you are mailed or handed informs you of the amount of the penalty and that you have 60 days to file an appeal. The procedure is similar to the appeal of an audit—you must file a written protest with the appeals office. (See Chapter 4.) If you don't appeal, after 60 days the preliminary notice becomes final and you will receive a formal demand for payment. (Internal Revenue Code § 6672.) If you don't pay, the IRS can go through its normal lien and levy process to enforce collection. (See Chapter 6.)

A sample protest letter is shown below, followed by the case history that led up to this letter.

Sample Letter to Appeal Trust Fund Recovery Penalty

September 20, 20xx

Internal Revenue Service
P.O. Box 408
Church Street Station
New York, NY 10008

Protest of Trust Fund Recovery Penalty
Sandy Swinger
SSN: 555-55-5555

VIA CERTIFIED MAIL–RETURN RECEIPT REQUESTED

Dear Sir or Madam:

This is a protest of the proposed assessment of a Trust Fund Recovery Penalty. I request a hearing. I have enclosed copies of IRS Letter 1153 (DO) and Form 2751 dated September 10, 20xx.

I deny that I was a responsible person and/or was willful in not paying over employment taxes for Crazy Calhoun's Incorporated under Internal Revenue Code Section 6672.

I never had any authority to make any tax payments to the IRS or to order another person to do so while I was employed by Crazy Calhoun's. I never had a financial stake in the business, other than as a salaried employee. I was never an officer or director of the corporation. I was only the manager of the bar operation and subject to the direction of the president, Tom Ranoff.

Under penalties of perjury, I declare that I have examined the statement of facts presented in this protest and to the best of my knowledge and belief, they are true, correct, and complete.

Sincerely,

Sandy Swinger
Sandy Swinger

Copy to Manuel Indiana, Revenue Officer

Enclosed: IRS Letter 1153 (DO) and Form 2751

Sandy and Crazy Calhoun's—A Case History

Crazy Calhoun's was a popular singles spot owned by three partners. At the height of its glory, the least competent of the partners, Tom, bought out the other two partners. Tom lived in the fast lane and preferred play to work. He let his employees run the business. His neglect and expensive tastes caused the business to fall behind in its bills—including federal payroll taxes.

Sandy was a longtime employee of Crazy Calhoun's. She worked her way up from cocktail waitress to bar manager. Because C.O.D. liquor deliveries during Tom's frequent absences needed to be paid, Sandy was authorized to sign checks. She was uneasy about it, but went along because she knew if the bar didn't have any booze, she'd be out of a job.

One day, a revenue officer showed up asking for Tom, who was out. The officer said he was padlocking the doors if he didn't get immediate payment of at least $2,000 for back payroll taxes. Sandy replied that she had authority to write checks for liquor deliveries only, unless Tom specified more. Several times in the past, Tom had phoned the bookkeeper saying that Sandy could sign payroll checks. Sandy asked her fellow workers what to do. They all agreed Tom would want her to write the check to the IRS, so she did.

Several months later Crazy Calhoun's was padlocked by the same revenue officer. By then, Tom had disappeared. Suppliers had stopped making deliveries for nonpayment; most employees had quit. Sandy got a new job. Eventually, Tom showed up in jail in Hawaii.

Sandy is found responsible

About two years later, a new IRS revenue officer paid a surprise visit to Sandy at home. Unlike the first guy, this man was very nice. He said he was investigating Crazy Calhoun's and needed to ask a few questions. He went through an interview and asked Sandy to sign a statement, thanked her, and left.

Two months later Sandy found in her mailbox an IRS notice of Proposed Assessment of Trust Fund Recovery Penalty. The nice man had found Sandy liable for $128,000 in payroll taxes of Crazy Calhoun's. She was hysterical. At 28 years old, Sandy owned a five-year-old Chevy, some old furniture, and a cat. She earned $350 a week as a waitress and was supposed to pay an IRS bill on which interest and penalties were running at over $1,500 per month.

Sandy and Crazy Calhoun's—A Case History (continued)

Sandy appeals

Sandy hired an attorney for her appeals hearing. The attorney felt that Sandy had a fair chance of winning an appeal. The most difficult thing to overcome would be the statement—Form 4180—that she had signed. The form is designed to virtually guarantee anyone interviewed will be found liable.

Her attorney sought out other former Crazy Calhoun employees, who backed Sandy's story that she never had authority to pay business taxes. The former manager, Jack, was living 2,500 miles away. Jack was sympathetic and said Sandy was telling the truth. He was afraid to put this in writing for fear the IRS would come after him.

Lois, the former bookkeeper, had prepared checks for the business but never signed them. She was not being pursued by the IRS. She gave a statement that Sandy could sign checks only to pay for liquor C.O.D.s and that Tom had sole authority to pay all other bills. Sandy's lawyer submitted a statement from Lois.

At the hearing, Sandy's lawyer presented a statement from Lois and her own statement summarizing the attorney's conversation with Jack. Also, Sandy stated she had paid the IRS only once, under the duress of the revenue officer. At the end of the hearing, the appeals officer stated that the case was closed. About 60 days later, Sandy received his report—she was not held to be responsible for the taxes.

TIP

Appealing a proposed TFRP assessment will buy time—even if you're clearly responsible. An IRS collector can't come knocking at your door while you are appealing. And interest does not run during the time an appeal is being considered. This is an unexplainable quirk in the law. For example, if you are eventually found responsible for $50,000 in unpaid payroll taxes and your appeal process takes a year, you'll avoid about $3,500 in interest. Of course, if you lose the appeal, interest starts to run again.

If You Lose Your Trust Fund Recovery Penalty Appeal

Many TFRP cases don't have endings as happy as Sandy's in the example above. If you really were a responsible person—that is, you knew about, had the authority to pay, and should have paid the payroll taxes—there may be no way to avoid the penalty. Nevertheless, if you find yourself in this awful predicament, keep reading to find your options.

Go to court. If you really believe you aren't liable, you can challenge a TFRP in court. You can sue in tax court (the easiest route), in the U.S. District Court nearest to you, or in the U.S. Court of Claims. (See Chapter 5.)

Tax court doesn't require you to pay the IRS any tax before filing your suit. However, to sue in a district court or the court of claims, you must first pay at least some of the taxes claimed due and then file a lawsuit seeking a refund. The minimum amount you must pay is equal to the unpaid payroll taxes due for one employee for one quarter of any pay period. This means that if you are found liable for a large amount—say $50,000—under the TFRP, you only need to pay the taxes for a minor employee—perhaps only $100—to contest the whole $50,000.

While you can go to tax court without a lawyer, as a practical matter, you will need an attorney to sue in either a district court or the court of claims. (See Chapter 5, "Other Federal Courts–Paying First Is Required.") Expect to pay a minimum of $10,000 in legal costs.

File for Chapter 13 bankruptcy. A TFRP can't be discharged, or wiped out, in a Chapter 7 bankruptcy. However, you can include a TFRP in a Chapter 13 repayment plan. See Chapter 6 for a description of bankruptcy. To try to get the TFRP partially wiped out in Chapter 13, consult a good bankruptcy lawyer.

Pay or compromise. If you throw in the towel, just deal with the TFRP as with any other kind of tax bill. See Chapter 6 to find out your options. Your best bets may be either an installment agreement or an Offer in Compromise.

Request a nonassessment or nonassertion. A little-known tax code provision allows people found responsible for TFRPs to request a "nonassessment" or "nonassertion." (Internal Revenue Code § 6672; *Internal Revenue Manual* 5.7.5.1 et seq.) I have had this request granted when my client showed she was broke and the IRS concluded it wasn't worth the effort to try to collect the penalty—even though she was clearly responsible for the payroll tax.

Are Other People Responsible?

If you or your tax professional submits a written request to the IRS, the agency must disclose the names of other people found responsible for the TFRP. Furthermore, the IRS must describe in writing its efforts to find and collect from each of them. It's clearly in your best interest to give the IRS any information you have regarding the location of assets of other responsible persons—unless you are feeling charitable.

Also, if you end up paying more than your proportional share of the TFRP, you can sue the others for the difference. For example, you and two other people are found responsible for a TFRP of $33,000. The IRS grabs your $15,000 IRA. Since your share is only $11,000, you may sue the other two people for the $4,000 difference. But don't look to the IRS for help in collecting from the two others; it's not their job. (Internal Revenue Code § 6672.)

Cash Transactions Over $10,000

As part of a government campaign against the underground economy and money laundering, all cash and cash equivalent *business* transactions over $10,000 must be reported to the IRS, using Currency Transaction Reports, or CTRs. Some state tax agencies have similar reporting laws and forms.

Cash equivalents include traveler's checks, money orders, and bank drafts. Personal checks of any amount are exempt from CTR reporting, presumably because banks keep copies of personal checks, thereby creating a paper or electronic trail the IRS can follow.

All businesses that receive cash or cash equivalents must report each customer's name and Social Security number for each transaction over $10,000 on IRS Form 8300. Banks report these transactions on Form 4789. (For details, see IRS Publication 1544.)

CTRs are used by the IRS to identify people who unload nontaxed money by purchasing luxury goods—such as cars, yachts, and jewels—or by taking lavish trips.

Within 15 days of receiving over $10,000 in cash or cash equivalents in a business transaction, you must send Form 8300 to the IRS. And when you deposit that money into your bank—or if your total cash deposits for one day exceed $10,000—your bank will report it to the IRS unless you are specifically exempt from this law. Large grocery stores and a few other types of businesses are exempt from CTR reporting.

> **CAUTION**
>
> **There is a law against "structured transactions."** This entails separating one $10,000 transaction into several smaller ones to avoid currency transaction reports. If multiple small transactions from the same source exceed $10,000 in total, you still must file a CTR. Similarly, if you make three cash deposits of $4,000 over a short period of time, your bank is obligated to report the total on a CTR.

Failing to file a Form 8300 can get you fined, audited, or both. And CTR violations may be sent to the IRS criminal investigation division. (See Chapter 10.) In short, not filing a CTR can cause you more problems than if you had reported the cash in the first place.

Chapter Highlights

- Self-employed people have the highest audit risk so they should keep very good records.
- If you hire others for your small business, be aware of the tax rules for independent contractors and employees.
- Hiring employees means you have to withhold taxes from their pay and follow all federal and state payroll tax requirements.
- Cash transactions in your business must be reported to the IRS if they are over $10,000.

Penalties and Interest

RS-imposed penalties and interest charges are discussed throughout the book. These fines can be very expensive. I once saw a $7,000 tax bill with $15,000 (eight years' worth) of interest and penalties. Tax penalties, from the IRS's perspective, are explained in Notice 433, *Interest and Penalty Information*. (A copy is available on the IRS's website at www.irs.gov.)

Some questions I frequently get:

Is it possible to get the IRS to drop a penalty?

What can I do about the interest on my audit bill?

How many different ways can the IRS penalize me?

Can I negotiate a penalty down?

Does the IRS ever have to pay me interest?

Penalties Added to Tax Bills

When the IRS hits you with an additional tax bill (from an audit, for example), it usually adds penalties and interest. Penalties are added automatically by IRS computers or by IRS personnel at their discretion. Interest charges are required by law (and are discussed below).

Penalties are authorized whenever you file or pay your taxes late, have been found to owe additional taxes, or have failed to file all required tax forms.

Although penalties were originally meant to punish errant taxpayers—that's why they are called penalties—they are now considered a regular and dependable source of revenue in our national budget. Reflecting this, in the past decade, the total dollar amount of penalties imposed on taxpayers increased by 1,000%. In a recent year, 25 million penalties were assessed for over $6 billion. In short, penalties have become a tax—on a tax.

> **TIP**
>
> **Take heart—you may be able to beat the IRS at the penalty game.** The IRS can remove a penalty if you can show that your failure to comply with the tax law was due to "reasonable cause."

IRS penalties fall into five basic categories—accuracy, fraud, failure to pay taxes, late filings, and a combined late-filing and -paying penalty.

Accuracy Penalties

The IRS can add a 20% accuracy-related penalty to your tax bill if IRS auditors find your tax return understated your tax liability. This is a commonly imposed penalty by the IRS "due to negligence or intentional disregard of the tax law." This means you didn't pay heed to the tax law or you were just plain careless.

Fraud Penalties

If the IRS concludes that you fraudulently omitted or underreported income, it can add a heavy fraud penalty. This penalty is 75% of the amount you underreported. For example, if you fraudulently underreported $10,000, the fraud penalty is $7,500.

Or, if the IRS finds that you fraudulently failed to file a return, it can penalize you—15% for every month you didn't file for up to five months—a total of 75% based on the taxes owed. This penalty is rarely, if ever, imposed. The IRS usually just hits you with a late-filing penalty of 5% per month for a maximum of five months, a total of 25%.

Failure to Withhold, Deposit, or Pay Taxes

This is a stiff penalty on employers who do not withhold or pay over their employees' Social Security, Medicare, and income taxes. This happens when employers aren't timely filing IRS Form 941 and making the deposits. The penalty varies by how late the payments are made. (For details see *Tax Savvy for Small Business*, by Frederick Daily (Nolo).)

Failure to File Information Returns

This penalty is on business owners who don't file reports with the IRS, most often Form 1099 showing payments to service providers like independent contractors. The penalty varies depending on the type of form and the number of nonfiled forms.

Failure to Pay Penalties

The IRS can add to your bill a penalty of ¼% to 1% per month of the amount you failed to pay on time. The penalty starts off at ½% per month. If you enter into an installment agreement to pay the taxes, the IRS drops the penalty to ¼% per month. If you don't pay and the IRS later issues a Notice of Intent to Levy (see Chapter 7), it can raise the penalty to 1% per month on the balance due.

This penalty starts on the day after the original due date, April 16 for individual tax returns. It is imposed on the unpaid balance and added to your bill on the 16th day of each month thereafter. This penalty is imposed monthly and is not prorated daily.

Late Filing Penalties

Did you file your individual tax return late and didn't request an extension? The IRS can impose a penalty of 5% per month on any tax balance due, up to 25% of the bill. You max out on this penalty if, on September 16—five months and one day after April 15—you still haven't filed your individual tax return. *If you file late but don't owe any taxes, there is no federal penalty.* For some information-type forms (such as 1099s) filed late, the IRS can impose a penalty in varying amounts according to specific tax code provisions.

Combined Penalties

Did you both file late and pay late? The IRS can impose a combined penalty of 5% per month (½% per month less than the separate penalties for each). The combined penalty is based on the unpaid tax balance for each month your return is late. When you reach 25%—five months—for filing late, the penalty for late filing stops. The failure-to-pay portion of the combined penalty continues at ½% per month until it reaches a total of 22½%. Thus, the maximum combined penalty is 47½%. Note that tax penalties *do not* include charges for interest, which never stops running.

Late-filing penalties, late-payment penalties, or the combined penalty can be stacked—imposed in addition to other penalties, such as accuracy or fraud penalties resulting from an audit of your tax return.

Interest on Tax Bills

The second unwelcome addition to every overdue tax bill is IRS-charged interest. By not paying your taxes on time, you are considered to be borrowing from Uncle Sam. Congress does not like to lend money interest free (except to various dictators and deadbeat foreign countries), so it requires the IRS to charge interest.

The interest rate is also set by Congress and is adjusted by formula four times a year and compounded daily. Compounding means interest is charged on interest. For older tax bills, interest calculations cannot be easily verified without a computer that emulates the IRS's program. In recent years, the interest rate has ranged between 3% and 6% per year. Interest is computed on *both* the tax and penalties due.

Understanding Penalty and Interest Notices

When you receive a tax bill from the IRS, it usually states penalty and interest charges separately. If you don't understand the IRS computation—it's unlikely you will—call the taxpayer assistance number (800-829-1040) or write or ask your local IRS office to mail you a detailed penalty and interest explanation, called a PINEX transcript (Form CP-569).

The PINEX is a multipage computer printout showing:

- your tax account (by Social Security number or employer identification number) showing all tax penalty and interest computations
- dates, interest rates, penalties assessed, and any credits—payments or refunds
- principal tax amounts on which interest and penalties were charged
- explanations of which penalties were applied, and
- a summary of your account with balance due, including up-to-date penalty and interest amounts.

Check the figures on the transcript to see that you agree with the amount of the taxes shown, and that you have been credited for all payments you made.

Reducing or Eliminating Penalties and Interest

The IRS can eliminate or reduce a penalty for a *reasonable cause* if you request it. The term the IRS uses for wiping out a penalty is *abatement*. About one-third of IRS-imposed penalties are later canceled (abated).

Interest, however, is rarely abated. By law, interest can be canceled only if it was erroneously applied or if it was due to lengthy IRS delays. Additionally, if you qualify for an offer in compromise, the IRS may reduce an interest charge or a penalty along with the tax due. (See Chapter 6.)

Abatement requests can be granted at any IRS level—IRS campus, automated collection system, or personnel at local IRS offices. However, local IRS offices can only grant abatements up to $100.

Approximately 20% to 25% of all IRS penalties are subsequently abated on request.

Reasonable Cause for a Penalty Abatement

The key to having a penalty removed is to show the IRS some *reasonable cause* for your failure to follow the tax law. Reasonable cause is any excuse that an IRS officer will buy. The *Internal Revenue Manual* (IRS Policy Statement P-2-7) says:

> *Any sound reason advanced by a taxpayer as the cause for delay in filing a return, making deposits … or paying tax when due will be carefully analyzed …. Examples of … reasonable cause:*
> 1. *Death or serious illness of the taxpayer or … immediate family. In the case of a corporation, estate, [or] trust … death or serious illness must have been of an individual having sole authority to execute the return or make the deposit or payment.*
> 2. *Unavoidable absence of the taxpayer ….*
> 3. *Destruction by fire or other casualty of the taxpayer's place of business or records.*
> 4. *Taxpayer was unable to determine amount of deposit of tax due for reasons beyond taxpayer's control ….*
> 5. *Taxpayer's ability to make deposits or payments has been materially impaired by civil disturbances.*

6. *Lack of funds is an acceptable reasonable cause for failure to pay any tax or make a deposit … only when a taxpayer can demonstrate the lack of funds occurred despite the exercise of ordinary business care and prudence.*

7. *Other explanations may be acceptable …. Acceptable explanations of delinquency are not limited …. Any reason … established that the taxpayer exercised ordinary business care and prudence but was nevertheless unable to comply within the prescribed time will be accepted as reasonable cause.*

Practical suggestions. If possible, choose one or more of the first six items when requesting a penalty abatement. Also mention Number 7, that you acted with "ordinary business care and prudence" but still couldn't file or pay your taxes on time.

Here are some explanations the IRS has accepted:

- You relied on a tax professional who steered you wrong. For example, if your accountant or bookkeeper caused the tax problem by giving you bum advice or filing the wrong form, say so. Bear in mind that the IRS might counter that because you picked the tax professional, you are responsible for his or her action.

- The IRS wouldn't help you earlier. If you called, wrote, or visited the IRS and got the wrong information or no response when you tried to clear things up, make the point. Be sure to provide copies of letters you sent, the names and IRS identification numbers of all IRS personnel you spoke with, and the dates and summaries of your conversations.

- Someone else caused your problem. For example, if your employer submitted an incorrect 1099 or W-2 form, be sure to tell that to the IRS.

- If your penalty is from a late payment, plead that you would have suffered an undue hardship if you had paid on time. Be warned that this is a tough sell to the IRS. You will need to show that had you paid your taxes on time, you would not have been able to put food on the table. The IRS is often sympathetic if the hardship is medically related, including alcohol or drug abuse. Again, supply documentation, such as letters from doctors explaining your condition.

If it's true, stress your clean past IRS record: You've never before requested an abatement, had a penalty, or been behind in paying your taxes.

How to Request a Penalty Abatement

For penalties imposed by IRS mailed notices, start the abatement process by mail. As soon as you receive a tax bill with penalties, write back and ask for an abatement. Use a letter like the sample, below. Alternatively, use IRS Form 843, *Claim for Refund and Request for Abatement.* (A copy is available on the IRS's website.) Attach to your letter a copy of the IRS notice showing the penalty.

Also attach copies of substantiating documents—such as a doctor's statement, fire department report, insurance claim, or death certificate of a family member. Without supporting papers, your abatement request may not get serious consideration.

If possible, enclose payment for the underlying tax, and write on your check that the payment is for the tax portion only. Paying the tax stops the accrual of interest on that balance. Send the letter with enclosures to the IRS address in the notice, and use the IRS enclosed bar-coded envelope.

Keep copies of any letters or documents sent to the IRS. The IRS is notorious for ignoring or losing taxpayer correspondence. Send the additional copies if you get another IRS billing before getting a reply to your initial abatement request.

For penalties imposed in an audit, ask the auditor or a manager to drop them before you sign the report. If that doesn't work, you can protest the penalty to the Appeals Office. (See Chapter 4.)

If Your Abatement Request Is Rejected

If the IRS officially rejects your abatement request, you will get a written notice. You then have four options besides accepting your fate.

Appeal. File a protest—a letter requesting an appeal. See the sample letter, below.

Send your appeal letter to the IRS. Unlike an appeal of an audit, the IRS does not grant you an in-person appeal hearing after an abatement request is rejected. The appeal is handled by mail or telephone.

Sample Letter Requesting Abatement of Penalties

November 3, 20xx

Penalty Abatement Coordinator
IRS Campus
P.O. Box 9941
Ogden, UT 84409

RE: Request for Penalty Abatement
    SSN: 555-55-5555

To Whom It May Concern:

I am requesting an abatement of penalties in the IRS notice enclosed dated 5/5/xx in the amount of $2,312.10.

The reason I [*select one*] filed late, paid late, didn't report some income was that [*fill in your reason, such as*]:

- I was suffering from a nervous breakdown

- my wife had just passed away

- my house burned down on April 14 with all of my tax records

- I was a hostage in Lebanon, or

- any other excuse.

Enclosed is a [*describe your documents, such as*]:

- letter from Dr. Freud explaining my condition which prevented me from filing my tax return on time

- death certificate confirming my wife's passing

- report from the fire department

- letter from the U.S. State Department confirming my status as a hostage, or

- other documentation.

I have also enclosed payment that covers the amount of the underlying taxes I owe. [*Optional, but a good idea if you can afford to make the payment.*]

Sample Letter Requesting Abatement of Penalties (continued)

Please abate these penalties for reasonable cause. I can be reached at
801-555-3444 during daytime hours.

Thank you,

Sanford Majors
Sanford Majors
43 Valley Road
Salt Lake City, UT 84000

Enclosed: IRS Tax Notice; doctor's letter, death certificate, fire report, letter from
State Department [*or whatever*]

Sample Letter Appealing Denial of Abatement of Penalties

January 15, 20xx

IRS Campus
P.O. Box 9941
Ogden, UT 84409

Re: Appeal of Penalty Abatement Denial
   SSN: 555-55-5555

To Whom It May Concern:

I wish to appeal the denial of my penalty abatement request, which I received on January 10, 20xx. A copy of the denial is attached.

The grounds for my appeal are that I had a reasonable cause for [*state type of penalty*] filing late, paying late, not reporting some income because [*state reasons*]:

- I was in a coma
- my tax preparer had just died, or
- any other excuse.

I can prove my condition with [*state type of proof*]:

- letter from Dr. Stein proving my condition
- death certificate confirming my tax preparer's death, or
- any other documentation.

Thank you,

Sanford Majors

Sanford Majors
43 Valley Road
Salt Lake City, UT 84000
Telephone: 801-555-1212

Enclosed: IRS Tax Notice; Dr. Stein's letter; death certificate [*or whatever*]

Request a transfer of your file. Write the IRS requesting that your file be transferred to your local IRS office. Then request a meeting with a revenue officer to try and convince the officer that your penalty should be removed.

Pay and claim a refund. Pay the penalty and then file for a refund. Despite what you may think, paying first does not hurt your chance of getting a refund granted. Your refund request should be submitted to your IRS campus on Form 843, *Claim for Refund and Request for Abatement.* You can either attach a letter of explanation similar to the one you tried in your original abatement request, or give your reasonable cause explanation in the small space provided on Form 843.

If your Form 843 claim is refused, you can sue in a U.S. District Court or the court of claims. (See Chapter 5.) Rarely, however, are tax penalties large enough to justify the costs of going to court.

Make an Offer in Compromise. An Offer in Compromise is a formal procedure for contesting or negotiating any IRS bill, including a penalty. (See Chapter 6.)

Abating Interest

Congress makes the IRS charge interest on a tax bill. Of course, if a tax or penalty is canceled for any reason, interest on it is wiped out as well. Usually the IRS computer does this automatically, but check your bill to make sure.

The tax code authorizes the abatement of interest only in the following circumstances:

(a) The IRS was wrong in charging interest—meaning that either you paid the tax when it was due or didn't owe any taxes on which interest could be charged. If this happens to you, write to the IRS, explain what is wrong, and ask for an interest abatement. If that doesn't work, call the Taxpayer Advocate Service at your local IRS office. (See Chapter 8.) You also can sue in U.S. District Court or the Federal Court of Claims to recover interest already paid, but this is too costly to be a practical alternative.

(b) The IRS incorrectly sent you a refund, wants its money back, and is charging you interest all the way back to the time the check was issued. This is not so unusual. Computer-generated tax refunds sometimes come out of the blue. You are entitled to an interest abatement as long as your actions did not cause the refund. Once the IRS asks for its money back, it can, however, charge you interest, but only from the date of the request, until you repay it. (Internal Revenue Code § 6404.)

(c) The interest resulted from delays of the IRS in performing ministerial acts. For example, the IRS delays sending a tax bill after you agree to an audit report. You are entitled to an interest abatement of all but the first 30 days of the delay. (Revenue Procedure 87-42; IRS Regulation 301.6404-2T.) So if, following an audit, a bill with interest arrives 90 days after you agree to the result, you can have the last 60 days of interest abated.

The exception for ministerial acts does not cover interest while you challenge a bill or while the IRS audits you, or while you appeal or go to tax court. This interest cannot be abated, unless you win your case.

(d) The interest accrued more than 18 months after the original due date of a tax return or the date the return was filed, and the IRS did not notify you that additional tax was due during that period. (Internal Revenue Code § 6404.)

(e) The interest accrued on a return you filed late because you were living in a federally declared disaster area when the return was due.

As with taxes and penalties, interest also may be reduced or eliminated by an Offer in Compromise or through bankruptcy. (See Chapter 6.)

How to Request an Interest Abatement

To request an interest abatement for an IRS error in billing (a) or (b) above, follow the sample form letter appealing denial of abatement of penalties. Instead of alleging reasonable cause, as the form letter does, state something like, "The IRS wrongfully sent me a refund and is charging interest. I should not have to pay interest because my actions did not cause the refund to be sent." Although interest is seldom abated except when the IRS has made the mistake, it never hurts to ask and you are only out the cost of a first-class stamp.

If you are requesting an abatement because of IRS delays ((c) or (d)), use Form 843. If you are in a disaster area, call the IRS for instructions at 800-829-1040.

Designating Late Tax Payments

If you can't pay in full, be sure to tell the IRS how a late payment should be applied to your tax account. If you don't, the IRS allocates it first to taxes, then to penalties, and last to interest. Payments are automatically applied to the oldest tax period for which you owe. For example, you owe $10,000 in taxes, penalties, and interest for several of the past eight years. You make a $1,500 payment. Tell the IRS in writing that it is to be applied to the most recent year.

Advantages of Designating Your Payments

On the date income taxes are assessed, the IRS has ten years to collect these taxes, penalties, and interest. If part of your tax bill is for a year for which the ten-year limit is about to expire, then be sure to designate in writing that your payments are to be applied to your most recent tax debts. For example, suppose in 2012 you want to make a payment to a tax debt for years 2003 and 2004. Designate the payment to 2004, because the 2003 tax debt expires on April 16, 2014, assuming you filed your 2003 tax return by April 15, 2004. (See Chapter 6.)

Another reason to designate payments to the most recent years is your right to reduce some tax bills in bankruptcy. Generally, older tax bills are more easily reduced or eliminated in bankruptcy than newer ones. (See Chapter 6.)

How to Designate a Payment

When making an income tax payment by check or money order, write in the lower left-hand corner your Social Security number and the tax period or year you are paying. For a business tax, use your taxpayer identification number instead of your Social Security number.

Unless the payment is for the current tax bill, enclose a letter with the payment clearly stating that payment is to be applied to the tax period or year noted on your check or money order. Otherwise, the IRS will apply the payment to the oldest tax period. If you're concerned that the IRS has misapplied the funds, you can request an account statement, called a Record of Account for individuals with Social Security numbers or businesses with separate identification numbers. (See Chapter 1.)

If the account statement shows that the IRS ignored your designation request, send photocopies of your letter and the checks to show that payments were not misapplied. With proof of your designation of payment, the IRS will correct its records.

If the IRS refuses or ignores your request, complain to the taxpayer advocate. (See Chapter 8.)

 CAUTION

Only voluntary payments can be designated to particular tax periods.
If the IRS levies your wages or bank account or withholds a refund, you have no right to designate how it's applied.

Chapter Highlights

- The IRS can add penalties to your bill for a variety of tax misdeeds.
- Interest is always added to a tax bill if the bill isn't paid on time.
- You may get the IRS to remove a penalty for "reasonable cause."

CHAPTER 13

Help Beyond the Book:
Tax Professionals and Tax Information

This book gives you strategies for coping with most tax problems—audits, bills, and tax court. If you need more help, try any of these:

- **Tax professionals.** An enrolled agent, a certified public accountant, or a tax attorney can prepare tax returns or provide a tax information, guidance, or representation before the IRS.
- **IRS.** The IRS has free tax publications, telephone prerecorded and live information, Internet access, and taxpayer service representatives at many offices.
- **Library.** You can research tax questions in larger public libraries and law libraries in your community.
- **Internet.** You can do much research on tax issues at the IRS's and others' websites.

Finding and Using a Tax Professional

You can successfully take on the IRS alone most of the time. But if you feel over your head or want professional reassurance, consider consulting or hiring a tax professional.

Under the Taxpayer Bill of Rights (Chapter 15), you may have a representative handle any IRS matter for you. You never have to face the IRS alone if you hire a tax professional. You also have the right to call "time out" to consult a tax professional during the process whenever you are taking on the IRS by yourself. But you don't have the right to free help. You'll have to pay whomever you hire.

You can safely go it alone in the two most common, but serious, IRS situations:

- You are being audited and your records are in order, you can substantiate almost everything on your return, and you have nothing to hide.
- The IRS is seeking to collect an overdue tax bill of $10,000 or less and you can pay it off over time.

But before making any decision on proceeding alone or working with a tax professional, weigh the pros and cons of each.

Going it alone

Pro: You save professional fees.

Con: It takes a lot of time.

You may find it very stressful.

You may say or do the wrong thing.

Consulting a tax professional before facing the IRS on your own

Pro: You gain knowledge, strategy, advice, and confidence.

Con: Most tax professionals charge for a consultation, but it will be less than if you hire the tax professional to represent you.

Hiring a tax professional to represent you before the IRS

Pro: The IRS respects knowledgeable tax professionals.

You don't have to face the IRS in most cases.

Tax professionals know tax issues.

Con: Tax professionals are expensive if they are good.

You understand your tax records best.

You risk hiring someone who is inexperienced or incompetent.

How Tax Professionals Can Help

Myth: The IRS will think I am guilty of something if I hire a tax professional or will get mad at me for not facing them myself.

Fact: IRS auditors and collectors prefer dealing with experienced tax professionals. It makes their job easier. Good tax professionals know what the IRS wants and don't get overly emotional.

If you face an audit, collection of a tax bill, or a tax court hearing—and you've decided to find a tax professional—you should get the services listed here.

Consultation and advice. A tax professional can analyze your situation and suggest a strategy. Rarely is there only one way to handle an IRS matter. Once you know the alternatives, you can make an informed choice. Of course, a tax professional might pitch his or her services. Weigh the professional's advice against what you have learned by reading this book and your own judgment. If the tax professional suggests a course of action you believe is excessively expensive, is dishonest, or doesn't make sense, find someone else. There are good ones and bad ones, as in any profession.

Negotiation. An experienced tax professional should know what kinds of deals can and can't be made with the IRS.

Representation. Tax professionals know IRS procedures and how to maneuver around the IRS bureaucracy. They can neutralize the intimidation factor the IRS knows it holds over you. And, if you have something to hide, a tax professional usually can keep the lid on it better than you can.

Types of Tax Professionals

For an audit, a collection, or an appeals problem, you can choose among enrolled agents, tax attorneys, and certified public accountants. A fourth category—tax return preparers with no professional certifications—can help you around April 15, but may not have the right to represent you before the IRS.

Enrolled agent (EA). An EA is a full-time tax adviser and tax preparer who is licensed to practice before the IRS. Most EAs cannot represent you in tax court, however. They became enrolled agents by either passing a difficult IRS exam or having at least five years of IRS work experience. They also must participate in continuing education programs to retain their EA designations.

There are approximately 24,000 EAs in the United States. EAs are the least expensive of all tax professionals. For a cost-effective approach to handling a tax problem, consider an EA.

Tax attorney. Tax attorneys are lawyers who specialize in complex tax and estate planning; others focus on IRS dispute resolution and some do complex tax return preparation. Look for a tax attorney with either a special tax law degree (LL.M.-Tax) or a certification as a tax law specialist from a state bar association. If a great deal of money is at stake, the IRS is accusing you of fraud, or you're headed to court, call a tax attorney.

Certified public accountant (CPA). Like attorneys, CPAs are licensed and regulated in all states. They do sophisticated accounting and internal audit work and prepare tax returns. To become a CPA, an accountant must have a college degree and experience with a CPA firm and must pass a rigorous examination. Some CPAs have a great deal of IRS experience, but many never deal with the IRS. CPAs charge about the same as attorneys. As a rule, CPAs are not as aggressive as tax lawyers when facing IRS personnel.

> ⓘ **CAUTION**
> **Is your preparer legit?** As of January, 2011, *all* paid tax return preparers must have an IRS-issued Preparer Tax Identification Number (PTIN) and list it on all returns they prepare. If you're in doubt about your tax pro, ask to see the letter from the IRS showing his or her PTIN.

How to Choose a Tax Professional

There are several ways to find a good tax professional. Asking the IRS is not one of them.

Personal referrals. This is frequently the best source. Ask friends, relatives, and acquaintances whose judgment you trust for the names of tax professionals who helped them. If their tax professionals can't help, ask for a referral.

Your tax preparer or accountant. Your tax return preparer or accountant should know a good tax professional who can help you deal with an IRS problem.

Prepaid legal plans. Prepaid legal plans offer basic services for a low monthly fee and discounted fees for additional work. Few lawyers in prepaid legal plans have tax or IRS experience, however. Tax attorneys rarely participate because of relatively low fees paid by the plans.

Chain tax services. Some national outfits offer audit assistance free with their tax return preparation service. One chain says they will go with you to the IRS to explain how a return was prepared. This service may fall short of actual representation. And there is no guarantee the person going with you prepared your return or is a tax expert. Not all tax preparers are created equal—not by a long shot. These folks may know how to prepare simple tax returns, but I wouldn't rely on them to help with an IRS problem.

Advertising. Various directories, including phone books and newspapers, carry lists of tax professionals. Look under Accountants, Tax Return Preparers, Tax Consultants, and Attorneys-Tax. Some tax professionals offer a first consultation by phone or in their office at no charge. Bear in mind, however, that professionals heavily advertising or giving away their time may be new to the game.

Professional associations and referral panels. Most local bar associations will give out the names of tax attorneys who practice in your area. But bar associations don't meaningfully screen the attorneys listed; those who are listed may not be experienced or competent. To find an EA in your area, call the National Association of Enrolled Agents referral line at 800-424-4339. To find a CPA, try calling a local or state CPA society.

Direct solicitation. If the IRS has filed a Notice of Federal Tax Lien against you, you may receive a call or letter from a tax professional. Be wary. In general, good tax professionals are too busy to do this.

What to Look for in a Tax Professional

Once you have the name of a tax professional, call and ask to speak with the person directly. If he or she is too busy to talk to you—and your call isn't transferred to another tax specialist—assume the office is too busy to handle your case. Call the next person on your list.

When you speak to a tax professional, try to develop a rapport. Mention how you got his or her name, especially if it was a personal referral. Then get to the point—talk about your tax problem. If he or she doesn't handle your type of case, ask for the names of professionals who do.

Here are some other suggestions for making a good match:

- Don't rush to hire the first tax professional you speak to. Your decision is important, and rarely is there only one person for the job. Talk to a few. Choose the one you communicate with best—do you understand the advice and answers to your questions?
- Question the tax professional carefully about his or her IRS experience. No matter how well someone knows the tax code, prior IRS dealings are key. Previous IRS employment is not always a plus; it may have forever impressed the IRS point of view on the person. Also, be skeptical if the person hasn't been in practice at least five years.
- Does the tax professional seem to be aggressive or timid in discussing your case? If he or she seems awed by the IRS, find someone else.
- Does the tax professional give you a feeling of confidence? Ask about the likely outcome of your case. While no one can predict the future, this answer should create trust. Look for an honest response, not necessarily a rosy picture.

If you lose faith in your tax professional, find another one fast. But don't dismiss the first one until you get a second opinion on his or her work. And don't fire a tax professional simply because nothing is happening. Frequently, inaction is because the IRS is dragging its feet. Be patient—delay often works to your advantage in dealing with the IRS.

Tax Professionals' Fees

Get an understanding about the tax professional's fees at your first meeting. Will you be charged by the hour or a flat fee? Professionals can charge anything from $50 (for an enrolled agent) to $700 (for a top tax attorney) per hour, depending on where you live, the type of case, and the tax professional. To some extent, you can control costs. Tax professionals can be hired either as consultants, meaning you handle your own case and ask for advice as needed, or hired to represent you from start to finish. In other words, hiring a tax professional need not be an all or nothing affair.

Tips on Controlling a Tax Professional's Fees

- If you like the tax professional but not the fee, ask if it can be done for less. If the person isn't very busy, he or she may be flexible on fee and payment arrangements. Small tax firms or solo practitioners are more likely than professionals in large offices to negotiate their fees.
- Ask for a written fee agreement and monthly billings with itemized statements of time and services rendered. This will keep the tax professional honest and keep the large-bill shock down. In many states, attorneys are required to give you a written fee agreement before starting work.
- If you disagree with a bill, call your tax professional. If the firm is interested in retaining your business, it should listen to your concerns, adjust the bill, or work toward satisfying you. If the tax professional won't budge, call your state or local CPA society or your state's bar association. Many groups have panels that help professionals and clients mediate fee disputes.

Although uncertainty about open-ended fee arrangements leaves most folks uncomfortable, many good tax professionals won't quote a flat fee. But they should be able to ballpark a range of hours necessary for your case. For example, I usually figure five to 15 hours of my time for full representation in an office audit or a collection matter. For appeals, field audits, and tax court cases, I put in ten to 60 hours on average.

Most tax professionals require a fee and cost retainer paid in advance, often equal to the minimum time estimated as needed on the case.

Tax Pros for Serious Audits

If you're being pursued by a tax collector or you're headed to tax court, the information in this chapter, and in Chapters 5 and 6, should guide you in your decision about using a tax professional. Audits, however, require special attention: Spending a small percentage of your potential IRS exposure for professional help can be a wise investment for the peace of mind and confidence that good advice brings. Before reading this information, however, read the information above and Chapter 3.

If you consult a tax professional, bring your IRS audit notice, tax return, and documents on which the return was prepared to the first meeting. If you face an *office*—as opposed to a field—audit, go over the audit letter checklist with the tax professional—explain why you reported your income as you did or took the deductions that the IRS is now questioning. Ask the tax professional what documentation will help you prove your position.

If you face a *field* audit, your audit will likely go beyond any pre-prepared list of items to be examined. This makes a field audit more difficult to prepare for than an office audit. Show an audit-experienced tax pro your return and ask which items he or she would expect the IRS to question. Next, ask if he or she sees any legal problem areas and how to deal with them. You might ask the person to provide some supporting tax law authority or prepare a memorandum of law pertaining to your case to show the auditor.

Finally, ask the tax professional for suggestions on how best to explain and present your documents to the auditor. You may want assistance in making summaries or spreadsheets showing your business or investment transactions. The more clearly you present information, the less time you will spend with the auditor. Auditors appreciate and, more importantly, reward well-prepared taxpayers.

If your tax professional was the preparer of the tax return, ask him or her to explain all figures and schedules to you. If workpapers or notes were used to prepare your return, ask for copies and interpretations, if needed. You won't necessarily show them to the auditor; they may be just for your reference.

The Right Type of Tax Professional

Using an enrolled agent is a cost-effective choice when you need representation in an audit. But if you face complex legal or accounting issues or if the IRS accuses you of fraud, hire a tax attorney or CPA. In some cases, you may need both.

Your tax return preparer may legally represent you at an audit. Or an immediate family member or business partner or employee can with written permission on IRS Form 2848. (Call 800-829-3676 to get this form.) Bringing any of these people along for support is okay, but I don't recommend having any of them represent you at an audit.

Tax Professional Analysis After an Audit

If you handled your own audit and it did not turn out well, you might want to ask a tax professional why. The tax pro can analyze the examination report, tax return, and documents you produced at the audit. Tell the tax pro what you said and what the auditor said about items that are disputed. The tax professional can then evaluate the strengths and weaknesses of your legal position.

If the person believes you are at least in a legal gray area, he or she may examine the quality of the documents and consider the credibility of your explanations. In an hour or so, the tax pro should be able to decide whether you should contest the IRS's report. He or she may advise you to try again with the auditor or the auditor's manager, or to make a formal appeal or go to tax court. (See Chapter 4.)

Hiring a Tax Return Preparer

IRS problems often stem from the accuracy of your tax return and who prepares it. Over half of all tax returns are professionally prepared. The commissioner of the IRS has said that the "tax system has become so complex … something must be done to make it less burdensome." Until this happens, consider having a tax professional prepare your returns, especially if you are self-employed.

You might also lessen your chance of being audited by having a professional preparation. Insiders say that IRS personnel (see Chapter 3) are more likely to pick self-prepared returns for audit than those signed by a reputable tax professional.

Enrolled agents, tax attorneys, and CPAs are the cream of the crop. Others may call themselves tax preparers, too. But unless they are admitted to practice before the IRS, they cannot represent you there. Fees for preparing individual income tax returns range from $50 to $2,500 and up, depending on the complexity of your return and the professional qualifications of the tax preparer.

Whether you hire a tax preparer or do it yourself, you alone are responsible for the accuracy of the tax forms. So check out the qualifications of the preparer you hire. The IRS and most states don't license tax preparers, but states do license attorneys and CPAs. Almost anyone can call him or herself a tax return preparer.

Internet and chain tax preparers' fees are the lowest, but their work product is inconsistent. These McTax outfits depend on inexperienced seasonal employees earning minimum wage. Emphasis is on quantity, not quality, and workers earn bonuses for turning out a lot of returns. You may never meet the actual preparer of your return. And even if you do, chances are he or she won't be around after April 15 if you—or the IRS—have questions about your return.

For most people, enrolled agents are the best bet to prepare a tax return. They are licensed by the IRS. Their prices are higher than chains, but lower than CPAs and tax attorneys. If you want a tax preparer for many years down the road, start looking long before the tax season starts. Don't switch tax preparers unless you have a good reason.

CAUTION

Avoid certain tax preparers. Never hire a tax preparer who bases his or her fee on a percentage of the refund you will receive, guarantees refunds in all cases, or will not sign your tax return as the preparer. If the IRS designates someone as a problem preparer, it casts out its audit net to bring in the preparer's clients.

Researching Tax Questions

Although most tax matters require no research, some do. Your auditor may go beyond looking at your records. For instance, the question may be whether or not the deductions are legally allowable. Your home office expenses may be disallowed not because you didn't prove them, but because the auditor says that you don't qualify for a home office deduction. To find out if the IRS is correct, you must know what the legal requirements are to qualify for a home office.

There are many good sources to augment the information in this book.

Free IRS Information

The IRS offers free publications and telephone and face-to-face help. To meet with someone from the IRS in person, call your nearest local IRS office. At larger IRS offices, there are Taxpayer Assistance Centers where you can sit down and talk to a taxpayer service representative. Check the IRS website at www.irs.gov or call 800-829-1040 for the closest Taxpayer Assistance Center. Just don't expect any tax savings tips or sophisticated advice from the IRS.

IRS Publications

The IRS distributes free taxpayer pamphlets, nicknamed pubs, numbered from 1 to 1000. Pubs contain tax information on all kinds of issues—from the IRS's point of view, of course. For example, Publication 334, *Tax Guide for Small Businesses*, has rules from how to claim depreciation of a business vehicle to reporting losses on the sale of assets.

These pubs are free at IRS offices or by calling 800-829-3676 or at the IRS's website at www.irs.gov. Start with Publication 910, *Guide to Free Tax*

Services, to request the tax information you need. Expect to wait several weeks to get them by mail.

IRS Telephone Information

The IRS toll-free numbers are 800-829-1040 or 800-829-8815. Live people answer questions on tax preparation and tax notices. You'll be asked to give your Social Security or employer ID number if you need information about your account.

The IRS toll-free prerecorded tax information number is 800-829-4477. IRS Publication 910 has a list of the topic numbers and subjects that correspond to the prerecorded messages.

The best thing I can say about these telephone services is that they are free. They will give you only the official IRS position, which is conservative and not necessarily beneficial. And many times the answers are misleading or outright wrong (although the IRS Commission claims IRS answers are accurate over 80% of the time). Start, but don't stop here, with your tax law research.

Tax Information on the Internet

Many legal and tax resources intended both for lawyers and the general public are available online through the Internet. Visit any of the following websites, each of which provides links to other tax and legal information resources:

- **www.nolo.com.** The Nolo site includes tax and legal information. There are FAQs (frequently asked questions) on a wide variety of legal topics and articles on legal issues. Nolo's Legal Encyclopedia includes a section devoted exclusively to tax issues.
- **www.law.cornell.edu.** This site, another law pointer, is maintained by Cornell Law School. Click on "Law About" and then "taxation."
- **www.irs.gov.** This is the home page for the IRS. You can read articles on current topics, download most IRS forms and publications, peruse summaries of many tax topics, and read tax statistics or tax regulations. You can also email simple tax questions to the IRS; you'll get an email response in a few days. The response will be fairly generic, but will help you get started researching a question.

- **www.el.com.** Click on "elinks" and then "taxes." The Essential Links tax section points you to just about every tax site on the Internet.
- **www.unclefed.com.** This site features a number of good tax links, federal and state tax forms, and articles (including some by me).
- **www.quicken.com.** Click on "taxes" for a link to TurboTax.com, which has a "tips and resources" section.

Last but not least, there is always www.google.com.

Private Tax Guides

For hard-copy research, there are numerous privately published tax guides that are widely available.

Popular Guidebooks

You've probably seen the annual tax guides, including *The Ernst & Young Tax Guide* (Ballantine Books) and *J.K. Lasser's Your Income Tax* (Prentice Hall).

These guides are sold just about everywhere during tax season. They cover the most current tax rules for income reporting and deduction taking. They are easier to read than IRS publications and have better examples of how the tax law works. I like *The Ernst & Young Tax Guide* because it's the most comprehensive, although it is not the easiest to understand. These guides are inexpensive and can be found in most libraries as well.

Tax Professional Deskbooks and Guides

Accountants, IRS agents, and attorneys use more sophisticated tax desk-books. The three top professional guides are the *Master Tax Guide* (Commerce Clearing House), *Master Federal Tax Manual* (Research Institute of America), and *Federal Tax Guide* (Prentice Hall). They are all about 600 pages of fine print. Don't let this scare you, as you may need to read only a few pages. These deskbooks summarize the law on the most common tax law problems. They are available online at www.amazon.com, in libraries, especially law libraries, and they are sold in larger bookstores.

IRS personnel seem to prefer the *Master Tax Guide*. If you have a choice of which of the three to consult, you may want to use that one.

Other Research Materials—Using the Library or Internet

The original source materials for the tax law are the Internal Revenue Code and Congressional committee reports. IRS regulations and federal court decisions interpret the law and show how it is applied to a set of facts. The IRC and reports are found in federal building libraries, large public libraries, and law libraries as well as on the Internet (www.irs.gov). Tax court decisions are available online at www.ustaxcourt.gov. Most are technical in the extreme and are only recommended as a cure for insomnia. The guidebooks listed above are an attempt to make sense out of this mass of legalese and are your better bets.

Nevertheless, if you want to look at court decisions or legal treatises, find a law library or go online. To find a library, call your local courthouse or college or a lawyer and ask where the nearest law library open to the public is located. Many private law libraries only allow use by lawyers, judges, and law students.

If you go to a library, look in the card catalogue or computer database for:

- tax
- Internal Revenue Code
- IRS regulations
- U.S. tax court and other federal court opinions, and
- books by research companies and legal scholars explaining the tax law, such as this book and the tax guides mentioned earlier.

Use the site www.el.com or the IRS website at www.irs.gov to get this material. Or, use a search engine like www.google.com.

Start your research with the number of an Internal Revenue Code section, an IRS regulation, or a name of a case you have run across.

If you go the library route, once armed with the call numbers and the citation or topic, head for the material or throw yourself on the mercy of the library staff. A librarian might even show you how to use the books. But, few law librarians have great familiarity with tax law, so don't expect too much.

Further Reading for Dealing With IRS Problems

- *Representing the Audited Taxpayer Before the IRS, Representation Before the Collection Division of the IRS,* and *Representation Before the Appeals Division of the IRS* (Thomson West). All three are loose-leaf and supplemented annually. They are written clearly by experienced people in the field although they are too expensive for anyone but a serious tax professional. I especially recommend the collection book.
- *Tax Management Tax Practice Series* (Bureau of National Affairs, 800-223-7270). This is a top-of-the-line pricey research resource tool on CD-ROM. It is most likely to be found at a law library or a tax professional's office.
- My website, www.taxattorneydaily.com.

Chapter Highlights

- Usually you can file tax returns and deal successfully with the IRS on your own, but sometimes you should hire a tax professional.
- The best tax professionals are enrolled agents, certified public accountants, and tax attorneys.
- There are free and low-cost sources of good tax information, including books, the IRS, and some websites.

When You Owe State Income Taxes

A ll states except Alaska, Florida, Nevada, New Hampshire, Tennessee, South Dakota, Texas, Washington, and Wyoming impose an income tax. Usually the filing requirements, penalties, and collection techniques mirror those of the federal IRS. For more specific information, write or call your state taxing authority. Even if you live in a state without an income tax, there may be helpful information in this chapter—for example, your state may tax business entities or estates.

The IRS and State Taxing Authorities

States' agencies have computer links with the IRS. Only Nevada does not share residents' data with the IRS.

Most state taxing authorities act quickly when they receive IRS information if it means the taxpayer will owe the state more, too. In fact, many states act on IRS-supplied information before the IRS does. By the time the IRS comes to collect, you may have set up a state installment plan or lost your property to a state tax collector, leaving little for the IRS. Why the IRS gives this information to the states before it acts on it is a mystery.

Audit adjustments. Because of the computer linkage, if you are audited by the IRS, your state automatically finds out. Based on IRS adjustments, the state can change your state tax bill without conducting a separate audit.

TIP

If you contest an IRS audit in tax court, notify your state's income tax department to prevent a premature state tax assessment. Send the state agency a copy of your tax court petition. (See Chapter 5.) Request that no further action be taken until your case has been decided.

States seldom audit individual taxpayers. They prefer to let the IRS audit you and then tag on a bill. States are more likely to audit businesses for sales or employment taxes. If you are audited by your state taxing authority, most of the general principles of this book will apply.

Most state tax assessments can be appealed, as with IRS audits. If your appeal of a proposed state assessment is rejected—even an assessment following a state audit—you cannot contest the tax bill in most state courts unless you pay the bill first.

Collections. If the IRS pursues you as a nonfiler, so probably will your state. Most states automatically dun taxpayers based on IRS bills. So, if the IRS makes a mistake in the bill, the state will, too.

Does Your State Have a Taxpayer Bill of Rights?

Some states have enacted their versions of the federal Taxpayer Bill of Rights. To find out if your state has one, and to obtain a copy, call or write your state taxing authority. Many of the state bills include grievance procedures. The California bill, for example, provides an administrative hearing to protest an improper seizure of property.

Also, ask if your state has a taxpayer advocate who acts much the same as an IRS taxpayer advocate. (See Chapter 8.) For example, taxpayer advocates may get state wage levies released or property returned, if they are convinced that the seizures threaten the taxpayers' health or welfare.

If your state has a taxpayer advocate whom you want to contact, first try by phone. If that fails, show up at the advocate's office or write and tell them your home and work telephone numbers and the best times to reach you.

If your state doesn't have a taxpayer advocate, contact your state representative or assemblyperson.

State Time Limits to Assess and Collect Income Taxes

As you've learned, once you file a federal return, the IRS generally has three years to assess additional taxes by way of an audit. In some situations, the IRS has six years. (See Chapters 3 and 6.) Similarly, state time limitations vary from one to five years.

Once additional taxes are assessed, the IRS has ten years to collect them. Again, state limitations differ tremendously.

Beware—in many states, the period to collect the tax is renewable; that is, it is not limited. In California, for example, the ten-year period can be renewed twice, for a total of 30 years.

State Tax Collection Departments

Like the IRS, most states have computerized collection systems that spit out a series of notices. If you don't respond, involuntary collection starts. Just like the IRS, your state files liens and seizes your property. (See Chapter 7.) States act quickly at grabbing property, often much faster than the IRS. And some states hire private collection agencies, usually to go after debtors who have moved beyond the state line.

If you disagree with the state's assessment notice, there is likely an appeals process similar to the IRS's. If your state doesn't have a specific form to appeal, follow the sample protest letter in Chapter 4.

The state may have an informal conference or appeal hearing. If you are unsuccessful, you must pay the tax and then file a claim for a refund or sue in state court. Some states let taxpayers go to court without first paying a tax bill, similar to tax court.

Many state tax agencies don't run as smoothly as the IRS. That's pretty scary, huh? Letters are lost and calls not returned. Most state taxing authorities must respond to your inquiries within a certain number of days. If the agency denies receiving your letter or won't return calls, however, what can you do?

Avoid lost mail and unreturned phone calls by dealing with the state taxing authority in person. Always get the name and direct telephone number of any employee you talk to. This fixes some responsibility and may keep him or her from vanishing when you call back. If you reach any agreement over the phone or in person, immediately send a confirming letter. Later, if anyone disputes the agreement, speak to a supervisor or the state taxpayer advocate. Consider asking for political help.

State Tax Bills

Most state tax collectors operate similarly to the IRS—they may accept installments, seize assets, or settle tax bills for less than the full amount owed. States can also suspend collection for hardship. Some states, such as California and New York, are especially tough to deal with.

Getting a State Payment Plan

Most tax collectors will grant installment agreements if they don't believe you can make a full payment. As with the IRS, you may be able to get a time payment agreement over the phone or by writing. You might have to visit the state tax office in person. Call to make an appointment or go to the office and wait in line.

You may be required to complete financial disclosure forms showing your assets, bank accounts, and sources of income.

Many states use an abbreviated version of the IRS financial disclosure Form 433. (See Chapter 6.) State forms usually don't have enough room for listing all expenses. Therefore, before meeting with a state tax collector, thoroughly review the material in Chapter 6 on Forms 433-A and 433-B if you own a business. Gather together your proof of expenses, such as credit card bills and rent receipts. Expect an argument if you list expenses the collector does not think are absolutely necessary. Charitable contributions, cigarette expenses, and entertainment are usually in this category.

Provide a copy of your most recent pay stub. If your pay varies due to bonuses or overtime, take the lowest recent stub. If self-employed, take in your last tax return—unless your income has dropped lately. In that event, write up a projection of your income and expenses for the next three months to a year.

States don't usually verify the information in a financial statement as stringently as the IRS. State tax offices tend to accept any documentation that appears to be genuine. This doesn't mean, however, that you should be less than truthful. Let your conscience be your guide.

State tax collectors often display a take it or leave it attitude. They demand payment plan commitments on the spot, without much negotiating. They may reject requests for agreements to last more than 12 months. If you need longer, you may have to agree for now and ask for more time later. Most can give you more time to pay, regardless of how tough they talk. And even if you get an installment agreement, the state may record a tax lien, just like the IRS.

Enforced Collection—Seizing Assets

States often act quicker than the IRS in seizing property of tax delinquents. State laws vary as to the amount of wages that the state can take. In California, for example, the state can grab 25% of your net pay.

Keeping your bank account from tax collectors—state or federal—is always a concern. (See Chapter 6 about protecting your bank accounts from collectors.)

If you have made financial disclosures, the state will have a list of your assets, such as your bank accounts, car, and home. Most states have the power to seize houses, but you may be entitled to full or partial protection under the state homestead exemption.

Homestead exemptions never protect you from the IRS, however. In some states, if tax collectors take a house, they must pay the homeowner the amount of his or her statutory homestead exemption. Every state is different, so check with an attorney or do some legal research. (See Chapter 13.)

Bankruptcy

State tax bills, like IRS debts, can be handled under federal bankruptcy law. If the state is about to take your property, filing for bankruptcy could give you a reprieve. Collection activities must stop. State tax debts may or may not qualify for discharge in a Chapter 7 bankruptcy. See a bankruptcy lawyer in your area for details. But, if the state taxes don't qualify for Chapter 7, you can force a payment plan on the state in a Chapter 13 bankruptcy. (See Chapter 6.)

Compromising a State Tax Assessment

You must settle an IRS tax bill through the offer in compromise procedure. (See Chapter 6.) Many states, too, will consider settling a tax bill you can't afford to pay. Contact your state tax agency and ask if it can be done and, if so, how. There is probably a form for making the request. If you are told it can't be done, speak to the clerk's supervisor. Keep going up the ladder until you are satisfied you have received the final word.

Coordinating Installment Plans With the IRS and Your State Tax Department

If you owe both federal and state income taxes, coordinate your payment plans. Let each taxing agency know you owe the other. Make your federal and state financial disclosure forms match. Propose installment plans simultaneously with payments in proportion to your total tax debt.

> **EXAMPLE:** Hamlet owes Minnesota $3,000 for state income taxes and the IRS $12,000. Although it's a strain, he can scrape together $500 a month for back taxes. He offers $100 to the state and $400 to the IRS. When questioned about his allocation, Hamlet says, "What could be more fair? I owe the IRS four times as much as I owe Minnesota. I should pay in that proportion."

Assuming the usual case—you owe the state far less than you owe the IRS—consider stalling the IRS and paying off the state first. Negotiating is simpler when your monster has one head, not two. Typically, states seize wages and property more quickly than the IRS. Finally, if you borrow money to pay off the state, this is another debt and expense to list on your IRS financial disclosure form.

Suspending Collection

If you can convince the state that paying would be a hardship, you may get a collection reprieve. You will likely have to tell a sob story and make a financial disclosure, in person, in writing, or perhaps on the phone. Expect the state to balk, so be persistent with your request. If you are unemployed, have health problems or other serious difficulties, you should prevail.

When All Else Fails, Try Your Political Connections

If the state tax agency is treating you unfairly, use whatever political connections you can muster. Someone in your broad circle of friends, relatives, acquaintances, or business associations may know a state legislator. Contact the elected official's office even if you don't have a connection. State tax agencies tend to be more sensitive to political pressures than the IRS. It's certainly worth a call to your state representative's office.

Chapter Highlights

- IRS computers automatically exchange your tax data with all states except Nevada.
- Most state tax agency procedures are modeled after the IRS.
- State tax agencies generally have the same powers of audit and tax collection as the IRS.

The Taxpayer Bill of Rights

n 1988, Congress passed the first of three Taxpayer Bills of Rights. Senator Pryor announced that:

[This law will] stem the abuse of taxpayers by the IRS and provide redress when abuse does occur. It marks a victory for the little taxpayer. It levels the playing field.

Well, you know how politicians get carried away with the sound of their own voices. TBOR I, as it is known, was a step in the right direction. TBOR II added a few more taxpayer protections, and TBOR III, passed in 1998, finally made real progress in giving taxpayers rights.

The IRS now must let taxpayers know that they have certain rights when facing the agency. Congress required the IRS to publish a plain-English pamphlet summarizing these rights, which is Publication 1, *Your Rights as a Taxpayer*. Take time to read this pamphlet if you are being audited or dealing with an IRS collector. It is reprinted at the end of this chapter.

Taxpayer Bill of Rights I

The following summarizes some of the key features of TBOR I.

The Good

- The IRS created the position of ombudsman, now called taxpayer advocate. This IRS official is empowered to issue Taxpayer Assistance Orders (TAOs) stopping the IRS from taking certain actions against taxpayers. For instance, the taxpayer advocate can stop a seizure of your property if you can show that it will cause a significant hardship. This advocate works through the Taxpayer Advocate Service (see Chapter 8).
- The IRS developed Publication 1, *Your Rights as a Taxpayer*. The IRS must enclose it with your first notice concerning delinquent taxes. Oddly, it doesn't have to be sent with an audit notice. This pamphlet summarizes your rights during any IRS noncriminal interview, such as an audit, an appeal, or collections matter.
- You can propose an installment plan to the IRS if you can't pay a bill in full. This doesn't mean you can force the IRS to accept your deal, but the IRS must fairly consider your request.

- You generally don't have to meet with the IRS personally if you send a qualified representative—a lawyer, a CPA, or an enrolled agent. (See Chapter 13.)
- You can stop an audit or other IRS meeting to contact a tax professional for advice. (See Chapter 3.) This is the IRS equivalent of your right to an attorney before talking to the police. The IRS won't furnish you a free tax professional, however.
- You generally can't be forced to meet with an IRS auditor at an inconvenient time or place. Congress was concerned about a small business being forced to close during an audit. In this situation, the IRS must hold the audit at its office or elsewhere. The IRS can, however, visit your business to verify items on your tax return, such as inventory or equipment. (See Chapter 3.)

The So-So

- Dollar amounts of property and wages exempt from IRS seizure were increased a bit. (See Chapter 7.)
- The district director—your IRS local chief—or the director's assistant must personally approve seizures of your principal residence. Revenue officer Rambo cannot decide on his or her own to take the roof over your head.
- You must be sent a Notice of Intent to Levy before the IRS seizes your property. You have 30 days to contest the seizure. In practice, if you owe the IRS, you'll have no legal grounds to contest. This freeze period, however, gives you time to negotiate further with the IRS.

The Window Dressing

- Penalties can be removed from your tax bill if they resulted from your relying on incorrect IRS *written* advice. The IRS rarely provides written advice.
- You can *audio record* most meetings with the IRS. Taping a meeting would probably make the IRS agent apprehensive and hard to deal with. You can't legally videotape or record telephone conversations with the IRS.
- You can sue any IRS employee who intentionally disregards the law, up to $100,000, plus legal costs. In the decade this has been law, 20 taxpayers

(at most) have won such cases. And, if you sue and lose, the IRS can get its costs awarded against you.

Taxpayer Bill of Rights II

TBOR II is a supplement to TBOR I, not a replacement. Here is a summary of some of TBOR II's provisions, which I have also put into the categories of the Good, the So-So, and the Window Dressing.

The Good

- Taxpayers can formally appeal liens, levies, and seizures to the IRS Appeals Office, which is totally independent of the collection division. The appeals office can either stop a lien, levy, or seizure if collectors did not follow correct procedures, or it can consider less drastic actions. Collectors are now more respectful of taxpayers, knowing there is another department looking over their shoulders.
- The IRS can withdraw a Notice of Tax Lien or return seized property in any of the following cases:
  - The IRS action was premature.
  - The IRS action was not in accord with established procedures.
  - The taxpayer enters into an installment agreement.
  - It would facilitate collection of the tax debt.
  - It is in the best interests of the taxpayer.
- The IRS can forgive penalties for failing to timely deposit payroll taxes for first-time offenders. Also, the IRS can abate penalties for sending the payment to the IRS instead of depositing it with a proper financial institution. These should ease the burden somewhat for the small business person just starting off.
- If you personally owe payroll taxes under the Trust Fund Recovery Penalty, the IRS must now inform you of the efforts it makes to collect taxes from any other people who may be liable for the same taxes. (See Chapter 11.) Before, the IRS often made little effort to collect from all but the easiest target. Now, collectors must conscientiously pursue others

as well and tell you of the efforts being made. TBOR II also establishes a federal basis for a lawsuit by one codebtor against the others.

- For married or divorced couples with joint tax bills, the IRS must tell both spouses what collection efforts have been made to get payment from the other spouse. The IRS typically pursues whichever divorced spouse is easier to find, usually the ex-wife with the kids, while the ex-husband with no children skips town. The IRS may now more seriously pursue the other ex-spouse than in the past.

The So-So

- Interest or penalties on tax bills won't begin for 21 days after an assessment. If the added tax is $100,000 or more, the interest-free period is dropped to ten business days. This is an incentive to encourage payment by audit victims as soon as the audit ends. It could save you a few bucks, but not many.
- Courts can more easily award attorneys' fees and legal costs to taxpayers who run up against the IRS. The IRS must prove it was substantially justified in bringing a case. While this sounds good, it is still within the discretion of the judge, not a jury, to allow recovery of your legal costs in fighting the IRS. In the past, few people have ever been awarded fees against the IRS, even when they won their cases.
- If you dispute the validity of income attributed to you on a Form 1099 or W-2—for example, a business incorrectly reports money paid to you as an independent contractor—now the IRS, not you, must hash it out with the third party.
- The IRS must notify a taxpayer within 60 days if it has a credit it can't match up with a tax bill. The IRS sometimes misapplies payments to accounts. At least now the agency must try to straighten it out in a reasonable period of time. We'll see.
- Married taxpayers who previously filed separately and owe taxes can amend their returns to file jointly, without paying the taxes due. Paying first was required to file this type of amendment.

The Window Dressing

- The term ombudsman from TBOR I was replaced with taxpayer advocate. The problems resolution office is now also known as the Taxpayer Advocate Service. Proponents failed, however, in making this job independent of the IRS.
- Taxpayers can sue anyone who files a false Form 1099 or W-2 with fraudulent intent—that is, someone who falsely and deliberately reports to the IRS that you were paid money. Some militia groups have filed reports on IRS officials and other perceived enemies; this provision is the IRS's version of revenge.
- The amount you can sue an IRS collector for illegal acts is $1 million. This sounds good, but just try to get it.
- The tax court can decide whether or not the IRS's failure to abate interest was in error. I can't imagine an ordinary taxpayer taking this issue to court, but for multimillion-dollar cases, this could be significant.
- You can file your tax return by certain private delivery services, such as UPS, FedEx, or Airborne, as well as by the U.S. mail.
- Annual notices must be sent to anyone owing the IRS, showing a current balance due. I'm not sure most people are especially eager to get this information, if they need it. More trees sacrificed on the IRS altar.

Taxpayer Bill of Rights III

In 1998, the most significant IRS reform ever became law. While the outcome for the taxpayer was not perfect, it was far better than I expected. I supplied data to Congress and sat through the hearings in Washington.

The Good

- Innocent spouse help became easier to get for joint return filers. And, a "separate liability election" is now possible for an ex or a legally separated spouse or one living apart for at least 12 months. The election limits the tax just to items relating to the innocent spouse (typically a wife). But there's no help if assets were transferred fraudulently or if the hubby and wife both knew of the tax cheating. This is one of the real highlights of the reform act.

- The tax court can now hear disputes about innocent spouse relief.
- The monthly penalty for paying a tax bill under an installment agreement was cut from 0.50% to 0.25%. Anything helps.
- The IRS can't charge interest or certain penalties unless it contacts the tax debtor at least once a year. Usually this just means a computer generated notice. This rule doesn't apply to the failure to pay a penalty or tax fraud.
- A tax notice showing a penalty must indicate its source (the tax law section) and how it was computed. But, this doesn't apply to failure to file, failure to pay, or a few other types of penalties.
- Every IRS notice that includes interest must show how it was computed. This has helped cut down on the number of famous IRS "mystery" bills of the past.
- The IRS must notify individuals when a Notice of Federal Lien is filed. And, more importantly, for the 30-day period after the mailing of the notice, the taxpayer can go before an appeals officer. Could be of significance in a few cases.
- All Notices of Intent to Levy must be sent by registered or certified mail, return receipt requested. No levy can take place within 30 days of the mailing. The taxpayer can contest it before an appeals officer. Great added taxpayer protection.
- There can be no seizure of a principal residence without a court order and prior notice of the hearing. At the hearing, the IRS must show that there is no reasonable alternative for the collection of the tax. This provision has virtually eliminated residence seizures by the IRS. Hooray!
- The attorney-client confidentiality of communications privilege is extended to anyone authorized under federal law to practice before the IRS. Theoretically, this puts CPAs and enrolled agents on the same footing as attorneys. Sounds good, but not really very important in practice.
- IRS auditors can't use financial status or economic reality probes to find unreported income without a reasonable indication that there is a likelihood of it. What the heck is a "reasonable indication"?
- The IRS may not contact anyone other than the taxpayer during an audit or a collection investigation without providing reasonable notice

to the taxpayer those contacts are being made. Not much change in IRS procedures, just extra paperwork.

- IRS supervisory approval is required for any lien, levy, or seizure to affirm that the collector's action is appropriate under the circumstances. Circumstances include the amount due and the value of the asset. Restricts gunslinger collectors from acting on their own. Since levies and seizures decreased dramatically after the IRS reform act, this provision may deserve part of the credit.

- Levy exemption amounts for property are indexed for inflation and adjusted annually. These amounts are still pretty minimal.

- The IRS must provide a written accounting of sales of seized property, whether real or personal, to the tax debtor. The IRS has always done this anyway as a matter of policy, and now it's law.

- The IRS can't seize a residence for a tax debt of $5,000 or less. No big deal as the IRS isn't seizing residences anymore anyway.

- The IRS must exhaust all other payment options before seizing the taxpayer's business assets. May slow down a few rogue IRS collectors.

- The IRS can't force a debtor to agree to extend the ten-year statute of limitations on collections. However, extensions may be required as part of an installment agreement. So, the doubletalk here is that IRS really can force you to extend the collection period after all.

- For folks undergoing an audit, the IRS may request an extension of the normal (three-year) audit period. If it does so, the IRS must also tell the audited person that he or she has the right to refuse to sign or to limit the extension to particular audit issues. Well, if you don't sign, it usually means the IRS will disallow deductions or find you didn't report all your income and hit you with a bill.

- The IRS must allow folks making offers in compromise enough money for basic living expenses. The IRS can't reject an offer just because it is low. This is so vague, it's a source of amusement at IRS offices.

- IRS levies are prohibited during an Offer in Compromise, 30 days following the rejection of an offer, during an appeal, or while an installment agreement is in force.

- IRS must have internal review procedures when rejecting requests for installment agreements. Good protection in theory as it requires supervisors to approve actions of their underlings.

The So-So

- The IRS now has the burden of proof in any *court proceeding* on a factual issue once a taxpayer presents credible evidence to the contrary. Four conditions must be met. The taxpayer must (1) substantiate the item, (2) maintain records, (3) cooperate with reasonable IRS requests for meetings, information, and documents, and (4) for entities (not individuals) meet certain net worth limitations. Congress considered, but unfortunately rejected, the original part of this law which placed the burden of proof on the IRS in audits.
- A federal court can award up to $100,000 to a taxpayer if an IRS employee negligently breaks the law in collecting a tax bill and up to $1 million if the employee willfully violates the bankruptcy code automatic stays or discharge provisions. In reality, I've seen very few cases where taxpayers got a dime. However, IRS collectors seem to have become more timid since the law passed.

The Window Dressing

- IRS will adopt a liberal acceptance policy for offers in compromise. From what I've seen the IRS has completely ignored this "suggestion" from Congress.
- Tax audit losers must be told of the deadline date for taking their bill to tax court. This date wasn't always easy to figure out for someone not in the tax world and is more important than it might appear to be.
- Certain fair debt collection practices were made applicable to the IRS (for example, a prohibition against harassing or abusive communications).
- An installment agreement must be granted if (1) the tax bill is under $10,000, (excluding penalties and interest), (2) in the previous five years, the debtor has had another installment agreement and didn't default on it, (3) the debtor submits financial statements, if requested, showing he or she can't pay in full; and (4) the installment agreement provides for full payment within three years.
- Joint and several liability rules must be explained to married tax debtors. The spouses must be told about electing separate liability and how to get out of the debt altogether.

- Taxpayers' rights must be set forth in Publication 1 clearly, including the right to be represented.
- Explanations to taxpayers of the audit, appeals, and collection processes are required. And folks must be informed about the taxpayer advocate whenever the IRS proposes a new tax bill.
- Annual statements must be sent to debtors on IRS installment agreements showing the past year's payments and the remaining balance.
- IRS correspondence (other than routine notices) must include the name, telephone number, and ID number of an IRS employee the taxpayer may contact. IRS employees calling on the phone must give their telephone number and IRS badge number.
- IRS employees may use pseudonyms only if there is adequate justification, such as protecting personal safety, and IRS management has approved. This stops over-zealous employees from abusing taxpayers while hiding behind phony names.
- Illegal tax protester designations are prohibited. These permanent character stains can't be listed anywhere in the IRS files or in its computer. The IRS only can designate folks as "nonfilers," but must remove this designation after the taxpayer has filed tax returns and paid all taxes.
- Any person (whistleblower) providing confidential information to Congress can't be punished if he or she believes such information relates to misconduct or taxpayer abuse.
- Local IRS telephone numbers and local IRS offices must be listed in directories. Believe it or not, the IRS did not do this before Congress ordered them in the law.

Chapter Highlights

- A federal law known as the Taxpayer Bill of Rights establishes certain rights for individuals and entities in dealing with the IRS.
- Your primary rights are to be treated fairly and in a prompt manner and to have a representative deal with the IRS for you.
- Read the two-page IRS Publication 1, *Your Rights as a Taxpayer*, whenever you have a problem with the IRS.

Publication 1, *Your Rights as a Taxpayer*

Department of the Treasury
Internal Revenue Service

Publication 1
(Rev. May 2005)

Catalog Number 64731W

www.irs.gov

Your Rights as a Taxpayer

The first part of this publication explains some of your most important rights as a taxpayer. The second part explains the examination, appeal, collection, and refund processes. This publication is also available in Spanish.

Declaration of Taxpayer Rights

I. Protection of Your Rights

IRS employees will explain and protect your rights as a taxpayer throughout your contact with us.

II. Privacy and Confidentiality

The IRS will not disclose to anyone the information you give us, except as authorized by law. You have the right to know why we are asking you for information, how we will use it, and what happens if you do not provide requested information.

III. Professional and Courteous Service

If you believe that an IRS employee has not treated you in a professional, fair, and courteous manner, you should tell that employee's supervisor. If the supervisor's response is not satisfactory, you should write to the IRS director for your area or the center where you file your return.

IV. Representation

You may either represent yourself or, with proper written authorization, have someone else represent you in your place. Your representative must be a person allowed to practice before the IRS, such as an attorney, certified public accountant, or enrolled agent. If you are in an interview and ask to consult such a person, then we must stop and reschedule the interview in most cases.

You can have someone accompany you at an interview. You may make sound recordings of any meetings with our examination, appeal, or collection personnel, provided you tell us in writing 10 days before the meeting.

V. Payment of Only the Correct Amount of Tax

You are responsible for paying only the correct amount of tax due under the law—no more, no less. If you cannot pay all of your tax when it is due, you may be able to make monthly installment payments.

VI. Help With Unresolved Tax Problems

The Taxpayer Advocate Service can help you if you have tried unsuccessfully to resolve a problem with the IRS. Your local Taxpayer Advocate can offer you special help if you have a significant hardship as a result of a tax problem. For more information, call toll free 1–877–777–4778 (1–800–829–4059 for TTY/TDD) or write to the Taxpayer Advocate at the IRS office that last contacted you.

VII. Appeals and Judicial Review

If you disagree with us about the amount of your tax liability or certain collection actions, you have the right to ask the Appeals Office to review your case. You may also ask a court to review your case.

VIII. Relief From Certain Penalties and Interest

The IRS will waive penalties when allowed by law if you can show you acted reasonably and in good faith or relied on the incorrect advice of an IRS employee. We will waive interest that is the result of certain errors or delays caused by an IRS employee.

THE IRS MISSION

PROVIDE AMERICA'S TAXPAYERS TOP QUALITY SERVICE BY HELPING THEM UNDERSTAND AND MEET THEIR TAX RESPONSIBILITIES AND BY APPLYING THE TAX LAW WITH INTEGRITY AND FAIRNESS TO ALL.

Publication 1, *Your Rights as a Taxpayer* (continued)

Examinations, Appeals, Collections, and Refunds

Examinations (Audits)

We accept most taxpayers' returns as filed. If we inquire about your return or select it for examination, it does not suggest that you are dishonest. The inquiry or examination may or may not result in more tax. We may close your case without change; or, you may receive a refund.

The process of selecting a return for examination usually begins in one of two ways. First, we use computer programs to identify returns that may have incorrect amounts. These programs may be based on information returns, such as Forms 1099 and W-2, on studies of past examinations, or on certain issues identified by compliance projects. Second, we use information from outside sources that indicates that a return may have incorrect amounts. These sources may include newspapers, public records, and individuals. If we determine that the information is accurate and reliable, we may use it to select a return for examination.

Publication 556, Examination of Returns, Appeal Rights, and Claims for Refund, explains the rules and procedures that we follow in examinations. The following sections give an overview of how we conduct examinations.

By Mail

We handle many examinations and inquiries by mail. We will send you a letter with either a request for more information or a reason why we believe a change to your return may be needed. You can respond by mail or you can request a personal interview with an examiner. If you mail us the requested information or provide an explanation, we may or may not agree with you, and we will explain the reasons for any changes. Please do not hesitate to write to us about anything you do not understand.

By Interview

If we notify you that we will conduct your examination through a personal interview, or you request such an interview, you have the right to ask that the examination take place at a reasonable time and place that is convenient for both you and the IRS. If our examiner proposes any changes to your return, he or she will explain the reasons for the changes. If you do not agree with these changes, you can meet with the examiner's supervisor.

Repeat Examinations

If we examined your return for the same items in either of the 2 previous years and proposed no change to your tax liability, please contact us as soon as possible so

we can see if we should discontinue the examination.

Appeals

If you do not agree with the examiner's proposed changes, you can appeal them to the Appeals Office of IRS. Most differences can be settled without expensive and time-consuming court trials. Your appeal rights are explained in detail in both Publication 5, Your Appeal Rights and How To Prepare a Protest If You Don't Agree, and Publication 556, Examination of Returns, Appeal Rights, and Claims for Refund.

If you do not wish to use the Appeals Office or disagree with its findings, you may be able to take your case to the U.S. Tax Court, U.S. Court of Federal Claims, or the U.S. District Court where you live. If you take your case to court, the IRS will have the burden of proving certain facts if you kept adequate records to show your tax liability, cooperated with the IRS, and meet certain other conditions. If the court agrees with you on most issues in your case and finds that our position was largely unjustified, you may be able to recover some of your administrative and litigation costs. You will not be eligible to recover these costs unless you tried to resolve your case administratively, including going through the appeals system, and you gave us the information necessary to resolve the case.

Collections

Publication 594, The IRS Collection Process, explains your rights and responsibilities regarding payment of federal taxes. It describes:

- What to do when you owe taxes. It describes what to do if you get a tax bill and what to do if you think your bill is wrong. It also covers making installment payments, delaying collection action, and submitting an offer in compromise.

- IRS collection actions. It covers liens, releasing a lien, levies, releasing a levy, seizures and sales, and release of property.

Your collection appeal rights are explained in detail in Publication 1660, Collection Appeal Rights.

Innocent Spouse Relief

Generally, both you and your spouse are each responsible for paying the full amount of tax, interest, and penalties due on your joint return. However, if you qualify for innocent spouse relief, you may be relieved of part or all of the joint liability. To request relief, you must file Form 8857, Request for Innocent Spouse Relief no later than 2 years after the date

on which the IRS first attempted to collect the tax from you. For example, the two-year period for filing your claim may start if the IRS applies your tax refund from one year to the taxes that you and your spouse owe for another year. For more information on innocent spouse relief, see Publication 971, Innocent Spouse Relief, and Form 8857.

Potential Third Party Contacts

Generally, the IRS will deal directly with you or your duly authorized representative. However, we sometimes talk with other persons if we need information that you have been unable to provide, or to verify information we have received. If we do contact other persons, such as a neighbor, bank, employer, or employees, we will generally need to tell them limited information, such as your name. The law prohibits us from disclosing any more information than is necessary to obtain or verify the information we are seeking. Our need to contact other persons may continue as long as there is activity in your case. If we do contact other persons, you have a right to request a list of those contacted.

Refunds

You may file a claim for refund if you think you paid too much tax. You must generally file the claim within 3 years from the date you filed your original return or 2 years from the date you paid the tax, whichever is later. The law generally provides for interest on your refund if it is not paid within 45 days of the date you filed your return or claim for refund. Publication 556, Examination of Returns, Appeal Rights, and Claims for Refund, has more information on refunds.

If you were due a refund but you did not file a return, you generally must file your return within 3 years from the date the return was due (including extensions) to get that refund.

Tax Information

The IRS provides the following sources for forms, publications, and additional information.

- *Tax Questions:* 1–800–829–1040 (1–800–829–4059 for TTY/TDD)
- *Forms and Publications:* 1–800–829–3676 (1–800–829–4059 for TTY/TDD)
- *Internet: www.irs.gov*
- *Small Business Ombudsman:* A small business entity can participate in the regulatory process and comment on enforcement actions of IRS by calling 1-888-REG-FAIR.
- *Treasury Inspector General for Tax Administration:* You can confidentially report misconduct, waste, fraud, or abuse by an IRS employee by calling 1–800–366–4484 (1–800–877–8339 for TTY/TDD). You can remain anonymous.

The 25 Most Frequently Asked Questions

1. How long should I keep my tax papers?

At least three years, but six years is preferable. The IRS has three years after you file a tax return to complete an audit. For example, if you filed on April 15, 2010, for 2009, keep those records until at least April 16, 2013.

The IRS can audit you for up to six years if it suspects that you underreported your income by 25% or more. If the IRS suspects fraud, there is no time limit for an audit, although audits beyond six years are extremely rare.

Keep records of purchases of real estate, stocks, and other investments for at least three years after the tax return reporting their sale was filed. (See Chapter 3.)

2. How long should I worry if I haven't filed tax returns that I should have filed?

At least six years. The government has six years from the date the nonfiled return was due to *criminally* charge you with failing to file. There is no time limit, however, for assessing *civil* penalties for not filing. If you didn't file for 1958, you still have an obligation if you owed taxes for that year. Not until you actually file a return does the normal audit time limit—three years— and collection time limit—ten years—start to run.

Don't overworry about a nonfiled return due more than six years ago if you haven't heard from the IRS. The IRS usually doesn't go after nonfilers after six years—unless the IRS began its investigation before the six years elapsed. After six years, the IRS transfers its computer files to tape for storage. (See Chapter 2.)

3. Do many people cheat on their taxes?

According to the IRS Oversight Board, 13% of Americans admit to believing that tax cheating is okay. Presumably, these folks—as well as the ones who don't admit it—are practicing their beliefs, keeping the IRS audit mills churning. Small business owners and self-employed people have the most opportunities to play fast and loose—and they get audited the most.

Arguably, cheating by self-employed people approaches 100%. It may just be a question of degree—did you ever mail a personal letter with a business-bought stamp?

4. If I can't pay my taxes, should I file my return anyway?

Yes. Filing saves you from the possibility of being criminally charged or, more likely, from being hit with a fine for failing to file or for filing late. Interest continues to build up until you pay. Of course, filing without paying will bring an IRS collector into your life—who may be friendlier if he or she doesn't have to hunt you down. The sooner you start filing, the better. (See Chapter 6 for an explanation of the benefits of filing even when you can't pay.)

5. Can I get an extension to pay a tax without penalties and interest?

Probably not. Although you can get an extension to file your tax return until October 15, you still must pay by April 15 or the IRS can impose a penalty and charge interest. Try pleading hardship on IRS Form 1127 to get up to six months extra to pay. Few payment extensions are granted. Even then, only penalties, not interest, stop accruing. Form 1127 works best in requesting an extension to pay estate taxes. (See Chapter 6.)

6. My state had an amnesty period for nonfilers. Can I ever hope the IRS will have one?

Maybe—it is frequently kicked around in Congress. The IRS has always opposed tax amnesty legislation—which lets nonfilers come forward without being criminally prosecuted or civilly fined. The IRS's reasoning is that after the amnesty period expires, significant numbers of people won't file, expecting another amnesty. Based on the success of various states' trying amnesty programs, I think the IRS is wrong.

7. Who has access to my IRS file?

Federal law makes IRS files private, not public records. The law has many exceptions, however. IRS files can be legally shared with other federal and state agencies. Most leakage comes as a result of sloppy state agencies that are granted access to IRS files. Furthermore, IRS employees have been caught snooping, and computer hackers have broken into government databases. While violation of the privacy act is a crime, rarely is anyone prosecuted for it, though IRS personnel can be fired if caught.

8. Is it true that the IRS pays rewards for turning in tax cheaters?

Yes. The IRS rewards snitches. The catch is that payments are made only if and when the IRS collects the taxes due from the miscreant. More often than not, this means little or no reward at all. If it comes, it will likely be years after the report is made. The good news for squealers is that the IRS can pay up to 15% of the amount collected, with a maximum of $10,000,000. Good luck. (IRC 7623.) Any reward you recover is taxable income. Identities of informers are kept secret, but tax cheats usually know who reported them—mostly ex-spouses or disgruntled business associates.

The IRS places low priority on investigating tips and paying rewards. Typically, you will never know what action, if any, is taken on your tip. If you want to try it, submit IRS Form 211 or call 800-829-0433, the IRS tip line.

P.S. Rumor has it that turning someone in to the IRS can result in the informant's being investigated as well. (See Chapter 10.)

9. Should I notify the IRS when I move?

Report your new address on IRS Form 8822. A post office change of address form may *not* work. Notifying the IRS ensures that you will get audit letters and other vital notices, which often have strict time limits for replies. (See Chapter 3.)

10. What should I do if I don't get my refund?

If you filed your tax return and it's been eight weeks, call the IRS tax refund hotline at 800-829-4477, Monday–Friday, 7 a.m. to 11:30 p.m. Or, call the 24-hour assistance number at 800-829-1040 and request assistance from the taxpayer advocate.

If you filed your return on or before April 15 and don't receive your refund until after May 31, the IRS must pay you interest.

If you never get a refund, it may have been intercepted to pay other state or federal taxes you owe; a defaulted student, SBA, or other federal government loan; delinquent child support; or a public benefit, such as HUD, VA, or Social Security overpayment. In these situations, you are supposed to be notified in writing, but don't count on it. (See Chapter 8.)

11. What should I do if I encounter a dishonest IRS employee?

Report any employee who lies or suggests you give him or her any favors. Dishonest employees are a rarity at the IRS. If you find one, however, call the chief inspector at 800-366-4484 or write to P.O. Box 589, Benjamin Franklin Station, Washington, DC 20044-0589. You can make your complaint anonymously or sign your name. Either way, don't expect to hear the results of the investigation.

12. Can the IRS charge me interest if I was incorrectly sent a refund and the IRS now wants it back?

It depends on who was at fault. The *Internal Revenue Manual* states that "taxpayers should not be held liable for interest on ... erroneous refunds if the IRS was clearly at fault ... and the taxpayer is cooperative in repaying." But if you caused the erroneous refund by your actions and now can't repay it, the IRS can and will charge interest. (See Chapter 12.)

13. How legitimate are the claims by "tax experts" that you don't have to pay income taxes?

Not at all. These con artists are very convincing, but if they were legit, I'd be first in line to stop paying taxes. Constitutional arguments against the tax laws are routinely dismissed by courts, and their proponents are fined or jailed. More sophisticated scams involve multiple family trusts, limited partnerships, and credit cards issued by offshore banks. While these schemes can confuse and slow down the IRS, they are bogus, period. Would a federal judge—whom you will appear before if you are prosecuted for tax evasion and whose salary comes from the federal government—ever uphold one of these schemes? Get serious. (See Chapter 2.)

14. Do auditors use computers? If so, does it make it harder to beat an audit?

Yes—computers are used by all auditors to prepare their final reports. No— it doesn't make it harder to beat an audit. Computers are just machines; it's the person operating the computer who counts. Computers can't make the judgments that are at the heart of the tax audit process. (See Chapter 3.)

15. What are my chances of getting through an audit without owing additional taxes?

A minority of audit victims make a clean getaway. The IRS, thanks to its sophisticated computer selection process, only audits returns in which adjustments are almost a certainty. Realize the odds are against you and focus on limiting the damage from an audit. (See Chapter 3.)

16. I am being audited and the deadline for filing this year's return is fast approaching. Should I file?

Not if you can help it. The danger in filing is that the auditor may expand the audit to include that return.

Instead of filing, submit IRS Form 4868 by April 15 to obtain an automatic extension to delay filing until October 15.

If the audit is still alive on October 15, don't file until it is completed. As long as you have paid all the taxes due, you won't incur any penalties or interest for not meeting the deadline. If you owe additional taxes, send in your payment with your extension form. Auditors can't make you file a return. If requested, simply say, "I am not yet ready to file." (See Chapter 3.)

17. I am being audited and haven't heard from the auditor for months. What can I do to get the audit over with?

Don't be overanxious. IRS auditors are instructed to close examinations within 28 months of the date you filed your tax return. For example, if you filed your 2009 return on April 15, 2010, the IRS wants the audit completed by August 15, 2011. Legally the IRS has until April 14, 2012 (or longer in the case of fraud), but auditors are instructed to allow at least eight months for processing any audit appeals.

If you haven't heard from the auditor, it could mean any number of things. Maybe the auditor was ill, transferred, or terminated. Or your file may be lost in the system. When your case resurfaces, a new auditor is under a deadline to close it, which can work in your favor. In the best of all worlds, the three-year time limit for completing the audit may expire while your file is in IRS never-never land. So why not leave the sleeping dog alone? (See Chapter 3.)

18. The auditor or collector is impossible to get along with. What can I do?

Calm down and use some basic psychology. Put yourself in the auditor's shoes. Most IRS employees are 9-to-5 types just trying to do a job. Their pay is often too low to support a family in many urban areas. They deal with hostile and untruthful citizens all day long. Understandably, IRS morale is low. Would you like this kind of job?

And even if an agent hates you, he or she doesn't get paid bonuses for giving you a hard time. So, if you've exchanged harsh words through an audit or collection interview, instead of escalating the war, offer an olive branch. For instance, say, "I'm sorry we can't get along. But let's work it out, okay?"

If conciliation fails, speak to the auditor's manager, whose job is to close cases and smooth things over with taxpayers.

19. I have always deducted a certain expense. During a recent audit, the deduction was denied and now I know I was wrong all those other years. What should I do?

Let your conscience be your guide. If your audit is still open, the auditor can make adjustments in other open years—periods for which the three- or six-year time limit from the date you filed your return hasn't yet expired. The auditor may ask you for copies of your tax returns for those years. You're not legally obligated to provide them. If you don't, he or she may request them from IRS record centers. But if the auditor is facing a deadline, he or she may just let it pass. Don't worry about being audited on returns filed more than three years ago—unless you understated your tax liability by 25% or more or committed outright fraud.

If you feel guilty, give the auditor copies of your tax returns for the open years and accept the disallowances. Or file amended tax returns and pay the additional taxes after the audit is completed. (See Chapter 3.)

20. Do I have to let the IRS into my home?

No. IRS employees can't enter your home without an express invitation from a rightful occupant. The only exception is if the IRS has a court order, which is very rare. A field auditor may ask to come in to verify your home office deduction. You don't have to let the person in, but he or she may disallow the deduction. Your choice.

21. Can the IRS take my house?

Yes, but the Taxpayer Bill of Rights discourages the IRS from seizing primary residences (your vacation home or rental property is fair game). The IRS must obtain a court order to take your house, which you can contest. And you can request help to stop the seizure from the Taxpayer Advocate Service.

The IRS doesn't like publicity about taxpayers losing their homes, so a call to the newspaper might help. Typically, the IRS seizes homes only if you are a druglord or tax protestor or just totally failed to communicate or cooperate with the IRS collectors. Your state homestead law, which might entitle you to keep all or some of the equity in your house if you were sued or filed for bankruptcy, won't protect you from the IRS. (See Chapter 7.)

22. I recently got married. Am I responsible for my spouse's past taxes?

Maybe. Your wages and property might be at risk of IRS seizure for your spouse's tax bill, depending on the laws of the state where you live. In most states, property owned by one spouse before marriage remains that spouse's separate property during marriage. Assets acquired during marriage, however, are generally considered joint property. When couples own property together, IRS problems can arise. The IRS can legally go after jointly owned assets to cover the tax debt of just one spouse. The IRS cannot, however, take the share of the nondebtor spouse. See a local attorney for help.

Be particularly aware of these specific problem areas:

- **Gifts.** If a spouse without an IRS tax debt gives a spouse who has a tax debt an interest in property, the IRS can grab it. For example, Tiffany deeds her separate property boat to her husband, Bobbo, and herself as joint tenants. The IRS can seize the boat for Bobbo's debt, although the IRS would have to pay the wife for her half interest in the boat once it was sold.

- **Commingled property.** If spouses deposit funds into a joint account and use that account to pay joint expenses, the funds are commingled. The IRS can take the *entire* account to satisfy the tax debt of one spouse.

  However if the couple uses commingled funds to purchase property, and the IRS seizes it for only one spouse's tax debt, the IRS must give the nondebtor spouse one-half of the sales proceeds.

- **Wages.** The IRS, quite unfairly, can take the wages of one spouse to pay for the sole tax debt of the other spouse. Some couples have divorced just to stop the IRS from taking the wife's wages for taxes owed by the husband prior to marriage. They may continue to live together after the divorce, but the wife's earnings are no longer within the IRS's grasp. (See Chapter 9.)

23. How likely am I to get in trouble for tax fraud?

Not very. Fewer than 2% of us are ever investigated for tax fraud. And if you are, the likelihood of a civil fine or criminal charge is under 20%. The unofficial minimum amount of taxes owed before the IRS will file criminal fraud charges is over $70,000 and involves at least three years of fraud. To some extent, whether you are charged depends on your line of work or visibility in the community. Most of those prosecuted for tax fraud work in organized crime or are public figures. (See Chapter 10.)

24. Can I make a deal with the IRS to pay less than my tax bill?

Maybe. Consider filing Form 656, *Offer in Compromise.* The IRS will thoroughly investigate your finances before deciding if settling for less than what you owe is in the best interests of the government. About 15% to 20% of all offers are accepted by the IRS. A filing fee and a down payment are required. You can greatly increase your chances of success by carefully following the IRS rules for offers and submitting all of the paperwork correctly. (See Chapter 6.)

25. If I win, can I recover my accountant's and lawyer's fees for fighting the IRS?

It's possible, but difficult. Legally, if you win, you may get reimbursed for your costs. But the IRS seldom pays attorneys' fees, and when it does, it's at a rate lower than what most tax lawyers charge. Absent special circumstances, the maximum attorneys' fee allowed is $125 per hour. The judge makes the final determination of the reasonableness of the entire bill. And, to win, you must "substantially prevail" in court, the IRS must have taken an unreasonable position, and you must have exhausted all procedural remedies within the IRS before going to court.

Fees paid for representation in an IRS administrative proceeding, such as an appeals hearing, can be recovered only if the IRS brought an unreasonable claim. So far, few taxpayers have gotten the IRS to admit it was wrong. No surprise.

Glossary of Tax Terms

Note: These terms are defined as they are used in this book. They may have different meanings in other contexts.

Abatement. The IRS's partial or complete cancellation of taxes, penalties, or interest owed by a taxpayer.

ACS. *See* Automated Collection System.

Adjustment. Change to your income tax liability as you reported in your tax return by an IRS auditor or Service Center. Typically adjustments result from disallowed deductions.

Amended Tax Return. A tax return filed within three years to make one or more changes to a previously filed tax return. Taxpayers usually file amended tax returns to claim a refund. Amended individual income tax returns must be filed on IRS Form 1040X.

Appeal. The IRS formal administrative process for taxpayers to contest decisions, such as an audit, within the IRS. Most, but not all, administrative decisions can be taken to the IRS Appeals Office. If the appeal is lost, a taxpayer may be able to contest the IRS decision in a court of law.

Assess. The IRS process of recording a tax liability in the account of a taxpayer.

Asset. Any property, real or personal, that you own and that has a monetary value.

Audit. An IRS review of the correctness of a tax return. The IRS official term for an audit is "examination." *See also* Field Audit, Office Audit.

Auditor. An IRS Examination Division employee who reviews the correctness of a tax return. *See also* Revenue Agent, Tax Auditor.

Automated Collection System (ACS). A computerized collection process in which IRS collectors contact delinquent taxpayers by telephone and mail.

Bankruptcy. A federal law—separate from the Internal Revenue Code—which, in limited circumstances, can be used by taxpayers to eliminate their tax debts (Chapter 7 bankruptcy). In other instances, taxpayers can use bankruptcy to pay off their tax debts over three to five years (Chapters 12 and 13 bankruptcy).

Basis (Tax Basis). For tax purposes, this is the cost of an asset, which may be adjusted for tax reporting purposes downward by depreciation or upward by improvements.

Certified Public Accountant (CPA). CPAs are the most highly skilled of those in the accounting profession. They do sophisticated accounting and business audit work, and prepare tax returns and financial statements for clients. To earn the professional designation of CPA, an accountant must have a college degree and work experience with a CPA firm and must pass a series of rigorous examinations. CPAs are regulated by state law and are allowed to practice before the IRS.

Claim for Refund. Taxpayers who feel that they have overpaid their taxes may file a claim to the IRS for refund consideration. The IRS provides Form 843 for claims. An amended tax return (Form 1040X) may also be treated as a claim for a refund. If the claim is denied, the taxpayer can bring a "refund suit" in a federal district court or the U.S. court of claims. *See also* Amended Tax Return.

Code. *See* Internal Revenue Code.

Collection Division. The branch of the IRS that is staffed by tax collectors at the IRS Service Center, Automated Collection System, or local IRS office.

Commissioner of Internal Revenue. The head of the entire IRS organization.

Correspondence Audit. An IRS examination conducted by mail.

Criminal Investigation Division (CID). The branch of the IRS that investigates individual and business entities to determine whether or not they have committed tax crimes. *See also* Fraud.

Death. The other certainty.

Deduction. An expense which the Internal Revenue Code allows taxpayers to subtract from their annual gross income to reduce the amount of their tax liability.

Delinquent Return. A tax return not filed by the legal due date or by the dates allowed through the IRS extension periods.

Dependent. *See* Exemption.

Depreciation. A tax deduction allowed for the wear and tear on an income-producing asset, such as a business automobile or rental real estate.

Disallowance. An IRS finding that you weren't entitled to a tax benefit claimed on your tax return, usually a deduction or loss. *See also* Adjustment.

Discriminant Function (DIF) Scoring. An IRS computer program that measures tax returns for audit potential. The Discriminant Function assigns each tax return a DIF score; the higher the DIF score, the higher the audit possibility.

Documentation. Any tangible proof that substantiates an item on your tax return, usually an expense claimed as a deduction. Documentation is ordinarily something in writing. *See also* Records.

Enrolled Agent (EA). An EA is a tax adviser and tax preparer permitted to practice before the IRS. An EA earns the designation either by passing a difficult IRS exam testing tax knowledge or by having at least five years of employment by the IRS. EAs also must participate in annual continuing education programs to retain their designations.

Examination. Official IRS terminology for an audit. *See also* Audit.

Exemption. Exemption has two meanings in this book. First, exemption refers to the dollar amount that all taxpayers may subtract from their income on their tax returns corresponding to the number of people they support as dependents (including themselves). Second, exemption refers to the limited list of property that the IRS cannot legally take if it levies on your property to satisfy your tax debt. *See also* Levy.

Extension to File. Income tax returns are normally due to the IRS by April 15. An extension to file gives a taxpayer extra time to file a return but not to pay the taxes owed. A taxpayer can obtain an automatic extension until August 15 by filing a form with the IRS. A taxpayer can request a second extension until October 15 by filing another form with the IRS. The second extension is discretionary with the IRS. A taxpayer can also request an extension to pay taxes, but such a request is rarely granted.

Failure to File Tax Return. The most frequently charged tax crime. Defined as intentionally failing to file a return when you were obligated to do so. A misdemeanor punishable by up to one year in jail and/or a fine of $25,000 for each year not filed.

Fair Market Value. The price a buyer and seller of real or personal property would agree upon as fair, when neither is under any compulsion to buy or sell.

Field Audit. An examination that takes place outside the IRS offices—at your business, home, or tax representative's office. *See also* Audit, Revenue Agent.

Fifth Amendment Right. A well-known right guaranteed by the U.S. Constitution that protects people from being forced by the government to incriminate themselves. You can assert your Fifth Amendment right against the IRS by refusing to answer questions or provide certain documents.

Filing. The act of giving in person or otherwise delivering to the IRS a tax return or another IRS document.

Fraud. Conduct meant to deceive the IRS in the determination of any tax liability. Fraud can be either (a) civil (resulting in a penalty of 75% of the taxes owed), or (b) criminal (tax evasion, a felony with a maximum prison sentence of five years and a maximum monetary fine of $100,000; or filing a false return, a felony with a maximum prison sentence of three years and a maximum monetary fine of $100,000), or (c) both civil and criminal.

Fraud Referral. A transfer to the IRS Criminal Investigation Division from another department when IRS personnel suspect a taxpayer of tax fraud. *See also* Criminal Investigation Division.

Freedom of Information Act. A federal law giving people the right to see U.S. government documents, including their IRS files.

Gift. Transfer of property without any financial payment in return. A true gift is not taxable to the recipient but may cause tax consequences for the giver, depending on the size of the gift.

Gross Income. Income from all sources which taxpayers must report on their income tax returns. Not all money received is income for tax purposes, however. *See also* Taxable Income.

Group Manager. The immediate superior of an auditor or a tax collector at an IRS office.

Income. All monies and other things of value you receive, except items specifically exempted by the tax code. For example, a gift or an inheritance is not considered income. *See also* Gross Income, Taxable Income.

Independent Contractor. A self-employed worker. Income taxes and Social Security contributions are not withheld or made by the business for which the services are performed. Each year, businesses that hire independent contractors must file a Form 1099 with the IRS for each independent contractor paid more than $600 for the preceding year.

Information Return. A report filed with the IRS showing monies paid by or to a taxpayer. The most common information returns are Form W-2 (wages) and Form 1099 (independent contractors and other income, such as interest paid by a bank, stock dividends, or royalties).

Installment Agreement (IA). An IRS monthly payment plan for past taxes.

Internal Revenue Code (IRC). The tax laws of the United States as enacted by Congress. Also called the "tax code."

Internal Revenue Manual (IRM). A collection of handbooks which set forth the internal operating guidelines for IRS personnel. Most, but not all, of the manual is now public information and may be found at the IRS website.

Internal Revenue Regulations. *See* Regulations.

Internal Revenue Service (IRS). The tax law administration branch of the U.S. Treasury Department.

Jeopardy Assessment. An expedited procedure by which the IRS determines your tax liability without first notifying you. A jeopardy assessment is rare and usually limited to when the IRS believes you are about to flee the country or hide assets.

Joint Tax Return. An income tax return filed by a married couple.

Levy. An IRS seizure of your assets or wages to satisfy a delinquent tax debt.

Lien. *See* Tax Lien.

Limitation on Assessment and Collection. *See* Statute of Limitations.

Market Value. *See* Fair Market Value.

Negligence. Whenever you have carelessly disregarded the tax law in preparing a tax return, the IRS can deem your conduct negligent and impose a penalty (fine) against you. Also called an accuracy related penalty.

Nonfiler. A person or an entity who does not file a timely tax return even though required by law to do so.

Notice of Deficiency. *See* 90-Day Letter.

Notice of Federal Tax Lien. *See* Tax Lien.

Offer in Compromise. A formal written proposal to the IRS to settle your tax account balance for less than the amount the IRS says you owe. An Offer in Compromise must be submitted on IRS Form 656.

Office Audit. An IRS examination of your tax return by a tax auditor at a local IRS office. *See also* Audit, Field Audit, Tax Auditor.

Payroll Taxes. Federal income tax and FICA contributions—which include both Social Security and Medicare—that a business owner must deposit regularly and report quarterly to the IRS for each employee. These are also called trust fund taxes. *See also* Trust Fund Recovery Penalty.

Penalties. Civil fines imposed by the IRS on a taxpayer who disobeys tax laws, such as by filing a form beyond the time limit set by law.

Personal Property. Any item of property that is not real estate—such as cash, stocks, cars, and the shirt on your back. *See also* Asset, Real Property.

Petition. A written form filed with the U.S. Tax Court to contest a proposed IRS tax assessment. *See also* Tax Court.

Power of Attorney. A form you sign appointing a tax representative to deal with the IRS on your behalf.

Problems Resolution Officer (PRO). Former title of the taxpayer advocate.

Property. *See* Personal Property, Real Property.

Protest. A written or an oral request to appeal a decision within the IRS. *See also* Appeal.

Real Property. Real estate, consisting of land and structures attached to it.

Reconsideration. A discretionary IRS procedure which lets you reopen a closed audit or another tax assessment previously made.

Records. A collection of tangible proof, usually in writing, which shows income, expenses, and financial transactions. Records are one form of documentation.

Refund Suit. *See* Claim for Refund.

Regular Tax Case. A tax court case in which a taxpayer contests $50,000 or more per tax year. This is a complex proceeding, in which formal rules of procedure and evidence apply. *See also* Petition, Small Tax Case, Tax Court.

Regulations. IRS written interpretations of selected Internal Revenue Code provisions. *See also* Internal Revenue Code, Revenue Procedures, Revenue Rulings.

Representative. *See* Tax Professional, Tax Representative.

Return. *See* Tax Return.

Revenue Agent. An IRS employee who conducts a field, as opposed to an office, audit. *See also* Audit, Field Audit, Office Audit.

Revenue Officer. A tax collector who works out of a local IRS office.

Revenue Procedures. IRS interpretations of selected Internal Revenue Code provisions which specify the procedures taxpayers must follow to comply with certain sections of the code. *See also* Internal Revenue Code, Regulations, Revenue Rulings.

Revenue Rulings. IRS interpretations of selected Internal Revenue Code provisions as applied to specific factual circumstances. *See also* Internal Revenue Code, Regulations, Revenue Procedures.

Seizure. *See* Levy.

Self-Employed. Anyone who works for him- or herself, not receiving wages from an employer; synonymous with small business owner. *See also* Independent Contractor.

Service Centers. Regional IRS facilities where tax returns are filed and processed. Most IRS bills and notices come from service centers.

Small Business Owner. *See* Self-Employed.

Small Tax Case. A tax court case in which a taxpayer contests less than $50,000 per tax year. This is a simple, small claims court type proceeding, in which formal rules of procedure and evidence don't apply. *See also* Petition, Regular Tax Case, Tax Court.

Special Agent. An IRS officer who investigates suspected tax crimes. *See also* Criminal Investigation Division (CID).

Statute of Limitations. Differing time limits imposed by Congress on the IRS for assessing and collecting taxes, on the Justice Department for charging taxpayers with tax crimes, and on taxpayers who claim refunds.

Summons. A legal order issued by the IRS compelling a taxpayer or another person or entity (such as a taxpayer's employer or bank) to appear or provide financial information to the IRS.

Tax Attorney. A lawyer who does various types of tax-related work, including tax and estate planning, IRS dispute resolution, and tax return preparation. Usually, only an attorney may represent a taxpayer in a court proceeding against the IRS. A tax attorney should have either a special tax law degree (LLM) or a certification as a tax law specialist from a state bar association.

Tax Auditor. An IRS employee who conducts an office, as opposed to a field, audit. *See also* Audit, Field Audit, Office Audit.

Tax Code. *See* Internal Revenue Code.

Tax Court. The only U.S. federal court where a taxpayer can contest an IRS tax assessment without first paying the taxes claimed due by the IRS. *See also* Petition, Regular Tax Case, Small Tax Case.

Tax Fraud. *See* Fraud.

Tax Law. The Internal Revenue Code, written by Congress, and the decisions of all federal courts which interpret it. *See also* Internal Revenue Code.

Tax Levy. *See* Levy.

Tax Lien. Whenever you owe money to the IRS and don't pay after the IRS has demanded payment, the IRS has a claim against your property. This is called a tax lien, which arises automatically by "operation of law." The IRS has the right to inform the public that you are subject to a tax lien. This is done by recording a Notice of Federal Tax Lien at the county recorder's office or with your Secretary of State's office. A tax lien allows the IRS to seize (levy on) your property to satisfy your tax debt. Also most state tax agencies are given lien powers for state taxes due. *See also* Levy.

Tax Preparer. A person who fills in your tax return forms for a fee.

Tax Professional. Anyone working privately in the tax field, such as an accountant or a tax lawyer. *See also* Certified Public Accountant, Enrolled Agent, Tax Representative, Tax Attorney, Tax Preparer.

Tax Representative. A tax professional who is legally qualified to represent you before the IRS and whom you have authorized to deal with the IRS on your behalf. *See also* Certified Public Accountant, Enrolled Agent, Tax Attorney.

Tax Return. A form that individuals, partnerships, limited liability companies (LLCs), and corporations are required to file each year with the IRS stating income, exemptions, credits, and deductions. Tax liability, if any, is based on this form for individuals and corporations.

Taxable Income. The amount of money on which you must pay taxes each year. It's determined on your tax return by subtracting deductions and exemptions from your gross income. *See also* Deduction, Exemption, Gross Income.

Taxpayer Account. An IRS computer record containing your taxpaying history. Your tax account includes all tax assessments, penalties and interest, and credits for payments for each tax year.

Taxpayer Advocate. An IRS troubleshooter who acts for taxpayers whose problems were not solved through normal IRS channels. The taxpayer advocate works out of IRS local offices and service centers.

Taxpayer Assistance Order (TAO). An order that a taxpayer advocate can issue to override an action against a taxpayer by the IRS. *See also* Taxpayer Advocate.

Taxpayer Identification Number (TIN). An IRS-assigned number used for computer tracking of tax accounts. For individuals, it is their Social Security number (SSN). For other entities, such as corporations and trusts, it is a separate 13-digit number called the employer identification number (EIN).

Taxpayer Bill of Rights (TBOR). Federal laws imposing standards and limits on the IRS, and establishing your rights in dealing with the agency.

Tele-Tax. IRS prerecorded tax topic information, available by telephone.

Third Party. Any person or entity other than you who has knowledge of your finances, such as your bank, stockbroker, or employer.

Trust Fund Recovery Penalty (TFRP). A tax law giving the IRS the power to assess unpaid payroll taxes against "responsible" individuals involved in a business owing the taxes. *See also* Payroll Taxes.

Trust Fund Taxes. *See* Payroll Taxes.

Unreported Income. Any income you were required to report on your income tax return, but didn't.

Waiver. An agreement where you voluntarily give up a legal right, such as the right to have the IRS collection period on a delinquent tax debt expire. Often, the IRS requires waivers in exchange for granting installment agreements.

Willful. Intentional conduct which violates the tax laws and can subject the wrongdoer to criminal prosecution.

Workpapers. Notes made by accountants and IRS auditors that explain items or adjustments made on a tax return. *See also* Adjustment, Disallowance.

100% Payroll Penalty. *See* Trust Fund Recovery Penalty.

30-Day Letter. IRS written notice following an audit giving you 30 days to protest the audit by requesting an IRS appeals hearing.

90-Day Letter. The letter the IRS must send if it seeks to impose additional taxes—usually after an audit—which you don't agree to. The letter gives you 90 days to file a petition in U.S. Tax Court to protest the proposed assessment of taxes. If you don't file a petition, the tax assessment becomes final. Also called a "Notice of Deficiency." *See also* Petition, Tax Court.

Index

 **Keep Up to Date**

 Go to Nolo.com/newsletters to sign up for free newsletters and discounts on Nolo products.

- **Nolo's Special Offer.** A monthly newsletter with the biggest Nolo discounts around.

- **Landlord's Quarterly.** Deals and free tips for landlords and property managers.

 Don't forget to check for updates. Find this book at **Nolo.com** and click "Legal Updates."

Let Us Hear From You

 Register your Nolo product and give us your feedback at Nolo.com/book-registration.

- Once you've registered, you qualify for technical support if you have any trouble with a download or CD (though most folks don't).

- We'll send you a coupon for 15% off your next Nolo.com order!

SIRS11

⚖ NOLO *Online Legal Forms*

Nolo offers a large library of legal solutions and forms, created by Nolo's in-house legal staff. These reliable documents can be prepared in minutes.

Create a Document

- **Incorporation.** Incorporate your business in any state.
- **LLC Formations.** Gain asset protection and pass-through tax status in any state.
- **Wills.** Nolo has helped people make over 2 million wills. Is it time to make or revise yours?
- **Living Trust (avoid probate).** Plan now to save your family the cost, delays, and hassle of probate.
- **Trademark.** Protect the name of your business or product.
- **Provisional Patent.** Preserve your rights under patent law and claim "patent pending" status.

Download a Legal Form

Nolo.com has hundreds of top quality legal forms available for download—bills of sale, promissory notes, nondisclosure agreements, LLC operating agreements, corporate minutes, commercial lease and sublease, motor vehicle bill of sale, consignment agreements and many more.

Review Your Documents

Many lawyers in Nolo's consumer-friendly lawyer directory will review Nolo documents for a very reasonable fee. Check their detailed profiles at **Nolo.com/lawyers**.

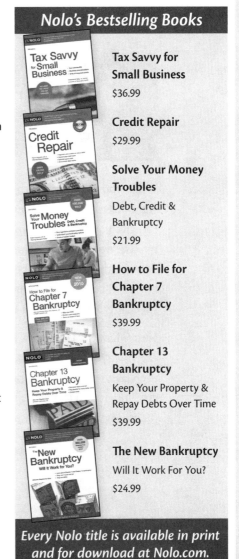